# FaXiang

法相

# FaXiang

## A Buddhist Practitioner's Encyclopedia

Venerable Tzu Chuang

Translated by Robert Smitheram

Buddha's Light Publishing, Los Angeles

© 2012 Buddha's Light Publishing
First edition

By Venerable Tzu Chuang
Translated by Robert Smitheram
Cover designed by John Gill

Published by Buddha's Light Publishing
3456 S. Glenmark Drive
Hacienda Heights, CA 91745, U.S.A.
Tel: (626) 923-5144
Fax: (626) 923-5145
E-mail: itc@blia.org
Website: www.blpusa.com

Printed in Taiwan.

Library of Congress Cataloging-in-Publication Data

Cizhuang.
  [Fa xiang. English.]
  Faxiang : a Buddhist practitioner's encyclopedia / Venerable Tzu Chuang ; translated by
Robert Smitheram. -- 1st ed.
      p. cm.
  ISBN 978-1-932293-55-5
  1. Buddhism--Encyclopedias. 2. Spiritual life--Buddhism--Encyclopedias. I. Smitheram,
Robert. II. Title. III. Title: Buddhist practitioner's encyclopedia.

  BQ128.C5913 2012
  294.303--dc23

                                    2012012595

# Contents

# Acknowledgments

Like all of Buddha's Light Publishing's endeavors, this project benefited from the contributions of many people. We would like to thank Venerable Tzu Jung, the Chief Executive of the Fo Guang Shan International Translation Center (FGSITC), Venerble Hui Chi, Abbot of Hsi Lai Temple, and Venerable Yi Chao, Director of FGSITC for their support and leadership.

Robert H. Smitheram provided the translation; John Gill and Nathan Michon edited the texts; Louvenia Ortega and Amanda Ling proofread the manuscript and prepared it for publication. The calligraphy on the cover was provided by Venerable Master Hsing Yun, and digitized by Wilson Yau. The book was designed by Wan Kah Ong. The cover was designed by John Gill.

Our appreciation goes to everyone who supported this project from conception to completion.

# Editor's Note

The present volume is a full English translation of Venerable Tzu Chaung's FaXiang. However, a great deal of Chinese text has been provided to assist English-language readers who wish to deepen their understanding of Chinese Buddhist writing, as well as Chinese-language readers who wish to learn about Buddhist doctrinal terms in English.

Articles are organized alphabetically by English title, and are accompanied by their corresponding Chinese titles. English translations of article titles were chosen to allow an English-language reader to most easily find what he or she is looking for, and as such are not direct translations. The corresponding Chinese titles are provided as they appeared in the 1997 Chinese edition of FaXiang to allow Chinese-language readers to easily reference the source text. Chinese characters provided in the body text and the article subheadings are much more directly translated.

The Chinese edition of FaXiang was organized numerically, in the tradition of the Ekottara Agama. Articles with two major doctrinal topics were grouped together, followed by articles with three topics, and so forth. A list of all the articles in the order they appeared in the Chinese edition with their Chinese titles, English titles, and corresponding page numbers is provided as an appendix.

# Preface to the 1997 Chinese Edition

Many people interested in gaining some understanding of Buddhism often face a perplexing problem: the vast array of Buddhist sutras contain complex doctrines expressed in an arcane terminology, and people are left not knowing how to appreciate their profound insights. Just how the Buddhist sutras can be made more accessible to the average reader has always remained the long cherished wish of Venerable Master Hsing Yun as embodied in his promotion of Humanistic Buddhism. In order to put this ideal into practice, he edited the *Buddhism* reference series so that people would no longer regard Buddhist studies as a daunting task to be avoided.

Actually, as early as 1964 after the founding Shoushan Buddhist Seminary, Master Hsing Yun was already vigorously engaged in encouraging a more practical and simplified Dharma for everyday life. Whenever one learns a new language, a new area of knowledge or scholarship, or a new skill, each of these entails its own specialized vocabulary and terminology, and religion is no exception.

Buddhism originated some 2,600 years ago on the plain of India, and the Buddha's teachings were preserved in Indic languages like Sanskrit and Pali. Since the time of the Han, Wei, and the Northern and Southern dynasties, many monastics have engaged in the work of translating the Buddhist sutras from Sanskrit and Pali into Chinese.

The sutras were translated into Chinese in a terse, yet precise manner. This style can be yet another obstacle that fosters incomprehension for modern people schooled in reading modern vernacular Chinese. For this reason, the compilation of a simple and clear dictionary for Buddhist studies or a glossary of terminology has become a matter of utmost urgency.

Thirty-three years ago, I took charge of the teaching work at the Shoushan Buddhist Seminary, just as interest in studying Buddhism was beginning to grow in Taiwan. To allow those many students who were interested in being able to study the Dharma directly to develop a solid foundation, Master Hsing Yun asked me to teach Buddhist terminology using a vivid and dynamic style, in hopes that these lectures could later be published in the monthly journal *Awakening the World* for the benefit of all.

Owing to my busy administrative duties at the temple, as well as my trips all around the world over the past ten odd years to establish more than one hundred Fo Guang Shan branch temples, I had no time to sift carefully through my lecture notes. On the thirtieth anniversary of the founding of Fo Guang Shan, Master Hsing Yun asked me to edit my teaching materials, now long covered in dust, into a book that can serve as a reference to others. Consequently, I have put together this volume by carefully selecting one hundred and twenty-one items from my lectures. This book is my offering to the thirtieth anniversary of Fo Guang Shan.

Given the shifting of conditions, mistakes and errors are unavoidable. It is my hope that the great practitioners and scholars of the world will be generous in their feedback. I would also like to express my gratitude to Venerable Man Yi who helped me prepare the manuscript and to my colleagues working at Fo Guang Cultural Enterprises Ltd. for editing and printing this work.

Tzu Chuang, April of 1997

# List of Articles

## A

## B

## C

## D

# N

# O

# P

# Q

## Abhidharma
阿毗達磨

*See:* Gem, triple; Tripitaka.

## Accomplishments, Six
六成就

The Buddhist teachings state that an effect can only manifest when all the necessary conditions are complete and present. This is the doctrine of dependent origination, an eternal truth which the Buddha realized when he attained awakening. Even when the Buddha gave teachings, the necessary conditions had to be present and these conditions are called the six accomplishments: faith, hearing, time, teacher, location, and assembly. Only when these six accomplishments were present, could the Dharma be taught.

All sutras begin with the phrase "Thus have I heard." This phrase shows that the six accomplishments are present:

### 1. The Accomplishment of Faith (信成就)

This accomplishment is signified by the characters *rushi* (如是), "thus," at the beginning of a sutra. The ocean of the Buddha's teachings can only be entered through faith. At the beginning of each sutra we accept on faith that the Dharma was spoken by the Buddha "thus" as it is written, and do not doubt it. It is by relying on the Dharma in this way that we can practice.

### 2. The Accomplishment of Hearing (聞成就)

The next characters are *wowen* (我聞), "I heard." This is to show that Ananda, the Buddha's attendant, was present to hear the Buddha give such a teaching.

### 3. The Accomplishment of Time (時成就)

The next characters in a typical sutra are *yishi* (一時), "one time." This refers to the time that the teaching was given. Whenever an assembly had gathered, if sentient beings were present, had the proper conditions, and made an appeal to him, the Buddha taught them the Dharma.

### 4. The Accomplishment of the Teacher (主成就)

The accomplishment of the teacher refers to the Buddha himself being present to teach. The Buddha is the teacher who gives teachings and guidance for both the mundane and supramundane worlds.

### 5. The Accomplishment of Location (處成就)

After the Buddha is mentioned, next comes the characters *zai mouchu* (在某處), "at some certain place." This refers to the location where the teachings were given. With the exception of the time when the Buddha gave teachings to his mother in the

Heaven of the Thirty-three Gods, the Buddha always gave teachings in the human world, at such places as Magadha and Sravasti in India.

### 6. The Accomplishment of the Assembly（眾成就）

Sutras continue with the characters *yuzhong ruoganren ju*（與眾若干人俱）, "along with a certain gathering of beings," followed by a list of those in attendance. This refers to all those present in the assembly who have come to listen to the Dharma. Bodhisattvas, *sravakas*, *pratyekabuddhas*, heavenly and human beings would gather in multitudes to listen to the Dharma.

The Dharma could only be taught because the six conditions above were present. If even one was lacking, the transmission of the true Dharma could not have taken place. Therefore, teaching at a Dharma assembly is not something that any single individual can accomplish, for the conditions of faith, hearing, time, teacher, location, and assembly must be present. Those who teach the Dharma today should retain a sense of graciousness and sincerity when they teach, so that those who are assembled can increase their understanding and gain the benefits of the Dharma. Those who listen to the Dharma should understand how rare it is to have such an opportunity, and furthermore, should vow to uphold the true Dharma and see to the accomplishment of the Dharma assembly. This way the Buddha's light and the water of the Dharma will spread far and wide.

A

# Ages of the Dharma, Three
# 三時佛法

> When the Buddha was in the world, I was lost,
> After the Buddha passed into *nirvana* was I then
> born;
> I repent for all my many karmic obstacles,
> That have prevented me from seeing the
> Tathagata's golden body.

The above verse gives a portrait of sentient beings in this current age of declining Dharma, and how they regret missing the time when the Buddha was in the world. Cultivation is more difficult in the era after the Buddha's *nirvana*, such that "being born when no Buddha is present" is even mentioned as one of the eight difficulties for practicing Buddhism.

Though it is impossible now to go back and be present when the Buddha was in the world, the Buddha's teachings have been passed down for generations since the Buddha entered *nirvana*. Sentient beings still have the opporunity to hear the Dharma and practice according to the teachings; however, the conditions following the Buddha's *nirvana* change over time. These changes can be divided into the three ages of the Dharma: the Age of Right Dharma, the Age of Semblance Dharma, and the Age of Declining Dharma

## 1. Age of Right Dharma (正法)
The Age of Right Dharma is the period not long after the Buddha has passed into final *nirvana*, during which his disciples are still able to maintain monastic discipline and uphold the Buddha's

teachings in form and essence without misinterpretation. During this age, sentient beings are provided with the Right Dharma and have a great capacity to learn. Many of those who have the will to practice diligently will attain awakening.

## 2. Age of Semblance Dharma（像法）

The Age of Semblance Dharma is the period after the Buddha's final *nirvana* has receded into the past, and the esteem and admiration that sentient beings hold for the Buddha's teachings has waned. Different ideas and understandings of the Buddha's teachings appear, and this leads to ideas about the Buddha's teachings which only *resemble* the Right Dharma. During this age, sentient beings lack the solid foundation of positive karma possessed by those alive during the Age of Right Dharma, and as a result, even though the teachings still exist, very few attain awakening.

## 3. Age of Declining Dharma（末法）

The Age of Declining Dharma is the period when the Buddha's teachings go into decline. Sentient beings misunderstand and cannot distinguish between true teachings and false ones, and become stubborn and difficult to teach. Meanwhile, non-Buddhist teachers that invoke the name of the Buddha do as they please. During this age the Buddhist teachings remain in the world, but most people have no faith in them, do not practice, and attain nothing. During this age the Dharma has weakened, and Mara has become stronger.

According to the Buddhist sutras, the Age of Right Dharma and the Age of Semblance Dharma each last about one thousand years, while the Age of Declining Dharma lasts for ten thousand years. According to the Buddhist calendar, the year 2011 of the common era is 2555 years after the Buddha's final *nirvana*, so we have already entered the Age of Declining Dharma.

In the work *Encouragement for Generating the Aspiration for Enlightenment*, the eighteenth-century monastic Master Xingan wrote: "The Age of Right Dharma and the Age of Semblance Dharma have already passed. What remains is only the Age of Decling Dharma." He went on to say, that during the age of declining Dharma, the teachings will exist but no one will practice them, that no one will be able to distinguish true teachings from false ones nor tell right from wrong, and that people will struggle and fight amongst themselves in pursuit of fame and fortune. The Age of Declining Dharma is lamentable indeed. Over twenty-five hundred years ago, the Buddha said to Ananda that, during the Age of Declining Dharma, sentient beings will attempt to out maneuver and betray one another as they contend for power, wealth, fame and fortune, even to the point where they will brutally kill one another. Such people are as senseless as crows fighting over a piece of rotten meat.

In particular, there are many non-Buddhist groups who proclaim to be Buddhist and dress themselves in the guise of Buddhism and do all kinds of harm to Buddhism.

In today's society selfishness, fame, and fortune reign supreme. Greed has become ingrained in the human heart, and our morals have declined. There is little distinction between the teachings that are right and those that are wrong. People with dangerous doctrines about supernatural powers and spirits now assume the name of "Buddhism" to cheat others out of their money to the point that real Buddhists have become victims. We can see the fulfillment of the Buddha's prediction today.

Moreover, the government lacks the proper policies to set things right. The media, too, disregards morality and only concerns itself with commercial profit. The media only reports exaggerated and unsubstantiated stories that mislead their audience, resulting in an ever more chaotic society with more and more social problems that will plague the future for generations. Venerable Master Hsing Yun once remarked, "The government has no law, the media has no morals, Buddhism has committed no fault, and the believers have no choice."

To address the above abuses, the world's governments should truly create some policies regulating religious organizations as soon as possible so that they will have some legal basis, and that illegal activity will be thwarted before it happens. This will also allow orthodox Buddhism the space it needs to disseminate its teachings. The media too should develop its professional ethics and report more on the brighter side of human character to edify its audience. Buddhist followers should be more self-aware and united as a whole, and should actively spread Buddhism to develop the contributions that Buddhism can make to purifying the mind and giving people guidance. There is no way to avert the decline of the Dharma, but in this way, we can lay the groundwork for the Right Dharma to return in the future. This would be a great blessing for Buddhism and for all sentient beings.

## Aggregates, Five
## 五蘊

The five aggregates are also known as the "five heaps" or "five components," for they are the five factors that make up the self. What are the five aggregates? "Aggregate" here refers to accumulation, and the term refers to the accumulations of five kinds of conditioned phenomena: form, feeling, perception, mental formations, and consciousness.

### 1. Form（色）

"Form" refers to anything that obstructs. The aggregate of form includes anything that occupies space, can hinder or obstruct, or can be divided into parts. This includes all matter that has shape and can be broken down, as well as the five sense organs (eyes, ears, nose, tongue, and body) and the five sense objects (sight, sound, smell, taste, and touch).

### 2. Feeling（受）

"Feeling" refers to sensation, the function whereby the mind grasps external phenomena to produce a response. Feelings can be either painful, pleasurable, or neither painful nor pleasurable.

### 3. Perception（想）

"Perception" refers to cognizing an object. Conceiving of objects from external phenomena, conceptualizing, making associations, remembering the past, and imagining the future. These are the mental functions through which we perceive all objects. One could say that perception is the formation of mental concepts.

### 4. Mental Formations（行）

"Mental formations" refers to our fabrications. These are the activities that are fabricated from the apprehension of objects, the various actions that are relegated to one's body or speech after mental deliberation and judgment. Mental formations can be either wholesome or unwholesome.

*5. Consciousness*（識）

"Consciousness" refers to awareness. Consciousness is what recognizes, understands, and distinguishes between various mental states. For example, the eye can recognize and distinguish between blue, yellow, black, and white; the ear can distinguish between harsh and pleasing sounds; the nose can distinguish between fragrant and noxious smells; the tongue can distinguish what is sour, sweet, bitter, and spicy; and the body can distinguish between hot and cold, hard and soft. The mind and body are an accumulation of the five aggregates, an impermanent combination dependent upon causes and conditions that lacks both inherent essence and autonomy. The mind and body are neither free nor permanent. However, sentient beings remain deluded and unawakened, and believe that what they see as "me" and "mine" is real, and thus they sink into an ocean of suffering.

The *Ekottaragama* states, "Form is like a patch of foam, feelings are like water bubbles, perception is like a wild horse, mental formations are like a plantain trunk, and consciousness is like an illusion." The mind and body are an accumulation of the five aggregates; if they were truly the self, how could the self be as impermanent as foam, bubbles, a wild horse, a plantain trunk, or an illusion?

# Aging
老
*See:* Dependent origination.

# Ajita
長眉羅漢
*See:* Arhats, eighteen.

## Alaya Consciousness
阿賴耶識
*See:* Consciousness, eight kinds of.

## Alms Bowl
缽
*See:* Robe and bowl.

## Altruism
利行
*See:* Means of embracing, four.

## Amitabha Buddha
阿彌陀佛
*See:* Namo amitofo; noble ones of the West, three; rebirth in the
Pure Land, nine grades of; supports, three.

## Amoghavajra
不空
*See:* Translators, four great Chinese.

## Ananda
阿難陀
*See:* Disciples, ten great; questions of the Buddha, four; thus have
I heard.

## Angaja
布袋羅漢
*See:* Arhats, eighteen.

# Anger
## 憤怒
*See:* Poisons, three.

# Animals
## 畜生
*See:* Dharma realms, ten; difficulties, eight; lower realms, three.

# Aniruddha
## 阿那律
*See:* Disciples, ten great.

# Apara-godaniya
## 西牛貨洲
See: Continents, four geat.

# Arhats, Eighteen
## 十八羅漢

In the history of Buddhism, there have been many eminent, awakened monks who were said to have "inwardly kept their bodhisattva practice, while outwardly manifesting the form of an arhat." Such figures are known for their unrestrained, supernatural powers which they use to liberate beings throughout the human world. For this reason most Buddhists have a conception of an arhat as one who is unconventional, capricious, bizarre, and uncanny.

Actually, there were also arhats who were known for being very reserved and dignified. An *arhat,* or *luohan* (羅漢) in Chinese, is a practitioner who has attained awakening and achieved liberation.

Most arhats are described as renunciative, non-contentious, world-weary, and tranquility-loving. Quite a few of the Buddha's disciples had become truly awakened, great arhats. For example, the ten great disciples of the Buddha were each arhats. Listings of arhats grew to include a group of five hundred arhats, as well as 1250 arhats. Among the various groups, the most common listing of arhats is a list known as the "eighteen arhats."

The sutras contain no such listing of the eighteen arhats as a group. The *Record on Dharma Abiding as Spoken by the Great Arhat Nandimitra*, lists sixteen arhats commanded by the Buddha to remain forever in the world and protect the true Dharma. The names of the sixteen arhats are:

### 1. The Tiger Subduing Arhat （伏虎羅漢）
Also known as the Venerable Pindolabharadvaja. He once subdued a vicious tiger.

### 2. The Celebrating Arhat （喜慶羅漢）
Also known as the Venerable Kanakavatsa. Hse was a great debater in ancient India.

### 3. The Bowl Raising Arhat （舉缽羅漢）
Also known as the Venerable Kanakabharadvaja. He would carry his alms bowl as he liberated beings.

### 4. The Stupa Raising Arhat （托塔羅漢）
Also known as the Venerable Subinda. He was the Buddha's last personally-ordained disciple. He always raises the Buddha's reliquary *stupa* in remembrance.

### 5. The Meditating Arhat（靜坐羅漢）

Also known as the Venerable Nakula and as the "great strength arhat," because before he become a monastic he served in the military and was very physically strong.

### 6. The River Crossing Arhat（過江羅漢）

Also known as the Venerable Bhadra. Due to his supernatural powers he is able to cross rivers like a dragonfly skimming over the surface of the water.

### 7. The Elephant Riding Arhat（騎象羅漢）

Also known as the Venerable Kalika. Before he became a monastic he was an elephant trainer.

### 8. The Laughing Lion Arhat（笑獅羅漢）

Also known as the Venerable Vajraputra. Before becoming a monastic he was a hunter, but stopped killing living beings when he became a Buddhist. The lions came to express their gratitude, hence the name.

### 9. The Open Heart Arhat（開心羅漢）

Also known as the Venerable Jivaka. He is commonly depicted with a Buddha image on his chest to show that Buddhism lies in his heart.

### 10. The Raised Arm Arhat（探手羅漢）

Also known as the Venerable Panthaka. He would often raise his arms to stretch his tired back after completing his sitting meditation, hence the name.

### 11. *The Deep Thinking Arhat*（沉思羅漢）

Also known as the Venerable Rahula. He was the Buddha's son and also one of the ten great disciples, known as foremost in secluded practice.

### 12. *The Ear Picking Arhat*（挖耳羅漢）

Also known as the Venerable Nagasena. He was well-known for his teaching on "purifying the ear sense organ," and is thus often depicted as cleaning his ears.

### 13. *The Bag Carrying Arhat*（布袋羅漢）

Also known as the Venerable Angaja. He is said to have always traveled carrying a bag on his back, laughing as he went on his way.

### 14. *The Banana Tree Arhat*（芭蕉羅漢）

Also known as the Venerable Vanavasin. After becoming a monastic, he would often diligently meditate under a banana tree.

### 15. *The Long Eyebrow Arhat*（長眉羅漢）

Also known as the Venerable Ajita. He was born with two long eyebrows.

### 16. *The House Guarding Arhat*（看門羅漢）

Also known as the Venerable Cudapanthaka. He was known for his loyalty and faithfulness in performing his duties.

In addition to the sixteen arhats mentioned in the *Record on Dharma Abiding as Spoken by the Great Arhat Nandimitra,* two additional arhats are usually added: the Venerable Nandimitra, the "dragon subduing arhat" (降龍羅漢), and the Venerable Pindola, the "sitting-on-deer arhat" (乘鹿羅漢). One theory is that the Venerable Nandimitra mentioned above is the same Nandimitra who authored the text describing the sixteen arhats, and that the Venerable Pindola is the same monastic also known as the "tiger subduing arhat." In this regard, there are really only sixteen arhats.

Regardless of whether there are sixteen arhats or eighteen arhats, differences in popular customs and beliefs from ancient times to the present and from India to China, have thus resulted in various accounts. However, people today must not become bogged down in arguing over which numbers or names are correct. Arhats are simply those who have gained liberation through their spiritual practice and, as such, are worthy of our respect.

## Ascetic Practices
## 十二頭陀行

Mahakasyapa, one of the Buddha's ten great disciples, was known as "foremost in austerities." When Mahakasyapa had reached old age, the Buddha once tried, out of compassion, to convince Mahakasyapa to give up his ascetic practices. But Mahakasyapa did not consider his ascetic practices painful. On the contrary, they made him happy.

Mahakasyapa did not worry about food or clothing, nor did he experience any suffering from success or failure. Mahakasyapa only experienced purity and liberation.

Mahakasyapa regarded ascetic practices as the strictest possible lifestyle. Those who are able to condition themselves to this kind of life are better able to endure hardship and find joy in simplicity, and can thus more easily devote their lives to the Dharma and to helping others. Ascetic practices have a direct effect of bringing stability to the monastic order, and thus indirectly bringing benefit to sentient beings. It is for this reason that the Buddha also praised Mahakasyapa, for as long as he lived, Mahakasyapa vowed to never abandon his ascetic practice.

The Chinese word *toutuo* (頭陀), "ascetic practice," means to cultivate the body and mind by sacrificing the comforts of clothing, food, housing, and transportation. Such practices aim to rid one of defilments and afflictions. Prior to his awakening, the Buddha undertook ascetic practices for six years before discovering that they were not the path of ultimate liberation. However, the Buddha felt that excessive craving can overwhelm one's will to practice. Therefore, as long as one does not engage in ascetic practices to gain notoriety, Buddhism still commends living a life of renunciation and simplicity.

The following are twelve common ascetic practices undertaken by Buddhist monastics, though they can also be applied in our daily lives:

*1. Living in the wilderness* (在阿蘭若處)
Staying in a tranquil and quiet place, far from the homes of worldly people.

*2. Only eating what is given as alms* (常行乞食)
Not having thoughts of like or dislike with respect to the food placed in the alms bowl.

*3. Collecting alms in order* (次第乞食)
Taking the alms bowl from one house to the next, regardless of whether the households are rich or poor.

## 4. Receiving one meal per day（受一食法）

Taking only one meal per day, in order to prevent multiple meals from becoming an obstacle to one's spiritual devotion.

## 5. Eating a limited amount（節量食）

Knowing moderation in food and drink so that one does not eat too much. Indulging one's appetite leads to a swollen stomach and a bloated belly, which hinders spiritual practice.

## 6. Not drinking broth after noontime（中午後不得飲漿）

Not drinking broth after the noon meal. Doing so would instill pleasure in the mind, and one could not single-mindedly focus on practicing goodness.

## 7. Wearing robes of cast-off rags（著弊衲衣）

Wearing robes with no craving for what is new and fine, thereby preventing any decline in one's practice.

## 8. Wearing only the three robes（但三衣）

Not having any extra clothing except for the three robes: the inner robe, upper robe, and monastic robe.

## 9. Dwelling in cemeteries（冢間住）

Dwelling in or near cemeteries in order to practice the contemplations on impermanence, suffering, and emptiness, so that one may become weary of the three realms and wish to leave them.

## 10. Staying under a tree（樹下止）

Imitating the practice of the Buddha by seeking awakening under a tree.

*11. Dwelling in an open place*（露地住）
Sitting out in the open, allowing the mind to become clear and sharp so that one may meditate on emptiness.

*12. Only sitting and not lying down*（但坐不臥）
One does not lie down, for if one were to rest comfortably, then there is the danger that afflictions would have an opportunity to arise.

# Assembly, Sevenfold
# 七眾弟子

To be a Buddhist disciple it is not necessary to join the monastic order; one can be a lay disciple as well. There are five different classes of monastic disciples and two different classes of lay disciples, who are together known as the "sevenfold assembly." Being a Buddhist disciple is also open to both men and women. The sutras say that, "When members of the four castes join the monastic order, they all become part of the Buddha's family." Male or female, rich or poor, highborn or lowbred, anyone who believes and practices the teachings of the Buddha can be called a Buddhist disciple. The classes of disciples that make up the sevenfold assembly are as follows:

*Bhiksu*（比丘）
A *bhiksu* is a monk who has received the full ordination of 250 precepts after joining the monastic order. The term for a monk in India was *bhiksu*, which means a "male mendicant." They request of the heavens that truth be imparted to them from all Buddhas to nourish their wisdom, and they gather alms on earth from sentient beings to sustain their bodies. With shaven heads and monastic

robes, they shoulder the responsibility for maintaining the true Dharma. They strive to overcome their afflictions and strike fear in Mara. A *bhiksu* is a model teacher for human and heavenly beings.

## Bhiksuni（比丘尼）

A *bhiksuni* is a nun who has received the full ordination of 348 precepts after joining the monastic order. With shaven heads and monastic robes, they look like the male monastics and have all the same associated meanings of *bhiksu*.

## Sramanera（沙彌）

A *sramanera* is a junior monk: one who has joined the monastic order, but has yet to receive full ordination. Anyone age seven or older is called a *sramanera*, regardless of age, as long as they have yet to receive full ordination. *Sramaneras* aged seven to thirteen are called "scarecrow" *sramanera*, those aged fourteen to nineteen are called "Dharma responding" *sramanera*, and those aged twenty to seventy are called *sramanera* "in name." *Sramanera* only undertake ten precepts.

## Sramanerika（沙彌尼）

A *sramanerika* is a junior nun who has joined the monastic order but has yet to receive full ordination, and just as the *sramanera*, they only undertake ten precepts.

## Siksamana（式叉摩那）

This refers to the novices who are preparing to join the monastic order as nuns. They are above the *sramanerika* but a grade below the *bhiksuni*. The term means a female Buddhist student who observes six precepts for a period of two years. This period was developed because some women seeking ordination may have been previously married; the concern here is that they might already be pregnant, in which case their being a *bhiksuni* would invite ridicule and disapproval. If the six precepts are not violated during the two year period, they can then receive ordination as a *bhiksuni*.

## Upasaka（優婆塞）

This refers to male lay practitioners who observe the five precepts. It is also acceptable to observe only a subset of the five precepts. Those that observe one precept are called *upasaka* of "one step," those who observe two precepts are called *upasaka* of "fewer steps," those who observe three or four precepts are called *upasaka* of "more steps," and those who observe all five precepts are called *upasaka* of "full steps." *Upasaka* means "man who serves," that is, a man who serves the *bhiksus* to learn the path.

## Upasika（優婆夷）

This refers to the female lay practitioners of Buddhism who observe the five precepts. As in the above, *upasika* means "woman who serves," as in a women who serves the *bhiksus* and *bhiksunis* to learn the path.

Within the Hinayana precepts, the seven classes of disciples are strictly differentiated, but the Mahayana bodhisattva precepts apply to all seven classes of disciples as long as they vow to become bodhisattvas. The implications of the monastic bodhisattva vows and the lay bodhisattva vows are the same in both cases. Buddhism as a religion belongs to all seven classes of disciples, for all Buddhist disciples honor the Buddha's kindness above and alleviate the suffering of sentient beings below.

## Asura
## 阿修羅

*See:* Dharma realms, ten.

## Attendants
## 左右脅士

As Buddhist temples have grown in popularity a great variety of Buddha images can be seen in their shrine halls. There are far too many configurations of Buddha images to be listed here, but some of the most common three statue configurations will be listed.

The three image configuration is the most common in all shrines, with a main central image flanked by two attendants on either side. Attendants are most commonly bodhisattvas, but can include youths and arhats as well. For example, the main image of Avalokitesvara Bodhisattva is often flanked by the youth Sudhana and a *naga* maiden as attendants. The Radiant King Acala is attended by the two youths Cetaka and Kimkara; Sakyamuni Buddha is attended upon by his two direct disciples, Mahakasyapa and Ananda; and Ksitigarbha Bodhisattva is attended on by a father and son: the Elder Min and Daoming.

That being said, the most common configuration is a Buddha as the central figure and bodhisattvas as the attendants. For example, Amitabha Buddha is usually depicted with Avalokitesvara Bodhisattva and Mahasthamaprapta Bodhisattva, and this grouping is known as the "three noble ones of the west." The Medicine Buddha is attended by Suryaprabha Bodhisattva and Candraprabha

Bodhisattva (sunlight and moonlight), or Bhaisajyaraja Bodhisattva and Bhaisajyasamudgata Bodhisattva, and these grouping are called the "three noble ones of the Medicine master." Mahavairocana Buddha is commonly depicted with Manjusri Bodhisattva and Samantabhadra Bodhisattva, and they are called the "three noble ones of Huayan."

The attendants indicate the virtue of the central Buddha figure. For example, the attendants who flank Sakyamuni Buddha are the Venerable Mahakasyapa, known as the foremost in austerities, and the Venerable Ananda, known as the foremost in hearing. The Buddha is the noble teacher who emphasized both understanding and practice, and here Mahakasyapa and Ananda represent practice and understanding, respectively. The combination of listening and understanding with actual practice represent Sakyamuni Buddha's perfect practice and awakening.

In the three noble ones of the *Flower Adornment Sutra* configuration, Mahavairocana represents the Buddha's Dharmakaya, also called the absolute form of the Buddha. To his right stands Samantabhadra Bodhisattva of great practice, while to his left stands Manjusri Bodhisattva of great wisdom. This shows how only the completion of great practice and great wisdom can fulfill the Buddha's Dharmakaya. Among the three noble ones of the west configuration, Avalokitesvara Bodhisattva represents great loving-kindness and great compassion, while Mahasthamaprapta Bodhisattva represents great joy and great equanimity. Their combined accomplishment of the four immeasurable minds of loving-kindness, compassion, joy, and equanimity is seen in Amitabha Buddha's infinite merit.

In addition, the youth Sudhana and the *naga* maiden who are the attendants of Avalokitesvara Bodhisattva, and Elder Min and

Daoming who are the attendants of Ksitigarbha Bodhisattva indicate Buddhism's equality between male and female, and young and old.

The attendants are significant in another way, for they assist the central figure in the task of liberating sentient beings. This is particularly true in the case of Avalokitesvara Bodhisattva and Mahasthamaprapta Bodhisattva, who are "bodhisattvas in waiting," which means that, after Amitabha Buddha enters final *nirvana*, these bodhisattvas will be his successors. This relationship represents the continued transmission of Dharma from one generation to the next.

The relationships between each of the three image configurations mentioned above serves to show us the importance of balance in Buddhism, whether it is the balance of practice and understanding, the unity of knowledge and practice, or the cultivation of both merit and wisdom. Just like our two eyes or two feet, these virtues must complement and support one another, for only in this way can they be perfected.

## Avaivartika
## 阿鞞拔致

The *Amitabha Sutra* states: "All sentient beings who are reborn in the Land of Ultimate Bliss are *avaivartikas*." An *avaivartika* is a bodhisattva who will not regress on the path to Buddhahood. Only if such a person has made a vow to turn around their boat of compassion and return to the Saha world to liberate sentient beings will it be necessary to experience human life and undergo the suffering of birth and death.

*Avaivartika* means "not regressing." This means that the faith and understanding realized through practice has reached a point that it has become irrevocable, and it is no longer possible that someone will turn back from attaining Buddhahood.

There are fifty-two stages on the bodhisattva path: ten levels of faith, ten levels of dwelling, ten levels of practice, ten levels of dedicating merit, ten grounds, the stage of universal awakening, and the stage of wondrous awakening. The seventh level of the ten levels of dwelling is called "non-retrogression," but there are several ways that a bodhisattva is said not to regress:

1. Bodhisattvas of the seventh level of the ten levels of dwelling and higher do not regress in attainment, and will no longer regress to the state of *sravakas* or *pratyekabuddhas*.

2. Bodhisattvas of the eighth level of the ten levels of dwelling and higher do not regress in their practice. Bodhisattvas at this level practice what is conditioned and unconditioned, so they will not regress.

3. Bodhisattvas of the eighth level of ground and higher do not regress in their mindfulness, for they do not need to strive diligently. They naturally advance along the path without giving it any thought.

4. Bodhisattvas reborn in Amitabha Buddha's Pure Land will not regress in their abiding.

5. Bodhisattvas of the sixth level of faith and higher will not regress in their faith, and no longer hold wrong views.

6. Bodhisattvas of the first ground and higher will not regress in their realization.

7. Bodhisattvas at the stage of universal awakening no longer regress in the face of affliction.

The Buddhist sutras often liken the human mind to a field. Learning Buddhism is thus like cultivating the field of the mind, and to do so one must have mental resolve, or *bodhicitta*, the "aspiration for awakening." Regarding *bodhicitta*, it is said that "the inception of the aspiration for awakening is more than enough to attain Buddhahood."

Among the many obstacles along the Budhist path, those obstacles related to the mind are the most dire. The Buddhist sutras have many names for the obstructed mind, including a mind with closed doors, a shackled mind, a burdened mind, a delusional mind, a sorrowful mind, a dark mind, a narrow mind, a negative mind, an erroneous mind, a greedy mind, a confused mind, and a mind that does not know emptiness. Of particular importance is the obstruction to making the aspiration for awakening, for if doing so is difficult then persevering to completion will be even more so.

Students of Buddhism should not only develop their minds to make great vows and seek improvement, renunciation, awakening, compassion, and joy, but also develop a mind that is steadfast. Given that the Buddhist path is a long one and the attainment of Buddhahood takes three great incalculable *kalpas*, one's commitment can be easily lost when encountering difficulties without motivation to stay the course. There is a Chinese saying, "After practicing Buddhism for one year, the Buddha is before your eyes; after practicing Buddhism for two years, the Buddha is up in the sky; and after practicing Buddhism for three years, the Buddha is nowhere to be found."

The *Flower Adornment Sutra* says that when learning Buddhism, one must not forget one's initial resolve. Only by holding to the vow made at the outset of Buddhist practice, will one then be able to remain steadfast and patient enough to overcome all the various obstacles along the way and attain awakening. To succeed, one must practice what is hard to practice and bear what is hard to bear, cultivate both merit and wisdom, and put equal emphasis upon practice and understanding.

Being fearful of trouble and lacking patience is like planting a seed without giving it water and fertilizer: one cannot expect it to sprout, much less flower and bear fruit. To go from one's initial resolve to final completion is the path of achieving Buddhahood. As long as we do not regress in our faith, regress in our vows, or regress in our practice, attaining Buddhahood is not hard at all.

## Avalokitesvara
## 觀世音

*See:* Mountains, four great; noble ones of the West, three.

## Avici Hell
## 五無間罪

*See also:* Hell.

To be weary of suffering and gladdened by happiness is human nature. Who does not wish to live a fortunate and happy existence in this lifetime and be reborn in the heavenly realms after death, or find rebirth in a Pure Land? Who does not fear falling into hell?

There is a saying in Chinese: "Being reborn in heaven results from its own reward. Immortality is not attained just because one seeks it." By the same principle, rebirth in hell has its own karmic causes as well. Except from the application of supernatural powers or the power of a vow, sentient beings enter hell due to their negative karma from past deeds. Among these, commiting the five great violations in particular will lead one to hell after death—the most painful and horrifying of them all being *avici*, the hell of uninterrupted torment. Just as the five great violations can lead one to suffer in *avici* hell, *avici* hell is characterized by its five kinds of uninterrupted torment:

### 1. Uninterrupted suffering（受苦無間）
The tormented beings suffer the various painful punishments of burning, killing, searing, boiling, roasting, broiling, and so on, one after the other, again and again, without reprieve.

### 2. Uninterrupted physical form（身形無間）
The bodies of tormented beings fill all the hells at the same time; and all the painful sufferings of all the hells are applied to their bodies at the same time, such that their suffering defies description.

### 3. Uninterrupted time（時間無間）
After dying from their torture, the tormented beings are revived again by a gust of their karmic wind so they can be punished some more. In this way they die and are revived again and again continuously.

### 4. Uninterrupted implements of torture（罪器無間）
*Avici* hell is filled with all manner of torture implements for punishment. Tormented beings will suddenly climb up a hill of knives,

then suddenly fall into the vat of boiling oil, and then just as suddenly, they will be hugging a fiery pillar, or force-fed molten copper. The brutality of their suffering cannot possibly be imagined by us human beings.

## 5. Uninterrupted categories of beings （眾類無間）
Different kinds of sentient beings are suffering at the same time, without the slightest separation.

Buddhism's doctrine of karmic effects arising in accordance with causes and conditions may seem fair and impartial and clear in its application of fortune and misfortune, but what is most wonderful about Buddhism is the practice of repentance. The practice of repentance offers transgressors an opportunity to repent and reform. Repentance is an act of internal reflection and self-inquiry and, like Dharma water, it can wash away our negative karma.

Those who know to repent when they commit a fault will prevent even more serious negative karma from occurring, for those who know the importance of repentance are not likely to repeat their faults again so rashly. Through repentance, even those who commit the five great violations will be able to see the light of day again once the effects of their negative karma have been exhausted. There is a Buddhist saying, "lay down the butcher's knife and become a Buddha right there and then." This explains how rare and supreme the meritorious accomplishments of repentance are.

In contrast, if one commits a fault and does not repent, one may escape the sanctions of the law, but one cannot escape the prison of the mind. That is why the Buddhist belief is not that committing faults is the problem, but committing them and not reforming oneself is. There may be wrongdoing, but as long as there is sincere repentance, one can wipe away negative karma and receive back one's original, pure nature. Just as when polishing a mirror, once the dust has been cleaned, one can see one's reflection. Therefore, in one's everyday life, there is no telling how many wrongful deeds, how many wrongful words, and how many deluded thoughts have occurred, consciously or unconsciously, through our body, speech, and mind. We must always be mindful of repentance, and use Dharma water to clean our mind, for only in this way can we constantly protect our pure, bright mind.

# B

## Becoming
有
*See:* Dependent origination.

## Bhadra
過江羅漢
*See:* Arhats, eighteen.

## Bhiksu
比丘
*See:* Assembly, sevenfold.

## Bhiksuni
比丘尼
*See*: Assembly, sevenfold.

## Birth
生
*See:* Dependent origination.

# Bodhisattva
# 菩薩

*See:* Dharma realms, ten.

# Bodhisattva Path, Ten Grounds of
# 十地

Students, whether in primary school, secondary school, or college, are all assigned to certain levels such as first year, second year, third year, and so on, to distinguish degrees of accomplishment. In the same way, the development of a bodhisattva is divided into fifty-two stages. From beginning to end they are: the ten levels of faith, the ten levels of dwelling, the ten levels of practice, the ten levels of dedicating merit, the ten grounds, universal awakening, and wondrous awakening. In particular, bodhisattvas of the "ten grounds" are truly great bodhisattvas. But what are these levels, and what do they mean?

The Chinese character di (地) "ground," is used because the ground gives rise to all things: trees, flowers, and plants grow out of the ground; gold and copper ore are produced in the ground; and all sentient beings can only live by relying on the ground. Bodhisattvas can be categorized into these "ten grounds," for just as the ground gives rise to all things, these levels give rise to all merit. Bodhisattvas within the ten grounds are soon to become Buddhas. The ten grounds are:

## 1. The Ground of Joy (歡喜地)
Bodhisattvas of the first ground have eliminated the bonds of views of the body, views that attach to wrong views as truth, and doubt; they are no longer susceptible to fear, error, or illusion. They do not

worry about life nor do they fear death; and they do not complain when others slander them. Bodhisattvas of the first ground are said to have been "born into the Buddha's family." Such bodhisattvas base themselves on helping others, find joy in being generous, are able to perpetuate and enrich the seed of Buddhism and teach the Dharma to liberate sentient beings. Since they have perceived and experienced the Buddha's Dharmakaya and are in accord with the aspiration for awakening, bodhisattvas of this ground jump for joy.

### 2. The Ground of Freedom from Defilement（離垢地）

Bodhisattvas of the second ground have cultivated the ten wholesome actions and have also encouraged others to do so as well. They no longer violate the minor precepts and are free from worldly defilement. They have purified the three kinds of karma and are able to reach many with their compassion to benefit sentient beings.

### 3. The Ground of Radiance（發光地）

Bodhisattvas of the third ground diligently seek out the Dharma and put it into practice. Such bodhisattvas are able to bear all external circumstances and remain unperturbed. They thoroughly practice meditative concentration and the four immeasurable minds of loving-kindness, compassion, joy, and equanimity. They are no longer blinded by greed, hatred, and delusion, and their noble character grows like a bright light that drives away darkness.

### 4. The Ground of Brilliant Wisdom（燄慧地）

Bodhisattvas of the fourth ground persevere in the cultivation of the thirty-seven aspects of awakening (the four bases of mindfulness, the four right efforts, the four bases of spiritual powers, the five faculties, the five strengths, the seven factors of awakening, and the

Noble Eightfold Path). Except for lingering attachment to the self and phenomena, their understanding is free of delusion and their thinking is also without error. They are no longer defiled by greed nor disturbed by anger. The light of their wisdom is like a flaming torch, burning brightly, illuminating the path to Buddhahood.

### 5. The Ground of Mastery of Final Difficulties （難勝地）
Bodhisattvas of the fifth ground have not only fully mastered meditative concentration but have also realized the true principles of reality. Such bodhisattvas have abandoned sophistry and have realized the non-duality of emptiness and existence. They abide in neither the cycle of birth and death, nor *nirvana*. This is an extremely difficult ground to achieve.

### 6. The Ground of Manifesting Prajna-wisdom （現前地）
Bodhisattvas of the sixth ground have perfected *prajna*-wisdom and often find their repose in meditating upon cessation, where discrimination does not arise in their mind.

Such bodhisattvas have directly experienced the inherent emptiness of dependent origination and have completely realized the nature of all phenomena. Those who have attained this ground are said to have had the true Dharma manifest before them.

### 7. The Ground of Proceeding Afar （遠行地）
Bodhisattvas of the seventh ground find their repose in meditating upon cessation, and they can enter and leave this level of meditation at will. They effortlessly practice all the Buddha's teachings, and possess unlimited skillful means which they use to liberate sentient beings. Bodhisattvas of this stage are about to achieve their long, far-off goal.

B

### 8. *The Ground of Attaining Calm*（不動地）

Bodhisattvas of the eighth ground have virtues which increase of their own accord, and no longer have any afflictions. These bodhisattvas remain unmoved by fame and fortune and are not tempted by external attractions. For them, all that remains is their great vow to liberate all sentient beings.

### 9. *The Ground of Finest Discriminatory Wisdom*（善慧地）

The practice of bodhisattvas of the ninth ground is formless and effortless. Not only do they achieve their own realizations without effort, but they are able to effortlessly teach the Dharma to others as well. They apply the power of the Dharma which comes naturally to them for the sake of protecting the Buddhist teachings, which they reveal and proclaim to sentient beings with their superbly excellent wisdom.

### 10. *The Ground of the Dharma Cloud*（法雲地）

Bodhisattvas of the tenth ground are the true princes of the Dharma. They are still bodhisattvas, but are very near attaining Buddhahood. They possess great compassion and great supernatural powers. They are protected by a cloud of merit and wisdom which, in a hail of lightning and thunder, can release a downpour of Dharma rain to subdue the wicked people and outsiders. In the end, he will attain Buddhahood.

From their initial vow on through the ten grounds, bodhisattvas have completed three great *kalpas* of practice, and then wait to take their place as Buddhas.

# Breath
息

*See:* Contemplations, five.

**B**

# Buddha
佛

*See:* Contemplations, five; dharma realms, ten; gem, triple;
Maitreya Bodhisattva; marks of excellence, thirty-two; names
of the Buddha, ten; questions of the Buddha, four.

# Buddha's Progress, Eight Stages of
八相成道

The sutras say that, "All Buddhas appear in this world because of
one great matter." The Buddha lived in this world for eighty years,
and his life can be summed up well in the eight major events of his
life, also known as the "eight stages of the Buddha's progress":

## 1. Descent from Tusita Heaven（降兜率）
In a former life, Sakyamuni Buddha's eventual awakening was
predicted by Dipankara Buddha, who said that he would become
a bodhisattva and then later become the next Buddha of the Saha
world. Before attaining his final birth in which he would attain
awakening, he dwelt in the inner court of Tusita Heaven for four
thousand years, as he observed the conditions for bringing liberation to the Saha world.

## 2. Entry into the womb（入胎）
After he had dwelt in Tusita Heaven for four thousand years, the
Buddha came down from that heaven riding a white elephant,

and entered the womb of his noble mother, Queen Maya, from the right side of her body.

### 3. Birth（誕生）

On the eighth day of the fourth lunar month, as flowers bloomed in warmth of spring while a brilliant sun shined in the sky, the Buddha was born in the Lumbini Garden. After his birth, the Buddha took seven steps, pointed one hand towards the heavens and his other hand towards the earth, and said, "In the heavens above and the earth below, I am the sole honored one."

### 4. Leaving home（出家）

At the age of twenty-nine, the Buddha was moved by the impermanence of the world, how the weak are at the mercy of the strong, and the injustice of the world. Thereupon, courageously and with determination, the Buddha rode his horse out of the city-gate, leaving his home and renouncing his former life.

### 5. Subduing Mara（降魔）

As he meditated beneath the bodhi tree, the Buddha was plagued by the demon Mara. Mara came internally as the afflictions of greed and anger, and came externally as opportunities for carnal pleasure and wealth. Subduing Mara and remaining untouched by the seductions placed before him required great determination, heroism, wisdom, and fearlessness.

### 6. Awakening（成道）

After Mara was subdued, the Buddha attained awakening on the eighth day of the twelfth lunar month, as he sat beneath the bodhi tree gazing into the starry night.

**B**

### 7. Turning the Dharma wheel（轉法輪）

After he attained awakening, the Buddha taught the Dharma for forty-nine years and gave teachings at more that three hundred Dharma assemblies. He spread the truth to all of humankind and ensured that the Dharma wheel would always be turning in this world.

### 8. Final nirvana（涅槃）

On the fifteenth day of the second lunar month in the Buddha's eightieth year, his teaching career was complete. In the city of Kusinagara, along the banks of the Ajitavati River, between two sala trees, the Buddha entered final *nirvana*.

The "eight stages of the Buddha's progress" depict the transformative aspects of the Buddha's life. Among these, the major turning point was the Buddha's subduing of Mara: if he had been unable to conquer Mara, he would not have attained awakening, and without awakening, he would not have taught the Dharma and brought liberation to sentient beings. Because the Buddha was able to subdue Mara, the Triple Gem became complete, and the light of the Dharma shone upon the human world. "Mara," the demon, primarily refers to the demons to be found within the mind. If we can subdue these demons by cultivating the mind, then the light of the Triple Gem will shine forth.

## Buddha Statues
## 佛像

*See:* Attendants; shrine, main; structures and buildings.

# C

## Caodong School
### 曹洞宗
*See:* Chan schools.

## Cause and Condition
### 因緣
*See:* Contemplations, five; dependent origination.

## Chan Schools
### 五家七派

The Chan School of Buddhism is traditionally divided into a number of different sects, known as the "five houses and seven schools," all of which at one time stemmed from the Southern School of Chan.

The Chan School was first brought to China by Bodhidharma (d. 535 CE), the Twenty-eighth Indian Patriarch, where it was passed on through five patriarchs to Hongren (602-675 CE). After that, the school was divided into the Northern School of Shenxiu (605-706

CE) and the Southern School of Huineng. After Huineng, there came the further division into the "five houses" of Linji, Guiyang, Caodong, Yunmen, and Fayan. This period of profusion is historically known as "one flower opening with five petals."

During the Song dynasty (960-1279 CE), the Huanglong and Yangqi sects developed out of the Linji school. When added together with the previous five sects, they were known as the "seven schools." These distinctions solidified into what is commonly called the "five houses and seven schools" of Chan.

Each of these sects maintained their own lineage and style. The founders of each sect had their own unique way of transmitting their principal doctrines, and their own methods for training their disciples. Each sect can be characterized by its quickness or slowness, and its sternness or laxity:

### 1. The Linji School (臨濟宗)

This school was founded by Linji Yixuan (d. 867 CE), a disciple of Huangbo Xiyun (d. 850 CE). Linji would often shout as a way of teaching his students. Chan Master Fayan Wenyi (885-958 CE) once described Linji's style as "a thunderclap upon the five great violations." This means that Linji's shout was so powerful that it seemed to split one's head, just as a thunderclap might split apart anyone guilty of the five great violations. The Linji School's style is like an iron hammer striking a rock, making sparks fly, or like the crash of a thunderbolt that rattles one's conscience.

### 2. The Guiyang School (溈仰宗)

This school was founded by Guishan Lingyou (771-853 CE) and Yangshan Huiji (840-916 CE), both disciples of Baizhang Huaihai (720-814 CE). The Guiyang School uses a teaching method called the "ninety-seven symbolic circles," and has a mild style, unlike the fierceness of the Linji School. The *Eyes of Heaven and Humanity* states: "The Guiyang School is typified by the kindness of fathers and the obedience of its sons, in which those above give orders and those below carry them out. It is said, 'You want to eat something, then I'll cook for you; you want to cross the river, then I will row the boat.' See smoke over yonder hills and you know there's a fire; see a horn peek out over the wall and you know there's a bull." *On the Ten Rules for Disciples of Chan Master Fayan* states, "In the Guiyang School they show their agreement through symbols, like an echo resonating in a canyon or presenting a pass at the gate." This shows how mild the style of this school was.

### 3. *The Caodong School* （曹洞宗）

This school was founded by Dongshan Liangjie (807-869 CE) and his disciple Caoshan Benji (840-901 CE). *On the Ten Rules for Disciples of Chan Master Fayan* comments that "the Caodong School employs the method of knocking and receiving an answer." This implies that the style of this school employed the give and take of questions and answers, which can be refreshingly different from a more sharp approach. The third chapter of the *Eyes of Heaven and Humanity* states: "The Caodong School is typified by delicate work, in which words and deeds correspond to each other; where living beings are benefited in accordance with their spiritual capacity, and the right word is employed to initiate the student." There is an old Chan saying, "Linji for generals, Caodong for farmers." The style of the Linji School is more like a general who commands thousands of troops, while the style of the Caodong School is more like a farmer who manages a few fields here and there.

### 4. The Yunmen School （雲門宗）

The founder of this school was Chan Master Yunmen Wenyan (864-949 CE), whose style was described as "all-inclusive" and "ending outflows." This means putting an end to the outflow of merit life after life, as teacher and student become part of all-inclusive suchness. The Yunmen School styled itself after the act of bringing a rushing torrent to a sudden stop. The third chapter of the *Eyes of Heaven and Humanity* states: "The main doctrines of the Yunmen School were 'stopping all outflows,' 'disallowing judgment based upon conjecture,' 'negating any path for ordinary or awakened beings,' and 'going beyond emotion and logic.'" Such was the style of the Yunmen School.

### 5. The Fayan School （法眼宗）

The founder of this school was Chan Master Qingliang Wenyi (885-958 CE). His style was to guide his students using the "six characteristics" and the "four outlooks." The fifth chapter of the *Eyes of Heaven and Humanity* states: "For the Fayan School, when teacher and student perfectly interact, words and their meaning are perfectly matched. The beginning is bold and dashing and the end stimulating, for as the human mind is permeated, feelings and conceptualization are swept aside. Adjusting to capacity and circumstance, blockages are opened up and confusion ground away. All the various teaching stories cannot be fully detailed here. In general, the style of the Fayan School was one in which medicine was applied to treat the illness; and the teacher appeared tailored to the nature of the student's capacity, so that perception and comprehension were swept aside." Such was the style of the Fayan School.

### 6. The Yangqi School（楊岐派）

This school was an offshoot of the Linji School and its founder, Chan Master Fanghui (996-1049 CE), practiced his own style of teaching from Mount Yangqi near Yuanzhou. Later generations called it the Yangqi School. Fanghui's fundamental ideas were drawn from the doctrines of the Linji School, and he once said, "Fog locking away the vast sky; wind stirring across the open wilderness; all the plants and trees grow as tall as the lion roars—these are teachings on the great *prajna*-wisdom, while the Buddhas of the past, present, and future are all turning the great wheel of Dharma right under your feet. If you can realize this, then your efforts have not been wasted." This approach bears a great deal of affinity with the Yunmen School's doctrine on the "all-inclusive universe" in which everything is already done. In this way the Yangqi School combines the styles of the Linji and Yunmen schools.

### 7. The Huanglong School（黃龍派）

Chan Master Huinan (1002-1069 CE), an eighth-generation disciple of Linji, began as a student of the Yunmen School under Letan Huaicheng (ca. 10th-11th cent. CE). He later taught in the Linji style at Huanglong in Longxing prefecture. Subsequent generations have called this the Huanglong School. He once proclaimed, "Is the Way far off? Whatever can be seen is real! Is sagehood far away? One becomes divine through direct realization!" From these statements it can be seen that the Huanglong School reflects the Linji view that "whatever can be seen is real."

Classical writers have characterized the teaching styles of the "five houses" as follows:

- The Caodong School gives careful instructions.
- The Linji School overpowers one.
- The Yunmen School is abrupt and fast.
- The Fayan School uses skillful means.
- The Guiyang School applies interpretation.

C

Although the style of the five houses vary in their laxity or fierceness, quickness or slowness, each of their varying styles are skillful means through which the masters of these schools guided their students.

## Clinging
## 取

*See:* Dependent origination.

## Compassion
## 悲

*See:* Immeasurable minds, four; mountain gate.

## Comportment, Four Kinds of
## 四威儀

The observation of etiquette and comportment are fundamental aspects of what makes us human beings. Buddhists in particular should care about how they conduct themselves in everyday life; they should be courteous and polite; and they should ensure that their every action is in accord with proper comportment.

The sutras mention the "three thousand rules of proper manners and eighty thousand fine practices." As beginners, of course, there is no way for us to achieve such perfection, but we should at least follow the four kinds of comportment:

### 1. Walk Like the Wind（行如風）

When walking, one should not look around or let the body sway from side to side. One should lift the head, keep the chest squared, and look straight ahead as one moves forward just like the wind.

### 2. Stand Like a Pine（立如松）

When standing, one should not incline to one side or the other, nor lean against walls to prop oneself up. One should be remain steadfast as a pine tree.

### 3. Sit Like a Bell（坐如鐘）

When sitting, one should not bend at the waist, hunch the back, or cross one leg over the other and let it dangle and shake. One should keep the feet firmly planted on the ground, just as a bell is stable and dignified.

### 4. Sleep Like a Bow（臥如弓）

When sleeping, one should not lie on one's back or sleep on one's stomach, nor cover the head and fold up the legs. One should use the right hand as a pillow and lay on one's side like a bow.

The purpose of learning Buddhism is to purify the mind and body, and transform our temperament. Sometimes, when the body is positioned properly the condition of the mind will become proper, while sometimes the proper condition of the mind can promote the proper positioning of the body. A person who emphasizes comportment will naturally purify the body and mind, and his moral character will become elevated. We should routinely practice walking, standing, sitting, and sleeping as described above, as well as pay particular attention to our comportment when we recite Amitabha Buddha's name, venerate the Buddha, or chant sutras.

C

> While reciting the Buddha's name be like slow,
>     flowing water;
> When chanting the sutras be orderly as geese in
>     formation;
> Fold your hands together before your chest like
>     holding water;
> Stand still and straight like balancing a pot of oil
>     atop of your head;
> Look ahead and watch behind as you step
>     lightly;
> Turning left or right, look by glancing to the
>     side;
> If you can always conduct yourself like this, in
>     rest or activity;
> You haven't wasted your time as a Buddhist
>     monastic.

How civilized a person is can be determined by their comportment. The four kinds of comportment mentioned above are not only practiced by monastics, but lay people should observe them as well.

# Consciousness, Eight Kinds of
八識

*See also*: Aggregates, five; dependent origination.

> Of eight brothers, one is dimwitted;
> While another is the most clearheaded.
> Five others do business outside the door;
> While one remains indoors and makes all the
>   plans.

This verse describes the functions of the mind and serves as metaphors for the eight consciousnesses. The eight consciousnesses are as follows: the eye consciousness, the ear consciousness, the nose consciousness, the tongue consciousness, the body consciousness, the mind consciousness, the *manas* consciousness, and the *alaya* consciousness.

"Five others do business outside the door" refers to the first five consciousnesses that serve as the vanguards of the mind. Each of the first five consciousnesses is associated with a particular sense organ and sense object. For example, the eye consciousness relies upon the eyes to discriminate color and shape data. The ear consciousness relies upon the ears to discriminate sound data. The nose consciousness relies upon the nose to discriminate what is fragrant and malodorous. The tongue consciousness relies upon the tongue to discriminate tastes. The body consciousness relies upon the body to discriminate sensations as pain, itchiness, cold, and heat.

The line, "While one remains indoors and makes all the plans" refers to the sixth consciousness, the mind consciousness. The mind consciousness has the ability to think and discriminate. If

C

the first five consciousnesses were not processed by the thinking of the sixth or mind consciousness, then whatever the eyes saw, the ears heard, the nose smelled, the tongued tasted, and the body felt could not be processed into perceptions like beauty and ugliness, pleasing or discordant, fragrant or malodorous, sour or sweet, and fine or course. We would not cling to desirable objects or reject undesirable objects, and we would not have the afflictions of greed, anger, or ignorance. This constant churning of thoughts is the function of the mind consciousness.

The line "One is dimwitted" refers to the seventh, or *manas* consciousness. The *manas* consciousness is always focused on the self, and is the origin of selfishness, attachment, and ignorance. That is why it is called "dimwitted."

The eighth consciousness, the *alaya consciousness*, is the source of all phenomena in the universe. It is referenced in the verse as the "most clearheaded," because it stores within it the potential for Buddhahood.

In this context, these eight are referred to as *bashi* (八識), "eight consciousnesses." However, when talking about the various faculties of the mind there are many different words which are used, including *xin* (心), "mind," *yi* (意), "thought," and *shi* (識), "consciousness." In general usage, the first five consciousnesses are referred to simply as "eyes, ears, nose, tongue, and body." The sixth consciousness is referred to as "mind." The seventh, or *manas* consciousness, is referred to as "thought." The eighth, *alaya* consciousness is referred to as "consciousness."

Each of the eight consciousnesses has its own duties. The mind consciousness directs the consciousnesses of the eyes, ears, nose, tongue, and body to engage in various activities. This creates positive or negative karma, and the *manas* consciousness passes these karmic seeds onto the *alaya* consciousness. The *alaya* consciousness is also called the "storehouse consciousness" because it stores up all the positive and negative karma one creates, and thus acts like a storehouse or safe-deposit box. The *alaya* consciousness is the master of our life.

The *Verses on the Structure of the Eighth Consciousness* states: "It is the master; it comes first and leaves last." After death, the eye, ear, nose, tongue, and body will cease their functioning, but the *alaya* consciousness is the very last to leave the body. When the *alaya* consciousness enters the womb in the next rebirth, the eyes, ears, nose, tongue, and body will have already matured, but it is only when consciousness enters the womb that there can be any understanding of the external world.

Consciousness is the essence of our lives, for it is never destroyed nor is it ever lost. It is like a thread which links together the beads of a rosary, threading the past, present, and future together. Life in the past, present, and future relies upon it unceasingly to continue its endless cycle.

The *alaya* consciousness is like a field, for one will reap what has been sown. Such is the origin of the Buddhist expression, "Know the causes in your past lives by looking at what befalls you in the present life. Know your future outcome by looking at what you are doing now." Each one of us can become the master of our fate, for it all depends upon how you plant and cultivate the field of the *alaya* consciousness.

## Contact
觸

*See:* Dependent origination.

# Contemplations, Five
## 五停心觀

There are many sayings which describe the Buddha's wisdom of skillful means in teaching sentient beings, such as "teachings which adapt in accordance with the audience's capacity," and "the right medicine must be given for the right ailment."

Since sentient beings vary in their spiritual capacity, the Buddha gave various teachings to meet their needs. For example, for sentient beings with many desires, he taught the contemplation of impurity. For sentient beings with lots of anger, he taught the contemplation of loving-kindness and compassion. For sentient beings who are especially ignorant, he taught the contemplation of causes and conditions. For sentient beings with many obstacles, he taught the contemplation of the Buddha. For those sentient beings who are confused or distracted, he taught the contemplation of counting the breath. Together these are called the "five contemplations."

The five contemplations are beginning practices for developing meditative concentration. Each is given in detail below:

### 1. The Contemplation of Impurity (不淨觀)

The contemplation of impurity is used as an antidote for desire. One visualizes all the filth and muck contained within the physical body of oneself and others to remove the affliction of desire. Due to desire, sentient beings produce attachment to "me" and "mine," which lead to various forms of pain and suffering. That is why the Buddha taught us to visualize all the dirty filth related to one's own body, including the seed of impurity, abiding impurity, the essence of impurity, the impurity of external characteristics.

C

This will reduce sexual desire for one's own body and the body of others.

## 2. The Contemplation of Loving-Kindness and Compassion (慈悲觀)

The contemplation of loving-kindness and compassion is used as an antidote for anger. There are some who often get angry for no reason and do harm to sentient beings; this is known as unjustifiable anger. There are others who become angry when they are harmed by others, or see that while they do what is wholesome, others are unwholesome; this is known as justifiable anger. Some people believe that only they are right, and everyone else is wrong, and thus they angrily argue with others; this is called argumentative anger. Of these three types of anger, the Buddha taught that "loving-kindness for sentient beings" can put an end to unjustifiable anger, "loving-kindness based upon reality" can bring an end to justifiable anger, and "unconditional loving-kindness" can bring an end to argumentative anger.

## 3. The Contemplation of Causes and Conditions (因緣觀)

The contemplation of causes and conditions is used as an antidote for ignorance. For those who are ignorant of nihilism and eternalism, and mistakenly think that phenomena are destroyed or exist forever, the Buddha recommended contemplating the causes and conditions of the past, present, and future. For those who are ignorant of existence and non-existence, and mistakenly think that phenomena are truly existent or non-existent, the Buddha recommended contemplating the causes and conditions of karma. For those who are ignorant of the nature of the material world and become attached to the four elements, the five aggregates, and the labels applied to sentient beings and the world, the Buddha recommended contemplating the causes and conditions of a single thought.

### 4. The Contemplation of the Buddha (念佛觀)

The contemplation of the Buddha is used as an antidote to various karmic obstacles. By employing mindfulness of the Buddha's Nirmanakaya, Sambhogakaya, and Dharmakaya, one can clear away karmic obstacles. The negative karma that we have created with our body, speech, and mind will generate negative karmic effects in the future. Before these negative effects manifest themselves, we should cultivate merit and good deeds, for the manifestation of negative karma can often hinder the wholesome path. Such negative karmic effects are the "karmic obstacles" that contemplation of the Buddha can help to relieve. For example, by contemplating the Buddha's Nirmanakaya radiant appearance we can put an end to the obstacles of sloth and laziness. By contemplating the Buddha's Sambhogakaya with its majestic accomplishments we can put an end to the obstacles of negative thoughts and thinking. By contemplating the Buddha's tranquil Dharmakaya we can put an end to the obstacles of one's mental state.

### 5. The Contemplation of Counting the Breath (數息觀)

The contemplation of counting the breath is used as an antidote for confusion and distraction. By counting the in-breaths and out-breaths one can ease the mental talk that leads to confusion and distraction so that the mind can become settled. The process of contemplating the breath has six stages: counting the breath, following the breath, stopping illusion, contemplating truth, focusing the mind, and purification. This contemplation can only be considered complete when all six of the stages are fulfilled. These six stages are also known as *liu miaomen* (六妙門), "six wonderful methods."

There is a Buddhist saying that, "It does not matter whether the Dharma is high or low; the most profound is that which correlates with one's spiritual capacity. In the same way, it does not matter if the medicine is expensive or cheap; the best is the one which cures the disease." The Dharma consists of eighty-four thousand teachings, and though there are many skillful means, they all return to the same source. All Buddhist teachings are meant to guide us along the path to Buddhahood. All one needs to do is find the method of practice that is most suitable for oneself and follow it without distraction. When practicing in this way, one will surely get results.

## Continents, Four Great
## 四大部洲

According to the Jambu-dvipa chapter of the *Dirghagama*, at the center of the universe is a massive mountain called Mount Sumeru, which rises eighty-four thousand *yojana* above sea level (one *yojana* is between 4.5 and 5 miles). Mount Sumeru is surrounded by four continents, nine mountains, and eight oceans. Above Mount Sumeru lie the sun, moon, and stars, as well as the heavens of the first *dhyana*. Below Mount Sumeru lies a great wheel of wind that is located beneath the earth. All of these structures constitute a single minor "world-system," which is similar to a "solar system." It includes the human realm, hell realm, hungry ghost realm, animal realm, *asura* realm, the six heavens of the desire realm, and the three heavens of the first *dhyana*. Buddhist cosmology considers the great three thousandfold world system to be made up of many minor world systems, as described above.

Human beings live on one of the "four continents" that are oriented around Mount Sumeru in each of the cardinal directions. They are located by the salty ocean between the seven golden mountains and the great iron mountains. The four continents are:

### 1. Purva-videha （東勝身洲）

This continent is located in the salty ocean to the east of Mount Sumeru. The humans who live in this continent have extraordinarily fine bodies, and as such the continent is also called *shensheng* （身勝）, "superlative bodies." The Jambu-dvipa chapter of the *Dirghagama* says, "To the east of Mount Sumeru there lies a world named Purva-videha. The land is laid out in a perfect circle with a diameter that spans nine thousand *yojana*. The faces of the people there are also round, like the shape of their land." This continent is extraordinary in three ways: it is extremely vast, extremely grand, and extremely wondrous.

### 2. Jambu-dvipa （南贍部洲）

This continent lies to the south of Mount Sumeru. In Buddhist cosmology, this is the continent that we live on. It is a rich producer of gold and Jambu trees. Jambu-dvipa is shaped like a rectangle, similar to the trunk of a cart, and the people who live here have faces shaped the same way. The people who dwell on this continent have superior recollection and superior bravery. They can cultivate good karma and pure conduct, for Buddhas appear here. For this reason Jambu-dvipa is said to be superior to the other three continents and the various heavens.

C

### 3. Apara-godaniya（西牛貨洲）

This continent is situated west of Mount Sumeru. Sheep, cattle, and *mani* jewels are plentiful here, and serve as currency. The land is shaped like a full moon, and the people who live here also have faces shaped like the full moon. This continent is extraordinary in three ways: many cattle, many sheep, and many *mani* jewels.

### 4. Uttara-kuru（北俱盧洲）

This continent is found in the salty ocean north of Mount Sumeru. It is shaped like a square, with each side being two thousand *yojana* in length. The overall appearance is one of a lid, and it is surrounded by the seven golden mountains and the great iron mountains. The ground is made of gold, which shines brightly day and night. The land is even, tranquil, clean, and without brambles. The faces of the people who live there are square-shaped, like the continent itself, and they are of even complexion and great height, standing fourteen feet tall. The people of this land live a worry-free life of equality, peace, and joy. The continent is filled with various wonderful mountains, forests, rivers and streams, swimming pools, gardens, and fruited trees. The people use utensils made of gold, silver, glass, and crystal, which are shared by all. There is no robbery or bickering, nor are there any thieves, wicked people, or fighting. The people of this continent live to be a thousand years old, and when they die, they are reborn in Trayastrimsat or Paranirmita-vasavartin heavens. Among all the four continents, their karma is very fine. However, because no Buddha has appeared in this land, being born here is considered one of the eight difficulties for learning Buddhism.

We may live on this earth, but there is a vast number of stars in space with worlds so numerous that we cannot comprehend them. In this same way, Buddhist cosmology posits innumerable worlds. As the Buddha underwent many *kalpas* of practice he directly experienced the vast numbers of worlds over limitless time and space, so many that they cannot be calculated.

## Craving
愛
*See:* Dependent origination; desires, five.

## Cudapanthaka
看門羅漢
*See:* Arhats, eighteen.

# D

## Death
## 死
*See:* Decay, five signs of; dependent origination.

## Decay, Five Signs of
## 五衰相現
*See also:* Heaven.

Most people hope to go to heaven after they die, but for Buddhists, rebirth in heaven is not the final goal by any means. Even though the rewards of living in heaven are the highest among the  six realms of existence, once heavenly beings have exhausted their merit they suffer "the five signs of decay" and re-enter the cycle of birth and death among the six realms of existence.

The "five signs of decay" refer to two sets of five unusual phenomena, the five major marks and the five minor marks, that appear when the life of a heavenly being is about to end. The five major marks are as follows:

## 1. Clothes become filthy（衣服垢穢）

The splendid and magnificent clothing of heavenly beings is always lustrous and clean, but once their merit is exhausted and their lives draw to an end, their clothing becomes sullied.

## 2. Garland atop the head fades（頭上華萎）

Heavenly beings are adorned with garlands of jewels whose pearls and jade sparkle with multicolored light. But once the merit of these beings is exhausted and their lives draw to an end, the garland crown atop their head will naturally darken and fade.

## 3. The armpits become sweaty（腋下出汗）

The marvelous and sublime bodies of heavenly beings are delicate and immaculate, but once their merit is exhausted and their lives draw to an end, their armpits begin to sweat.

## 4. The body becomes foul-smelling（身體臭穢）

The wondrous and extraordinary bodies of heavenly beings are always clean and fragrant, but once their merit is exhausted and their lives draw to an end, their bodies begin to exude a foul smell.

## 5. The heavenly palace appears unpleasant（不樂本座）

The pleasures and luxuries of heavenly beings are far superior to those in our human realm, but once their merit is exhausted and their lives draw to an end, they begin to loath the palaces that they live in.

The appearance of these five signs of decay indicate the imminent death of a heavenly being. There are also five minor signs of decay:

*1. The music stops*（樂聲不起）
The heavenly realms are filled with music produced by self-playing instruments, but when the signs of decay appear the music stops.

*2. The body's radiance fades*（身光忽滅）
The bodies of heavenly beings radiate a dazzling light that shines day and night, but when the signs of decay appear, this radiance fades away.

*3. Bathwater clings to the body*（浴水著身）
The skin of heavenly beings is smooth, fragrant, and as sublime as a lotus flower, such that water does not cling to the skin. But when the signs of decay appear, the skin of heavenly beings remains wet after bathing and does not dry off.

*4. Attachment to their surroundings*（著境不捨）
Though heavenly beings are surrounded by an extraordinarily magnificent landscape, they are not infatuated with it. But when the signs of decay appear, they become attached to these surroundings and cannot give them up.

*5. The eyes start blinking*（眼目數瞬）
The vision of heavenly beings is such that they can see everything in the universe without obstruction, but when the signs of decay appear, their eyes begin to blink.

If the heavenly being has extraordinarily deep roots of goodness when the five minor signs of decay appear, then there is still a possibility that things will improve.

It is not only heavenly beings who experience signs of decay. According to the *Dirgha Agama*, those who break the precepts are beset by their own five signs of decay:

1. They will not gain wealth as they wish.
2. Even if they gain wealth, it will diminish daily.
3. They will not be respected no matter where they go.
4. Their bad reputation will be known throughout the world.
5. When they die they will fall into hell.

For this reason Buddhists should uphold the precepts, count their blessings, and foster good merit.

## Declining Dharma
## 末法
*See:* Ages of the Dharma, three.

## Dedication
## 回向

Those who are new to Buddhism often ask about the practice of "dedicating" merit to others each day. One may think, "My own efforts are not great and I have accumulated very little merit. Wouldn't there be too little merit left over for me?"

The practice of dedicating merit is actually quite extraordinary, and one that is unique to Buddhism. Dedication of merit is much like holding a candle to light another candle: not only is the light of the original candle not diminished in any way, but on the contrary, the light of the newly lit candle will ensure that the room becomes even brighter. In the same way, without diminishing anything of your own, the more merit is dedicated, the more people you will be able to help, and the more extraordinary your own merit will become.

The dedication of merit takes place in two parts:

**D**

*1. Storing up merit*（寄存）
One accumulates merit from practice in order to attain awakening. This merit is stored in the Buddha Land's field of merit.

*2. Sharing merit*（分享）
One offers and shares all the benefits of one's merit with all the sentient beings everywhere.

According to the sutras, dedication of merit can be categorized into six types:

*1. Dedicating phenomena to the absolute*（回事向理）
This is dedicating the merit of the phenomenal qualities of one's practice towards the attainment of absolute reality, which neither arises nor ceases.

*2. Dedicating cause to effect*（回因向果）
This is dedicating the meritorious practices which are the causes for awakening to the effect of supreme Buddhahood.

*3. Dedicating self to others*（回自向他）
This is the dedication of the merit of one's own practice to all sentient beings in the universe.

## 4. Dedicating the small to the large（回小向大）

This is the dedication of the Hinayana mind that is oriented towards self-realization and self-liberation to transform into the Mahayana mind of benefiting self and others.

## 5. Dedicating the few to the many（回少向多）

This is dedicating one's merit, as scarce as one's own roots of goodness may be, and sharing them broadly with joy and happiness, such that they can support all sentient beings.

## 6. Dedication of the inferior to the superior（回劣向勝）

This is dedicating the merit that comes from the joy of benefiting ordinary people, *sravakas*, and *pratyekabuddhas* and transforming it into an appreciation for supreme awakening.

Dedication of merit is the finest method of practice, and is part of the Mahayana bodhisattva path. It is a direct application of the concept of benefitting oneself and others, and treating friend and foe alike. Since we can dedicate our merit to all sentient beings, it is possible to dedicate merit to friend and foe alike, or even to one's creditors. In this way negative conditions can be transformed into positive ones, and misfortune can become good fortune. Dedication of merit is the embodiment of unconditional loving-kindness and compassion. Only those who have the spirit that the self and others are the same, and that friend and foe should be treated alike can dedicate merit. That is why a single thought of dedication is commended as supreme among all the acts of a bodhisattva. No matter what practice you do, or what merit you have achieved, all should be dedicated.

# Dependent Origination
# 十二因緣

*See also:* Karma.

Where do we come from when we are born and where do we go when we die? What is the source of sentient beings' journey through the cycle of birth and death? The Buddha's teaching on the twelve links of dependent origination can help solve this mystery.

The twelve links of dependent origination are twelve stages of life as it moves from past to present, and from present to future:

### 1. Ignorance（無明）

The Buddhist sutras say, "All phenomena arise through causes and conditions and cease due to causes and conditions. They arise when conditions come together and cease when conditions disperse." Not understanding reality in this way is ignorance. "Ignorance" in this instance is synonymous with delusion, and means being unable to understand causes and conditions.

### 2. Mental Formations（行）

Mental formations are that which generates karma of the body, speech, and mind. This karma is created from the ignorance of past lives.

### 3. Consciousness（識）

Relying upon previous karma as a cause, the present life comes into being. The moment that thought is embodied in the womb is the arising of consciousness. Consciousness is the entity that unifies one's mental faculties. The distinctions made by consciousness create a greater awareness of the outside world and heighten sensory perception. Consciousness also governs the thought process.

### 4. Name and form（名色）

"Name and form" refers to the five aggregates. "Name" is a collection of the mental aggregates of feeling, perception, mental formations, and consciousness, while "form" is the aggregate of form. Together the five aggregates are the mental and material components that make up life.

### 5. Six sense organs（六入）

The six sense organs are the eyes, ears, nose, tongue, body, and mind. They interact with the six sense objects of sight, sound, smell, taste, touch, and *dharmas.*

### 6. Contact（觸）

"Contact" refers to the consciousness generated when the six sense organs contact the six sense objects. For example, pleasure and pain, hunger and cold, or soreness and itchiness are all created by interaction between the body sense organ and touch sense objects.

### 7. Feeling（受）

There are three types of feeling generated with contact as a cause: painful feelings arise from things and people that are disliked, pleasurable feelings arise from things and people that are liked, and neither painful nor pleasurable feelings arise from things and people that are neutral.

### 8. Craving（愛）

Generating thoughts of greed towards what is desirable is "craving." For example, there is craving for wealth, for love, for life, for fame, and so on. Craving is the root of the cycle of birth and death.

The increase of craving leads to "clinging," and clinging made manifest as the conditions for behavior is "becoming," which leads to further travel in the cycle of birth and death.

### 9. Clinging（取）

"Clinging" refers to focusing on oneself in the mad pursuit of all things to the exclusion of every other consideration. This generates karma. There are four kinds of clinging: clinging to desire, clinging to wrong views, clinging to wrong rules, and clinging to the self.

### 10. Becoming（有）

There are two kinds of becoming: karmic becoming and life becoming. Physical, verbal, and mental actions generated in response to like or dislike that are wholesome or unwholesome are known as karmic becoming. Within this process are created effects which act as a force to propel future birth; this is life becoming.

### 11. Birth（生）

When a child is born from its mother's womb with a cry, this is birth. The subjectivity of the self with its five aggregates of form, feeling, perceptions, mental formations, and consciousness begins to develop and proceeds on to old age and death. This constitutes a single lifetime in the ongoing cycle of birth and death.

### 12. Aging and death（老死）

The physiological functions of the body will decline until the breath stops and the causes and conditions for the aggregates disperse and fade away. The reality of impermanence and change has finally arrived. This is old age and death. But this does not mean that the

entirety of the person is obliterated. After death and the separation of the five aggregates, consciousness combines with ignorance
and mental formations once again to begin another life. With one
thought of awakening, karma is no longer created by ignorance.
Otherwise, life will be just like the hands on a clock: turning round
and round endlessly with no beginning and no end.

D

The element that gives rise to an effect is called a "cause," and
the supporting elements are known as "conditions." A cause is like
a seed, and conditions are those functions that support its growth.
The causes and conditions of dependent origination continue in a
cycle as each link is the effect of the link that proceeded it, and the
cause for the next link.

The continuity of causation makes possible the continuity of
life. Changes in one's causes and conditions, whether they be positive or negative, will alter the course of future rebirths: some will
ascend to heaven and some will fall into hell; while others will
have their fortune or misfortune, their success or failure, and their
poverty or wealth. The content of one's life is formed from these
causes and conditions, which are in our hands to create. Therefore,
as long as one takes charge of the present by creating good causes
and good conditions, then one can certainly create a bright and
beautiful future.

## Desires, Five
## 五欲

Once there was a traveler who was being chased by a crazed elephant. The traveler was finally able to escape by climbing down
a vine into an old well, but as he descended into the well, four

poisonous snakes appeared and began climbing up the vine towards the traveler, ready to bite him. Just when he was about to climb back out again, there appeared above him two mice, one black and one white, who began gnawing away at the vine. The traveler was trapped from above and below, stuck between a rock and a hard place. Suddenly, from the top of the well, five drops of honey dripped into his mouth. At that moment, the traveler forgot all about the things that were threatening him, the crazed elephant and the poisonous snakes, for he had become intoxicated with the sweetness of the honey.

What were these five drops of honey, and how could they have possibly made the traveler forget about the dangers he was facing? In the story, the drops of honey are symbols for the five desires of wealth, sex, fame, food and drink, and sleep.

### 1. Wealth（財）

In today's materialistic society, everything costs money. We cannot pay one dime less than what we owe for the food, clothing, and transportation we enjoy. It even costs money to see a doctor or go to school. You cannot do without money in this life. There is no era in history that is without its greedy, corrupt officials, thieves, and bandits. Fighting and pillaging is all for the sake of money, just as mangling bodies so they are unidentifiable is all for the sake of money. People die over riches; the tragedies spawned by wealth are too many to count.

### 2. Sex（色）

Passionate feelings can sink sentient beings into an ocean of desire, and lead them to commit great wrongs. Suitors who have been thwarted have resorted to assault and even murder, and jilted lovers have sometimes resorted to suicide, all because of the desire for sex. Extramarital affairs ruin families, rape and seduction lead to courtroom accusations and lawsuits. It is not exterior form which beguiles these people, for they beguile themselves with their desire for sex which can lead to endless regrets.

### 3. Fame（名）

Fame itself is not bad—it is scrambling for fame, status, and renown that can lead one to heedlessly destroy friendships and make enemies. Many will not care if guns or knives are used if it is to gain power. Enmity and jealousy are generated for the sake of fame and status. Fawning and servile flattery are employed for the sake of fame and status. People behave with arrogance and blatant egotism for the sake of fame and status. People become covetous and obsessive for the sake of fame and status. There are a few sayings in Chinese, such as "The greatest trees are subject to the winds, the most famous are subject to jealousy." and "the higher the climb, the more serious the fall." When fame comes to those who have not actually risen to a level of distinction, the consequences can be quite grave.

### 4. Food and Drink（食）

Humans cannot live without food, but craving fine delicacies or gourmet meals will lead to disorders of the stomach and intestines, while the fondness for fine delicacies will poison the body and lead to death. Wars stem from the problem of hunger and scarcity; and human strife is often the consequence of a cup of soup shared unequally. Living beings are killed to satisfy our appetites, while family fortunes are squandered for unbridled gluttony. There is no telling how many crimes and negative deeds are hidden within rich fare and gourmet meals.

*5. Sleep*（睡）

After a day's work, people must rest and recuperate during the night, but too much craving for sleep will make one sluggish and lethargic the whole day through. Work and careers are neglected for the sake of sleep; and spiritual work is not practiced for the sake of sleep. The Buddha once chided Aniruddha saying, "How well you sleep! A snail in its shell will sleep a thousand years, never even hearing the Buddha's name!"

Sentient beings will become distracted and enamored by some temporary pleasure, and becoming slaves to the five desires, so that they are unable to free themselves from the three realms. For human beings, the five desires are like honey on the blade of a knife: trying to lick up the sweetness will cut our tongues. Only by having few desires and knowing contentment can one follow the path to peace and happiness.

## Dharani
**陀羅尼**
*See:* Om mani padme hum.

## Dharma
**法**
*See:* Gem, triple; giving; gratitude; harmony, six points of
  reverent; reliance, four kinds of; teaching, four modes of.

## Dharma Friends
**善知識**
*See also:* Friends, four kinds of.

The Entry into the Dharma Realm chapter of the *Flower Adornment Sutra* describes how the young Sudhana asked for instruction from fifty-three good Dharma friends so that he could learn to practice the bodhisattva path. "Good Dharma friend" (善知識) here refers to those individuals who have good moral conduct, can teach the true Dharma, and can lead others to follow the correct path. Those who teach in opposition to the Buddhist path and lead others astray are called "bad friends."

D

A good Dharma friend must have the right view and understanding of the Dharma, be well-versed in the sutras, and understand their principles. They must teach the Dharma joyfully and compassionately and to the capacity of listeners, such that they instill faith in their audience. The sutras describe good Dharma friends as "realizing the teachings and knowing true nature, teaching with compassion and skill." This means that the good Dharma friend must be virtuous and learned and have practiced and attained realization. Furthermore, they must be able to teach joyfully and skillfully, and excel in communicating the essentials of the Dharma to lead sentient beings to enter the Buddhist path, give up what is unwholesome, and practice what is wholesome. This is what a perfect Dharma friend can do. However, in the present Age of Declining Dharma it is difficult to find such good Dharma friends, so as long as someone's practice and understanding exceeds your own they can serve as your good Dharma friend.

Within Buddhist circles, teachers are often called "good Dharma friends." The term is also applied to those who act as companions on the path, or who support the Dharma financially, as both types of people are indispensable to the practice of the Buddhist path. These are known as the three kinds of Dharma friends:

*1. Good Dharma friends who give*（外護善知識）
These good Dharma friends provide material assistance and support for the path. They free others from non-essential tasks and from fear, so that they can practice the path in peace.

*2. Good Dharma friends who share in practice*（同行善知識）
These good Dharma friends accompany us on the path, so that we can learn from and encourage one another.

*3. Good Dharma friends who teach*（教授善知識）
These good Dharma friends teach the Dharma, help us resolve our doubts, and reveal right view to us. Under their guidance, we can remove what is unwholesome and pursue what is wholesome, and understand cause and effect.

Dharma friends exert the greatest influence on our own cultivation. The sutras offer many analogies to describe Dharma friends, saying that they sustain us like the earth, support us like a tall mountain, protect us like a nursemaid, mend our suffering like a doctor, destroy our fears like a brave general, and ferry us across the sea of birth and death like a ship's captain.

The *Sutra on the Great Assembly on the True Dharma* says, "The good Dharma is our Dharma friend." The phrase "good Dharma" here refers to the Dharma that accords with principles and benefits the world. Teachings such as the three Dharma seals, the Four Noble Truths, the six perfections, and the four immeasurable minds allow sentient beings to free themselves from suffering and obtain happiness, as well as create the causes and conditions for awakening. Ultimately speaking, the Dharma itself is the true "good Dharma friend" that can lead us to the good path, and so students of Buddhism should listen to the true Dharma teachings. In doing so they will truly get to learn from a good Dharma friend.

# Dharma Realms, Ten
# 十法界

D

The ordinary and noble beings in Buddhism are divided into the following ten categories, proceeding from the bottom to the top: hell-beings, hungry ghosts, animals, human beings, *asuras*, heavenly beings, *sravakas*, *pratyekabuddhas*, bodhisattvas, and Buddhas. Since each of these varieties of beings arises due to its own causes and conditions with clearly delineated boundaries, the collection of these beings is known as the "ten dharma realms."

### 1. Hell（地獄）

Among the three lower realms, the pain and suffering of the hells is the most intense. Most of these hells are situated underneath the southern continent of Jambu-dvipa, and they resemble the prisons of the human world. Beings there are constrained by instruments of punishment and cannot act freely. Hell is called *diyu* (地獄) in Chinese, but is also known as *kuju* (苦具), "collections of suffering," and *kuqi* (苦器), "container of suffering." Sentient beings who often commit the ten unwholesome actions, particularly the five great violations, will be reborn in hell.

### 2. Hungry Ghost Realm（餓鬼）

The beings of this realm are fearsome creatures who live by begging for food and drink from others, so they are called *egui* (餓鬼), "hungry ghosts." Those who commit the ten unwholesome actions and are governed by greed, jealousy, sycophancy, corruption, or even die from hunger and thirst, will be reborn in the hungry ghost realm.

### 3. Animal Realm（畜生）

Beings in the animal realm are inherently ignorant and, in the case of domesticated animals, cannot act independently and must be cared for by others. Animals appear through the six realms of existence and are of many varieties. One way to categorize them is separating them into three groups according to their habitat: those that live in the water, those that live in the air, and those that live on the land. Those who create negative karma because of their ignorance of cause and effect but only feel little regret are reborn in the animal realm.

### 4. Human Realm（人）

Human beings are known for their endurance, since they are able to endure the various forms of pleasure and pain of this world. A human existence is key in determining future rebirth, and it is the hardest rebirth to attain among the six realms of existence. Observing the five precepts and a moderate practice of the ten wholesome actions is the cause for rebirth as a human being.

### 5. Asura Realm（阿修羅）

Rebirth as an *asura* is second only to rebirth as a heavenly being, for *asuras* lack the moral character of heavenly beings. For this reason, the *asura* realm is also sometimes called *wutian* （無天）, "non-heaven." *Asuras* are those beings who at least had a meager practice of the ten wholesome actions in their previous lives, but could not be reborn in the heavenly realm because of

an overwhelming preponderance of hatred, arrogance, and sus-
piciousness. Furthermore, due to their jealousy of heavenly beings, the *asuras* make war upon Lord Indra. Asuras can be found
throughout the hungry ghost realm, animal realm, human realm,
and heavenly realm, and can be born from the womb, from an egg,
from moisture, or from transformation.

## 6. Heavenly Realm （天）

Rebirth in the heavenly realm is of the greatest merit among the
six realms of existence. There are twenty-eight heavens to be reborn in, depending upon how much one has generated positive
karma and removed affliction. Those twenty-eight are divided into
the six heavens of the desire realm, the eighteen heavens of the
form realm, and the four heavens of the formless realm. Heavenly
beings exceed other sentient beings in their beautiful appearance,
long lives, and superior meditative concentration and bliss. But
even so, when heavenly beings reach the end of their life they experience the five signs of decay and will be reborn in the lower
realms as they continue through the cycle of birth and death. Thus,
in the end, though the heavenly realms are truly extraordinary,
they are not the ultimate peace.

## 7. Sravaka Realm （聲聞）

Sravaka means "voice-hearer," for these are the beings who awaken
through hearing the teachings of the Buddha. There are four levels
of spiritual attainment for a *sravaka*, with the highest being the arhat, which is the highest attainment of the Hinayana. There are many
practices associated with the *sravaka*; some initial practices include the
attainment of meditative states, focusing the mind on a single point,
abiding in right knowlege and right view, and other such practices.

D

## 8. Pratyekabuddha Realm（緣覺）

*Pratyekabuddhas* are beings who awakened upon hearing the teaching on the twelve links of dependent origination during the time the Buddha dwelt in the world, and so they are known as "awakened through dependent origination." There are also *pratyekabuddhas* who awaken on their own without a teacher by contemplating the arising, ceasing, transformation, and change of phenomena in the external world. These are known as "self-realized beings." Though *pratyekabuddhas* may differ in this way, they all awaken through the contemplation of dependent origination and enjoy their solitary existence.

## 9. Bodhisattva Realm（菩薩）

Bodhisattvas are sentient beings who have an aspiration for supreme awakening, seeking Buddhahood from on high and liberating sentient beings below. Bodhisattvas have a compassionate disposition and an intellect imbued with *prajna*-wisdom. The spirit of a bodhisattva is steadfast and persevering. Unique to bodhisattvas is the practice of the six perfections and undertaking the four universal vows.

## 10. Buddha Realm（佛）

Buddhas are awakened beings who have realized the truth. Not only have they liberated themselves from the cycle of birth and death, but they also understand the causes of suffering and affliction of sentient beings, and have helped them to liberate themselves from the cycle of birth and death. Buddhas have awakened themselves and awakened others, and have completed the mission of awakening.

Within a single day, there is no telling how many times an ordinary person travels between the ten dharma realms. For example, a thought of torment and enmity brings you to the hell realm, a thought of hatred and conflict brings you to the hungry ghost realm, a deluded and ignorance thought brings you to the animal realm, a thought of jealousy and arrogance brings you to the *asura* realm, a thought to keep the precepts and do good brings you to the human realm, a thought of bliss and happiness bring you to the heavenly realm, a thought of selfless altruism brings you to the bodhisattva realm, and a thought of universal equality and tolerance brings you to the Buddha realm.

Where are heaven and hell located? In this very mind. The ten dharma realms also provide the philosophical basis for the Tiantai School's teaching on "one thought containing the three thousand-fold world system."

## Dharma Seals, Three
## 三法印

*See also:* Impermanence.

The Dharma is the truth of the universe and human life. "True" in this instance refers to principles which are universal, inherent, and eternal. The "three Dharma seals" certify that the Buddhist teachings are true in this way. They are:

*1. All conditioned phenomena are impermanent* （諸行無常）
Of all of the many kinds of events and things in the world, not a single one of them remains fixed and unchanging, for each and every one of them shifts and transforms from moment to moment. Since all conditioned phenomena arise into being through a

coming together of causes and conditions, they are empty, and lack an independent "self" or identity. They exist when conditions come together, and they pass away when conditions dissipate. Living things are born, grow old, get sick, and die. Material things like mountains, rivers, and the earth itself are formed, abide, change, and are destroyed. Even thoughts arise, abide, change, and cease. All phenomena arise and pass into extinction from moment to moment; they cannot linger even for an instant. The past is already gone, the future has yet to appear, and the present is arising and ceasing. Since all phenomena shift from the past, present, and future, it is said that they are impermanent.

## 2. All phenomena are without an independent self (諸法無我)
The Buddhist term "self" refers to something's true essence. For something to have a "self" it must have agency and be permanent, unchanging, and autonomous. But within this world of conditioned phenomena nothing like this exists. For example, most people become attached to their body as "self," but the body is just a combination of the five aggregates. This body is just a collection of karma and affliction, that it could be the "self" is an empty illusion. The body is like a house: a house needs posts and supports, roof-tiles and cross-beams all working together to make it a house. Without any of these there could be no house at all. The "self" is just a label, nothing more, for it lacks any real substance. Everything in the world came into existence through various causes and conditions and, as such, lacks an independent self or nature.

## 3. Nirvana is perfect tranquility (涅槃寂靜)
Nirvana is the third of the Four Noble Truths, and means the end of greed, anger, and ignorance. It is extinguishing the burning flames

of ignorance, affliction, suffering, and the separate self, so that one can reach a state of tranquility without defilement that is filled with happiness, light, freedom, and comfort. This is a state of liberation in which the mind and body are both tranquil, where the body is free of negative conduct and the mind is free of negative thoughts.

Human life in this world means constantly being disturbed by things and events. We are fettered by greed, anger, ignorance, affliction, and delusion just as a prisoner is confirmed by his chains and shackles. One can be liberated by removing these shackles, and this liberation is called *nirvana*. In this way it is important to emphasize: *nirvana* is not death. In Buddhism, it is the most perfect state.

The three Dharma seals—all conditioned phenomena are impermanent, all phenomena are without an independent self, and *nirvana* is perfect tranquility—are the basis upon which the Dharma is verified, and are the standard by which one distinguishes between Buddhist and non-Buddhist teachings. Among the teachings of early Buddhism, these three formed the philosophical basis for the doctrine of dependent origination, representing the earliest, fundamental Buddhist teaching. Therefore, by understanding the three Dharma seals, one can understand the basic ideas of Buddhism.

## Dharma Wheel, Three Turnings
### 三轉法輪
*See also:* Four Noble Truths.

The sutras say, "All Buddhas appear in this world for one great matter." The "great matter" mentioned here is to spread their teachings, and demonstrate the benefits and joys of their meaning and practice. The Buddha's purpose is to tell sentient beings the truth he has awakened to, so that they too can realize the perfect wisdom of the Buddha and overcome their suffering. This is why the Buddha appeared in the human world. After his awakening, he dwelt in this world for forty-nine years, during which he gave teachings at more than three hundred assemblies. "Buddhism" is thus the teachings of the Buddha, and the twelve divisions of the Tripitaka are a record of those teachings given to sentient beings through the Buddha's words and deeds.

Following his awakening the Buddha first gave the teaching of the Four Noble Truths to the group of five monks, including Kaundinya, at the Deer Park on the outskirts of Benares. In Buddhist history, this in known as the "first turning of the Dharma wheel."

The Four Noble Truths are the truth of suffering, the truth of the cause of suffering, the truth of the cessation of suffering, and the truth of the path leading to the cessation of suffering. On the day the Buddha first turned the wheel of the Dharma, he told the group of five monks that the world we live in is like a house on fire. It is filled with the pain and suffering of the cycle of birth and death. For this reason, we must not cling to it nor remain here for long. The cause of the pain and suffering of the cycle of birth and death is the accumulation of greed, anger, and ignorance. Fortunately, in each of our minds there resides a pure intrinsic nature, and once this intrinsic nature manifests itself, we can eliminate afflictions and the cycle of birth and death and attain the state of tranquility and happiness that is *nirvana*. The path that leads to *nirvana* is to cultivate the six perfections, observe the precepts, do good works, practice the Noble Eightfold Path, and so on.

After sharing this teaching, the Buddha was still concerned, and proceeded to give more personal instruction. The Buddha hoped that the five monks would understand suffering as a reality of human life, and thus be able to sever the karmic causes that generate suffering. He hoped that they would be able to attain the joy of tranquility and the unconditioned. He wanted them to practice the path with determination and diligence.

To inspire faith in the monks to seek the Dharma and the path to awakening, the Buddha then patiently took up the task once more and taught the Dharma by example. The Buddha taught from his own experience to show: I already know that life is suffering; I have also eliminated all the causes of suffering; and at the same time, I have attained the happiness of liberation, because I have already completed the path.

The Buddha then repeated the Four Noble Truths to the five monks in three different configurations, known as the "three turnings of the Dharma wheel."

The first is called "turning the Dharma wheel for instruction," in which the content and definition of the Four Noble Truths were given and explained, so that the group of five monks could comprehend them. The Buddha said: "Such is suffering, which is oppressive; such is the cause of suffering, which beckons; such is the cessation of suffering, which is attainable; such is the path, which can be practiced."

The second is called "turning the Dharma wheel for encouragement," in which the Buddha exhorted the group of five monks to put the Four Noble Truths into practice to remove afflictions and obtain liberation. The Buddha said: "Such is suffering, you should understand it; such is the cause of suffering, you should end it; such is the cessation of suffering you should realize it; such is the path, you should practice it."

D

The third is called "turning the Dharma wheel to share his realization," in which the Buddha tells the group of five monks that he himself has already realized the Four Noble Truths, to show them by example that with determination and diligence they too can realize the Four Noble Truths. The Buddha said: "Such is suffering, I have understood it; such is the cause of suffering, I have ended it; such is the cessation of suffering, I have realized it; such is the path, I have practiced it."

When we look at how the Buddha turned the Dharma wheel three times for the group of five monks, we can see the wisdom and compassion with which the Buddha used his teachings to liberate sentient beings. The Buddha was a great teacher with the best understanding of how to teach. The Buddha gently guides with a penetrating analysis of the principle of things; he gives the right encouragement based upon one's capacity, and excels in giving the right medicine for the given aliment. For sentient beings of any spiritual capacity he can give teachings that are true and in accord with circumstances so that they can benefit from the Dharma.

The Buddha did not abandon any being. There is a saying in Buddhism: "It does not matter whether the medicine is expensive or cheap, the best is the one that cures the disease. It does not matter whether the Dharma is high or low, the most profound is in accord with one's spiritual capacity." Only when one understands the method is it possible to do less work and get more results, and in this the Buddha left us the best example of a model educator.

# Difficulties, Eight
## 八難

A human birth is hard to obtain and a chance to hear the Buddhist teachings is hard to encounter. Even if one obtains a human birth, one does not necessarily get a chance to hear the Buddhist teachings, and even less so if one is reborn in other realms of existence. According to the sutras, there are eight kinds of difficulty that impede one's ability to learn Buddhism:

### 1. Hell（在地獄難）
Due to their past negative karma, beings reborn in the hell realms dwell in a long night of darkness, for they must endure hell's many forms of suffering without respite. Therefore, they cannot see the Buddha nor hear his teachings.

### 2. The Realm of Hungry Ghosts（在餓鬼難）
Some beings reborn as hungry ghosts do not even hear of water for *kalpas*, and some must wait and beg for wash water, blood, pus, and sewage sludge in the human world. Others may get their fill for a time, only to be driven away by knives and sticks. In multitudes that fill the rivers and plug up the seas, their suffering is infinite. Therefore, they cannot see the Buddha nor hear his teachings.

### 3. The Animal Realm（在畜生難）
There are many classes of animals, with each linked to a particular karmic cause. Some are raised as domesticated animals. Others live in the mountains and oceans or other places. They are beaten and killed or fall prey to one another and are eaten. The suffering they bear is limitless. Therefore, they cannot see the Buddha nor hear his teachings.

D

### 4. The Heavenly Realm (在長壽天難)

Beings reborn in heavenly realms live extremely long lives, with those reborn in the Unconscious Heaven living for five hundred *kalpas.* The beings reborn in this realm are completely without thought, like a hibernating animal. Many outsiders who cultivate non-Buddhist practices are reborn here, such that they cannot see the Buddha or hear his teachings.

### 5. The Excellent Continent (在邊地之鬱單越難)

In Buddhism there is a land adjacent to our own world of Jambu-dvipa called *uttara-kuru,* the "excellent continent." Those who are reborn in Uttara-kuru enjoy a life-span of one thousand years, and no one dies young. Those who live there only crave pleasure, and for that reason they cannot receive the teachings of liberation, and no sages appear there. As such they are unable to see the Buddha or hear his teachings.

### 6. Physical and Mental Disability (盲聾瘖啞難)

Though some people may be born in a place where the Dharma exists, their karmic impediments may prevent them from being able to see the Buddha and hear his teachings by being born blind, deaf, or dumb. Such people are not complete in their sense faculties, so even when the Buddha is in the world, they are unable to hear and see him.

### 7. Birth as a Philosopher (世智辯聰難)

Though philosophers may be intelligent, they can easily become enamored with the texts of non-Buddhist teachings. Many do not believe in the true, supramundane Dharma.

## 8. Birth Between Buddhas（生在佛前佛後難）

Burdened with karma and lacking positive conditions, some beings are born at a time when a Buddha has not appeared in the world. Therefore, one cannot see the Buddha nor hear his teachings.

According to the *Agamas*, undertaking the eight precepts can ameliorate the eight difficulties. Additionally, the *Treatise on Establishing the Truth* states that one can prevent these difficulties through four methods:

D

1. By dwelling in a good place, one will be born where the Dharma exists.
2. By relying upon good people, one will be born when the Buddha is in the world.
3. By making the right vows, one will be able to have right view.
4. By laying down wholesome roots for the future, one will become complete in physical and mental faculties.

Though these difficulties have been given as eight particular items, in reality they are each expressions of the fact that it is hard to be born when the Buddha is in the world, it is hard to hear the Buddha's teachings, and it is hard to be born as a human being. For this reason, one should have a penitent mind and remember the verse:

> When the Buddha was in the world, I was lost,
> After the Buddha passed into *nirvana* I was born.
> I repent for all my many karmic obstacles
> That have prevented me from seeing the
> Tathagata's golden-hued body.

**D**

One should also remember the difficulty of obtaining a human rebirth, as in the couplet:

> Hard it is to obtain a human body, but now I
> have obtained one;
> Hard it is to hear the Buddha's teaching, but now
> I have heard them.

It is important to value the rare opportunity to be born as a human being, see the Buddha, and hear the Dharma. If you are not liberated in this life, which lifetime will you be? Only by having this kind of attitude towards Buddhist practice will one ever come in direct contact with the truth.

## Disability
## 盲聾瘖啞

*See:* Difficulties, eight; field of merit.

## Disciples of the Buddha, Ten Great
## 十大弟子

During the time of Sakyamuni Buddha, the founder of Buddhism, many disciples came to take refuge in him, the most well-known being a group called the "ten great disciples." Each of the ten disciples was distinguished for being the best in a particular area of the Dharma:

### 1. Sariputra: Foremost in Wisdom （舍利弗）
Sariputra was born in Kalapinaka, in the Kingdom of Magadha. His father was a famous and learned Brahman, while his maternal

uncle was Kausthila. At the age of eight, Sariputra was already well-regarded for his knowledge of the Vedas. Upon encountering the *bhiksu* Asvajit, Sariputra became a disciple of the Buddha. He was almost eighty-one when he entered final *nirvana*, three months before the Buddha did.

### 2. Maudgalyayana: Foremost in Supernatural Powers （目犍連）

Maudgalyayana, a high-minded scholar, joined the monastic order together with Sariputra, and attained awakening in only seven days. Maudgalyayana possessed great supernatural powers, attaining awakening about ten days earlier than Sariputra. He was known for being a filial son. Maudgalyayana was ultimately stoned to death by a group of Nigranthas who attack him for being Buddhist.

### 3. Purna: Foremost in Teaching the Dharma （富樓那）

Purna was a pampered son from a rich family. After entering the monastic community, he became a persuasive speaker who would enthusiastically teach the Dharma.

### 4. Subhuti: Foremost in Understanding Emptiness （須菩提）

Subhuti was a kind person who found joy in doing good and enjoyed being generous. He practiced the *samadhi* of non-contention and would sit in a cave contemplating emptiness, inspiring heavenly beings to rain down flowers from the sky in admiration.

### 5. Mahakatyayana: Foremost in Debating the Dharma (迦旃延)

He came from Ujjeni in the southern Indian kingdom of Avanti, and was the nephew of the seer, Asita. He excelled at explaining the Dharma and was known for being foremost in debate.

### 6. Mahakasyapa: Foremost in Austerities (大迦葉)

Mahakasyapa was born to an extremely wealthy family. He was married to a beautiful wife for twelve years, though they were married in name only, as they both were celibate practitioners. After he joined the monastic order, Mahakasyapa was steadfast and conservative in his approach, and diligently practiced austerities. In the end, he received Dharma transmission from the Buddha, becoming the first Chan patriarch.

### 7. Aniruddha: Foremost in Heavenly Vision (阿那律)

Aniruddha was the Buddha's cousin and a descendent of the royal family. Owing to his diligent practice he became blind in both eyes, though afterwards attained heavenly vision.

### 8. Upali: Foremost in Monastic Discipline (優婆離)

Upali came from a lower class family and served in the palace as a barber for the royal princes, like Aniruddha. Later, after joining the monastic order, his position put him before the princes, as he was a more senior disciple and thus received the obeisance of the princely monks. This shows Buddhism's egalitarian spirit.

### 9. Ananda: Foremost in Having Heard Much (阿難陀)

Ananda was the younger brother of Devadatta and served as the Buddha's attendant. He was known for being particularly handsome, and also for requesting that the Buddha establish the *bhiksuni* order.

### 10. Rahula: Foremost in Esoteric Practices（羅睺羅）

Rahula was a very fortunate person, as he was not only the Buddha's son but had Sariputra as his teacher. Rahula was the first novice monk. Pure of heart and energetic, Rahula practiced hard and attained awakening all because the Buddha had severely reprimanded him.

D

# E

## Earth
地
*See:* Elements, four great.

## Effects of Karma of the Three Time Periods
三時業
*See also:* Karma of the three time periods; Karma, three types of.

Karma, cause and effect, is the law of the universe, as well as the moral law governing pleasure and pain in human life. Karmic effects control human destiny. The effects of karma are created by one's own actions rather than some supernatural power, giving equal opportunity to all without any special considerations. Karma offers us a bright future and limitless hope, and the effects of karma manifest regardless of social status.

There are those who feel that they have been loyal and cheated no one and yet have been poor their whole life, while others took advantage of every opportunity by trickery and became millionaires. There are also those who feel that they have been good sons and daughters who take care of their parents and yet are often sick, while others act badly towards their parents and yet are always healthy. What is the karmic explanation for this?

This is not the way that karma works. Loyalty and honesty versus opportunistic trickery are moral causes and effects; fame and fortune versus poverty are economic causes and effects; and a sound body versus a sick one are health-related causes and conditions. If a person is loyal and honest, but does not take care of his finances, he will certainly end up poor. The unfilial sons and daughters described above pay attention to their health and nutrition, so naturally they have healthy bodies. Karma cannot be understood by mixing these things together.

There is a Buddhist saying, "In the end, good and bad have their reward or retribution. The only question that remains is whether it comes sooner or later." The time between when an action is performed and its karmic effect reaches fruition varies. Just as some seeds may be planted in the spring and be harvested in the fall, while others may only be harvested next year or even many years after, there are three categories of time in which karmic effects manifest:

*1. Karmic effects in this life* （現報業）
Do good in this life and you will enjoy blessings in this life; do bad in this life and you will suffer disasters in this life. You help others and others will help you; you harm others and others will harm you. This is very direct; and as such karma is very realistic. No matter who you are, karma does not dole out special treatment.

## E

*2. Karmic effects in the next life*（生報業）

In some instances, doing good or bad will only manifest as positive or negative karmic effects in the next life, but there will certainly come a day when the planted seeds will sprout, flower, and bear fruit. If you have yet to experience the negative effects of a bad deed, don't count yourself lucky, for spreading vines grow quickly. Positive and negative causes and conditions follow us just like a shadow, for they cannot be escaped.

*3. Karmic effects in future lives*（後報業）

Everything in this world will one day disappear, except for karma. Whether it is the next life, the one after that, or billions of lifetimes later, if a karmic effect has yet to manifest, it surely will once the causes and conditions have matured. There is a Buddhist saying, "Good is rewarded with good, and bad is repaid with bad. Do not worry that there is no effect, for the time is not yet right."

Karma is absolute freedom, for one experiences the consequences of one's own actions, and no one can exchange theirs with another.

# Effort, Right
# 正勤

*See:* Path, noble eightfold; right effort.

# Elements, Four Great
# 四大皆空

Once while Chan Master Foyin of the Song dynasty (1032-1098 CE) was giving a teaching, the great scholar and poet Su Shi (1037-1101

CE) entered the hall. At the time, all the seats were occupied and so the Chan master spoke to Su Shi in the epigrammatic style of the Chan School: "There's no seat for the scholar!"

Since Su Shi had studied Buddhism and practiced Chan for many years, he also gave his reply in the Chan style: "How about I borrow the Chan master's four great elements and use them as a seat?"

The Chan master then countered with a question: "According to the Dharma, 'the four great elements are fundamentally empty and the five aggregates are without self,' so just where, sir, are you going to sit?" Despite all his knowledge of state policies and programs, Su Shi was struck dumb by this question.

So what are the four great elements, and why are they empty?

All the world's phenomena, be they plants, animals, or non-sentient things, and whether they are as massive as the universe itself or as small as a flower or a blade of grass, all are made up of the four great elements. The four great elements are earth, water, fire, and wind:

### Earth（地）

The earth element includes anything that has the quality of hardness and solidity. The earth element can support all things. Solid parts of the human body like hair, teeth, nails, skin, bone, muscle, and soft tissue all belong to the earth element.

### Water（水）

The water element includes anything that has the quality of wetness or fluidity. The water element can sustain all things. The fluids of the human body like spittle, mucus, pus, blood, saliva, phlegm, tears, and body fluids all belong to the water element.

*Fire*（火）

The fire element includes anything that has the quality of heat. The fire element can warm up all things. The human body's warmth and temperature belong to the fire element.

*Wind*（風）

The wind element includes anything that has the quality of movement. The air element can nurture all things. The parts of the human body that move, like the in-breath and the out-breath all belong to the wind element.

Human beings are not the only thing made of the four great elements; plants like flowers and grasses are as well. For these plants to grow they require some fertile "earth," a suitable amount of "water," the warming "fire" of the sun, and the "wind" of the air. If any one of these elements is lacking, then the plant will be unable to sprout and develop, let alone flower and bear seeds.

The reason human life can exist is because of the combination of the four great elements. Any imbalance amongst the four great elements will lead to illness, and when the four great elements disperse, death occurs. Another way to look at it is that things which are formed through the combination of conditions are destroyed when those conditions disperse. There are no exceptions.

When it is said that the four great elements are "empty," this does not mean that earth, water, fire, and wind have disappeared. Instead it means that all phenomena are formed out of a combination of dependent causes and conditions consisting of the four main elements of earth, water, fire, and wind. If this combination of causes and conditions is lacking, then no phenomena are produced. It is because all things arise through this process of dependent origination that the four great elements are said to be "empty."

It is important to note that the four great elements do not become empty only when the conditions supporting a phenomena have dispersed. Even when a flower has just bloomed or a person is in the best of health, from the perspective of dependent origination, the flower and the person are fundamentally empty.

Emptiness does not "destroy" existence, nor is it the same as non-existence. If one does not comprehend causality, then one will not understand the truth of the Dharma, that "the four great elements are fundamentally empty and the five aggregates are without self."

E

## Empathy
同事

*See:* Means of embracing, four.

## Emptiness
空

*See:* Elements, four great.

## Equanimity
捨

*See:* Immeasurable minds, four.

## Esoteric School
密宗

*See:* Schools of Chinese Buddhism, eight.

# F

## Faith
信仰

*See:* Practice, four stages of; spiritual wealth, seven kinds of; supports, three.

## Fame
名

*See:* Desires, five.

## Faxiang School
法相宗

*See:* Schools of Chinese Buddhism, eight.

## Fayan School
法眼宗

*See:* Chan schools.

# Feeling
# 受

*See:* Aggregates, five; dependent origination.

# Field of Merit
# 八種福田

*See also:* Merit and wisdom.

The Buddhist sutras often use planting a field as a metaphor for generosity. For example, a farmer must select a good field and work hard at ploughing and weeding before he can bring in a bountiful harvest. In the same way, in order for there to be merit when performing acts of generosity, one must select the appropriate recipient to give to and understand that the giver, the gift, and the recipient are empty.

According to the Buddhist sutras, there are eight categories of people in this world who are worthy recipients of our generosity: the Buddha, sages, the monastic community, individual monks, teachers, one's father, one's mother, and the sick. But in terms of our modern society, these are: the Triple Gem, spiritual practitioners, one's parents, teachers, the sick, the physically impaired, crisis victims, and groups helping the disadvantaged. These constitute the kinds of people worthy of our generosity and support.

## 1. The Triple Gem（三寶）

The Triple Gem is the Buddha, Dharma, and Sangha. The Buddha is the one who has realized the truth of the universe and human life. The Buddha has awakened himself, awakened others, and completed his mission of awakening. By respectfully making offerings to the Triple Gem, we can obtain all merit and eliminate wrongdoing. This is why it is called a field of merit.

### 2. Spiritual Practitioners (修道者)

The term "spiritual practitioners" includes those who vow to practice the bodhisattva path and liberate all sentient beings, but it also includes teachers of other religions such as pastors, nuns, and priests, as well as experts and scholars who possess specialized knowledge who can contribute their learning for the benefit of the people. All such people are worthy of our respect and support.

### 3. Parents (父母)

Our fathers are the source of our life, and kindly raise us. With discipline and guidance, they provide for us from the time we are toddlers until we grow up; such is the vastness of their kindness. Our mothers bear us in the womb and give birth to us. They expend great effort to feed us, protect us, support us, and raise us with caring thoughts and hard work; such is the vastness of their kindness. If we support our parents with filial love, then we will naturally obtain merit.

### 4. Teachers (師長)

Although parents raise our physical bodies, without the worldly and spiritual teachers to teach us, we would not know about reason and human sentiment; and a person without reason and human sentiment is no different from a wild beast. We should realize that our teachers are the parents of our wisdom and they should be respected and honored.

### 5. The Sick (病人)

The Buddha said, "Of the eight fields of merit, treating the sick is the greatest." This shows the Buddha's emphasis on caring for the sick. Treating the sick is not just a way of seeking merit; it is also a form of practice. Buddhist disciples should vow to become the doctors and nurses of all sentient beings. When we see a sick person, we should reflect upon their suffering, and devote ourselves to aiding their treatment and providing medicine. In this way, we will attain merit. Thus the sick are known as a field of merit.

### 6. The Physically Impaired (殘障)

Often those who are physically impaired cannot make a living. We can allow them to be more independent by supplying mental and physical treatment, providing them with certain skills, or offering them employment opportunities. In this way, we can provide help.

### 7. Crisis Victims (急難)

There is a saying that "It is better to help those in a crisis than those in poverty." In this instance, "crisis" refers to natural and human-made disasters such as wars, earthquakes, floods, or sudden emergencies that affect families. To extend a helping hand at the time when it is most needed, to aide those facing imminent disaster is truly a way to bring about infinite merit.

### 8. Groups Helping the Disadvantaged (弱勢團體)

In society today there are public welfare groups that are actively engaged in the relief work of assisting child prostitutes, providing protection against AIDS, helping mentally impaired children, facially disfigured people, and victims of child abuse or sexual violence against women. Many of these organizations suffer from a shortage of funds to cover their expenses, and they are unable to carry out their work. By donating funds to assist these groups we are indirectly engaging in social welfare and helping to solve social problems. The significance of such help is quite extraordinary and should be encouraged.

## Fire
火
*See:* Elements, four great.

## Flower Adornment Sutra
華嚴經
*See:* Schools of Chinese Buddhism, eight.

## Food
食
*See:* Desires, five; meal contemplations, five; offerings, four; robe and bowl.

## Form
色
*See:* Aggregates, five.

## Friends, Four Kinds of
友有四品
*See also:* Dharma friends.

Everyone in the world needs friends, but there are good friends and bad friends. Making good friends is like entering a room full of orchids; after a while you will no longer smell the sweet fragrance.

Making bad friends is like entering a fish shop; after a while you will no longer smell the pungent stench. We must be careful about our friendships.

The *Bei Sutra* states that there are four kinds of friendship:

## 1. Friendship Like a Flower（有友如花）

Friends who treat your friendship like a flower praise, flatter, and follow you when you possess power and wealth, but as soon as you are no longer useful or fall on hard times, they will turn their backs and abandon you. This kind of friend despises poverty and curries favor with the rich, treating you like a flower: When a flower is fresh and beautiful it is treasured, but when the flower wilts it is discarded. Such people draw near the rich and powerful, and abandon the poor and the lowly.

## 2. Friendship Like a Balance-scale（有友如秤）

There are some friends who treat their friendship like a balance-scale: if you are weighty and important, the scale will shift and they will bow their heads to you; but as soon as you lose importance they will tower above you. Just as a balance-scale tips in one direction with a heavy weight and tips the other way with a light weight, when you are successful, hold an important position, and wield power, such a friend will serve you on bended knee, bowing low to you as they flatter you to curry favor. But once your reputation and power are gone, they will hold their heads high and look down upon you.

## 3. Friendship Like a Mountain（有友如山）

Friends whose friendship is like a mountain are broad and open-minded, for they can support many friends, just as a mountain can support all the plant and animal life that lives upon it. Such friends are as valuable as a mountain of gold, for when they are powerful they honor others, and when they are rich they share their enjoyments.

## 4. Friendship Like the Ground （有友如地）

Friends whose friendship is like the ground take on responsibilities on your behalf whenever there is a need. They share in your troubles, and even give support regardless of the cost, never expecting anything in return, just like the solid ground. The ground supports all living things and bears flowers and fruit. It even allows people to walk over it, accepting all without the slightest complaint. Friends whose friendship is like the ground are generous and nurturing, just like the ground which provides grain and abundance, unstinting in kindness.

We make friends in order to improve one another's character and help each other out. As the saying goes, "good friends are one's best relations." As the examples stated above, we should stay away from friendships like flowers and balance-scales, and draw near those friendships which exert a positive moral influence as in the friendships like mountains and ground.

# G

## Gem, Triple
## 三寶

What is the Triple Gem? The Triple Gem is the Buddha, the Dharma, and the Sangha.

### Buddha（佛）

*Buddha* is a Sanskrit word which means "noble awakened one." The Buddha is one who has awakened himself, awakened others, and completed his mission of awakening. Generally, when "the Buddha" is mentioned, it refers to the founder of Buddhism, Sakyamuni Buddha.

Sakyamuni Buddha attained complete realization under the bodhi tree, attained true, unsurpassed awakening, and brought liberation to infinite sentient beings. With his great compassion, great wisdom, and great supernatural powers, he became the founder of Buddhism for this Saha world and the "teacher of human and heavenly beings."

*Dharma*（法）

*Dharma* is a Sanskrit word which refers to the Tripitaka, the collection of the Buddha's teachings, with its twelve divisions.

All the teachings the Buddha proclaimed at more than three hundred Dharma assemblies over the course of his forty-nine year teaching career in this world, were complied together by his disciples Ananda and Mahakasyapa into the sutra, vinaya, and abhidharma divisions of the Tripitaka, that have been circulating in the world until today. The Tripitaka contains explanations of the truths of life and the universe. It is a precious raft that ferries one across the ocean of suffering, leading us away from suffering and towards liberation.

*Sangha*（僧）

*Sangha* is a Sanskrit word which means community, peace and happiness, and purity. Generally, the male and female monastics are known as the sangha, the monastic community.

The sangha is heir to the work of the Buddha and teaches the Dharma for the benefit of living beings. The monastic community guides sentient beings as they eliminate afflictions and free themselves from the cycle of birth and death.

In addition to this standard formula, there are other groupings of the Triple Gem:

*The Manifested Triple Gem*（化相三寶）

In this formulation, Sakyamuni Buddha is the Buddha Gem, the Four Noble Truths and the twelve links of dependent origination are the Dharma Gem, and the group of the first five *bhiksus* is the Sangha Gem. This is also sometimes called the "Original Triple Gem."

*The Maintained Triple Gem*（住持三寶）
This refers to sacred images of the Buddha as the Buddha Gem, the Tripitaka as the Dharma Gem, and all *bhiksus* and *bhiksunis* as the Sangha Gem. This is also called the "Forever Abiding Triple Gem."

*The True Triple Gem*（真實三寶）
Here the Triple Gem is represented by the Dharmakaya, Nirmanakaya, and Sambhogakaya. This grouping has many names, including the "Triple Gem of Intrinsic Nature," the "Triple Gem of One Essence," and the "Fundamental Essence of the Triple Gem."

The Triple Gem possesses unsurpassed merit. When compared to the founder, teachings, and followers of other religions, the Triple Gem is the most perfect and pure. The Triple Gem is a light that shines in darkness, a ship that crosses the ocean of suffering, the sweet rain that douses the blazing house, and the guiding star that points the way for those who are lost. That is why we take refuge in the Triple Gem.

G

# Ghost
# 餓鬼
*See:* Dharma realms, ten; difficulties, eight; lower realms, three.

# Giving
# 三輪體空
*See also:* Means of embracing, four; perfections, six.

In order for an act of generosity to occur, there must be three key elements: the giver, the recipient, and the gift. In Buddhism, these are sometimes called *sanlun* (三輪), "three spheres." A Buddhist sutra says that, "As the mind, the field, and the object vary, so too can superior and inferior karmic results be distinguished." In this passage, the "mind" refers to the giver, the "field" to the recipient, and the "object" to the gift. These three components are the causes which determine if the karmic effect of the act of generosity will be great or small. Let us examine each one by one:

### 1. The Giver (施者)

The motivation of the person performing the act of generosity must be sincere, and must not be done in the hopes of seeking any favors in return, or any praise or glory. The correct attitude for someone giving a gift involves:

- Joy, such that the gift is given with a happy heart, and does not irritate oneself or others.
- Respect, such that the gift is given without pride or disdain, and demeans no one.
- Compassion, such that the giver sees all sentient beings as equal with him or herself, and wishes that they may be free from poverty and have their hopes fulfilled.

### 2. The Recipient (受者)

Giving is like planting a field: regardless of the seeds being planted, they must be planted in a good field to yield a good harvest. Therefore, when performing acts of generosity, it is important to select the best field of merit. There are two types of "fields" which are the most suitable:

- Those worthy of sympathy, such as helpless people who are in dire need of assistance like widowers, widows, orphans,

childless couples, the poor, the destitute, and the sick who
are unable to seek medical attention, as well as those who
have passed away but cannot afford a burial.

- Those worthy of respect, such as the Triple Gem, parents,
teachers, and elders. Among these, the Triple Gem is the
best field of merit.

### 3. The Gift (施物)

There are three main types of gifts: the gift of wealth, the gift of the
Dharma, and the gift of fearlessness. There is a saying that "the gift
of wealth and the gift of Dharma are equal and without any distinction." This refers to Buddhists providing the means of support
to a Dharma teacher while the teacher reciprocates with teachings
of the Dharma. In this instance, both are said to generate the same
unsurpassed merit. But speaking in a strictly comparative sense, as
the sutras say, "among all gifts, the gift of the Dharma is the best."
The gift of wealth is limited, finite, and defiled; it can only be of
benefit in this present life, and then only for a short time. The gift
of Dharma is limitless, infinite, and inexhaustible; it bestows benefit in this present life which continues on for lifetime after lifetime.
That is why it is said in the *Diamond Sutra* that if someone were to
give heaps of the seven treasures such that it filled the great three
thousandfold world system, the merit of this gift would not be as
great as having faith in the sutra's four-line verse and explaining
it to others. The merit of that gift of Dharma would be hundreds of
thousands of times greater than merit obtained through the giving
of wealth, food, and drink.

Though the merit of a gift will vary depending on the differences between the mind, the field, and the object given, the

**G**

greatest act of generosity is "generosity without notions." There is a Buddhist saying that "Wealth enters the temple gate and merit is credited to the generous benefactor." Acts of generosity should be empty and free of notions, such that there is no "I" who does the giving, no recipient, and no gift. In this way there no longer remains any thought of seeking favors in return. The greatest merit of all is generated only when the "three spheres" of giver, recipient, and gift are all empty.

# Gratitude, Four Kinds of
# 四恩總報

Appreciating kindness and showing gratitude is a fundamental part of being human. Buddhists in particular should emulate the Buddha's spirit of unconditional loving-kindness and compassion by expressing gratitude for the "four kindnesses" and rendering assistance to those in the three lower realms. The four kindnesses are:

### 1. Kindness of Parents（父母恩）

Our parents brought us into the world. They raised and educated us. If it were not for our parents we would not be here today. In particular, our mothers carried us in the womb for nine to ten months and fed us by hand for three years. They kept us dry and endured much bitterness and suffering for us. The kindness of a mother is higher than heaven and their love is deeper than the ocean. That is why the *Sutra on the Buddha's Gratitude to His Parents through Great Skillful Means* says that parents show the greatest kindness within the three realms. To express our gratitude for the kindness of our parents we should give to them true faith in Buddhism and offer them liberation, so that they may grow in wisdom towards awakening and put an end to the cycle of birth and death. This is the highest supramundane way of honoring one's parents.

## 2. Kindness of Sentient Beings (眾生恩)

Since beginningless time, all sentient beings throughout their numerous lifetimes have been each other's parents. In addition, sentient beings have shown us kindness through the various comforts and conveniences that they provide. To show our gratitude for the kindness of sentient beings we can practice the bodhisattva path in order to help sentient beings be liberated from the cycle of birth and death within the six realms of existence.

## 3. Kindness of One's Country (國家恩)

Our parents bore and raised our physical body, but it was society as a whole which provided for much of our daily needs. It is because of the protection that has been provided to us by our country, that we are able to live securely and be happy in our homes and jobs. If a country is destroyed, then its people will become lost as refugees, with no place to call home. That is why we should express gratitude for our country. Therefore each of us should serve our country faithfully and fulfill our duties in whatever position or post we hold. In this way we can repay the kindness of our country for safeguarding our lives.

## 4. Kindness of the Triple Gem (三寶恩)

The Triple Gem is the Buddha, Dharma, and Sangha. These three are the light of the world, and exhibit unimaginable kindness. The Buddha is described as having ten kinds of kindness:

G

1. The kindness of his resolve to bring universal liberation.
2. The kindness of his self-sacrifice in previous lives.
3. The kindness of consistent altruism.
4. The kindness of manifesting in six realms of existence.
5. The kindness of pursuing liberation for sentient beings.
6. The kindness of his great compassion.
7. The kindness of appearing as a human being in accordance with the capacity of his audience and concealing his true form.
8. The kindness of teaching provisional teachings before ultimate teachings in accordance with the capacity of his audience.
9. The kindness of entering final *nirvana* to inspire appreciation for the rare presence of a Buddha.
10. The kindness of living only eighty years rather than a full life-span of one hundred so that the remaining blessings could be left to Buddhists of later ages and that the teachings would remain so that they could be practiced.

The Dharma is the truth of the world that can guide sentient beings out of the ocean of the cycle of birth and death to the other shore of *nirvana*. All the Buddhas of the past, present, and future practice according to the Dharma so that they may end all obstacles, attain awakening, and benefit sentient beings forever. The sangha persistently brings benefit to sentient beings, for the monastic community is ever mindful of this task. The Triple Gem allows us to achieve ultimate liberation; this in and of itself is a great, vast act of kindness. Therefore, we should respect the Triple Gem with the utmost sincerity, and truly practice the Dharma.

A Buddhist sutra says, "Though those with gratitude are in the cycle of birth and death, their roots of virtue are not destroyed. Those who have no gratitude eliminate the roots of their virtue. That is why all Buddhas praise those with gratitude." Buddhism emphasizes gratitude, particularly filial piety, for not only should we repay the kindness of our parents of this lifetime, but we should widen our focus to our parents of all our lifetimes. Gratitude should begin with one's own family, but should expand to encompass society as a whole, and eventually grow to encompass all sentient beings, so that all one's parents and family members for all time can attain liberation. Buddhism is an expression of filial piety and gratitude in its ultimate form.

## Greed
貪
*See:* Poisons, three.

## Grounds, ten
十地
*See:* Bodhisattva path, ten grounds of.

## Guanyin Bodhisattva
觀音
*See:* Mountains, four great; noble ones of the West, three.

## Guiyang School
溈仰宗
*See:* Chan schools.

# H

## Hanshan, Master
憨山大師

*See*: Masters of the Ming dynasty, four.

## Harmony, Six Points of Reverent
六和合僧

It is said that, "As long as the precepts abide, so too will the monastic order; and as long as the monastic order abides, so too will the Dharma." The Buddhist monastic community is called the *sangha* in Sanskrit, which means "harmonious community." This is because the *sangha* practices and lives in harmony. All must eliminate the same afflictions and realize the same truth. They are unified in body, speech, and mind according to six points, called the "six points of reverent harmony." These points are as follows:

*1. Harmony in view through sharing the same understanding*
（見和同解）
This means to share a common view and share an understanding of the Dharma. The Dharma is accepted as the highest standard for all matters, a proper course that cannot be abandoned.

*2. Moral harmony through sharing the same precepts*
（戒和同修）
Everyone is equal under the monastic precepts, such that by developing the habit of observing the rules, life will be fair and reasonable.

*3. Economic harmony through sharing things equally*
（利和同均）
Equitable distribution of economic resources and sharing together in the benefits and welfare of those resources will ensure that everyone can live safely and contentedly.

*4. Mental harmony through shared happiness* （意和同悅）
Sharing the same goals and ideals, without comparing oneself to others, seeing things in terms of success or failure, or keeping score of who is right or wrong. This creates a harmony that is broad-minded in purpose.

*5. Verbal harmony through avoiding disputes* （口和無諍）
This is the harmony that comes from not using unwholesome speech: no one is dishonest, harsh, divisive, or speaking idle chatter. Instead people speak to one another sincerely and tactfully.

H

*6. Physical harmony through living together*（身和同住）
This means having conduct that does not violate others and is built upon mutual respect and support, so that the community can live together in equality and harmony.

The monastic community is a crucible that molds one's nature and character. It is a force that collectively maintains the true Dharma and brings liberation to sentient beings. This is how important the monastic community is. The six points of reverent harmony not only lay the foundation for the monastic community, but they also establish a family system that has been transformed by Buddhism, is pure and loving, and can be used as a basis for a peaceful and happy society.

# Heaven
# 三界二十八天

*See also*: Dharma realms, ten; difficulties, eight; heaven of the thirty-three gods.

There are many religions that believe in the existence of heaven and hell, and Buddhism too affirms their existence. In Buddhist cosmology, heaven is divided into twenty-eight levels. These twenty-eight heavens exist within three different realms: the desire realm, in which there exists six levels of heaven, the form realm, in which there exists eighteen levels of heaven, and the formless realm, in which there exists four levels of heaven.

*1. Six Heavens of the Desire Realm*（欲界六天）
The beings who live in the six heavens of the desire realm are very similar to human beings. They have material bodies and physical

needs just as we do, and they enjoy the spiritual life. These beings also excessively indulge in the desires for food, drink, and sex; this is why it is said that these heavens are located in the "desire realm." The six heavens of the desire realm are:

1. Caturmaharajika Heaven (四天王天), also known as the heaven of the four kings.
2. Trayastrimsat Heaven (忉利天), also known as the heaven of the thirty-three gods.
3. Yama Heaven (夜摩天), also known as the heaven of timely restraint.
4. Tusita Heaven (兜率天), also known as the heaven of contentedness.
5. Nirmanarati Heaven (化樂天), also known as the heaven of joyful creation.
6. Paranirmita-vasavartin Heaven (他化自在天), also known as the heaven of robbing others' pleasure.

In addition to the six heavens mentioned above, there are also five other domains within the desire realm: the human realm with its four continents, the *asura* realm, the animal realm, the hungry ghost realm, and the hell realm.

## 2. *The Eighteen Heavens of the Form Realm* （色界十八天）

The beings who reside in the heavens of the form realm lack the desire for sex, food, and drink. They also are superior to human beings in beauty, spiritual love, community, and social organization. These beings are sustained by the pleasure of meditation as we are sustained by food. This is why they are known as the heavens of the "form realm":

Heavens of the first *dhyana*:

1. Brahma-parisadya Heaven (梵眾天), also known as the heaven of the followers of Brahma.
2. Brahma-purohita Heaven (梵輔天), also known as the heaven of the ministers of Brahma.
3. Mahabrahma Heaven (大梵天), also known as the heaven of the great Brahma.

Heavens of the second *dhyana:*

4. Parittabha Heaven (少光天), also known as the heaven of limited radiance.
5. Apramanabha Heaven (無量光天), also known as the heaven of infinite radiance.
6. Abhasvara Heaven (光音天), also known as the heaven of radiant sound.

Heavens of the third *dhyana*:

7. Parittasubha Heaven (少淨天), also known as the heaven of limited purity.
8. Apramanasubha Heaven (無量淨天) also known as the heaven of infinite purity.
9. Subhakrtsna Heaven (遍淨天), also known as the heaven of pervasive purity.

Heavens of the fourth *dhyana:*

10. Punyaprasava Heaven (福生天), also known as the heaven produced by virtue.
11. Anabhraka Heaven (福愛天), also known as the heaven of lovers of virtue.

12. Brhatphala Heaven (廣果天), also known as the heaven of bountiful fruits.

13. Asamjnisattvah Heaven (無想天), also known as the heaven without thought.

14. Avrha Heaven (無煩天), also known as the heaven without affliction.

15. Atapa Heaven (無熱天), also known as the heaven without heat.

16. Sudarsana Heaven (善見天), also known as the heaven of skillful vision.

17. Sudrsa Heaven (善現天), also known as the heaven of skillful manifestation.

18. Akanistha Heaven (色究竟天等), also known as the supreme heaven of the form realm.

*3. The Four Heavens of the Formless Realm* (無色界四天)
Those beings who reside in the heavens of the formless realm have already completely transcended the impediments caused by sex, food, and the physical form. They are not attached to any form of appearance, and only have a purely spiritual existence. Just as in the form realm, these beings subsist on meditative bliss and consciousness itself. The heavens of the formless realm are:

1. Akasanantyayatana Heaven (空無邊處天), also known as the heaven of limitless space.

2. Vijnananantyayatana Heaven (識無邊處天), also known as the heaven of limitless consciousness.

3. Akimcanyaayatana Heaven (無所有處天), also known as the heaven of nothingness.

4. Naiva-samjnanasamjnayatana Heaven （非想非非想處
   天）, also known as the heaven of neither thought nor non-
   thought.

The twenty-eight heavens mentioned above may be considered superior or inferior to each other in terms of how pleasurable they are, but they are all still realms of delusion, for it is
impossible for heavenly beings to escape the cycle of birth and
death. That is why the *Lotus Sutra* says, "The turmoil of the three
realms is like a burning house, for they are filled with a host of
sufferings that are terrible and frightening to behold." The three
realms are full of the suffering of birth, old age, sickness, and
death, and these sufferings harass the bodies and minds of sentient beings like a house on fire, preventing us from dwelling
in peace. That is why sentient beings should look for a way out
of the three realms. Only by attaining *nirvana* can we be completely liberated.

## Heaven of the Thirty-Three Gods
## 三十三天
*See also*: Heaven.

> There is a heaven beyond: the heaven of the
>      thirty-three gods.
> Beyond the sky are the heavenly immortals.
> Such heavenly immortals were once ordinary
>      people,
> Though one doubts that the minds of ordinary
>      people are so resolute.

In Buddhist cosmology there are many layers of heavenly realms, but these realms are not so far away that they cannot be reached. As long as ordinary individuals strive to do good and accumulate merit, they have the same opportunity to be reborn in heavenly realms as heavenly beings.

There is one heavenly realm called *sanshisan tian* (三十三天), "heaven of the thirty-three," or "heaven of the thirty-three gods." This does not mean that there are thirty-three heavens. The heaven of the thirty-three gods is merely one heavenly realm among twenty-eight, including the six heavens of the desire realm, the eighteen heavens of the form realm, and the four heavens of the formless realm. The heaven of the thirty-three gods is one of the six heavens of the desire realm, and is ruled by Sakra-devanamin-indra, also known as Lord Indra. Within Chinese folk religion Lord Indra is aligned with figures such as the Jade Emperor or the Lord of Heaven.

This particular heaven is notable in Buddhism, because the Buddha once went there for three months to teach the Dharma to his mother, Queen Maya, to repay her kindness for giving birth to him. During this time when the Buddha was gone, King Udayana of Kausambi had fallen sick over his longing for the Buddha. His ministers consulted with the Venerable Maudgalyayana, known as the disciple who was foremost in supernatural powers. Maudgalyayana used such powers to transport craftsmen to where the Buddha was teaching so that they could directly observe the Buddha's glorious appearance and carve a five-foot tall statue of the Buddha using the best sandalwood. This is said to be the beginning of the tradition of carving Buddha images.

Among the six realms of existence, the heavenly realms are where living beings have the greatest karmic rewards and enjoy

H

the greatest pleasure. Heavenly beings are still subject to the five signs of decay and re-entry into the cycle of birth and death after they have exhausted their positive karma. But, when compared to the human realm, heavens still have many attractive qualities. For example, the bodies of heavenly beings emit light, and they can fly freely wherever they please. The extreme pleasures of their existence exceeds any pain: palaces and gardens are prepared for their use and their sublime clothing and food manifest at a single thought. There is no need to work or rush about as there is in human life, nor is there any worry of hunger or want.

The Buddhist sutras say that among the various distinctions of heavenly beings, those who are taller have garments that shine more brightly. For example, beings of the Brahma-parisadya Heaven do not wear clothing at all, for they are naturally cloaked in garments of sublime radiance.

The levels of meditative concentration that are possible in the heavenly realms are more enjoyable than those of the human realm. Heavenly beings are also considerably taller and live longer than human beings. In terms of height, a height of six feet is about average for modern humans, but beings in the Caturmaharajika Heaven reach a height of nine hundred feet if calculated in our measurements. With each successively higher heavenly realm, the average height of the beings who reside there increases, with the supreme heaven of the form realm being home to beings with the gigantic stature of 265,000 kilometers. The distance from Taipei to Kaohsiung in Taiwan is only 380 kilometers; which should give us an idea of the colossal height of these heavenly beings. If a human being were to gaze up at one, it would be like an ant looking up at one of us—we could not help but marvel at such perfection, and likely feel that such a state is far beyond our reach.

Considering the life span of heavenly beings, it is a blessing for a human being to live to the age of seventy, while anyone who lives to be one hundred is respected by all. Even Pengzu, the Chinese sage who was said to live for eight hundred years, would pale in comparison to the longevity of heavenly beings.

How long do heavenly beings live? Beings who reside in the Heaven of the Thirty-three Gods live for five hundred "heavenly years," which is equivalent of nine million human years. In the highest formless heaven of neither thought nor non-thought, beings live for eighty thousand large *kalpas*. Such longevity is beyond measure.

Buddhism does not say that we should be satisfied with rebirth in heaven, though a heavenly rebirth should still be praised, for it requires many lifetimes of cultivating the ten wholesome actions— entire *kalpas* of performing acts of generosity and upholding the precepts. To be reborn in the higher heavenly realms even requires attaining levels of meditative concentration. For this reason there is a Chinese saying, "Being reborn in heaven is its own reward. Immortality is not attained just by seeking it."

H

## Hell
十八地獄
*See also*: Avici hell; dharma realms, ten; difficulties, eight.

In Buddhism, doing good leads to rebirth in heaven and doing bad means falling into hell. Ideas about hell have long had a great and profound influence upon the folk beliefs of China, in addition to Buddhism having its own concepts of heaven and hell. In Buddhist thought there are eighteen levels of hell, which are comprised of the eight cold hells of Arbuda Hell, Nirarbuda Hell, Atata Hell, Apapa

Hell, Huhuva Hell, Utpala Hell, Padma Hell, and Mahapadma Hell; the eight hot hells of Samjiva Hell, Kaslasutra Hell, Samghata Hell, Raurava Hell, Maharaurava Hell, Tapana Hell, Mahatapana Hell, and Avici Hell; the isolated hells, and the adjacent hells. Details for each of the eighteen hells are listed below:

### 1. Arbuda Hell （頞浮陀地獄）
*Arbuda* means "blister," and in this hell, sentient beings are so tormented by the harsh cold that their skin breaks out in blisters.

### 2. Nirarbuda Hell （尼羅浮陀地獄）
*Nirarbuda* means "bursting blister," because the cold has penetrated the skin all the way to the bone, the blisters covering the body burst open.

### 3. Atata Hell （阿吒吒地獄）
Due to the intense cold of Atata Hell, sentient beings suffering there cannot move their lips, and are only able to utter the sound "atata" with their tongue.

### 4. Apapa Hell （阿婆婆地獄）
Due to the even more intense cold of Apapa Hell, sentient beings suffering there cannot move their lips, and are only able to utter the sound "apapa" with their tongue.

### 5. Huhuva Hell （喉喉婆地獄）
Due to the increasingly extreme cold of Huhuva Hell, sentient beings suffering there cannot move their lips, and are only able to utter the sound "huhuva" with their tongue.

## 6. Utpala Hell（漚波羅地獄）

*Utpala* means "blue lotus." This refers to how the skin of sentient beings suffering in Utpala Hell bursts open under the extreme cold, resembling blue lotuses.

## 7. Padma Hell（波頭摩地獄）

*Padma* means "red lotus." This refers to how the flesh of sentient beings suffering in Padma Hell bursts open under the increasingly extreme cold, resembling red lotuses.

## 8. Mahapadma Hell（摩訶波頭摩地獄）

*Mahapadma* means "great red lotus." This refers to how the flesh of sentient beings suffering in Mahapadma Hell splits open under the increasingly extreme cold, such that their whole body appears covered with giant, red lotuses.

## 9. Samjiva Hell（等活地獄）

*Samjiva* means "being revived." Sentient beings who have committed serious crimes fall into Samjiva Hell, where there are punished by being cut, stabbed, ground up, and flailed. After they have died, they are immediately revived and brought back to life by a cool breeze, so that they may continue to suffer.

## 10. Kalasutra Hell（黑繩地獄）

*Kalasutra* means "black rope." Just as a carpenter measures out lumber, the soldiers of hell first use a black rope to measure the bodies of those who have been consigned to this hell for punishment, after which they proceed to chop and saw their bodies into pieces.

### 11. Samghata Hell（堆壓地獄）

*Samghata* means "multitude," refering to the multitude of torture devices that are gathered together in order to punish those sentient beings who have committed serious crimes.

### 12. Raurava Hell（叫喚地獄）

*Raurava* means "wailing." In this hell the soldiers of hell throw sentient beings into a giant cauldron, where they are boiled alive and scream and wail in pain. This hell is filled with those who have committed acts of killing, stealing, sexual misconduct, and consuming intoxicants.

### 13. Maharaurava Hell（大叫換地獄）

*Maharaurava* means "loud wailing." In this hell, after the soldiers of hell have boiled sentient beings alive, the wind of their karma revives them and they are driven onto a hot iron plate where they are fried alive, screaming and wailing loudly from their extreme suffering. This hell is filled with those who have committed acts of killing, stealing, sexual misconduct, and lying.

### 14. Tapana Hell（燒炙地獄）

*Tapana* means "roasting fires." This hell is surrounded by a wall of iron that is heated by intense fires so that everything inside and outside is roasted and broiled, burning the flesh of the wicked beings reborn there.

### 15. Mahatapana Hell（大燒炙地獄）

*Mahatapana* means "great roasting fires." Here the soldiers of hell put wicked beings within a wall of iron, which is then burned with raging fires until its glows red-hot both inside and outside, roasting them alive. Next, the soldiers skewer the wicked with iron pokers so that they can be burned alive in the flames.

### 16. *Avici Hell*（無間地獄）

Avici means "uninterrupted torment," for the wicked condemned to this hell experience infinite suffering without respite or pause. This is the hell of extreme suffering; all those who commit the five great violations or slander the Mahayana fall into this hell.

### 17. *The Isolated Hells*（孤獨地獄）

The isolated hells are spread throughout the four directions and are generated by the negative karma of each individual. Some are located within the four continents, others are in mountain valleys, or on mountain tops, or in the open countryside. In these hells, one is isolated without any companionship.

### 18. *The Adjacent Hells*（近邊地獄）

The adjacent hells are isolated locations spread throughout the four directions, similar to the isolated hells. Some are near rivers, while others are underground, and some are situated in the open air; they have no set location.

Among the three lower realms, beings in hell receive the most suffering. Sentient beings fall into the hells and experience suffering in accordance with their karma. Buddhas, on the other hand, manifest themselves in the hell realms to liberate sentient beings in accordance with their compassion and vows. For example, Ksitigarbha Bodhisattva vowed: "Not until hell is vacant shall I become a Buddha; only when all sentient beings are liberated will I attain *bodhi*." Ksitigarbha Bodhisattva considered, "If I do not enter hell, then who will?" enabling him to teach liberation throughout the hell realm, liberating beings from suffering.

# History of Buddhism
## 部派佛教

*See also*: Chan schools; non-Buddhist schools, six; schools of Chinese Buddhism, eight.

India is the birthplace of Buddhism, but Buddhism disappeared from India after only about sixteen hundred years of development. The history of Buddhism that spanned these centuries can be divided into three periods:

### 1. *The Period of Early Buddhism* （原始佛教時期）
This period begins from the time of the Buddha until roughly one hundred years after the Buddha's final *nirvana*. This also includes the time when King Asoka was on the throne. During this period Buddhism retained much of the theory, system, and thought that was present during the time of the Buddha.

### 2. *The Period of Sectarian Buddhism* （部派佛教時期）
This period covers from roughly one hundred to four hundred years after the final *nirvana* of the Buddha. During this time the Indian state of Mathura produced Mahadeva, one of the great transmitters of Buddhism. He authored five controversial theses that lead to the first schism within the sangha. Those who approved of these five theses formed the Mahasamghika School, while those who disapproved formed the Aryasthavira School (which later became the Theravada School). These two schools continued a process of division, until there were ten sects that descended from

the Aryasthavira School and eight sects that descended from the Mahasamghika School (another source lists eleven Aryasthavira sects and nine Mahasamghika sects). This process following the first schism became known as the "secondary divisions." Because Buddhism during this time split into many different schools and sects, this is known as the period of Sectarian Buddhism.

### 3. The Period of Mahayana Buddhism（大乘佛教時期）

This period roughly covers from four hundred years after the Buddha's final *nirvana* until Buddhism disappeared from India. Having gone through the early and sectarian periods, Buddhism had become an academic institution that was strictly focused on the study of doctrine, resulting in a disconnect between Buddhism and society. At this time there were some who had the great aspiration of the bodhisattva, and thus inaugurated a new Buddhist movement with the goal of restoring the spirit of Early Buddhism while also adjusting to contemporary developments. As this movement was predicated on bringing benefit to others, it became known as *mahayana,* "great vehicle" Buddhism.

In contrast to Mahayana Buddhism, the Buddhism of the sectarian period became known as *hinayana,* "small vehicle" Buddhism. In *An Overview of the Sectarian Buddhist Thought of India*, Master Yanpei (1917-1996) puts forward ten major reasons for the divisiveness of this period:

1. The democratic freedoms of the monastic system.
2. Differences among the various teaching traditions.
3. Differences in each group's use of language.
4. The impact of current trends.
5. Regional cultural influences.

H

6. Lack of unanimity in viewpoint.
7. Growing division and complexity within the oral tradition
8. Diverse personal temperament
9. Disagreements between reformists and traditionalists.
10. Divergent doctrines within sutras themselves.

Regardless of the reasons behind Buddhist schisms, there is still a saying in Buddhism that, "While there are many skillful means, there is only one way back to the source." Fundamentally, Buddhism is the teachings of the Buddha, which at their core have their own consistent character. Even though there are differences between Mahayana and Hinayana, the Northern and Southern transmissions, esoteric and exoteric teachings, and other such differences, we can still say, "Differences can be found within what is the same, and similarities can be found amid what is different." Different types of Buddhism should be approached with a spirit of mutual respect and harmony, in which everyone is honored and appreciated. Only in this way can the continued survival of the true Dharma be assured, so that Buddhism will not fade away as it has in India.

## Houses, Five
五家
*See*: Chan schools.

## Huanglong School
黃龍派
*See*: Chan schools.

## Huayan School
## 華嚴宗

*See*: Schools of Chinese Buddhism, eight.

## Human Realm
## 人勝諸天

*See also*: Saha world; dharma realms, ten.

> Hard it is to obtain a human body, but now I
>     have obtained one;
> Hard it is to hear the Buddha's teaching, but now
>     I have heard them.
> If I do not liberate myself in this lifetime,
> Then in which lifetime will I ever do so?

The *Agamas* contain the parable of "the blind turtle and the floating ring of wood." which compares the difficulty of obtaining a human rebirth to a blind turtle poking its head through a wooden ring floating on a vast ocean. The turtle in the parable only rises to the ocean's surface once every hundred years, during which the ring of wood floats on the ocean's surface and is tossed around by the wind and waves. The chance of obtaining a human rebirth is as rare as the blind turtle poking its head through the wooden ring when it rises to the surface. This is how difficult it is to be reborn as a human being.

The Buddha has also said, "The chance of not being reborn as a human being is as vast as the great earth; while the chance of being reborn as a human being is as small as the dirt under one's fingernail." This clearly shows how precious human life is. A human rebirth is the key factor which determines whether one rises or

H

falls among the other realms of existence; and although the karmic reward of human life is not as pleasurable as that of the heavenly realms, it is superior to all the heavenly realms in three areas:

### 1. Superior Bravery（勇猛勝）

Heavenly beings are addicted to the pleasures of desire and thus make no further progress in cultivation. Human beings, on the other hand, have an incredible propensity to endure suffering. As long as human beings feel that what they do has significance, they can put up with all manner of trials and tribulations as they strive to put it into practice. The moral strength of humanity to carry on bravely and strive unceasingly is superior to heavenly beings.

### 2. Superior Recollection（憶念勝）

Heavenly beings are addicted to the pleasures of desire and are unwilling to use their minds to think and create. As a result, their wisdom is very dim. On the other hand, humanity can ponder and distinguish all phenomena. By remembering the past, contemplating the present, and planning for the future, human beings build up and improve their knowledge. This is what has allowed human civilization to advance by leaps and bounds.

### 3. Superior Pure Practices（梵行勝）

Since heavenly beings are addicted to the pleasures of desire, they no longer cultivate positive karma. The human realm is located on the cusp between what is noble and vulgar. With neither too much suffering nor too much pleasure, humanity is able to be self-aware and can know shame. Even when human beings fall down, they can still produce the energy required to move towards goodness, and thereby save themselves from the mire of wickedness.

Due to these three characteristics, not only is the human realm superior to heaven, but no other realm of existence can match it. According to the Buddhist sutras, all the Buddhas of the past became Buddhas in the human realm, and all Buddhas of the future will practice and attain awakening in the human realm as well. Therefore, now that one has been born a human being, one should fully utilize these advantages to make progress day by day: use bravery and perseverance to build up one's bodhisattva practice; use recollection and wisdom to confer benefits upon society; and apply the wisdom of liberation to pursue pure practices with diligence. Only in this way will one avoid being unworthy of this human birth.

## Hungry Ghost
餓鬼

*See*: Dharma realms, ten; difficulties, eight; lower realms, three.

H

# I

## Icchantikas Can Attain Buddhahood
## 闡提成佛

Upon awakening, the Buddha proclaimed: "Marvelous, marvelous! All sentient beings have the Tathagata's wisdom and virtue." This means that all sentient beings have "Buddha nature," and can thus become Buddhas. The *Mahaparinirvana Sutra* goes further and explains that even *icchantikas*, beings said to have no good roots at all, possess Buddha nature, which abides within them unchanging. They too can ultimately obtain Buddhahood.

The earliest proponent of the "*icchantikas* can attain Buddhahood" doctrine was Master Daosheng of the Eastern Jin dynasty. Daosheng was a student of Kumarajiva, and after studying the incomplete, six fascicle *Mahaparinirvana Sutra* translated by Faxian and Buddhabhadra (4th-5th cent. CE), Daosheng proposed the idea that *icchantikas* can attain Buddhahood.

However, at that time, the complete *Mahaparinirvana Sutra* had not yet been transmitted to China, and the general consensus among Buddhist scholars was that *icchantikas* had no Buddha nature, and therefore could not become Buddhas. Consequently, most orthodox scholars considered Daosheng's views heretical for diverging from the Buddha's teaching, and so they excommunicated him from the sangha. Three years later, in 421 CE, Dharmaraksa (385-433 CE) translated the forty fascicle version of the *Mahaparinirvana Sutra* in Liangzhou. This version of the sutra clearly states that "all *icchantikas* have Buddha nature, and they all can attain Buddhahood." It was only then that everyone felt unanimous admiration for the outstanding intellectual insight and profound achievement of Master Daosheng.

It is said that after Daosheng had suffered the rejection of the other scholars, he went to Mount Huqiu in Jiangsu Province where he gathered stones as disciples. When he explained that *icchantikas* can attain Buddhahood to these stones, so convincing was his argument that the stones bowed. This story has become popularly remembered in the phrase, "When Daosheng teaches even the stones bow in affirmation."

The Sanskrit word *icchantika* has been translated variously into Chinese as *duan shangen* (斷善根), "destroying good roots," *xin bujuzu* (信不具足), "lacking faith," *jiyu* (極欲), "extreme in desire," *datan* (大貪), "of great greed," *wu zhongxing* (無種性), "lacking the seeds of goodness," and *shaozhong* (燒種), "burnt seeds of goodness." In summation, *icchantikas* are considered to be incorrigible beings who have lost all roots of goodness and are unable to attain Buddhahood. According to the *Lankavatara Sutra*, there are two kinds of icchantika:

### 1. Icchantikas of Eradicated Goodness （斷善闡提）
This type of *icchantika* fundamentally lacks the causes for liberation, for they hold wicked views and have eradicated their good

roots through great misdeeds such that they are unable to attain Buddahood. Such people disparage the Mahayana Dharma, do not believe in the positive and negative effects of karma, and commit the five great violations.

### 2. Icchantikas of Great Compassion （大悲闡提）

These are the bodhisattvas who, in accordance with their compassionate vow to liberate all sentient beings, intentionally do not enter *nirvana*. For example, Ksitigarbha Bodhisattva vowed, "Not until hell is vacant shall I become a Buddha; only when all sentient beings are liberated will I attain *bodhi*," and so he belongs to this class of *icchantika* of great compassion.

Besides its presentation in the *Mahaparinirvana Sutra*, the doctrine that *icchantikas* can attain Buddhahood is also supported by the Tiantai, Huayan, and other Mahayana schools, which advocate that all sentient beings can attain Buddhahood, because Buddha nature always exists and is possessed by all beings. However, the Faxiang School still holds that there are sentient beings who cannot attain Buddhahood, and so the question of whether or not *icchantikas* can attain Buddhahood still remains a controversial issue within Buddhist circles. But given the story that when Daosheng taught even the stones bowed in affirmation, one must consider that, if even non-sentient things like stones can bow in affirmation, then clearly Buddha nature permeates the whole world and everything is vitally alive.

People sometimes ask questions like, "Can mountains, rivers, plants and trees attain Buddhahood?" For an answer, we can turn to Chan Master Zhenguan's (1269-1341 CE) reply to Dharma Master Daowen (ca. 13th-14th cent. CE): "You are so concerned as to whether plants and trees can attain Buddhahood, but what good does that do you? What you should be concerned about is how you will attain Buddhahood."

Thus, whether or not plants and trees can attain Buddhahood is not the important issue. As long as we are able to realize that this mind is the Buddha, then the mountains and rivers, plants and trees will attain Buddhahood together with us.

The basic spirit of Buddhism is this: as long as one generates the aspiration for awakening, anyone can attain Buddhahood. Therefore, we should not belittle ourselves, but rather affirm our own ability to attain Buddhahood. This is what is most important.

## Ignorance
無明煩惱

*See also*: Poisons, three; dependent origination; wisdom, three kinds of; wisdom, four kinds of.

The *Notes to the Compendium of the Mahayana* states, "The Dharma is nothing other than the practice of transforming ignorance into awakening and transforming defilement into purity, and the key to these transformations is wisdom." "Wisdom" here means an understanding of principles, most specifically an understanding of the principles of cause and effect. Conversely, not understanding cause and effect and misinterpreting karma is considered "delusion," or "ignorance." Ignorance is both the source of affliction, and an affliction itself.

Afflictions have many names. They are called "obstructions," because they obstruct the progress of students of Buddhism. They are called "obscurations" because they obscure our true Buddha nature. Afflictions are also called "entanglements" because they

I

can tie up the mind like a coiled rope, and are called "shackles" because they restrain the freedom of the body and mind. Since afflictions can pollute the nature of the mind, they are also called "stains," and because they gather like dirt as we do our daily tasks they are called "dust." Afflictions can act like a flood that washes away our morality, so they are called "violent torrents," and since they can propel us into the cycle of birth and death they are sometimes called a "force." In the sutras, afflictions are also compared to a burning flame, a poison arrow, a savage beast, and a dangerous chasm. Whatever they are called, afflictions are those things which torment the body and mind, cause us to act out of ignorance, and lead us back to the cycle of birth and death. To practice Buddhism means to fight against the afflictions, for if we wish to obtain the freedom of liberation, we must defeat them.

An ordinary person has many built up habitual tendencies. For example, we will naturally want to possess the people, activities, and things that please us; this is greed. In contrast, we want to get rid of the people we loath, the activities we don't like, and the things we find displeasing; this is anger. Because of this we are pleased when things go according to our wishes and are angry when things go awry. This shows a total lack of understanding of reality, and is ignorance. Greed, anger, and ignorance lead to a host of other afflictions, such as avarice, stinginess, jealousy, selfishness, hatred, attachment, animosity, carelessness, and tension. Buddhists must cultivate the threefold practice of morality, meditative concentration, and wisdom to eliminate the afflictions of greed, anger, and ignorance.

The sutras say that human beings have eighty-four thousand afflictions. The afflictions of human beings are as numerous as the grains of sand in the Ganges River, and without some form of spiritual cultivation, there is no way that these afflictions can be corrected. In the *Universal Gate Sutra*, the Buddha tells Aksayamati Bodhisattva, "If there be countless hundreds of millions of billions of living beings experiencing all manner of suffering who hear of Avalokitesvara Bodhisattva and call his name with single-minded effort, then Avalokitesvara Bodhisattva will instantly observe the sound of their cries, and they will all be liberated."

The Buddha tells us to engage in spiritual cultivation such as single-mindedly focusing on Avalokitesvara Bodhisattva for the sake of liberation, though there are many other forms of practice such as reciting Amitabha Buddha's name, chanting sutras, paying homage to the Buddha, visualizing the Buddha, listening to the Dharma, upholding the precepts, performing good deeds, and other such things. The faith, power, and joy that comes from spiritual practice can all eliminate and purify the affliction of ignorance.

Affliction is ultimately caused by the ignorant pursuit of things outside of the mind, for we are confused and deluded by external reality. To combat this we must let go of the self. By forgetting about the self we can merge our "small self" into the greater self, such that we can expand our self-centered mind into one that cherishes all sentient beings. In this way we can remove the affliction of ignorance and recover ourselves.

I

## Immeasurable Minds, Four
## 四無量心

The Buddhist path is a long one. If one lacks an immeasurable aspiration for awakening, it is like driving an automobile somewhere without enough gas: there is no way you will reach your destination. Therefore, students of Buddhism should aspire to develop the "four immeasurable minds."

The four immeasurable minds are four qualities that bodhisattvas should equip themselves with to liberate all sentient beings:

### 1. Immeasurable Loving-kindness（慈無量心）

There is a Buddhist saying that "Loving-kindness is what brings happiness." Loving-kindness is fundamental to Buddhism, for without loving-kindness, all of the Dharma is nothing more than the teachings of Mara.

Immeasurable loving-kindness is the wish that sentient beings be happy. However, many misunderstand the forgiveness of loving-kindness as indulging others. Loving-kindness requires wisdom. True loving-kindness is a kind of purified and refined love, and constitutes service and assistance that is selfless and wise. Loving-kindness is given without seeking anything in return, and tries to fulfill the wishes of others. Loving-kindness is the combination of love, wisdom, vow, and generosity.

### 2. Immeasurable Compassion（悲無量心）

There is a Buddhist saying that "Compassion is what relieves suffering." The mind of immeasurable compassion wishes to free sentient beings from suffering. If a bodhisattva cannot feel empathy and compassion towards those who are suffering, he will not seek to attain Buddhahood and guide those who are unawakened by relieving their suffering and making them happy. It would be impossible for such a bodhisattva to complete the path to awakening. Therefore, immeasurable compassion is a prerequisite for a bodhisattva's attainment of Buddhahood.

## 3. Immeasurable Joy （喜無量心）

While loving-kindness is to bring happiness to sentient beings, joy is to bring joy to all sentient beings. The distinction is that "happiness" comes from the five sense-objects (of sight, sound, smell, taste, and touch) while joy is entirely mental. The Buddha was born into this world for a great purpose, and this great purpose was "to demonstrate the teachings, and the benefits and joy of their meaning and practice." Therefore, in the Buddhist sutras we often read how the Buddha's disciples were "happily eager to hear" when they asked for teachings, and how they "jumped for joy" and "joyously gave praise" after teachings were given. Clearly, Dharma joy and meditative bliss are the true treasure of Buddhism.

## 4. Immeasurable Equanimity （捨無量心）

The four immeasurable minds can bring one wondrous happiness. However, as we develop loving-kindness and joy it is easy to also generate attachment, and as we become more compassionate it is easy to generate sorrow as well. That is why we must develop equanimity and an even mind so that we can eradicate discrimination and delusion, making it possible for all sentient beings to enter the Buddhist path. The mind of immeasurable equanimity is the unsurpassed wisdom of the essential emptiness of the three spheres. In Buddhism we commonly talk about "letting go." This is because one can receive only after having let go of things, just as one can only advance by loosening one's pace. Those who teach the Dharma and liberate sentient beings should stabilize themselves in equanimity and let go of all attachment to loving-kindness, compassion, and joy, for in this way even greater accomplishments can be achieved.

I

The *Flower Adornment Sutra* states: "Always enjoy the practice of gentleness and patience; find your repose in the four immeasurable minds of loving kindness, compassion, joy, and equanimity." Loving-kindness, compassion, joy, and equanimity are what we should rely on, and where we can find our repose. The development of the four immeasurable minds begins with the concept of putting ourselves in others' positions so that we develop the view of considering others. Next, by trying to understand the feelings of others through our own and by imagining what it would be like to be in their place, we will naturally develop the four immeasurable minds.

## Impermanence
## 無常苦空
*See also*: Mindfulness, four bases of.

"Impermanence," *anitya* in Sanskrit, is opposed to the concept of eternalism, and describes how all phenomena cannot remain fixed and constant, but undergo a process of arising, extinction, and change. Conditioned phenomena are impermanent because they arise through the coming together of causes and conditions and pass into extinction once those causes and conditions are finished. The doctrine of "impermanence" means that there is not one single thing in this world that is unchanging and exists forever.

All life must undergo a process of birth, old age, sickness, and death. All the things will exhibit the changes of formation, abiding, destruction, and cessation. Even the thoughts of sentient beings undergo the impermanence of arising, abiding, change, and extinction. Once impermanence shows up, even loving and caring couples and family members will find it impossible to remain together. Just like a flock of birds roosting together in the forest, once the disaster of impermanence arrives, each bird flies off on its own to save itself. Some people spend their whole lives currying favor as they toil away ceaselessly, and yet they realize nothing from such effort. Their lives are a constantly changing mirage, for they fully experience the suffering of not getting what they want. Some people achieve fame and fortune through their efforts, but can lose it all and become prisoners locked behind bars in a single night, a fate common to many. There are even some who struggle bitterly, barely achieving their long sought honor and riches, and with the sudden intervention of impermanence their life's work is for naught.

The *Treatise on the Perfection of Great Wisdom* likens the world's impermanence to a dream, a mirage, a bubble, a shadow, a dewdrop, and a flash of lightning. Impermanence is as terrible as a wolf or a tiger. Like a murderous demon, impermanence can rob the practitioner of his or her life at any time, and so the wind of impermanence, the knife of impermanence, and the messenger of impermanence never leaves our side.

If sentient beings gain a profound understanding that all phenomena entail suffering, emptiness, and impermanence, they will be able to remove themselves from the unreal world with all its many illusions and follow the path to liberation. When we recognize the implications of impermanence, suffering, and emptiness, such understanding will certainly lead to a more positive attitude towards the path. For example:

I

- Because of the world's impermanence, suffering, and emptiness, all change is uncertain. This helps us to realize that all beings' true Dharma nature is equal.

- As we recognize the truth of the world's impermanence, suffering, and emptiness, and know that all phenomena come about through causes and conditions, so we must grasp this present moment and broadly create wholesome connections for a positive future.

- As we have fixed this concept of the world's impermanence, suffering, and emptiness in our minds, so we will not be led astray by the claims of supernatural power and false teachings.

Because the world is impermanent, there is suffering. Because all phenomena lack intrinsic nature, there is emptiness. When success becomes failure this is impermanence, but when disaster is transformed into a blessing this is also impermanence. When we understand that even impermanence itself lacks intrinsic nature and practice diligently, we can transform adversity into good fortune and ignorance into awakening. In this way one can avoid catastrophe and enjoy peace and health.

## Impurity
不淨
*See*: Contemplations, five.

## Intrinsic Nature
明心見性

The ancient sages of the Chan School spent their lives journeying, disregarding their own safety as they crossed mountains and forded rivers in their quest to visit famous teachers. Though they suffered greatly, they did not complain. Their goal was to see their intrinsic nature by illuminating the mind, and attaining Buddhahood through awakening.

What is meant by the expression "see intrinsic nature by illuminating the mind"?

National Master Zhongfeng (1263-1323 CE) said:

> The mind is of several types. The physical mind is part of the body that we inherit from our parents. The conditioned mind creates distinctions between good and bad, and positive and negative in each moment. The spiritual mind is beyond worldly distinctions, is free from confusion, and unchanging. This mind is luminous, preeminent, and unique. The spiritual mind is not greater in sages or lesser among ordinary people. In the ocean of birth and death, it is like a bright pearl that illuminates the sea. On the shore of *nirvana*, it is like a moon that hangs in the sky.

"Intrinsic nature" means the part of us which is unchanging. It is a quality that is originally complete in and of itself, an intrinsic part of us that cannot be influenced or altered by external factors. It is the fundamental essence that pervades the universe, and the source of all being. Intrinsic nature has many names, including "Buddha nature," "Dharmakaya," "body of inherent purity," "Tathagata nature," and "awakened nature." It is the inherent nature of the Buddha and the awakened nature of sentient beings.

To "see intrinsic nature by illuminating the mind" means that we must reach a clear and thorough understanding of our intentions and how they change. That is why one must awaken through seeing intrinsic nature in order to attain Buddhahood.

The Buddhist sutras compare the mind to a mirror. If it is clear, it can reflect all things. However, if the mirror is obscured by the dust of affliction, then it cannot reflect what is real. The sutras also compare the mind to a treasure chest that stores many rare and precious gems, such that it can supply us with inexhaustible wealth. It is because the mind is diseased by greed, anger, and ignorance that we cannot be free.

Because sentient beings do not understand or know themselves, we so often hear people lament that they cannot express how they feel, that others cannot know the pain they bear, or that they do not know what they are thinking. But is the mind really that difficult to fathom? The mind produces all consciousness, so we must look for a mental cure to our mental illness.

How can we see intrinsic nature by illuminating the mind?

There is a saying that "the finest jade must be cut." The same can be said for polishing the mirror of the mind, for unless we put the effort in to polish it, how can we expect it to reflect clearly? The Buddha said, "All sentient beings have the Tathagata's wisdom and virtue, but they fail to realize it because they cling to deluded thoughts and attachments." Just as the light of the sun can be obscured by clouds, only by removing the clouds of affliction can the inherent nature of the mind be revealed in all its glorious brightness. How do we see intrinsic nature by illuminating the mind? The Dharma teaches us that we must practice, for only with practice will we be able to recognize our intrinsic nature.

Since ancient times, many great monks and sages have undertaken such practices as cultivating austerities, reciting sutras, chanting Amitabha Buddha's name, sitting in meditation, serving the community, and teaching the Dharma for the benefit of others. In this way, they have refined the nature of the mind, and in the end they attained supreme awakening, saw their intrinsic nature by illuminating the mind, and attained Buddhahood.

I

# J

## Jeta Grove
祇園
*See*: Vulture Peak and Jeta Grove.

## Jivaka
開心羅漢
*See*: Arhats, eighteen.

## Joy
喜
*See*: Immeasurable minds, four; winds, eight.

# K

## Kalika
騎象羅漢

*See*: Arhats, eighteen.

## Kalpa
三大阿僧祇劫

The sutras say, "The Buddha spent three great *kalpas* to perfect his merit and wisdom, and one hundred small *kalpas* to perfect his primary and secondary marks." This passages shows that it takes an incalculable amount of time to practice for the attainment of Buddhahood.

What is a *kalpa*? In the Buddhist reckoning of time the smallest possible unit of time is the *ksana*, which is a single moment; a split-second. The largest unit of time is the *kalpa*, of which there are three types: small *kalpas*, medium *kalpas*, and large *kalpas*. A medium *kalpas* is the length of twenty small *kalpas*. A large *kalpas* is the length of four medium *kalpas*. A large *kalpa* is the length of time that a world-system undergoes a cycle of formation, abiding, destruction, and void.

The sutras offer a metaphor to describe the length of a small *kalpa*. Imagine a ten year-old child. Suppose that this child only grows one year older for every one hundred years that elapse for the rest of us. Now suppose this child has aged in this manner to be 80,000 years-old. Now that he is 80,000 years old, he grows one year younger for every one hundred years that elapse for the rest of us. When this child is once again ten years old, a small *kalpa* will have elapsed.

Twenty of these small *kalpas* constitute a medium *kalpa*, and four medium *kalpas* equal a large *kalpa*. These four medium *kalpas* correspond to different stages in the life of a world-system: one medium *kalpa* in which a world system is formed, one medium *kalpa* in which a world system abides and flourishes, and one medium *kalpa* in which a world system is in decline, and one medium *kalpa* in which a world system is completely destroyed. This cycle constitutes a complete large *kalpa*. The four stages are described in greater detail below:

### 1. Kalpa of Formation（成劫）

During this period of time all matter arises, such as mountains, rivers, trees and plants, and the earth itself. Sentient beings arise afterwards. According to the *Sutra on the Generation of World Systems*, the formation of a world system begins with the stirring of the winds of sentient beings' karmic connections. This changes the natural world and creates mountains, rivers, and land. Later, sentient beings are reborn into the world, one after another.

### 2. Kalpa of Abiding（住劫）

During this period of time the matter and sentient beings in the world system have settled. The various small *kalpas* that occur within the *kalpa* of abiding may either be characterized by beings living longer lives or beings living shorter lives. Sometime during this *kalpa* will occur the "three minor calamities" of war, pestilence, and famine.

### 3. Kalpa of Destruction （壞劫）

During the *kalpa* of destruction the world system will be destroyed by the three calamities of water, fire, and wind. First all sentient beings will be destroyed, followed by all matter. The three calamities of fire, wind, and water will each last for a small *kalpa*, destroying various parts of the world system. The Buddhist sutras say, "fire will burn the heavens of the first *dhyana*, water will flood the heavens of the second *dhyana*, and wind will blow away the heavens of the third *dhyana*." During the *kalpa* of destruction, the desire realm will be completely destroyed, and only the heavens of the fourth *dhyana* of the form realm and the heavens of the formless realm will remain.

### 4. Kalpa of Void （空劫）

During the *kalpa* of void, the world system has been destroyed. Only those beings in the heavens of the fourth *dhyana* continue to exist, for everything else enters a long period of void. This period of time is when a world system has yet to be formed, and phenomena have not yet come into being.

K

At the conclusion of the *kalpa* of void, another cycle of formation, abiding, destruction, and void begins. Each stage in the cycle lasts for approximately 320 million years. For the entire cycle to reach its conclusion requires about 1.28 billion years.

The *Sutra in Forty-Two Sections* states that human life hangs between an in-breath and an out-breath, indicating how short and impermanent human life is. But regardless if life lasts for three large *kalpas* or a single instant, we should make the best use of our time, so that we can use our limited time to support and realize the value of life.

## Kanakabharadvaja
## 舉鉢羅漢
*See*: Arhats, eighteen.

## Kanakavatsa
## 喜慶羅漢
*See*: Arhats, eighteen.

## Karma of the Three Time Periods
## 三世因果

> Know the causes in your past lives,
> By looking at what befalls you in this;
> Know your future outcome,
> By looking at what you are doing now.

The verse above summarizes the teaching of karma, one of the most important teachings of Buddhism: the success or failure, wealth or poverty of this lifetime are the result of one's actions created in the past, and that the positive or negative actions performed now will determine how fortunate or unfortunate one's future will be.

Buddhism emphasizes that cause and effect are carried throughout the "three time periods," the past, present, and future.

There is a saying that, "The karma one creates does not disappear even after a hundred thousand *kalpas.* One will still garner reward or retribution when cause and condition come together." Cause and effect in the past, present, and future is the basis of the cycle of birth and death. The karma that one creates does not go away, no matter how much time has elapsed, and will manifest itself when the conditions are right.

Karma of the three time periods does not necessarily refer to past lives, present life, and future lives; it could also mean last year, this year, and next year; or yesterday, today, and tomorrow; or even the previous moment, this moment, and the next moment. In short, the three time periods are the past, the present, and the future.

However, Buddhism teaches that "all conditioned phenomena are impermanent," and since all phenomena in the world are impermanent, they certainly cannot exist forever and never be destroyed. How is it that karma can persist throughout past, present, and future in an endless cycle?

In the Buddhist sutras karma is often compared to a seed. Consider a soy plant: through the process of planting, sprouting, maturation, and fruition, a soy plant will produce seeds in reserve. After a period of time the stem of the soy plant that has flowered and produced seeds will dry up as the whole plant withers and dies. But, once the seeds it had been holding meet the right conditions, they will sprout, put forth shoots, flower, and generate seeds once more. How the karma of sentient beings continues to produce effects is very much like this process.

Karma can also be seen as our habitual tendencies. Just as a bottle of perfume retains its fragrance long after the perfume has been used up, karmic effects will continue to influence future

K

causes. Whenever there is a cause, once the proper conditions mature, there will surely be a karmic effect.

The doctrine of karma in the past, present, and future not only enables our lives to have a future, to have hope and light, but at the same time, it also proves that Buddhism is not a religion that believes in "predestination." Buddhism holds that the actions of each individual can determine their own destiny. Whether a person's life is blessed or cursed is all created by their own karma, and one experiences the consequences of their own actions in terms of positive and negative causes and effects. One who commits many injustices will come to a bad end, while always performing good deeds will increase one's virtue and wisdom. It is better to perform good deeds than to accumulate wealth, for in the end, you can only take your karma with you. Doing good deeds and creating positive causes is the only everlasting wealth.

## Karma, Three Types of
三業

As human beings, we all live in one world together and possess similar learning and abilities, yet there is a wide disparity over the amount of fortune or misfortune we experience. Why is this? This is because of the differences in our past karma.

All sentient beings are endowed with the same life force and inherent nature, yet some enjoy all the freedoms of the heavenly realms while others suffer through cyclic existence in the lower realms. Why is this? Because each and every sentient being has created their own karma.

Karma is the action produced by one's body, speech, and mind. Thus karma is often separated into the "three kinds of karma":

physical karma, verbal karma, and mental karma. Examples of each are as follows:

## 1. Physical Karma（身業）

Any act in which your own happiness is built upon the suffering of others, constitutes an unwholesome act of physical karma. Examples include: using knives, guns, or poison to kill living beings; using sticks, clubs, and rocks to injure and wound; using trickery to rob or steal from others; swindling and embezzling; using money or good looks to seduce men and women; and violating ethics and morality.

Any act that is of benefit to others constitutes a wholesome act of physical karma. Examples include: helping others out of difficulty; letting others off the hook so they can be happy; donating financial resources; giving others any kind of advantage; respecting ethical standards; and refraining from committing any wrongdoing.

## 2. Verbal Karma（口業）

Examples of unwholesome acts of verbal karma include: habitually employing harsh words and sowing discord; regularly spouting falsehoods and worthless chatter; harping solely on the shortcomings of others; reporting solely on the mistakes of others; uttering artful deceptions; harming others through rumors and innuendo; and harming, deceiving, or embarrassing others.

Examples of wholesome acts of verbal karma include: encouraging others; commending others; overlooking the faults of others; making known the good that others do; expressing useful opinions, speaking with honest words; and praising, helping, or benefiting others.

K

### 3. Mental Karma（意業）

Any mental state that involves greed, anger, or wrong views constitutes an unwholesome act of mental karma. Examples include: scattered and fanciful desires, wishes that benefit oneself by harming others, angry and vicious hatred, personal resentment that blames heaven or other people, wrongheaded and dangerous delusions, and wrong views that deny cause and effect.

Examples of wholesome acts of mental karma include: treating others equally; expressing joy to others; refraining from venomous thoughts of resentment; curbing meaningless rage; holding reasonable and correct views; having pure and good wisdom; and keeping one's mind away from greed, hatred, and wrong views.

Buddhism's doctrine of karma is a wondrous teaching that is both sensible and reasonable. The fortunes and misfortunes of life are all generated by one's own body, speech, and mind. There is no one else who can control our fate; the only one who can control that is ourselves.

There is a saying in Buddhism, "You can take nothing with you except your karma." So let us create more wholesome karma through our body, speech, and mind!

## Kindness
恩

*See*: Gratitude; means of embracing, four; virtues of the Buddha, three. *See also*: Loving-kindness.

## Ksitigarbha
地藏

*See*: Mountains, four great.

# Kumarajiva
**鳩摩羅什**
*See*: Translators, four great Chinese.

K

# L

## Labor, Communal
## 出坡

Communal labor in a Chan temple, variously referred in Chinese as *chupo* (出坡), *puqing* (普請) or *pupo laozuo* (普坡勞作), refers to a system of rules by which the entire monastic community, including both senior and junior members, perform manual labor together. The system of communal labor was implemented throughout China during the Tang dynasty and encompassed chores like hauling firewood, bringing in water, sweeping the temple grounds, picking flowers and tea, harvesting crops, temple construction, airing out the sutra library, and other forms of manual labor.

During communal labor everyone from the abbot on down to those living in the monastery dormitories, except those assigned to official monastery business, gathers at the designated location. This practice truly shows what the monastic community can accomplish when they come together as well as exemplifying the ideals of self-reliance, democracy, and equality.

In Buddhism, communal labor is a kind of religious practice and a method of learning. Through communal labor one comes to understand the sanctity of work and the importance of service, and will come to feel that one is a valuable person.

There are many stories of the great monastics of the past and their achievements through practicing communal labor. For example Huineng, the Sixth Patriarch of the Chan School, came to know Buddha nature while pounding rice with a mortar and pestle. Chan Master Fayuan (991-1067 CE) served as a monastic cook at Guangjiao Temple in Ye County, Ruzhou, where he attained awakening after suffering many hardships.

Chan Master Baizhang Huaihai's *Rules of Purity for a Chan Temple*, an early system of Chinese monastic rules, features a passage describing communal labor:

> The monastic community shall form ranks and proceed to the designated location for communal labor. On both the way out and way in, no one should engage in idle chatter or frivolous behavior; nor shall there be any careless wandering about or whispering among the ranks. Everyone must go out together and come back together; no one is permitted to run off on their own. While engaged in communal labor, everyone should be hardworking and diligent.

Communal labor in a monastery setting is not the same as worldly manual labor. Communal labor is actually a unique form of spiritual practice, and is one of many methods for attaining awakening put forth by the Chan School.

Today the practice of communal labor has expanded beyond the monastic community to include lay volunteers, and the nature of the work itself has also become more varied. Examples include participating in temple mailings and publications, setting up the assembly hall, serving food and tea, working in the kitchen, ushering people during events, and even cleaning the Buddha statues before the lunar New Year and tidying up the temple grounds. All this work requires that members of the laity be sought out to join in such communal labor, thereby ensuring that the monastic community will have more time for the social outreach work of spreading the Dharma.

When members of the laity participate in communal labor, not only do they maintain the upkeep of the temple or monastery, but through such communal work they can forge connections, develop wisdom, gain experience, and mature in their understanding. This is the best form of practice for developing one's merit and wisdom.

During the time of the Buddha, the elder Sudatta not only donated Jeta Grove Monastery to house the Buddha and support his teachings, but he also went to the monastery every day to sweep the stupas and courtyards and keep the monastery grounds clean. This attitude of treating the monastery or temple like one's own home is the best model to follow for those who help to maintain a temple.

**L**

## Lianchi, Master
## 蓮池大師
*See*: Masters of the Ming dynasty, four.

## Linji School
## 臨濟宗
*See*: Chan schools.

# Lotus Sutra
## 法華經
*See*: Parables of the *Lotus Sutra;* schools of Chinese Buddhism, eight.

# Loving-Kindness
## 慈
*See*: Contemplations, five; immeasurable minds, four; mountain gate.

# Lower Realms, Three
## 三途
*See also*: Avici hell; dharma realms, ten; hell; realms of existence, six.

Among the ten dharma realms, four are supramundane realms while the other six, also known as the "six realms of existence," are mundane realms. Among these six realms, three are fortunate rebirths and three are unfortunate rebirths. The three unfortunate realms are also known as the "three lower realms," and include the animal realm, the realm of hungry ghosts, and the hell realm.

## 1. Animal Realm （畜生）
In Chinese, rebirth into the animal realm is called *chusheng* (畜生), "domesticated birth," referring to the many animals that have been domesticated by humans. Rebirth in the animal realm is also sometimes called *bangsheng* (傍生), "sideways birth," because most animals do not walk upright as humans do, and are more often horizontal or "sideways."

L

Animals are stupid and lack knowledge; they injure and kill each other, are made to bear burdens, are beaten, and are killed for food by humans. In this way, they suffer from all manner of pain and torment.

Animals are sometimes categorized by where they live, into those that fly, walk on land, or swim in water, or in terms of when they are active into those that are primarily active during the day (diurnal), during the night (nocturnal), or those who can be active during the day or night (cathemeral). There are five karmic causes that can lead to rebirth as an animal: breaking the precept against stealing, failing to repay loans, killing living beings, disliking to hear and receive the teachings, and using any means to prevent people from gathering to hear the Dharma.

## 2. Realm of Hungry Ghosts （餓鬼）

Beings in this realm are always starving and are cowardly with many fears; thus they are called *egui* (餓鬼), "hungry ghosts." They are impeded from eating or drinking in three ways. First, they are subject to external impediments, for due to their karma, the springs and lakes that they see are transformed into blood and pus, which they cannot consume. Second, they are subject to internal impediments, because their throats are as narrow as a pin, their mouths burn with fire, and their bellies are as big as drums; even if they try to eat or drink, they still cannot chew or swallow. Third, even if there are no physical impediments, because of the effects of their karma, whatever they chew and swallow is transformed by fire into burning charcoal, so they still suffer bitterly from thirst and hunger.

There are ten karmic causes the lead one to suffer rebirth as a hungry ghost: minor acts of negative physical, verbal, and mental karma, having many desires, having ill-intentioned desire, jealous-ly, holding wrong views, dying while still attached to the necessi-ties of life, dying from hunger, and dying from thirst.

### 3. Hell Realms（地獄）

Hell is the most despicable domain of all in the desire realm. In Chinese it is sometimes called *di* (底), "bottom," for among all things it is the lowliest. It is also called *ju* (局), "limited," for be-ings reborn in hell feel constricted and lose their freedom. Since hell has no advantages or benefits it is also called *wuyou* (無有), "non-possession."

There are many forms of hell known by a plethora of names, but classically they are divided into a group of eighteen hells. Among these, the pain and suffering of Avici Hell is the most horrifying. The karmic causes that can lead to rebirth in Avici Hell are:

1. Committing any of the five great violations: killing one's father, killing one's mother, killing an arhat, shedding the blood of a Buddha, and creating a schism in the monastic community.
2. Malicious slander against the Triple Gem or disrespecting the sutras.
3. Misappropriating the property of the monastic order, insulting monks and nuns, indulging in sexual desire within a monastery, or killing members of the monastic community.
4. Impersonating a monastic, squandering monastic prop-erty, cheating the laity, or disobeying the monastic rules and precepts.

5.  Stealing property from the monastic order.

Since the torment of those in hell is so extreme, their minds are in turmoil and cannot spare any effort to receive the Dharma. The minds of animals are dominated by ignorance, and thus they cannot be inspired by the Dharma. As hungry ghosts are subject to extreme hunger and thirst, and their bodies are burned by great flames, they too are unable to accept the Dharma. Even in the heavenly and *asura* realms, beings are able to indulge in so many pleasures that they do not comprehend the value of listening to the Dharma. Only the human realm, where happiness and suffering are roughly equal, offers the best opportunity for diligently listening to the Dharma. That is why it is said that among the six realms of existence, rebirth in the human realm is the most rare and admirable.

L

# M

## Mahakasyapa
**大迦葉**
*See:* Disciples, ten great.

## Mahakatyayana
**迦旃延**
*See:* Disciples, ten great.

## Mahasthamaprapta
**大勢至**
*See:* Noble ones of the West, three.

## Mahayana
**大乘**
*See:* History of Buddhism; Mahayana and Hinayana.

# Mahayana and Hinayana
大乘小乘

*See also*: History of Buddhism.

In Sanskrit, *yana*, "vehicle," is symbolic of how sentient beings are transported from the afflictions of this shore over to *nirvana* of the other shore.

The terms "Mahayana" and "Hinayana" appeared sometime after the Buddha's final *nirvana* with the rise of what came to be known as Mahayana Buddhism. *Mahayana*, the "great vehicle," is also called the "bodhisattva vehicle," the "supreme vehicle," the "excellent vehicle," and the "foremost vehicle." In contrast with the Mahayana, *hinayana*, "small vehicle," means a minor or narrow vehicle, referring to those teachings that can carry sentient beings with a spiritual capacity for self-benefit to the minor level of realization. It is also sometimes called the "*sravaka* vehicle."

Hinayana thus became a derogatory reference to the early Buddhist sects. Hinayana Buddhism considers Sakyamuni Buddha its religious leader and denies the reality of an independent self. The main goal for the Hinayana is self-liberation and, as such, the Hinayana constitutes the path for the *sravakas* and *pratyekabuddhas* who only eliminate their own afflictions and liberate themselves. Mahayana Buddhism, on the other hand, conceives of innumerable Buddhas spread across the ten directions throughout the past, present, and future, denies the reality of independent phenomena, and considers *nirvana* to have a positive meaning. The Mahayana advocates the path of the bodhisattva, a mode of practice that can be followed by both monastics and the laity and emphasizes benefiting both oneself and others.

**M**

Hinayana Buddhism reveres texts such as the *Agamas*, the *Four-Part Vinaya* and the *Five-Part Vinaya*, as well as the many treatises such as *Great Compendium of the Abhidharma*, the *Six Treatises of the Sarvastivada School*, the *Treatise on Generating Wisdom*, the *Treasury of the Abhidharma*, and the *Treatise on Establishing the Truth*, among others.

Mahayana Buddhism reveres texts such as the *Prajnaparamita Sutra*, the *Lotus Sutra*, the *Flower Adornment Sutra*, the *Treatise on the Middle Way*, and the *Compendium of the Mahayana*, among others. Although followers of the Mahayana acknowledge the value of Hinayana sutras, they still see them as secondary to the Mahayana sutras. Hinayana followers on the other hand do not consider the Mahayana sutras and treatises to have been taught by the Buddha.

Generally, we speak of the northern transmission of Buddhism into China and East Asia as Mahayana, with the southern transmission into Sri Lanka and Southeast Asia as Hinayana. Mahayana is the bodhisattva vehicle, which can carry many people with its great capacity and limitlessly powerful teachings. Hinayana Buddhism is only concerned with the individual practice, and as a vehicle is more like a bicycle, only able to carry a single person.

Today, Buddhism has spread throughout the world, and Buddhists should not condemn or disparage each other. We should be more ecumenical when referencing Mahayana or Hinayana, and instead refer to "Southern Buddhism" to refer to the Buddhism of places like Sri Lanka, Burma, and Thailand, and "Northern Buddhism" to refer to the Buddhism of places like China, Korea, and Japan.

Buddhist traditions vary according to the unique historical, environmental, social, and cultural background of the many

**M**

countries it has traveled to. But in terms of Buddhism's general principles, everyone is still united. For example, all Buddhists share a belief in the Triple Gem of the Buddha, Dharma, and Sangha, and share a respect for the Buddha as the religious leader of Buddhism. There is a shared acceptance of the Tripitaka with its collection of sutras, vinayas, and sastras preserved in both the Pali Canon and the Chinese Canon, which both contain the teachings of Early Buddhism. The community of practitioners for both traditions include the monastic order and the laity, and in both cases, the monastic order plays the leadership role with the laity serving as protectors of the Dharma. The monastic orders of both traditions must rely upon senior Dharma teachers and the giving and receiving of monastic rules and precepts. Both traditions share the same basic precepts of monastic precepts, the five precepts, and the eight precepts, and share a body of common doctrine including the three Dharma Seals, the Four Noble Truths, the Noble Eightfold Path, the twelve links of dependent origination, the threefold training, the five aggregates, the six sense organs, objects, and consciousnesses, the thirty-seven aspects of awakening, and the Middle Way.

All Buddhists take refuge in the Triple Gem, and then proceed to receive and observe the five precepts. There is the shared body of ceremonies which includes sutra chanting, *mantra* recitation, veneration of the Buddha, and sitting meditation. All Buddhists celebrate the Buddha's birthday. Both traditions share the tradition of the triple robe and alms bowl, and have the ending of affliction and attainment of liberation as their final goal. All monastics in the northern tradition and southern tradition shave their heads, and are ranked by the number of years since their ordination and their spiritual attainments.

M

The monastics of both traditions treat the cultivation of compassion and wisdom as their main spiritual practice, walking the Middle Way that is neither painful nor pleasurable. Likewise, the monastics of both traditions see teaching the Dharma as their responsibility, and benefiting sentient beings as their career. It is important that the northern and southern transmissions, the Mahayana and Hinayana, stand together in the spirit of ecumenical unity, so that they can marshal an even greater force for the expansion of Buddhism.

## Maitreya Bodhisattva
## 龍華三會

The first day of the first month in the lunar calendar is the birthday of Maitreya Bodhisattva, who will descend to this world in the future. Long ago, Maitreya Bodhisattva and Sakyamuni Buddha practiced together, but because of differences in their vows Sakyamuni Buddha has already attained Buddhahood while Maitreya Bodhisattva is still cultivating the bodhisattva path in the inner court of Tusita Heaven.

Maitreya Bodhisattva is this world's future Buddha. His awakening was prophesized by Sakyamuni Buddha himself: When Maitreya's four thousand year life in the heavenly realm comes to an end (that is about five billion, seven hundred and sixty million years in the human world), he will descend and be reborn in this Saha world. He will attain Buddhahood under the dragon-flower tree and teach the Dharma in three assemblies, known as the "three dragon-flower assemblies."

During the three dragon-flower assemblies, all of those who have not yet obtained awakening through Sakyamuni Buddha's

M

teachings in the past will obtain awakening in the order of their spiritual capacity: first those of high capacity, followed by medium and then low. According to the *Sutra on the Bodhisattva Dwelling in the Womb*, the three dragon-flower assemblies will liberate the following groups:

The first assembly will contain 9.6 billion sentient beings, and consist of all members of the monastic order who keep the precepts, since liberation should be brought to this group first.

The second assembly will contain 9.4 billion sentient beings, and consist of those who have not yet joined the monastic order, but who have already taken refuge in the Triple Gem and conduct themselves in accordance with the precepts and make offerings with respect. All such people in the assembly will be liberated.

The third assembly will contain 9.2 billion sentient beings and consist of those who have yet to observe the precepts, though they offer incence and pay homage to the Buddha, and may perhaps have recited the Buddha's name and made a few offerings, but did so with true faith. All such people in the assembly will be liberated as well.

Belief in both Maitreya Bodhisattva and Amitabha Buddha has been valued by Buddhist followers for centuries. Maitreya's Pure Land in Tusita Heaven possesses the following rare and superlative qualities:

1. Maitreya's Pure Land in Tusita Heaven is not far from this Saha world, and since it is also part of the desire realm, its practice of cultivation is somewhat easier. As long as one takes refuge in the Triple Gem, observes the precepts, acts with proper generosity, and in addition makes the vow to seek rebirth there by reciting *"Namo danglai xiasheng*

*Milefo,"* which means "Taking refuge in the future Buddha Maitreya," then one can gain rebirth in Maitreya's Pure Land in Tusita Heaven. It is not necessary, as in the case of Amitabha Buddha's Pure Land, to recite the name with single-minded devotion before one can attain rebirth there.

2. It is not necessary to generate the aspiration for awakening nor the mind of renunciation to seek rebirth in Maitreya's Pure Land. Human and heavenly beings with good roots of high, medium, and low spiritual capacity who are intent on self-improvement can be reborn there.

3. Those who are reborn in the Pure Land of Tusita Heaven will come face to face with Maitreya Bodhisattva himself. They can hear him give teachings and will no longer backslide in their progress. Seeing the Buddha and receiving the teachings is much faster there than in Amitabha Buddha's Pure Land.

Seeking rebirth in the Pure Land of Tusita Heaven does not mean that one wishes to enjoy the pleasures of Tusita Heaven, but that one wishes to be reborn to learn from Maitreya Bodhisattva. When Maitreya Bodhisattva descends to the human world, one can hear his teachings during the three dragon-flower assemblies. By seeing the Buddha and listening to his teachings, one can eliminate suffering and liberate oneself from the cycle of birth and death. Only in this way will Maitreya Bodhisattva's compassionate vow to establish a Pure Land in the heavens of the desire realm not have been made in vain.

**M**

## Manas Consciousness
末那識
*See:* Consciousness, eight kinds of.

## Manjusri Bodhisattva
文殊師利菩薩
*See:* Mountains, four great; non-duality.

## Mantra
咒
*See:* Om mani padme hum; schools of Chinese Buddhism, eight.

## Marks of Excellence, Thirty-Two
三十二相

It has been more than two thousand years since the Buddha passed into final *nirvana*, and sentient beings living in this Age of Declining Dharma are unable to personally venerate and look upon the major and minor marks of the Buddha's glorious appearance. The "major and minor marks" refer to the Buddha's bodily appearance. Those characteristics that can be observed in a glance are known as "major marks," while those that are not directly perceived but produce a feeling of pleasantness are known as the Buddha's "notable characteristics." As recorded in the *sutras*, the Buddha was endowed with thirty-two marks of excellence and eighty notable characteristics. The thirty-two major marks are as follows:

1. Feet that are planted flat on the ground without hollow spots.

M

2. Dharma wheels on the soles of the feet like with a thousand spokes.
3. Long, slender fingers that are as white as snow.
4. Flexible limbs that are neither coarse nor stiff.
5. Webbed fingers and toes that have connecting tissue.
6. Perfectly round heels without hollow or protruding spots.
7. Arched insteps that are perfectly formed front and back.
8. Thighs that are fine and round like those of a royal stag.
9. Arms reaching below the knee as stately as a mountain.
10. Retracted male organ that is concealed within the body.
11. The height of the body and the span of the arms being equal.
12. Each and every hair being dark in color.
13. Body hair is fine and curls up.
14. A golden complexion.
15. Light that radiates from the body in all directions for ten feet.
16. Fine lustrous skin that is as soft as oil.
17. Feet, palms, shoulders, and crown that are perfectly formed and proportioned.
18. Both armpits are full without hollow or protruding spots.
19. Perfectly balanced body of solemn appearance.
20. Firm and erect stature without bends or humps.
21. Full and proportioned shoulders that are extraordinarily well-developed.
22. Mouth containing forty teeth.
23. Teeth that are white, close together, clean, and firm.
24. Teeth that are perfectly aligned with nothing out of place.
25. Full cheeks like those of a lion.
26. Saliva that can make food taste delicious.

**M**

27. Broad and long tongue that is soft and thin.
28. Voice that can be heard from afar.
29. Eyes that are dark blue and as clear as the great ocean.
30. Eyelashes that are uniquely special and extraordinary.
31. White tuft of hair between the eyes that emits light.
32. Fleshy protuberance on the head.

In the sutras it is said that "It takes one hundred *kalpas* to perfect the primary and secondary marks of the Buddha, and the three incalculable *kalpas* to perfect the merit and wisdom of the Buddha." The Buddha's thirty-two marks did not simply appear, rather, they were achieved after ninety-one *kalpas* of practice. As stated in the *Sutra on the Adornments of the Hundredfold Merits*, a single mark adorned the Buddha's body only after the practice of each of hundred types of merit. Even the Buddha's broad and long tongue was only achieved after over hundreds and thousands of lifetimes of practicing the precept against lying. Clearly, becoming a Buddha requires the extensive cultivation of merit and wisdom before one can attain the perfect results.

## Masters of the Ming Dynasty, Four
明末四大師

There have been generations of eminent monks throughout the history of Chinese Buddhism who, through their teaching, not only became famous in their own time, but left a model for future generations to emulate. Towards the end of the Ming dynasty (1368-1644), there were four eminent monks who were well-known for both their scholarship and their moral conduct, and who later became known as "The Four Great Masters of the Late

**M**

Ming Dynasty." They were masters Hanshan, Zibo, Lianchi, and Ouyi.

### 1. Master Hanshan (憨山大師)

Master Hanshan (1546-1623 CE) had a given name of Deqing (德清), a courtesy name of Chengyin (澄印), and came from Quanjiao in Anhui Province. At the age of twelve, he studied the sutras with Master Yongning (1483-1565 CE) at the Baoen Monastery in Nanjing. At the age of nineteen, he received full ordination and went to Mount Louxia where he received training in the Chan School from Master Fahui (1500-1579 CE).

That same year while listening to Master Wuji Mingxin's (1512-1576 CE) teachings on the *Profound Meaning of the Flower Adornment Sutra*, Master Hanshan Deqing experienced a sudden realization. As the passage "eternal abiding of the ocean-seal array of phenomena" was being discussed in connection with the "ten gates of profundity" he experienced the perfect non-obstruction of the dharma realm. The following year, he gave his explanation of the *gongan* "reciting the Buddha's name with depth and sincerity," during a seven-day meditation retreat and, from then on, his training with his teachers began to bear fruit.

In 1583 CE, Master Hanshan Deqing lectured on the *Profound Meaning of the Flower Adornment Sutra* in which nearly ten thousand people attended, for which he was honored by those both inside and outside the imperial court. Moreover, he once wrote out a copy of the *Flower Adornment Sutra* using his own blood to repay his parent's kindness. Emperor Shenzong praised and commended his effort, and presented him with gold leaf paper.

In 1600 CE, Master Nanshao Daozhu (ca. 1600 CE) invited Master Hanshan Deqing to come to Baolin Monastery at Caoxi

M

and re-establish the Chan School. He selected monks to undergo ordination, established a monastic seminary, and codified the Chan monastery rules, thereby reinvigorating the Chan tradition. In 1603 CE, Master Hanshan Deqing was implicated in the trumped up charges that imprisoned Master Zibo and was exiled to Leizhou. General amnesty issued in 1606 CE allowed him to return to Caoxi. However, while restoring the main hall of the Nanhua Monastery, he was falsely charged with misappropriation of donated funds and was held on a boat in the Furong River for two years awaiting judgment, during which he fell very ill and nearly died.

In 1614 CE, the empress dowager died and an imperial edict was especially issued permitting him to return to the monastic order. Later on, he built a small hermitage beneath Wuru Peak, where he devoted himself to the Pure Land practice of reciting the name of Amitabha Buddha.

Hanshan Deqing's thought combines elements of Chan and Huayan philosophy, and he promoted the idea of practicing both Chan and Pure Land Buddhism, and the unification of the three religions of Confucianism, Daoism, and Buddhism. He was a prolific writer, and authored such works as the *General Explanation of the Surangama Sutra*, *Outline of the Flower Adornment Sutra*, *Commentary on the Perfect Enlightenment Sutra*, and the *Commentary on the Prajnaparamita Sutra*, among others.

Hanshan Deqing died in 1623 CE at the age of seventy-eight. Later generations called him "Master Hanshan." This honorific title derives from a particular journey he took to Mount Wutai, in which he was struck by the sublime beauty of Mount Han (*hanshan*) to the north, and thus named himself after the mountain. Furthermore, he so admired the personal character of Master Qingliang Chengguan (738-839 CE), that he gave himself the courtesy name Chengyin.

## 2. *Master Zibo* (紫柏大師)

Born with the given name Zhenke (真可), his courtesy name was Daguan (達觀), and he gave himself the name Zibo. Later generations would call him Master Zibo (1543-1603 CE). In his youth he was a wandering hero, driving away the wicked and protecting the good. At the age of seventeen, he joined the monastic order under the direction of Master Mingjue (ca. 16th cent.) at Yunyan Monastery in Huqiu, and received full ordination at the age of twenty. He went on a three-year retreat in the Jingde Monastery in Wutang.

Master Zibo arrived in the capital in the first year of Emperor Shenzong's reign (1573 CE) and spent the next nine years as a close disciple of Master Pianrong (ca. 16th cent. CE) of the Huayan School and Master Xiaoyan (1512-1581 CE) of the Chan School.

Master Zibo saw that Buddhists had difficulty reading the old loose-leaf format of the Tripitaka, so he worked towards creating a bound woodblock edition. He started his preparations at Mount Wutai, basing the bound edition on the Ming dynasty Northern Tripitaka with supplementary reference to the Ming dynasty Southern Tripitaka to create what is known as the "Fangce Tripitaka." Four years later, he moved to Jizhao hermitage on Mount Jing, where work on the printing blocks continued. This is why the edition is known as the "Mount Jing Edition."

Master Zibo strictly observed the monastic rules throughout his life as a monk. As abbot of the old Tantou Monastery, he once was visited by an old friend whom he had not seen in many years. The two were enjoying their conversation and when mealtime arrived, they were still deeply engrossed in their conversation, such that Master Zibo unconsciously picked up his chopsticks and began eating. After taking a few bites, he then realized that he had

M

forgotten to make an offering to the Triple Gem before the meal. Master Zibo thereupon consigned himself to punishment with the cane, personally ordering an attending monk to give him thirty vigorous strokes of the cane while kneeling on the ground. He used the opportunity to warn others, saying, "The habitual tendencies of sentient beings from beginningless time are like oil that seeps into bread, so difficult it is to break these habits. Without painful punishment, they cannot be easily controlled!"

Master Zibo shared a warm and sincere friendship with Master Hanshan Deqing, and the two of them once discussed working together to expand the *Great Ming Record of the Transmission of the Lamp* as a way of reinvigorating the Chan School. This collaboration regrettably never came to be. Master Hanshan Deqing was falsely accused of unauthorized temple construction and exiled to Leizhou in Guangdong Province. By the thirty-first year of Emperor Shenzong's reign (1603 CE), internal strife had erupted within the imperial court, and jealous individuals took advantage of the situation to slander and disparage others. As a consequence, Master Zibo was unjustly imprisoned and sentenced to death. Upon hearing his death sentence, he maintained his composure and said, "If this is the way of the world, why remain any longer?" He then composed the following verse:

> A smile for some other reason,
> Who could know that the great earth would
>      tolerate no dust?
> Now everything is arranged, this life my mother
>      bore me is done,
> For an iron tree to bring forth flowers awaits no
>      spring.

**M**

After reciting the verse he then sat down, closed his eyes, and passed away. He was sixty-one years old, and had been ordained for forty-one years.

### 3. *Master Lianchi* (蓮池大師)

Master Lianchi (1532-1612 CE) is considered the Eighth Patriarch of the Pure Land School. Coming from Renhe in Hangzhou, his given name was Zhuhong (袾宏), his courtesy name was Fohui (佛慧), and he gave himself the name of Lianchi (蓮池). He studied Confucianism from a young age, and became an imperial scholar at the age of seventeen, having become renowned for his scholarship and upright conduct. Under the influence of a neighbor, he devoted himself to the Pure Land practice, and he would inscribe the words *shengsi shida* (生死事大), "the great matter of life and death," to encourage himself to move forward.

At thirty-two, Lianchi Zhuhong joined the monastic order under Master Xingtian (ca. 16th cent. CE) of Wumen Monastery in Xishan, and received full ordination from Master Wuchen (ca. 16th cent CE) at Zhaoqing Monastery. Not long afterwards, Master Lianchi Zhuhong journeyed around visiting different teachers, living the life of a wandering mendicant. In 1571 CE, he moved to Mount Yunlou in Hangzhou, where he lived in a deserted, ruined monastery and refined his practice of *samadhi* through reciting Amitabha Buddha's name. Here and there he taught the Dharma, gathering disciples, and later build a temple.

In 1584 CE, Lianchi Zhuhong composed the *Rebirth in Pure Land Anthology* in three fascicles; and in 1602 CE he authored the *Varying Impressions of the Surangama Sutra* in one fascicle. At that time the full ordination ceremony had long been proscribed, so Master Lianchi Zhuhong had those seeking ordination to furnish

M

themselves with a complete set of monastic robes and receive ordination in front of the Buddha image as authoritative confirmation. He also composed liturgies for the *Water and Land Dharma Service* and *Yogacara Flaming Mouth Dharma Service* to bring relief to those suffering in the lower realms. He established pools for freeing living beings inside and outside the city, and wrote *On Freeing Living Beings and Refraining from Killing*, to warn against harming life.

All his life, Master Lianchi Zhuhong advocated the practice of reciting Amitabha Buddha's name. He condemned the variety of "crazy Chan," and took pains to explain how Chan and Pure Land could be cultivated together with an emphasis on the sutras. Later in life he suffered from illness, but this only strengthened his resolve to do good works. He wrote the texts *Three Regretables* and *Ten Lamentables* to give his disciples direction

In 1612 CE, Lianchi Zhuhong fell ill and died at the age of eighty-one. He became known to later generations as "Monk Yunqi" and "Master Lianchi."

### 4. *Master Ouyi* (蕅益大師)

Master Ouyi (1599-1655 CE) is considered the Ninth Patriarch of the Pure Land School. His given name was Jiming (際明), his courtesy name was Ouyi (蕅益), and he gave himself the name Babu Daoren (八不道人). He came from Mudu in Wuxian, and studied Confucianism from an early age. He had written several dozen articles condemning Buddhism, but at the age of seventeen, he read Master Lianchi's *On Self-Knowledge* and *Casual Notes by the Bamboo Window*. These texts made him realize he had been wrong about Buddhism, and he burned all his previous writings. At the age of twenty, he became inspired to join the monastic order while chanting the *Sutra on the Original Vows of Ksitigarbha Bodhisattva*. He was tonsured under Master Xueling (ca. 16th cent. CE), a disciple of Master Hanshan Deqing, and changed his name to Zhixu.

He received the bodhisattva vows at the age of twenty-six, and spent the next year reading widely from the Vinaya. At times he would fall seriously ill, and so he focused his attention on gaining rebirth in the Pure Land. At the age of thirty, he became profoundly aware of the corrupt practices of the various schools of Buddhism, and henceforth was determined to spread teachings on the Vinaya. At the age of thirty-two, he wished to produce a commentary on the *Brahma Net Sutra*, so he put four lots before an image of the Buddha and drew the one indicating the Tiantai School; and then proceeded to make an in-depth study of the Tiantai doctrines.

As a person, Master Ouyi Zhixu was stern and meticulous. He despised fame and fortune, was firm in his observation and the precepts, and widely taught the Vinaya. He spent his days reading sutras and writing. He made a comprehensive study of the doctrines of the Faxiang, Chan, Vinaya, Huayan, Tiantai, and Pure Land schools, but placed special emphasis upon the Tiantai School. He also advocated the unification of Buddhism, Daoism, and Confucianism. In particular, he was well aware of the schisms and divisions among the various schools of Buddhism of his day, and therefore strived vigorously to bring ecumenical harmony to them.

His thought could be summarized in his doctrine of "the threefold training in a single thought" and the equivalency of reciting Amitabha Buddha's name with the Buddha's lifetime of teachings. During the Qing dynasty (1644-1911), the Tiantai School began to rely upon Master Ouyi Zhixu's sutra commentaries to teach their

**M**

doctrines, resulting in the formation of the Lingfeng School that integrated Chan, the sutras, and the Vinaya into the Pure Land teachings. This movement continues to this day.

In 1655, Master Ouyi died at the age of fifty-seven. He would be known by later generations as "Master Lingfeng Ouyi."

Master Ouyi Zhixu was well versed in the sutras and honored the Tiantai School in his studies. He was also conversant in the doctrines of the Huayan and Faxiang schools. His thought was a synthesis of nature and form, Chan and Pure Land, Confucianism and Buddhism, and provisional and ultimate truth.

Master Ouyi Zhixu was also deeply concerned with the decline of the Dharma, which he saw as a result of the long neglect of the Vinaya. Thus he dedicated his life to furthering the spread of the Vinaya. After he received his bodhisattva vows at the age of twenty-six, Master Ouyi Zhixu was determined to read widely from both the Mahayana and Hinayana Vinaya, which laid the foundation for his study of the Vinaya. He also strictly observed the precepts, making him a *bhiksu* of superb moral conduct. Master Ouyi Zhixu spent his entire life revitalizing the purity of the Chinese Buddhist schools, and for this he will always be remembered.

Reading about the remarkable conduct of great monastics can inspire the minds of Buddhist disciples and as such, in addition to reading Buddhist sutras, students of Buddhism should learn more about the lives of great monastics.

**M**

## Maudgalyayana
目犍連
*See:* Disciples, ten great.

# Meal Contemplations, Five
# 食存五觀

In the life of a monastic, walking, standing, sitting, and lying down are all forms of practice. Even the most ordinary tasks like getting dressed and eating food are also opportunities for practice. During meals, monastics practice what are called the "five contemplations." Some monasteries even call their dining halls the "hall of the five contemplations." The five contemplations are:

*1. Consider the work that went into the food and where it came from*（計功多少量彼來處）

We should consider that every agricultural product requires the planting, irrigation, weeding, and harvesting of a farmer. Next, merchants ship and sell the food, which is then prepared by a cook into a fine meal. Then and only then is it placed before us. Moreover, all the tools, clothing, and supplies used by the farmers, merchants, and cooks every day are supplied by other groups of people. There is a Buddhist saying that, "In the contemplation of the Buddha, one grain of rice is a big as Mount Sumeru." Not a single plate of food comes easily.

*2. Reflect on my virtues and conduct, and if they merit this offering*（忖己德行全缺應供）

During mealtime, one should reflect upon what one has done, even including one's intentions and thoughts. Do they meet the expectations of proper moral conduct? Are they worthy of the donations of the faithful?

M

*3. Guard the mind against faults, greed in particular* (防心離
過貪等為宗)
Guarding against faults means avoiding the three poisons. When
we eat, we should not generate thoughts of greed, anger, or delusion, but rather generate thoughts of kindness, compassion, joy,
equanimity, and wisdom.

*4. Regard it as wholesome medicine for healing the weakened
body* (正事良藥為療形枯)
In this world, hunger and thirst are unavoidable. Buddhism
seeks to "practice the supramundane teachings by means of
the mundane world," and as such the vast variety of foods
should be seen as medicine for the body. There is then no need
to discriminate as to how good, how clean, or how much food
there is.

*5. For the sake of attaining the Way, I shall receive this food*
(為成道業應受此食)
The food and drink is taken for the sake of allowing one to persevere in one's practice in hopes of fulfilling the Buddhist path
in the future and teaching the Dharma for the benefit of living
beings.

Though five contemplations specifically mention aspects of
monastic life, lay people should perform these contemplations as
well. For only in this way will one be able to express gratitude for
the four kinds of kindness and help those who are suffering in the
three lower realms.

# Means of Embracing, Four
## 四攝

The four means of embracing are four different skillful means that are cultivated by bodhisattvas to provide benefit and bring relief to sentient beings. The four means of embracing are giving, kind words, altruism, and empathy:

### 1. Giving (布施)

For those who are poor, give them money, clothing, shelter, food, drink, and medicine. For those seeking knowledge to improve themselves, teach them and train them in skills, provide them with Buddhist sutras, and teach them the Dharma. For those who are fearful by nature, eliminate the fears that threaten and torment them and give aid, comfort, and protection in crises and natural disasters to ensure their security and freedom both materially and spiritually. By giving in this way people may generate faith, learn the correct path, and practice the Dharma.

### 2. Kind Words (愛語)

Praise those who have a moral character. Console those who have hardships. Give relief to those who are downcast, and encourage them to improve themselves. Help others obtain what they want, and provide them with limitless support. That being said, it is important to emphasize that kind words should not be hypocritical or dishonest. Kind words should be sincere and honest. A bodhisattva should come to know people's interests, so he can give teachings that are interesting and in accordance with their capacity. He should praise the accomplishments of the Buddha and of practices such as generosity, so that the wealthy are charitable and the

M

ignorant are awakened. This will lead to faith in the true Dharma and happiness for all.

### 3. Altruism (利行)

Altruism means to help others resolve their difficulties. It means to assist and facilitate the work of others and to help them complete worthy goals. When people become sick, give them medicine; when people fall on hard times, give them financial assistance. Generate a sense of sympathy and empathy. Create job opportunities for people to help and foster their success. In particular, apply the appropriate skillful persuasion to those who do not believe in the Dharma, to those who have broken the precepts, to those who are greedy and stingy, and to those with impaired intelligence. This will allow them to become secure in their faith and to understand how wholesome actions of body, speech, and mind can help to benefit both themselves and others. This will allow others to be happy and to rely upon the Dharma.

### 4. Empathy (同事)

"Empathy" in this sense means to use one's wisdom to observe the conditions of others and assume the form that is most suitable to liberate them. In the case of soldiers, talk with them about military science, while as for business people, talk to them about business expertise. There is a Buddhist expression, "For those that can be liberated by a certain physical form, then teach the Dharma by manifesting that physical form." Work with them in the same place and do their same job, become their good friend and show them how to turn away from unwholesome conduct. Join with them in practicing good deeds and share equally with them the benefits of the Dharma.

The fourth of the four universal vows is, "Sentient beings are limitless, I vow to liberate them." The hope is that everyone will learn from the compassion of the bodhisattvas and help to liberate all sentient beings by utilizing the four means of embracing.

## Medicine
### 湯藥

*See:* Field of merit; offerings, four; parables of the *Lotus Sutra*.

## Meditative Concentration
### 禪定

*See:* Merit and wisdom; path, noble eightfold; perfections, six; *samadhi*; spiritual wealth, seven kinds of; stopping and seeing meditation; training, threefold.

## Mental Formations
### 行

*See:* Aggregates, five; dependent origination.

## Merit
### 福

*See:* Dedication; field of merit; giving; merit and wisdom.

## Merit and Wisdom
### 福慧雙修

*See also:* Dedication; field of merit; giving; perfections, six; *samadhi*.

Merit and wisdom are two qualities that should be cultivated together. "Cultivation of merit" includes all forms of positive karma

**M**

that benefits others, such as the first five of the six perfections: giving, morality, patience, diligence, and meditative concentration. Cultivating wisdom is the development of the last of the six perfections: *prajna*-wisdom, and include those truths and concepts which benefit oneself.

According to the ninth chapter of the *Treatise on Establishing Consciousness-Only*, those great practices of a bodhisattva which are related to wisdom are the "cultivation of wisdom," while all others are the "cultivation of merit." It is often said that to attain Buddhahood, bodhisattvas seek awakening from above (i.e. cultivate wisdom) and bring liberation to sentient beings below (i.e. cultivate merit). Since the cultivation of both merit and wisdom are known as the supreme practices for attaining Buddhahood, they are known as the "supreme practices."

In Buddhism there is a saying that one who cultivates merit but not wisdom is like an elephant wearing a jeweled necklace, while one who cultivates wisdom but not merit is like an arhat who receives few offerings. Buddhists should take heed and cultivate both merit and wisdom, for neither one should be discarded. There are passages throughout the sutras that underscore the need to cultivate both merit and wisdom. Even those seeking rebirth in the Western Pure Land cannot do so without merit and the roots of goodness as their causes and conditions. The second chapter of the *Five Essays on the Flower Adornment Sutra* says, "As for the actual practice contained within the final teachings (of the Mahayana), one who makes the initial aspiration for awakening cultivates both merit and wisdom, which is why there is nothing else to cultivate upon attaining Buddhahood."

There is no special form of practice to attain Buddhahood other than just the cultivation of merit and wisdom. How can we cultivate merit and wisdom in our everyday lives? The best way is through cultivating the six perfections:

### 1. Giving (布施)

Whether one gives the gift of wealth, the gift of the Dharma, or the gift of fearlessness, to do so in a way that the giver is empty, the recipient is empty, and the gift itself is empty is to achieve the highest state of giving.

### 2. Morality (持戒)

To cultivate morality does not just mean to observe the precepts in their external form. The cultivation of morality is emphasizing the true spirit and meaning of the precepts, with their principle of not violating others, but rather respecting and benefiting them.

### 3. Patience (忍辱)

Patience does not mean passively not striking back when beaten, or not talking back when cursed. Patience is an attitude for dealing with affairs that is active, accountable, accommodating, engaged, and carefree.

### 4. Diligence (精進)

To correctly apply diligence means to remove unwholesomeness that is present, prevent unwholesomeness that has yet to arise, develop wholesomeness that has yet to arise, and strengthen wholesomeness that is present. Diligently cultivating merit requires the guidance of wisdom for, in this way, one will not practice blindly.

M

## 5. Meditative Concentration (禪定)

People who have cultivated meditative concentration well do not act rashly, do not speak foolishly, nor think impulsively. Such people do not interfere with others and develop wisdom, thereby gaining the respect and support of others.

## 6. Prajna-wisdom (般若)

By unceasingly cultivating giving, morality, patience, diligence, and meditative concentration guided by wisdom, one will certainly attain great *prajna*-wisdom.

As indicated above, merit must be guided by wisdom, and wisdom requires the accumulation of merit. Merit and wisdom are like the two wings of a bird, for it is impossible to rely upon one alone. That is why we must cultivate both at once.

# Mind
一心不亂

*See also*: Consciousness, eight kinds of.

What we are most intimate and have the closest relationship with is our own mind. The mind is in charge; and yet most people know nothing about the mind. They have no idea about their own intrinsic nature, so they cannot be in charge of the mind. Only by understanding the mind, can we know ourselves, and so it is said that "practicing the Dharma requires cultivating the mind."

The Buddhist sutras speak extensively about the power of the mind, and the importance of cultivating and purifying it. The *Samyukta Agama* says, "If the mind is afflicted then sentient beings are afflicted. If the mind is pure, then sentient beings are pure." The

*Vimalakirti Sutra* says, "When the mind is pure, the land is pure." The *Treatise on the Awakening of Faith in Mahayana* says, "When the mind arises, all phenomena arise. When the mind ceases, all phenomena cease." The *Platform Sutra* says, "The deluded mind is mastered by the *Lotus* [Sutra]. The awakened mind masters the *Lotus* [Sutra]." The *Flower Adornment Sutra* says, "If one wishes to know the Buddha's state, then purify the mind so it is like empty space." The *Sutra of the Teachings Bequeathed by the Buddha* says, "If one can focus the mind in one place, there is nothing that can't be done."

The sutras also say, "The Buddha said the mind is primary," "The three realms are mind-only, and all phenomena are consciousness-only," "All phenomena in the universe arise from the mind," "Ignorance and awakening are not separate from one's own mind," and "The Buddha taught many kinds of Dharma to cure all minds—without all the different kinds of minds, how could he teach the Dharma?"

The Buddhist sutras describe the mind in many different ways, including offering many metaphors for the mind. Some examples are:

1. The mind is like a monkey, for it is hard to control.
2. The mind is as fast as a flash of lightning.
3. The mind is like a wild deer chasing the sense objects.
4. The mind is like a thief who steals our positive karma.
5. The mind is like an adversary, for it causes us suffering.
6. The mind is like a servant of the afflictions, for it is ordered about by worldly temptations.
7. The mind is like a powerful king, for it has supreme control over the body.

8. The mind is limitless, like an ever-flowing spring.
9. The mind is like an artist who can paint all things.
10. The mind is boundless, like the vastness of space.

The sutras also offer many other names for the mind, including the Dharmakaya, the dharma realm, the nature of all phenomena, *tathagatagarbha*, Buddha nature, true reality, *prajna*-wisdom, as well as many others. The many names of the mind point to the fact that the ordinary mind is subject to delusion, and is ever-changing. The mind is erratic, and often leads the eyes, ears, nose, tongue, and body to engage in all manner of wrongdoing. This causes us suffering and hardship, and leads us to journey further in the cycle of birth and death. That is why the *Eight Realizations of a Bodhisattva Sutra* says, "The mind is the source of unwholesomeness."

However, the mind is also called "inherently pure," for the fundamental nature of the mind is pure. The mind is our own intrinsic Buddha nature, which belongs to each one of us and cannot be found externally. The mind is like the surface of a lake: if there are no waves, then the surface is clean and clear, and can reflect the full moon hanging in the sky. In the same way, if the mind is undisturbed by deluded thoughts and uncontaminated by the five desires, then the mind will be calm, harmonious, and unmovable. When we maintain the serenity of the mind, it will reflect our intrinsic nature, just as a calm lake reflects the moon. How then can we come to know the true mind? The key lies in being able to establish single-minded concentration.

How can we bring this mind that can ascend to heaven or plunge into hell into a state of single-minded concentration? Each of the many Buddhist schools and sutras have their own unique methods for achieving this state. For example, the Pure Land School encourages the recitation of Amitabha Buddha's name. Through this practice one is able to achieve single-minded concentration by focusing the six sense organs and maintaining a continuum of pure thoughts. Then, at the time of death, the practitioner will be received by Amitabha Buddha and be reborn in the Pure Land.

The Chan School's main practice is the cultivation of meditative concentration. There is a verse that indicates the primacy of meditation in the Chan School:

> Sitting in quiet meditation for even a moment,
> Is superior to building stupas of the seven trea-
> sures as plentiful as grains of sand in the
> Ganges River.
> In the end, the stupas will crumble into dust;
> But a single thought from a tranquil mind can at-
> tain awakening.

The Tiantai School has the doctrine of "one thought containing the three thousandfold world system," which shows how a single thought can encompass all phenomena of the dharma realm, such that all things can be contained within the mind. According to this doctrine, one need not seek precious jewels outside of oneself, nor look for some kind of bright light elsewhere, for this distracted, perturbed, and deluded mind of ours actually contains all things.

If we attain single-minded concentration, contemplate the self, return to intrinsic nature, and develop our innate virtue we can become an awakened being and attain liberation in the here and now. The Consciousness-only philosophers pulled off a bold stroke by developing the system of the "five categories and the one

M

hundred *dharmas*" to analyze the activities of the mind, transform consciousness into wisdom, and realize liberation.

Even with all of the methods put forth by the various schools, to truly achieve single-minded concentration is far from easy. This is especially true for those of us living an everyday life and dealing with the confusion and turmoil of worldly events and human emotion. It is difficult not to be affected by such surroundings.

However, there is a way. We can maintain good relations with others by doing good deeds naturally and happily. We can refrain from disputing with others, or comparing ourselves with others and feeling envy. We can strive to remain unaffected by praise or blame, success or failure, and suffering or happiness. We cannot waste our mental energy discussing the arguments and disputes of others or in pursuing fame and fortune. Further, we can find repose in practices that benefit others, like cultivating the four immeasurable minds, feeling gratitude for and contentedness for what we have, and being of service to society. If we regularly practice in this way, then we will not be caught up in the external events or the emotions of others and have a calm, peaceful life. In this way one can attain the freedom of liberation.

## Mindfulness, Four Bases of
### 四念處
*See also:* Impermanence

When the Buddha was about to enter final *nirvana*, it was the general consensus of the four groups of Buddhist disciples that the Venerable Ananda ask the Buddha for instruction:

"Lord Buddha, during your time in this world we have relied upon you for our abiding; after the Buddha's final *nirvana*, upon what should we rely for our abiding?"

The Buddha gently replied, "After my final *nirvana*, everyone should find their abiding in the four bases of mindfulness."

What are the four bases of mindfulness?

### 1. Contemplate the impurities of the body (觀身不淨)

The human body is a stinking bag of skin that is formed from a combination of the four great elements and five aggregates in accordance with causes and conditions. The body is impure both inside and outside, including such things as the skin, bones, blood, flesh, phlegm, and excretory substances. When awaking from sleep, the whole mouth is sticky with saliva and so unbearably filthy. If one gets drunk, the internal organs are obstructed and one vomits. When one is sick, sores and ulcers fester and burst, while pus and blood leak and ooze. When going to the toilet, one excretes feces and urine with offensive odors.

### 2. Contemplate the suffering of feelings (觀受是苦)

There are three kinds of feelings: painful feelings, pleasurable feelings, and neither pleasurable nor painful feelings. Each of these feelings has its own kind of suffering.

Painful feelings create the "suffering of suffering." Painful emotions such as sorrow, grief, and worry inherently lead to suffering, and thus they are known as the "suffering of suffering."

Pleasurable feelings create the "suffering of loss." Pleasurable things like health, fame, and wealth can make us feel happy, but since the body can become sick, fame can fade, and wealth can be lost, these pleasant things can lead to the "suffering of loss."

Feelings that are neither painful nor pleasurable create the "suffering of formation." Through spiritual practice one can live

**M**

a simple and tranquil life. However, our world is still subject to conditions and always changing, and having yet to end the cycle of birth and death we are still subject to the suffering of formation.

### 3. Contemplate the impermanence of the mind (觀心無常)

The mind is subject to many negative qualities, such as worries, delusion fatigue, defilement, impermanence, discrimination, distortion, and duality. The mind is like a mirage or an illusion that arises moment by moment and is then extinguished. The mind is like the frantic antics of a monkey or a wild horse, for such are their changeable and impermanent qualities. The *Diamond Sutra* states: "The mind of the past cannot be attained, the mind of the present cannot be attained, the mind of the future cannot be attained."

### 4. Contemplate the non-selfhood of phenomena (觀法無我)

For something to truly be called the "self" it must fulfill the four conditions of autonomy, permanency, universality, and freedom. However, what we think of as our "self" is formed through a combination of conditions, and therefore it is not autonomous. Because our "self" is created through dependent origination, it cannot be permanent. Our "self" is obstructed from all angles, therefore it cannot be universal, and because the self is subject to karma it is not absolutely free. All that is possessed by the self can be destroyed, all that the self knows can be wrong, and all that the self controls can change. In reality, all phenomena are falsely clung to by the self. The self wanders in the cycle of birth and death, built of the five aggregates. When its conditions are dispelled, just where is this self?

The four bases of mindfulness above teach us that all phenomena in the world are impure, suffering, empty, impermanent, and without a self. As Buddhists, we should regularly recall the four bases of mindfulness, examine our own bodies and minds, diligently cultivate ourselves, and seek to realize *nirvana* which is permanent, blissful, pure, and has an inherent self.

## Mountain Gate
## 山門
*See also*: Teaching, four modes of.

There is a saying in Buddhism, that "Wealth enters the mountain gate and merit is credited to the generous benefactor." The term "mountain gate" refers to the main entrance of a Buddhist temple or monastery, since many monasteries were once built in mountain forests. Later monasteries came to be built on flatter terrain, but the term "mountain gate" persisted as a way of referring to Buddhist monasteries regardless of locale.

It is said that in the past, one could enter the mountain gate of Shaolin monastery, but not leave. Only those with superior *gongfu* would be able to traverse the high surrounding walls, and if they could not they would not be permitted to leave. The mountain gate represents a transition from the ordinary to the sagely, from ignorance to awakening, and from darkness to the light, symbolizing the entrance of the worldly into the Buddhist sphere. So they do not return empty handed, those who enter the mountain gate must leave their habitual tendencies at the door.

The mountain gate is also sometimes called the "triple gate," as it represents the gate of faith, the gate of wisdom, and the gate of compassion. The gate of faith is entered by means of the Buddha,

M

the gate of wisdom is entered by means of the Dharma, and the gate of compassion is entered by means of the sangha. This is what it means to enter the Way by the Triple Gem.

The "triple gate" can also represent faith, understanding and practice, or the three ways of liberation: through wisdom, compassion, and skillful means. These "three ways of liberation" are methods used by bodhisattvas to attain awakening. In more detail, they are:

### 1. The Gate of Wisdom (智慧門)

The Chinese word for wisdom, *zhihui* (智慧), is made up of two characters: *zhi* (智), "knowledge," and *hui* (慧), "insight." Knowledge means knowing when to advance, when to hold, and when to retreat; insight is knowing emptiness and "non-self." By relying on knowledge one will no longer seek out self-pleasure, and by relying on insight one can turn away from the attachment to desire.

### 2. The Gate of Compassion (慈悲門)

The Chinese word typically used for compassion, *cibei* (慈悲), is made up of two characters: *ci* (慈), "loving-kindness," and *bei* (悲), "compassion." Loving-kindness means sharing your joy with others, while compassion means removing others' suffering. By relying on loving-kindness one shares peace and joy with all sentient beings, and by relying on compassion one eradicates the pain and suffering of all sentient beings.

**M**

### 3. The Gate of Skillful Means (方便門)

The Chinese word for skillful means, *fangbian* (方便), is made up of two characters: *fang* (方), "straight," and *bian* (便), "convenience." "Straight" refers to using a straightforward approach, and "convenience" means being concerned with others rather than oneself. By relying on a straightforward approach, one is compassionate towards all sentient beings, and by relying upon the exclusion of self, one turns away from self-aggrandizement.

In monasteries of the past, a statue of the smiling Maitreya Bodhisattva was almost always placed at the main gate, representing a joyful welcome to visitors. However, for the more recalcitrant sentient beings who are unable to receive the Buddha's compassion, more forceful methods must be employed. That is why, in many monasteries, after passing through the main gate one enters the Hall of the Four Heavenly Kings, which honors those who protect Buddhism such as the four heavenly kings or the bodhisattvas Qielan or Weituo. This shows that although Buddhism emphasizes compassion, it is a compassion that must be powerful. Again and again in this world, the strong abuse the weak and the weak are at the mercy of the strong. At such times, what is needed is the severe presence of Dharma protectors to counter the violence of the wicked. In addition to having the compassionate heart of a bodhisattva, practitioners must also be equipped with the forceful authority of the Dharma protectors. Only by exerting both compassion and authority and by applying both leniency and strictness, can the survival of the Dharma be assured.

## Mountains, Four Great
## 四大名山

Pilgrimage is a common practice among Buddhists, with many Buddhists considering an opportunity to visit the sacred sites of India to be a dream of a lifetime. In China four of the main

M

pilgrimage sites are mountains, each associated with a bodhisattva and a Buddhist virtue. They are Mount Putuo, Mount Wutai, Mount Jiuhua, and Mount Emei.

## 1. Mount Putuo (普陀山)

Mount Putuo is located on one of the Zhoushan Islands in the East China Sea near Dinghai County in Zhejiang Province, and is also known as Mount Pota, Mount Potalaka, Mount Meiling, and Mount Xiaobaihua. The mountain is known as a site where Avalokitesvara Bodhisattva manifests.

Avalokitesvara Bodhisattva, whose name is translated into Chinese as *guanshiyin* (觀世音) or *guanzizai* (觀自在), has vowed to bring relief to sentient beings and is a representation of great compassion. The Universal Gate chapter of the *Lotus Sutra* mentions that Avalokitesvara Bodhisattva has thirty-three manifestations with which to alleviate twelve kinds of danger. Avalokitesvara Bodhisattva is said to respond to those who call his name, and thus many Buddhists recite the name of Avalokitesvara Bodhisattva in times of distress, wishing for intercession.

The Chinese translation as Guanshiyin (觀世音), literally means "observing the sounds of the world." Notably the character *guan* (觀), "observe," is used rather than *wen* (聞), "hear." Why? The bodhisattva does not only use his ears to observe the sounds of the world, but uses all of his six sense organs together. Hearing may refer to superficially listening with one's ears, while *guan* refers to deep contemplation.

There is a Chinese saying that, "In every family there is a Guanyin, in every home there is an Amitabha Buddha." Faith in Avalokitesvara Bodhisattva as "Guanyin" is so deep in China that it has become integrated with Chinese folk beleifs. In the lunar calendar, Guanyin's birthday is celebrated on the 19th day of the second month, Guanyin's awakening on 19th day of the six month, and Guanyin's ordination on the 19th of the ninth month. Each holiday is commemorated with various Dharma services. Even non-Buddhists scramble off to the temples to join in the celebrations and to pray for good fortune.

Depictions of Avalokitesvara Bodhisattva in Chinese art tend to be quite varied, given the descriptions of his many manifestations. The most common depictions include Avalokitesvara riding on the back of a dragon or sea turtle, Avalokitesvara with a thousand arms and eyes, Avalokitesvara holding a child, Avalokitesvara holding a fish basket, and Avalokitesvara contemplating the moon in water.

## 2. Mount Wutai (五台山)

Mount Wutai is located northeast of Wutai County in Shanxi Province. The mountain is named *wutai* (五台), "five terraces," after the five treeless peaks located in the east, west, south, north, and center that rise high into the sky. The five peaks tower majestically above the surrounding mountains. Atop the peaks it is never too hot, and there is wind-blown snow even in summer, earning the mountain its other nicknames, *qingliangshan* (清凉山), "cold mountain." Since ancient times this mountain has been home to manifestations of Manjusri Bodhisattva.

Manjusri Bodhisattva, whose name means "wondrous virtue" or "wondrous auspiciousness," is the wisest and most eloquent of bodhisattvas. He has served as the teacher of seven Buddhas, and symbolizes *prajna*-wisdom. Among the fifty-three pilgrimages of the young Sudhana described in the *Flower Adornment Sutra*, the very first one was to Manjusri Bodhisattva, in which Sudhana

**M**

expressed his wish to enter the Buddhist path and the bodhisattva responded with the guidance of *prajna*-wisdom. Manjusri Bodhisattva is given the title of "Dharma prince," and his birthday falls on the 4th day of the fourth month in the lunar calendar.

Manjusri Bodhisattva is often paired with Samantabhadra Bodhisattva as attendants on the left and right of the Buddha. Throughout Sakyamuni Buddha's teaching career, from the teaching of the *Flower Adornment Sutra* at the very beginning to the teaching of the *Nirvana Sutra* at the very end, Manjusri Bodhisattva was present at all Mahayana Dharma assemblies. This shows his incredible contribution to the Mahayana teachings.

Depictions of Manjusri Bodhisattva show him with his hair braided into five coils to symbolize the five ultimate wisdoms and the five wisdoms of non-attainment. His left hand holds a lotus flower which contains a copy of the *Prajnaparamita Sutra*, indicating that *prajna*-wisdom is completely undefiled, while his right hand wields a jeweled sword, that represents how great wisdom can cut away ignorance. In some images he is sitting on a lotus flower that represents purity; in others he rides a lion and peacock, indicative of his mastery.

### 3. Mount Jiuhua (九華山)

Mount Jiuhua is located to the southwest of Qingyang County in Anhui Province. It was originally named *jiuzi* (九子), "nine children," but the name was changed to jiuhua (九華), "nine flowers," during the Tang dynasty because of the resemblance of the mountain's nine peaks to stone lotus flowers. It is associated with Ksitigarbha Bodhisattva.

The Chinese name of Ksitigarbha Bodhisattva is *dizang* (地藏), "earth treasury." The *Sutra on the Ten Wheels of Ksitigarbha* explains the name as follows, "Patient and unmovable like the great earth, quiet and profound like a hidden treasury."

The *Sutra on the Original Vows of Ksitigarbha Bodhisattva* records how Ksitigarbha Bodhisattva was once instructed by Sakyamuni Buddha to liberate beings during the period after the Buddha's final *nirvana* and before the birth of Maitreya Buddha. Thus he made this vow: "If the hells are not emptied then I vow not to become a Buddha; only when sentient beings have all been liberated, will I attain awakening." From this he is known as "Ksitigarbha of great vows."

The depiction of Ksitigarbha Bodhisattva is different from most other bodhisattvas because he is shown in the attire of a Buddhist monk. Representations of the bodhisattva have him sitting cross-legged or standing, the right hand holding a monk's staff to show his care for sentient beings as well as his strict adherence to the precepts, and the left hand holding the wish-fulfilling mani-jewel that shows his intention to fulfill the wishes of sentient beings. He rides on a white dog named *shanting* (善聽), "Excellent Listener," for he listens to the hells. The 30th day of the seventh lunar month is Ksitigarbha Bodhisattva's birthday.

## 4. Mount Emei (峨嵋山)

Mount Emei is located to the west of Emei County in Sichuan Province. It is named *emei* (峨嵋), "arching eyebrows," because the two peaks face each other like a pair of tall eyebrows. The mountain contains one hundred twenty-four stone niches, eleven major grottoes, and twenty-eight minor ones. On top of the mountain there is Guangxiang Monastery, which is the site of the Samantabhadra Bodhisattva's manifestation.

M

Called *puxian* (普賢), "universally worthy" and *pianji* (遍吉), "all-encompassing auspicious" in Chinese, Samantabhadra encompasses the practices of all Buddhas. He is paired with Manjusri Bodhisattva's great wisdom, for they both serve as attendants on either side of Sakyamuni Buddha. Samantabhadra Bodhisattva made ten great vows to practice, and is thus known as the "bodhisattva of great practice."

He is depicted riding a white elephant with six tusks. The steady gait and quiet seriousness of a marching elephant is a symbol for the bodhisattva's progress and learning through practice. The great elephant is also a symbol of the vastness of his vows and the perfection of his merit. The 21st day of the second lunar month is Samantabhadra Bodhisattva's birthday.

Among the four great bodhisattvas, Ksitigarbha Bodhisattva is the only one who appears as a monastic. The other three appear as members of the laity, demonstrating the equality between monastics and laity in Mahayana Buddhism. For this reason, Buddhists today should champion the harmony between the monastic and lay communities to ensure that the true Dharma will long remain.

M

# N

## Nagasena
**挖耳羅漢**
*See*: Arhats, eighteen.

## Nakula
**靜坐羅漢**
*See*: Arhats, eighteen.

## Name and Form
**名色**
*See*: Dependent origination.

## Names of the Buddha, Ten
**佛陀十號**

The Buddha is a great awakened being. So impressive are his achievements that people have given him various epithets to extol his greatness. There are eleven commonly used epithets:

| | | |
|---|---|---|
| 1. | Thus-Come *(tathagata)* | 如來 |
| 2. | Worthy One *(arhat)* | 應供 |
| 3. | Truly All-Knowing | 正遍知 |
| 4. | Perfect in Knowledge and Conduct | 明行足 |
| 5. | Well-Gone | 善逝 |
| 6. | Knower of the World | 世間解 |
| 7. | Unsurpassed | 無上士 |
| 8. | Tamer | 調御丈夫 |
| 9. | Teacher of Heavenly and Human Beings | 天人師 |
| 10. | Awakened One *(Buddha)* | 佛 |
| 11. | World-Honored One | 世尊 |

Among the various sutras the eleven epithets are typically presented as the "ten names of the Buddha," by combining some of the above. For example, sometimes "Well-Gone" and "Knower of the World" are combined into a single name. In other instances "Knower of the World" and "Unsurpassed" are combined, and in others "Unsurpassed" and "Tamer" are combined. Each name is given a detailed description below:

### 1. Thus Come（如來）

In Chinese, this name is rendered as *rulai* (如來). *Ru* (如), "such" or "thus" means that the Buddha's essence is unchanging; that it is such as it is. *Lai* (來), "come" refers to the Buddha's ability to change and transform as a skillful means to liberate beings. The Buddha has used his wisdom to know the Way and attain awakening. Because of his experience, he can realistically indicate the path of liberation to others, and in that sense he has already "come" from intrinsic nature.

N

## 2. Worthy One（應供）

The Buddha has eliminated all the afflictions within and beyond the three realms, and has perfected his virtue and wisdom. Therefore, he is worthy of veneration and offerings, such as food and drink, clothing, bedding, medicine, banners, adorned canopies, incense, flowers, lamps, and fruit. Such offerings are made by all sentient beings, which is why the Buddha is called a "worthy one."

## 3. Truly All-Knowing（正遍知）

The wisdom of the Buddha is both perfectly true and perfectly complete. It is all-inclusive, extending everywhere and covering all things. For example, the Buddha knows the names of all the world systems. He knows the names of all sentient beings, the causes and conditions of their previous lives, as well as where they will be reborn. He also knows all phenomena in the world, including all the characteristics of the mind, all afflictions, and all roots of goodness.

## 4. Perfect in Knowledge and Conduct（明行足）

"Knowledge" in this instance refers to the three supernatural knowledges of the Buddha: the knowledge of past, present, and future lives, the visual knowledge of all things (heavenly vision), and the knowledge that all defilements have been ended. "Conduct" refers to physical and verbal karma.

## 5. Well-Gone（善逝）

The Buddha's wisdom has eliminated all confusion. The Buddha has transcended the mundane world and arrived at the other shore of *nirvana*. There is no more returning to the ocean of the cycle of birth and death, and in this sense he is "well-gone."

N

## 6. Knower of the World（世間解）

The Buddha knows all the characteristics of living beings and material things. The Buddha knows that the material world is neither permanent nor impermanent, neither limited nor unlimited, and neither coming nor going.

## 7. Unsurpassed（無上士）

The Buddha has perfected all merit and wisdom through the three-fold practice of morality, meditative concentration, and wisdom. Because of his level of attainment, none can surpass him.

## 8. Tamer（調御丈夫）

The Buddha excels at applying skillful means to guide sentient beings to liberation. In doing so he allows them to be happy in this life and the next life, and even eventually attain the happiness of *nirvana*.

## 9. Teacher of Heavenly and Human Beings（天人師）

The Buddha teaches all sentient beings what is proper and improper to do, and what is right and wrong. If sentient beings practice these teachings and do not abandon them, they can gain liberation from affliction. Among all sentient beings, human and heavenly beings are the most inclined towards the Dharma, such that they are most likely to transcend the cycle of birth and death.

## 10. Awakened One（佛）

*Buddha* is Sanskrit for "awakened one." The Buddha has awakened himself, awakened others, and completed the mission of awakening. He knows all mundane and supramundane phenomena, and is a noble one who has attained unsurpassed, perfect awakening.

N

*11. World-Honored One*（世尊）

Because the Buddha has accomplished so much to such a perfect degree, there is no one in the world more honorable than him.

# Namo Amitofo
## 六字洪名

*See also*: Noble ones of the West, three; supports, three.

"Namo Amitofo" (南無阿彌陀佛) is a magnificent phrase containing thousands upon thousands of merits. Though only six Chinese characters in length, it includes endless meanings.

The first two Chinese characters, *namo* (南無) are a transliteration of the Sanskrit word *namo*, meaning "to take refuge." The phrase "Namo Amitofo" then means taking refuge in and relying upon Amitabha Buddha.

*Amitofo* (阿彌陀佛) is a Chinese translation of the Sanskrit name of Amitabha Buddha, a name which means "infinite light" and "infinite life." The infinite light of Amitabha Buddha is not limited by space, and the infinite life of Amitabha Buddha is not limited by time. As Amitabha Buddha is not limited by time or space, he transcends time and space, and as such embodies the truth of the universe itself.

The noble title of Amitabha Buddha contains within it endless virtue. If one can single-mindedly focus upon this great name, then wrongdoing will decrease, merit will increase, and one will attain rebirth in Amitabha Buddha's Pure Land, transcend the three realms, and become free of the cycle of birth and death.

The name of Amitabha Buddha contains the heart of all language. When we see each other in the morning and say "Amitofo," it means "good morning." When we must part and say "Amitofo,"

N

it means "goodbye." If one receives a gift and says "Amitofo," it is an expression of gratitude. When greeting guests one may say "Amitofo" to welcome them. Upon seeing pigs or sheep being slaughtered one may unconsciously utter "Amitofo" as a way of expressing sympathy for them. If one is in shock at witnessing murder or mayhem, one may recite "Amitofo" repeatedly as one commiserates over the victims. Amitabha Buddha is compassion and truth, and the father of perfect virtue. Amitabha Buddha is one's arrival at supreme truth and goodness.

There is no other name in this world so beautiful and moving as that of Amitabha Buddha. There is no other name in this world that contains as much meaning as that of Amitabha Buddha.

Amitabha Buddha was originally the ruler of a large kingdom during the time of a previous Buddha named Lokesvararaja. Later on, that ruler abandoned his kingdom to join the monastic order and became Dharmakara Bhiksu. In order to give to Dharmakara the teachings of twenty-one billion Buddha realms, Lokesvararaja Buddha used his supernatural powers so that Dharmakara Bhiksu could observe them all. Dharmakara Bhiksu then made forty-eight vows to adorn a Pure Land. After mindfully cultivating for five *kalpas,* he finally attained Buddhahood, and the realm he adorned became the Western Pure Land of Ultimate Bliss.

Chan Master Chewu (1741-1810 CE) said, "'Namo Amitofo' is itself the essence of the Buddha mind, for it plumbs the 'five periods' and spans the 'eight teachings.'" These six characters do indeed constitute a great name of thousands upon thousands of merits.

N

# Nirvana
涅槃

*See also*: Questions of the Buddha, four.

There are various Buddha images that are venerated in Buddhist temples and monasteries, including those that are sitting, standing, and reclining. The reclining posture is meant to represent the Buddha's final *nirvana*, indicating his perfection of merit and wisdom.

"Perfection" here means liberation from the cycle of birth and death, the transcendence of time and space, the extinction of the duality of self and others, and union of the self and others into a single essence. Thus, *nirvana* is not death, but rather life at its most real and valuable. *Nirvana* is the highest, awakened state in Buddhism.

There are many who confuse the Buddhist concept of *nirvana* with death. For this reason, it is common to see "obtained great *nirvana*" written at funerals. There is great misunderstanding of the meaning of *nirvana*.

*Nirvana* is a Sanskrit word that means "extinction," "transcendence," and "birthlessness." The *Nirvana Sutra* states, "The elimination of all affliction is *nirvana*." Simply put, *nirvana* is a state of peace and freedom beyond birth and death, a state of perfect brightness without the distinction between the self and outside things. This state can be realized through practice, by eliminating afflictions such as greed, anger, ignorance, delusion, wrong view, and discord. *Nirvana* is also the third of the Four Noble Truths, and the final goal of Buddhist practice.

*Nirvana* is realization of awakening, but it is distinguished into various types by different Buddhist schools. For example, the

N

Tiantai School distinguishes three aspects of *nirvana* based upon their system of essence, form, and function. Thus, the Tiantai School speaks of the full and complete "pure *nirvana* of inherent nature," which we all inherently have, the "prefectly pure *nirvana*" realized through practice, and the "skillfully pure *nirvana*" which manifests through the guidance of others. The Faxiang School distinguishes four kinds of *nirvana*: pure *nirvana* of inherent nature, *nirvana* with remainder, *nirvana* without remainder, and non-abiding *nirvana*.

Regardless of the many classifications of *nirvana* and what they are called, no type of *nirvana* is the same as death. If *nirvana* was simply death, then all the hard work of Buddhists over many *kalpas* of practice would be just for the sake of achieving death. That would be pointless.

*Nirvana* is also not something which can only be realized after death. For example, at the age of thirty-one the Buddha had already achieved *nirvana* while sitting under the bodhi tree. This was "*nirvana* with remainder," for the karma of his physical body continued to exist. The Buddha realized "*nirvana* without remainder" when he passed away at the age of eighty underneath the sala trees. The Buddha realized "non-abiding *nirvana*" in his forty-nine year teaching career as he responded to the spiritual capacities of all living beings without defilement or attachment. As the Buddha said in the *Lotus Sutra*, "Many *kalpas* ago, as many *kalpas* as all the dust in the universe, I had already become a Buddha. Since that time, I have been constantly teaching the Dharma in this Saha world. I have also been guiding and benefitting sentient beings in other places, domains numbering in the countless millions and millions of trillions." Manifestations such as the Buddha's birth, his renunciation, conquering Mara, attaining awakening, teaching

N

the Dharma, and entering final *nirvana* are all applications of the "skillfully pure *nirvana*" and the "non-abiding *nirvana*." What we seek when we seek *nirvana* is to recover the "inherently pure *nirvana*" that we intrinsically have.

*Nirvana* is liberation. It is eternal happiness and the state that is permanent, blissful, pure, and has an inherent self. *Nirvana* can actually be realized in everyday life: when we face a difficult situation, undergo a great deal of suffering and hardship, and finally come to some sort of resolution—one could say that is *nirvana*. How about those who urgently need to use the restroom or those who have been constipated for a long time? Being able to successfully find relief is also *nirvana*. When someone who has no appetite can finally enjoy a good meal or someone with insomnia can get a good night's rest, this wonderful feeling is not unlike *nirvana*.

*Nirvana* is when painful problems can be resolved and one is liberated from the cycle of birth and death. When we are no longer bound by the afflictions of greed, anger, and ignorance, that is the liberation of *nirvana*. In this way *nirvana* can be realized by everyone in this very moment.

## Noble Ones of the West, Three
## 西方三聖

*See also:* Namo Amitofo.

Among the many Pure Lands of Buddhism, the Western Pure Land is the most well-known, and the place where many vow to be reborn. The leader of this Buddha land is Amitabha Buddha, and assisting him in liberating sentient beings are his two attendants: Avalokitesvara Bodhisattva, who represents loving-kindness and compassion, and Mahasthamaprapta Bodhisattva, who represents

N

wisdom. Together, these three are known as the "three noble ones of the west." Avalokitesvara Bodhisattva and Mahasthamaprapta Bodhisattva are also "bodhisattvas in waiting," for in the future they will succeed Amitabha Buddha and become leaders of the Western Pure Land.

The Western Pure Land was generated in all its beauty through Amitabha Budha's forty-eight great vows over the course of his many lives of pious conduct. The details of this are recorded in *Infinite Life Sutra*, which along with the *Contemplation Sutra* and the *Amitabha Sutra* are collectively known as the "three sutras of the Pure Land School." Among these, the *Amitabha Sutra* describes the various extraordinary adornments of the Western Pure Land, and functions as a sort of "guidebook" to the Pure Land.

How did Avalokitesvara Bodhisattva obtain his name? Why does he transform himself into billions and billions of manifestations, and why is he endowed with such awe-inspiring spiritual powers that enable him to travel to the various Buddha Lands to seek out those who cry out in pain so that he can liberate them? These questions are answered in the Universal Gate chapter of the *Lotus Sutra*. Due to people's faith in Avalokitesvara Bodhisattva, the Universal Gate chapter was circulated as a separate sutra called the *Universal Gate Sutra*, which is part of the morning chanting for many Buddhists.

In addition, the *Compassionate Flower Sutra* records how during the course of his many lives of pious conduct in the past, Amitabha Buddha was once born as a king. At that time Avalokitesvara Bodhisattva was the crown prince named *Buxun,* who later came to be called Avalokitesvara after joining the monastic order. Under the guidance of Amitabha Buddha, Avalokitesvara Bodhisattva attained the thousand-arm and thousand-eye manifestation to assist

**N**

the Buddha in liberating sentient beings. When Avalokitesvara Bodhisattva attains Buddhahood, he is said to be named "Mountains of All Radiant Virtues Tathagata."

However, according to the *Great Compassion Repentance*, Avalokitesvara Bodhisattva has already attained Buddhahood in the past under the name "Tathagata of Illuminating Right Dharma." However, the bodhisattva cannot bear to witness the sufferings of sentient beings, so he has returned to the Saha world out of compassion to teach the Dharma. This is why people praise the compassion and great conduct of Avalokitesvara Bodhisattva as the "compassionate vessel of universal liberation."

Among the three noble ones of the west, Mahasthamaprapta Bodhisattva is the least familiar to most Buddhists. According to the *Compassionate Flower Sutra*, before Amitabha Buddha became a Buddha, Avalokitesvara Bodhisattva and Mahasthamaprapta Bodhisattva served as his attendants. Over the course of his many lives of pious conduct, Mahasthamaprapta Bodhisattva practiced the *samadhi* or mindful recitation of Amitabha Buddha's name and developed the "patience of the non-arising of phenomena," the highest level of patience. This is why he teaches sentient beings how to recite Amitabha Buddha's name, and thereby receives those beings who recite Amitabha Buddha's name into the Pure Land.

Reciting the name of Amitabha Buddha can gain one rebirth in the Western Pure Land, but single-minded recitation of Avalokitesvara Bodhisattva or Mahasthamaprapta Bodhisattva's names will also gain one rebirth in the Western Pure Land. The form of practice taught by Mahasthamaprapta is to "Focus the six sense organs and always maintain pure thoughts, thus attaining *samadhi*. This is the preeminent method." This method

N

of practice has become a very important one for Pure Land practitioners.

The Pure Land School's practice of reciting Amitabha Buddha's name is simple, easy to do, and erases the three roots of negative karma. Whether one is literate or illiterate, lay or monastic, one can recite Amitabha Buddha's name at any time and in any place as long as one has the right intention. According to the *Amitabha Sutra*, anyone who vows to be reborn in the Pure Land and who recites Amitabha Buddha's name with single-minded concentration will, upon death, be received by Amitabha Buddha and a host of noble ones bearing a lotus flower to lead that person to the Pure Land. This is why faith in the Pure Land has become deeply rooted in Chinese folk beliefs, and the names Amitabha Buddha and Avalokitesvara Bodhisattva have become so firmly planted in people's minds. There is a Chinese saying: "In every family there is an Amitabha Buddha, and in every household an Avalokitesvara Bodhisattva." The omnipresence of these two figures within Chinese folk religion has ensured the continued preservation of Pure Land thought over the generations.

# Non-Buddhist Schools, Six
# 六師外道

Ancient India was a country of advanced philosophy with many non-Buddhist schools. During his time in the world, the Buddha was often tested with questions calculated to confound him and even harassed by these non-Buddhist philosophical schools. Even among the Buddha's disciples there were quite a few individuals who were formerly disciples of these schools; but because they had received the Buddha's teachings and compassion and been transformed by his truth, they went on to join the Buddhist order. For example, both Sariputra and Maudgalyayana among the Buddha's ten great disciples were originally of the Sanjaya-Vairatiputra Sect.

The "Six Major Non-Buddhist Schools" refer to the six non-Buddhist philosophies that were the most influential in India during the time of the Buddha. They were made up of free thinkers who opposed the Vedic philosophy of the Brahmans:

### 1. The Sanjaya-Vairatiputra Sect (珊闍耶毘羅胝子)
Members of this sect were skeptics. They did not think that anything could be truly "known," and promoted agnosticism. They believed that one need not cultivate, because spiritual attainment will come automatically after eighty thousand *kalpas*.

### 2. The Ajita-Kesakambala Sect (阿耆多翅舍欽婆羅)
This sect believed in materialism and hedonism. It denied causality and negated the doctrine of an everlasting soul. The sect believed that happiness was the goal of life, and they condemned all strict ethical ideas. This group was thus only concerned with the mundane world.

### 3. The Maskari-Gosaliputra Sect (末伽梨拘舍梨)
This sect was the progenitor of the non-Buddhist school focused on the improper means of livelihood. It promoted the idea of a fatalistic existence and belonged to the Jainism movement. The sect was very influential during the time of the Buddha, and except for the Nirgranthas, it was the most prominent of the schools.

N

## 4. The Purana-Kasyapa Sect（富蘭那迦葉）

This sect did not believe in any moral system and denied that there were wholesome or unwholesome karmic effects from virtuous or non-virtuous acts.

## 5. The Kakuda-Katyayana Sect（迦羅鳩馱迦旃延）

This sect believed in a type of worldly eternalism; that spirit and matter can never be destroyed. They believed that everything was composed of independent entities of earth, fire, water, air, space, pain, pleasure, and soul.

## 6. The Nirgrantha-Jnatiputra Sect（尼乾陀若提子）

The Nirgranthas were precursors to the modern religion of Jainism, and they believed that pain or pleasure, fortune or misfortune, were all created by one's previous lifetimes. One simply had to accept one's karmic effects, for no spiritual practice of this lifetime could dispel them. In terms of actual practice, this sect was characterized by extreme asceticism and the strict prohibition against killing living beings.

These six non-Buddhist schools mentioned above may falsely hold that phenomena are the same or different, that the world is permanent or impermanent, that causality exists or does not exist, that pain is self-generated or generated outside oneself, and other such speculative views. In terms of their practice, most of these schools either took the approach of extreme austerities or extreme sensuality and hedonism. They differ from Buddhism which adopts the Middle Way between the extremes of pleasure and pain. It is for this reason that Buddhism sees these six schools as non-Buddhist and sees their teachings as false and operating outside of the Dharma.

N

Even today there are many groups that are non-Buddhist, but operate under the name of Buddhism. Some of these groups have professed magical and supernatural powers to confuse and seduce people, while others have amassed fortunes through columbarium mausoleum schemes.

When such groups operate under the guise of Buddhism and develop bad reputations, it creates a situation in society today in which people are doubtful of religion. Yet few Buddhists give it a second thought. If we consider the past, Venerable Master Daosheng was denigrated for his doctrine that "even icchantikas can attain Buddhahood." Daosheng was the leading teacher of his era, but since his ideas and understanding differed from that of his day, he and his ideas were rejected. This shows how deeply the Dharma was held in esteem at that time. But nowadays, no matter how many pernicious doctrines appear, no one is willing to stand up for the Dharma in stern and forceful terms to prevent such wrongheaded ideas from festering and growing. When we compare the present to the past, one is left feeling nostalgia for the past and regret for the present.

## Non-Duality
## 不二法門

> This gate is called "non-duality,"
> Duality or non-duality, both are one's true face.
> This mountain is Vulture Peak,
> Mountain or no mountain, nothing is not my
> pure body.

The couplet above is within an entryway called the "non-duality gate" inside Fo Guang Shan monastery in Taiwan. The term "non-

**N**

duality," or literally *buer* (不二), "not two," has several implications, including that there is only one way to enter the Dharma, not two or three, and that there is one truth, not two. In this instance, "non-duality" simply means "one and only."

But the term "non-duality" can refer to the broader Buddhist teaching of non-duality, which appears in the Entry into the Gate of Non-Duality chapter of the *Vimalakirti Sutra*, among other places. The general outline of this chapter is as follows:

When the Buddha dwelt in the world, there was a certain elder by the name of Vimalakirti who lived in the kingdom of Vaisali. It was said of him that, "Though a layman, he is not attached to the three realms. Though married, he always cultivates purity." He was the very model of a lay Buddhist follower of his day.

One day, the Buddha was giving teachings at the Amra Park in Vaisali when he learned that Vimalakirti was indisposed. He then asked his principle disciples to go as his representative to inquire after Vimalakirti's health, but as it turned out, none dared to undertake the task. The reason for this was that everyone had at one time or another undergone Vimalakirti's cross-examination. In the end, the Buddha could only ask Manjusri Bodhisattva, known for his great wisdom, to undertake the trip. Once everyone heard this, they knew that the encounter between Manjusri Bodhisattva and Vimalakirti would surely lead to a brilliant dialogue, and so they all came streaming along behind him.

They were not disappointed. As soon as Manjusri Bodhisattva arrived at Vimalakirti's abode, a series of questions and answers ensued between the two. The sublime profundity of the discussion left everyone with bated breath, as they carefully pondered what had been said. Suddenly, the topic of conversation shifted when Vimalakirti asked: "Gentlemen, how does a bodhisattva enter the

N

teaching of non-duality? Let everyone speak freely on this question as each one understands it."

One after the other, the thirty-one bodhisattvas assembled there each answered the question. Finally, no one had anything more to say. Then Vimalakirti asked Manjusri Bodhisattva, "Manjusri, how does a bodhisattva enter the teaching of non-duality?"

Manjusri Bodhisattva replied, "My understanding is that all phenomena are beyond words, beyond speech, beyond expression, and beyond knowledge. When one turns away from questioning and answering, this is the teaching of non-duality." This means that the one true path cannot be examined or speculated about by such logical methods as inference, comparison, induction, or deduction. One must have a direct and concrete experience of it, which can only be discovered by looking within. Only in this way will one be able to enter the teaching of non-duality.

After he had spoken, Manjusri Bodhisattva then asked Vimalakirti the same question, "How does a bodhisattva enter the teaching of non-duality?" At that moment, Vimalakirti remained silent and did not answer. This surprised all who were present, but only Manjusri Bodhisattva, with his superior wisdom, was able to understand Vimalakirti's profound meaning. Manjusri Bodhisattva then spoke to everyone, "Wonderful! This is indeed the way to enter non-duality."

This shows us that the teaching of non-duality is beyond words or description. How are we supposed to talk about it? Whatever could be expressed through words and speech cannot be the true teaching of non-duality. Vimalakirti's silence evokes this marvelous path that cannot be expressed in words, for his silence transcends the obstacles of formality and delves directly into the

N

source. Doing such is the only way for a bodhisattva to enter the teaching of non-duality.

Vimalakirti's silent response conceals within it a profundity of limitless meaning. In this way it not only negates the answers of the previous thirty-one bodhisattvas, but it even demolishes the response of Manjusri Bodhisattva, leaving to posterity the story of "Vimalakirti's thundering silence."

## Non-Retrogression
**不退轉**
*See*: Avaivartika.

## Non-Self
**無我**
*See*: Dharma seals, three.

N

# O

## Offerings, Four
## 四事供養

One day when the Buddha was teaching at the Jeta Grove Monastery, the lay woman Visakha came to pay homage to the Buddha, and to beseech the Buddha to grant her eight wishes, which were:

1. That the Buddha would permit her to offer rain clothes to the *bhiksus* to wear when it rained.
2. That the Buddha would permit her to offer support to the *bhiksus* who had newly joined the monastic order.
3. That the Buddha would permit her to offer food and money to those *bhiksus* going out on a journey.
4. That the Buddha would permit her to offer medicine to those *bhiksus* who were sick.
5. That the Buddha would permit her to offer appropriate food to those *bhiksus* who were sick.
6. That the Buddha would permit her to offer support for those *bhiksus* who were looking after the sick.

7. That the Buddha would permit her to regularly send thin porridge to the monastery as an offering to the *bhiksus.*

8. That the Buddha would permit her to offer bathing clothes for the *bhiksunis.*

Upon hearing this, the Buddha was extremely happy and granted her eight wishes.

To "make an offering" means to supply material support. As a Buddhist follower, not only must we offer support to our parents and elders, but even more so we should respectfully make offerings to the Triple Gem of the Buddha, Dharma, and Sangha, such as offering rice or land. Even things like incense, flowers, lamp oil, and fruits can be offerings. But for those members of the sangha who teach the Dharma for the benefit of sentient beings, the most necessary and practical offerings are Visakha's eight wishes listed above. The eight wishes above can be summarized as four kinds of offerings: food and drink, clothing, bedding, and medicine.

### 1. Food and drink（飲食）

People cannot live without eating, and if monastics had to rush about every day to prepare their meals, there would be no way for them to focus their attention upon their responsibilities for carrying on the Buddha's mission. Therefore, the task of offering food and drink to the sangha is borne by the laity.

### 2. Clothing（衣服）

To remain dignified and be protected from the cold, people must wear clothing. The robes of a monastic are not elegant dress, but realistically, dressing oneself in rags in today's society would be seen as disgraceful. It is said that "the Buddha must be clad in gold," and in the same way people must wear clothes. Therefore, the task of offering clothing to the sangha is borne by the laity.

### 3. Bedding（臥具）

This refers to the offering of bedding and cotton quilts to the monastic community. After a whole day of diligent practice, it is necessary to rest and get some sleep at night. Without bedding, one cannot get appropriate sleep and will lack the energy to awaken oneself and others. Therefore, the task of offering bedding to the sangha is borne by the laity.

### 4. Medicine（湯藥）

Sickness is an unavoidable part of life. As the saying goes, "Ministering to the sick is the foremost field of merit." In order to restore *bhiksus* to good health so that the light of the Buddha's lamp may continue the task of offering medicine to the sangha is borne by the laity.

As lay Buddhist followers we must learn from Visakha's exemplary devotion in making offerings, but we must also remember to make offerings with a sense of equality. Moreover, when offerings are made, we should feel joy in our hearts and respect for the Triple Gem. We must not have an arrogant attitude, nor should we expect any thanks or any reciprocated favors from the recipients of our generosity. If we can make offerings in this way, then not only will we obtain the reward of happiness for ourselves, but the recipients of our generosity will be happy as well.

O

# Om Mani Padme Hum
## 六字真言

Mantra recitation is the main practice of the Esoteric School of Buddhism. *Mantra*, also sometimes called *dharani*, means "true words," meaning they are the true language spoken by the Buddha. Another explanation of the word *mantra* is that it means "holding all," in the sense that a mantra can contain all meaning. There are five virtues to be gained from reciting mantras:

1. One develops wisdom.
2. One increases in right mindfulness.
3. One prevents disasters.
4. One brings together all that is wholesome.
5. One is protected from unwholesomeness.

Among the mantras handed down by the Esoteric School, the most common one is the six-syllable *mantra* of Avalokitesvara Bodhisattva, also known as the *dharani* of great brightness: *om mani padme hum*. It is known as the mind *dharani* of Avalokitesvara Bodhisattva and as such is endowed with deep meaning and virtue, and is practiced by many Buddhists.

According to one explanation, *om mani padme hum* means "taking refuge in the *mani* pearl atop the lotus." Tibetan Buddhists pray to Padmapani Bodhisattva to attain future rebirth in the Western Pure Land of Ultimate Bliss and so recite the mantra.

According to another explanation from the texts of Tibetan Esoteric Buddhism, the merit of reciting the syllable *om* brings an end to rebirth in the heavenly realm. Likewise, reciting the syllable *ma* will bring an end to rebirth in the *asura* realm. Reciting the syllable *ni* will bring an end to further rebirth in the human realm, reciting the syllable *pad* with bring an end to rebirth in the animal realm, reciting the syllable *me* will bring an end to rebirth in the realm of hungry ghosts, and reciting the syllable *hum* will bring an end to rebirth in the hell realm.

Such a *mantra* is the source of wisdom, liberation, aide, and happiness. Just by reciting this *mantra*, one can avert disaster, extend one's life, dispel negativity, and assure rebirth in the highest level of the Western Pure Land of Ultimate Bliss. Reciting the *mantra* will also ensure that whatever else one seeks will be fulfilled as wished.

In addition, the *Mahayana Dignified Treasure King Sutra* states: "This six-syllable *dharani* of great brightness is the wondrous intrinsic mind of the Great Avalokitesvara Bodhisattva. Those who come to know this wondrous intrinsic mind will then know liberation." It also states: "If one can obtain a wish-fulfilling *mani* pearl such as this [*mantra*], then one's ancestors as far back as seven generations will attain liberation." This shows how great the virtue of reciting this esoteric *mantra* can be.

The Esoteric School of Buddhism emphasizes that it is the recitation of the *mantra* itself that matters, for there is no need to understand its meaning. Regardless of which *mantra* is being recited, one should remain firm in one's faith and not harbor any doubts.

When reciting, it is important to combine the "three esoteric elements," which are 1) the physical esoteric element in the form of hand gestures or *mudras*, 2) the verbal esoteric element in the form of reciting the *mantra*, and 3) the mental esoteric element in the form of visualizing the mantra's seed-syllable. Coordinating these three elements means that as one verbally recites the *mantra* at the same time as one performs the *mudras* and mentally visualizes the seed-syllable of the Buddha or bodhisattva, one activates the three karmas of body, speech, and mind. Practicing *mantra* recitation by coordinating the three esoteric elements will make one's merit even greater.

# Omniscience (of the Buddha)
## 佛智如海

Since ordinary people lack great wisdom, we cannot comprehend the omniscience and omnipotence of the Buddha. Consider the following story:

Once, when the Buddha was traveling about teaching the Dharma, he came across two merchants. The merchants asked the Buddha, *"Sramana*, we have lost our camel. Have you seen it?"

The Buddha asked, "Was that camel blind in the left eye and lame in the left foot; and were its front teeth broken?"

The merchants were delighted, "Yes! That's our camel alright."

The Buddha then said to them, "No, I have not seen it." The merchants became suspicious, and asked the Buddha, "Your knowledge of the camel's appearance is so detailed, how is it possible that you haven't seen it? You probably stole it!"

The merchants then took the Buddha to court. After hearing the merchants' story, the judge posed a question to the Buddha: "How did you know that the camel's left eye was blind?"

The Buddha answered, "I knew because I saw how only the grass on the right side of the road showed signs of having been eaten by a camel. This led me to believe that the camel's left eye was blind."

The judge then asked the Buddha, "How did you know that the camel's left foot was lame?"

The Buddha responded, "I saw the camel's footprints on the road. The impression of the right foot was deep, the left foot's was shallow. This led me to believe that the camel's left foot was lame."

The judge continued his inquiry by asking the Buddha, "Then, how did you know that the front teeth of that camel were broken?"

The Buddha responded once more to the judge, "I saw that of the clumps of grass the camel had chewed, little patches were left in the center. This led me to believe the front middle teeth of the camel were surely broken."

After the Buddha offered his explanation, the two merchants were left speechless. The Buddha then went on to say, "Oh, there is no need to worry, merchants. Your camel was not stolen by anyone. I know this because I saw that there were no human footprints beside those of the camel."

Having heard all of the testimony, the judge said to the merchants, "I see no way that this *sramana* stole your camel. You should not form such suspicions of others based on your shallow knowledge. The Buddha's wisdom is as vast as the ocean, such that ordinary people like us cannot possible conceive of it."

After practicing over hundreds of millions of *kalpas*, the great Buddha truly knows and sees all.

## One Mind Opens Two Doors
一心二門

*See also*: Intrinsic nature; mind.

The sutras say, "The Buddha is a sentient being who has awakened. Sentient beings are Buddhas who have yet to awaken." In regards to the mind, the sutras also say, "The mind, the Buddha, and sentient beings are not different." As indicated in both of these quotations, sentient beings and the Buddha are each endowed with the same nature of mind. It is only because of ignorance's power to delude us that the phenomena of arising, abiding, change, and extinction as well as the distinctions between ignorance and awakening and defilement and purity exist.

The *Treatise on the Awakening of Faith in Mahayana* explains this characteristic of the mind by dividing all phenomena experienced by the mind of sentient beings as having been experienced by two different aspects of the mind: The door of suchness (心真如門) and the door of arising and ceasing (心生滅門). This distinction is often referred to as "one mind opens two doors" (一心二門).

## The Door of Suchness (心真如門)

The "door of suchness" refers to all things being just as they are. It is the fundamental essence of the mind, and cannot be characterized by relative distinctions like arising, abiding, change, extinction, ignorance, awakening, defilement, or purity. The door of suchness has as its essence absolute equality, and this essence neither arises nor ceases, and does not increase nor decrease, but is always present.

## The Door of Arising and Ceasing (心生滅門)

The "door of arising and ceasing" refers to the dynamic aspects of the mind, which arise and cease according to conditions. It is from this aspect of the mind that the phenomena of arising, abiding, change, and extinction and the distinctions between ignorance, awakening, defilement, and purity arise.

The essence of the mind is the primary cause which leads to the arising of all phenomena, but ordinary, deluded people do not perceive the essence of equality which underlies them. When delusion is removed the essence of the absolute appears on its own. The door of suchness and the door of arising and ceasing should be understood as neither the same nor different. They are different in the sense that the door of suchness has as its essence absolute equality while the door of arising and ceasing encompasses all phenomena with their relative distinctions, and as such they are considered to not be the same. However, at their essence there is no phenomena that arises or ceases outside of the fundamental essence of all things, and in this sense the door of suchness and the door of arising and ceasing are the same, and so the two are said to not be different.

Another way to explain this relationship is by the metaphor of water and waves. Water is passive, while waves are active, and in this sense the two are not the same. However, without water there can be no waves, and so the two are not different. We must come to realize that "not the same" and "not different" are two doors of one mind.

This should lead us to conclude that the essence of the universe with its myriad phenomena are the singular mind, and that both sentient beings and Buddhas are endowed with this mind. The mind is different only in terms of awakening and non-awakening, and that is how it can be differentiated into these two different aspects. The awakened mind is the door of suchness, while the unawakened mind is the door of arising and ceasing.

Fundamentally, the essence of the mind does not arise or cease and does not increase or decrease; it has no distinctive characteristics whatsoever. The dynamic aspect of the mind does arise and cease as well as increase and decrease, and as such possesses relative distinctions. These are two sides of the same coin, and are often referred to as "the one mind opens two doors."

The Chan *gongan* "Huike's settled mind" also features this concept. When Huike, who would become the second patriarch, encountered Bodhidharma for the first time, he told him, "My mind is not yet settled. Please, patriarch, settle my mind for me."

Bodhidharma replied, "Bring forth the mind. I will settle it for you!"

Huike said, "I cannot find the mind."

Bodhidharma replied, "I have already settled the mind for you."

In this *gongan*, the mind before it was settled is the door of arising and ceasing, and the mind after it is settled is the door of suchness. All one needs to do is bring one's consciousness to tranquility and eliminate delusion; then one will attain awakening by seeing intrinsic nature.

## One Thought Contains the Three Thousandfold World System
一念三千

> Three dots that look like stars,
> A stroke like a crescent moon;
> One becomes cloaked in skin and hair because
>     of it,
> One also attains Buddhahood due to it.

This riddle is describing the Chinese character *xin* (心), "mind." Throughout the day, there is no telling how many times our mind wanders among the ten dharma realms, and so all the phenomena of "three thousandfold world system," the Buddhist term for the universe, exists within a single thought.

The term "three thousandfold world system" refers to all wholesome and unwholesome phenomena in their essence and outward characteristics on the mundane and supramundane levels. According to Tiantai thought, the minds of both sages and ordinary people all contain the ten dharma realms, and each of the ten dharma realms contains the ten dharma realms, and each of the ten dharma realms possesses the ten qualities, existing in the three continuums. When these divisions are taken together (10 x 10 x 10 x 3), they constitute the "three thousandfold world system."

To fully understand the significance of the phrase "one thought contains the three thousandfold world system," each of these divisions must be examined. The ten dharma realms and the ten qualities each have their own entries, so what will be focused on here is the three continuums and the doctrine of "the mutual containment of the ten dharma realms."

## Mutual Containment of the Ten Dharma Realms （十界互具）

The Tiantai doctrine of "mutual containment" means that each of the ten dharma realms contain one another, such that each of the ten dharma realms contain the ten dharma realms. This means that what seemed like the hell realm yesterday can become the human realm of today, and what seems like the animal realm now can become the Buddha realm tomorrow. This endless cycle of transformation proceeds upward to the highest realm and downwards to the lowest one. To ascend up through the ten dharma realms is to come closer to awakening, and to sink down through them is to draw closer to ignorance.

O

The hell realm contains the other nine realms, just as the Buddha realm contains the other nine realms as well. For example, when one's mind is filled with greed, anger, or ignorance, this is the mind of the three lower realms. When the mind is inclined towards the ten wholesome actions, this is the heavenly realm, and a mind imbued with compassion is the bodhisattva realm. All of our thoughts can be found to correspond to either the six realms of ordinary existence or the four noble realms of existence, and in this way we can see the doctrine of "mutual containment" at work.

## Three Continuums（三世間）

In this instance "continuum" refers to a combination of space and time: space stretching in the ten directions, and time across the past, present, and future. Within this span we can consider three different "continuums":

1. The continuum of sentience, which refers to all sentient beings.
2. The continuum of matter, which is where all sentient beings dwell, and encompasses all mountains, rivers, land, and all other material things.
3. The continuum of the five aggregates, which is all form, feelings, perceptions, mental formations, and consciousness.

There is a saying in Buddhism: "The Buddha gave all teachings in order to quell the afflictions of the mind. Without all minds, of what use would the teachings be?" Buddhist practice emphasizes cultivating the mind. For this reason, each thought with its three thousandfold world system can serve as the basis of our practice.

# Ordination
## 三壇大戒

*See also*: Retreat; robe and bowl.

The triple platform ordination ceremony is an ordination ritual unique to China, and includes being given three sets of precepts:

1. The *sramanera* precepts of novice monastics.
2. The *bhiksu* or *bhiksuni* precepts of fully ordained monastics.
3. The bodhisattva precepts for monastics.

According to the tradition maintained by Chinese Buddhism, all those who shave their heads and put on robes to join the monastic order must receive ordination through the triple platform ordination ceremony in order to be officially recognized as legitimate members of the monastic community.

The Buddhist historical texts are able to give us a sense for how the various systems of precepts were maintained within the Chinese tradition. The earliest transmission of the precepts in China occurred in 250 CE, using *Heart of the Mahasamghika Vinaya*, a vinaya text translated by Dharmakala at White Horse Monastery. Indian monastics were invited to officiate at the ceremony and confer the precepts, making this the first transmission of the precepts in China according to the vinaya. The first Chinese person to receive full monastic ordination was Zhu Shixing (203-282 C.E.), who became the first Chinese monk.

The beginning of the ordination of Chinese nuns occurred a number of years later in 357 C.E. when Dharmakala held an ordination ceremony upon the Si River, in which four nuns from the

Zhulin Monastery participated, including the nun Jingjian (ca. 313-357 C.E.). The ceremony was based upon the *Mahasamghika Liturgy for Nuns* and the body of monastic precepts that Dharmagata had worked on in Luoyang.

The earliest joint ordination of monks and nuns in China was held in 434 C.E. at Nanlin Monastery by the monk Samghavarman (5th cent. C.E.) and the nun Tiesaluo (ca. 433 C.E.). More than three hundred monks and nuns, including the nuns Huiguo (5th-6th cent. C.E.) and Jingyin (5th-6th cent. C.E.), were ordained together.

The bodhisattva precepts began to spread throughout China when they were translated by Kumarajiva in the fourth century. The bodhisattva precepts were propagated far and wide, bolstered by their adoption by Emperor Wu of the Liang dynasty (r. 502-549 C.E.), Emperor Wen of the Chen dynasty (r. 560-566 C.E.), and Emperor Wen of the Sui dynasty (r. 581-604 C.E.), who all called themselves disciples of the bodhisattva precepts.

Chinese ordination ceremonies feature a system in which ten monastics, three presiding masters and seven witnesses, officiate over the ordination of new monastics. This practice was first instituted in 765 C.E., when Emperor Daizong (r. 762-779 C.E.) of the Tang dynasty requested Da Xingshan Monastery in Changan to establish a universal ordination platform, and subsequently ordered all the monastics in the capital to name their preceptors to serve as their ordination officiates. Additionally, in 856 C.E., intending to maintain the moral integrity of the monastic order through the certification process, Emperor Xuanzong (r. 846-859 C.E.) of the Tang dynasty began ordering that monks and nuns receive official ordination certificates. The triple platform ordination ceremony itself began in 1010 C.E. The Vinaya Master Yunkan (d. 1061 C.E.) created a Mahayana ordination platform at Cixiao Temple in Kaifeng, so that those monastics who had only previously received the *bhiksu* or *bhiksuni* ordination would be able to ascend the platform once again and receive the bodhisattva precepts for monastics. This innovation of adding the bodhisattva precepts was better aligned with the spirit of the Mahayana teachings, and the practice evolved into the triple ordination ceremony observed by later generations.

By the beginning of the Republic of China, the most famous ordination platform was at Mount Baohua, as celebrated in this comic verse:

> If you want to get ordained at Baohua,
> Be ready to work: bring your carrying pole and
>     rope.
> You make donations for fine vegetarian meals,
> Yet you eat pungent salted vegetables.
> You pay the lamp oil money,
> Yet you bow and scrape in the dark.
> Yes, whoever gets ordained at Baohua
> Is truly a righteous monastic.

This goes to show, that newly ordained monastics must undergo a complete and full ordination, and that they receive strict training at the hands of the precept master before they are able to extend their limitless wisdom.

# Ouyi
## 蕅益
*See*: Masters of the Ming dynasty, four.

# P

## Panthaka
## 探手羅漢
*See:* Arhats, eighteen.

## Parables of the Lotus Sutra
## 法華七喻

The *Lotus Sutra* employs a number of easy-to-understand parables to illustrate its profound truths. This is one of the most important characteristics of the *Lotus Sutra*, and explains why it has been singled out as one of the sutras with the greatest literary value. One could say that parables are employed throughout all twenty-eight chapters of the *Lotus Sutra*, but there are seven which are most well-known:

### 1. The Parable of the Burning House（火宅喻）
The parable of the burning house, featured in the Parables chapter, is also known as the "parable of the three carts." The parable describes a house consumed by fire with young children playing

P

inside, not knowing that they need to escape danger. Their father employs skillful means and tells his children that outside there are goat drawn carts, deer drawn carts, and ox drawn carts they have long hoped to ride. Having enticed the children out of the house in this way, they then all ride a cart yoked with a white ox and escape from the burning house. In this parable, the burning house represents the three realms, which are filled with the five impurities and the eight kinds of suffering. The children represent sentient beings, who have cravings for the three realms and who are so enamored with the pleasures of life that they do not realize the dangers they face. The father represents the Buddha, while the goat drawn cart represents the *sravaka* vehicle, the deer drawn cart represents the *pratyekabuddha* vehicle, the ox drawn cart represents the bodhisattva vehicle, and the cart yoked with the white ox represents the one Buddha vehicle.

## 2. The Parable of the Poor Son (窮子喻)

The parable of the poor son appears in the Belief and Understanding chapter. The parable concerns the son of a rich man who wandered off at a young age and grew up in poverty. Unaware of his own background, the poor son eventually arrives at the door of his father after the many twists and turns of his wandering life. Upon seeing the imposing richness of his father's great manor, the poor soon becomes fearful and tries to leave as soon as possible. The father recognizes his son immediately, and employs various skillful means to make the boy his heir, and enable him to learn who he is. This story shows how the Buddha employs various skillful means to help those who consider themselves to be *sravakas* to transform and realize themselves as bodhisattvas.

**P**

### 3. The Parable of the Medicinal Herbs（藥草喻）

The parable of the medicinal herbs appears in the chapter of the same name, and describes several herbs that vary in name and appearance. Although all the different herbs receive the same amount of rainfall, the tall plants and short plants each grow according to their nature, and depending on their different roots, stalks, branches, and leaves, they all end up looking quite different. The parable is a metaphor for the various spiritual capacities of sentient beings. The Buddha teaches and imparts wisdom to sentient beings in all their many forms according to their capacity, mending their delusions and enabling them to attain awakening.

### 4. The Parable of the Manifested City（化城喻）

The parable of the manifested city appears in the chapter of the same name, and describes a group of travelers who are journeying towards a great treasure, representing awakening, some five hundred *yojana* away. But as they approach midway through their journey, they wish to stop due to exhaustion. Their leader then creates a projection of an imaginary city some three hundred *yojana* in size, representing skillful means, to entice the travelers to reach the treasure. This parable shows how the Buddha guides sentient beings to the one Buddha vehicle by employing the teaching of the three vehicles as a skillful means.

### 5. The Parable of the Pearl in the Clothing（衣珠喻）

The parable of the pearl in the clothing appears in the "Five Hundred Disciples Receive their Prophecy" chapter. The parable describes a man who, while visiting a close friend, became drunk and passed out. The friend then had to leave on a long journey

P

to deal with some official matter, so he sewed a priceless pearl within the lining of his guest's clothing. As the man was asleep in his drunken stupor he was unaware of any of this and went on to experience all manner of suffering while seeking out food and clothing. It was not until the close friend told him about the gift of the pearl that the man's life improved and he became free from want. The parable demonstrates how sentient beings have always possessed Buddha nature, and yet in their confusion are unaware of it. As a result they wander through the cycle of birth and death and endure the full measure of suffering, and yet a single thought can lead them to liberation.

## 6. The Parable of the Pearl in the Topknot（髻珠喻）

The parable of the pearl in the topknot appears in the Peaceful Practicing chapter, and describes a wheel-turning monarch who removes the pearl from his topknot and presents it to his best ministers. This shows how, in teaching the *Lotus Sutra*, the Buddha exposes what are skillful means and reveals what is absolute, proving to those who practice as *sravakas* and *pratyekabuddhas* that they will attain Buddhahood.

## 7. The Parable of the Good Doctor（醫子喻）

The parable of the good doctor appears in the Lifespan of the Tathagata chapter. The parable features a group of children who unknowingly drink poison, and though their father tries to cure them with medicine, the children have lost all reason and are unwilling to take it. The father then leaves on a long journey and sends back false news that he has died. Shocked, the children are restored to their senses, take the medicine, and are cured. The parable demonstrates how the Buddha proclaims the *Lotus Sutra* for

**P**

the sake of sentient beings confused by wrong ideas. The Buddha also enables sentient beings to feel a deep sense of admiration and longing, so that they will advance towards *nirvana*.

## Paramartha
真諦
*See*: Translators, four great Chinese.

## Parents
父母
*See:* Field of merit; gratitude, four kinds of; violations, five great.

## Path, Noble Eightfold
八正道
*See also*: Mindfulness, four bases of; merit and wisdom; right effort; *samadhi*.

Qian Lou was a Daoist scholar who lived a life of poverty, simplicity, and virtue. After he passed away, many statesmen came to pay their respects, but his burial shroud was not long enough to cover his body. One suggested that the shroud be laid out crooked so that it could cover the entire body, but Qian Lou's wife said, "I would rather it be right (正), and have there be not enough, than for it to be crooked and have more than enough."

To be successful and achieve something in our journey through life, we need to go down the right path. If we go down the wrong path, our life could be over without a second thought. Those who wish to become Buddhas practice the "Noble Eightfold Path," those who move against this way will find it impossible to achieve their goal. The eight parts of the path are as follows:

P

## 1. Right View（正見）

A person's ideas go a long way to determining if they succeed or fail in life. Buddhist "right view" means having the right kinds of ideas, and right understanding. Right view is formed through having faith in the Dharma, and having the right view of cause and effect, positive and negative karmic results, impermanence, suffering, emptiness, and the enduring quality of the Buddhist teachings. Only when armed with right knowledge and right view can we see the life and the universe as they are, and avoid having mistaken or biased ideas and conduct.

## 2. Right Thought（正思）

Right thought is having thinking based on true principles. In the Buddhist sutras, the mind is commonly compared to a field: good thoughts are like grain seedlings, and delusional thoughts are like weeds. Just as the grain will not grow unless the weeds are removed, Buddhahood cannot be attained unless delusion is removed. Therefore those studying Buddhism should take good care of their thoughts and make sure they are aligned with the Dharma. The mind should be flexible, compassionate, pure, and without anger, such that our thoughts do not become tied up in arguments or disputes with others.

## 3. Right Speech（正語）

Speaking good words is the best form of practice for creating karmic connections with others. Conversely, by speaking in a sarcastic and vindictive tone, or resorting to dishonest, harsh, divisive, or idle speech, language becomes a weapon to harm others. Students of Buddhism should speak constructive words that benefit others, words that are true and compassionate such that they awaken faith in others, and words that praise and gladden others.

**P**

## 4. Right Action（正業）

Right action refers to creating positive karma with the body, which means turning away from unwholesome conduct like killing, stealing, and sexual misconduct. This also means having good life habits, such as getting the appropriate amount of sleep, food, drink, exercise, rest, and work.

## 5. Right Livelihood（正命）

Right livelihood means engaging in proper work to obtain the necessities of life. For example, this means not opening a gambling parlor, a bar, a slaughterhouse, a fishing tackle store, a gun shop for hunting, or traffic in human beings or drugs, and so on. Right livelihood also means having a respectable moral life, harmonious social relations, and a pure emotional life.

## 6. Right Effort（正勤）

Right effort is the exertion of diligence, such that one remains focused on advancement and does not lose ground. Right effort also means striving to do good and refrain from doing bad. In the *Treatise on the Perfection of Great Wisdom* this goal is broken down into four components: developing wholesome qualities that have not yet arisen, strengthening wholesome qualities that have already arisen, preventing unwholesome qualities that have yet to arise, and renouncing unwholesome qualities that have already arisen.

## 7. Right Mindfulness（正念）

Right mindfulness refers both to having pure ideas that accord with the Dharma, as well as the practice of the "four bases of mindfulness." Just before the Buddha's final *nirvana*, he taught the

P

gathered disciples to abide in the following four contemplations: contemplating the impurity of the body, contemplating the suffering of feeling, contemplating the impermanence of the mind, and contemplating the non-selfhood of phenomena. It is through these four bases of mindfulness that one can come to understand the reality of suffering, emptiness, and impermanence in order to realize *nirvana*, which is permanent, blissful, pure, and has an inherent self.

*8. Right Meditative Concentration*（正定）
Right meditative concentration is the focusing of one's mind and body to foster a moral character. "Meditation" should not be constrained by the formalities of sitting meditation, for any form of meditation that can ease the body and mind, enhance concentration, end confusion, and manifest Buddha nature can be called "right meditative concentration."

The Noble Eightfold Path includes elements of faith and morality. It is both the direct path to Buddhahood, as well as the standard for how we should behave in this very life. Therefore everyone can practice the Noble Eightfold Path and cultivate the Dharma.

## Patience
## 忍辱
*See:* Merit and wisdom; perfections, six.

## Perception
## 想
*See:* Aggregates, five.

# Perfections, Six
## 六度
*See also*: Giving; merit and wisdom.

The six perfections are six methods of practice that bring liberation to oneself and others. They are giving, morality, patience, diligence, meditative concentration, and wisdom.

There are some who believe that it is difficult for ordinary people to engage in bodhisattva practices like the six perfections, because they see them as only benefiting others, but not benefiting those who practice them. This makes it hard to actually put the six perfections into practice. In actuality, while the six perfections are beneficial to others, they are even more beneficial to those who practice them.

### 1. Giving (布施)
Is giving about giving to others, or giving to yourself? Sometimes the thought of giving to others and gaining nothing for oneself makes people unwilling to give. However, giving is actually like planting a seed of good karma that can be harvested later. Giving may look like only giving to others, but it is actually giving to oneself.

### 2. Morality (持戒)
Is morality about being constrained or being free? Sometimes people think following moral precepts is a constraint, and thus are unwilling to do so. Following Buddhism's moral precepts is more like following the law; without following the law, how can you be free? People in prison are under constraints because they have not behaved morally or followed the law. If one does not violate the

law, then you are protected. Morality may look like a constraint, but in actuality it is freedom.

### 3. Patience (忍辱)

Does patience put us at a loss or an advantage? Sometimes people think that having patience with others means taking a loss, but having a moment's patience can allow the storm to clear, and taking a step back can open infinite possibilities. Adversity provides a recipe for enhancing our practice. While patience may at times seem like a loss, in actuality we gain an incredible advantage.

### 4. Diligence (精進)

Is diligence drudgery or delight? Sometimes it seems that working with diligence is painful, whether it is at one's job or part of one's spiritual practice. But what is done today is finished today, allowing one to advance. What may seem like drudgery is actually unsurpassed delight in the Dharma.

### 5. Meditative concentration (禪定)

Is meditative concentration dull or energetic? "Meditation" generally makes people think of the dull image of sitting with one's eyes closed in deep contemplation. In actuality, hauling firewood and carrying water are meditation as well. Walking, standing, sitting, and lying down can all be meditation. The wind through the swaying trees and a boat sailing upon flowing water both evoke the energetic sense of meditation.

### 6. Wisdom (智慧)

Is wisdom found within oneself or outside? "Wisdom" can make us think of people who are richly informed or possess extraordinary

**P**

skill. In reality, there is no phenomenon which exists outside the mind; everything outside of the mind is illusory and unreal. After awakening, one will know everything. Only the wisdom that comes from within is truly beneficial.

## Perseverance
精進

*See:* Merit and wisdom; spiritual wealth, seven kinds of.

## Philosophy
世智辯聰

*See:* Difficulties, eight.

## Pindolabharadvaja
伏虎羅漢

*See:* Arhats, eighteen.

## Poisons, Three
三毒

*See also:* Ignorance.

The three poisons are three unwholesome elements that are entrenched in our minds that cause us harm again and again. The three poisons of greed, anger, and ignorance are what keep us from feeling happy and carefree and make nothing but trouble for us.

*1. The Poison of Greed*（貪毒）
The poison of greed arises from liking something. This defiles the mind and we create attachments and see all things as "mine" or "myself." For example, the mind becomes filled with "my" relatives,

P

"my" wealth, "my" reputation, "my" possessions, and so forth. With greed in the mind, one becomes enamored with the past, infatuated with the present, and hopeful for the future. From greed for food we kill living things. From greed for pleasure we pursue women and song. From greed for comfort we become lazy and listless. The harm caused by the poison of greed is great indeed.

Greed leads to infatuation, defilement, desire, and clinging. Attachment, avarice, sycophancy, and arrogance all follow in its wake. There is a saying that "When one no longer has desires, one naturally has heightened morality." It is because of greed that our refined moral character can sink into immorality.

### 2. The Poison of Anger (瞋毒)

The poison of anger arises from disliking something: one is dissatisfied with the present state of the world and one's personal relationships. When the poison of anger is concealed, one speaks sweetly but carries a dagger in one's breast. When the poison of anger is externalized, one glares with a ferocious expression. An angry person will verbally and physically abuse others, railing against heaven and earth, and cursing the gods.

Anger towards family leads to leaving home and running away. Anger towards friends leads to hurting or even killing them. Anger towards everyday things leads to destroying them. Anger towards one's circumstances leads to blaming others. The harm caused by anger is great indeed. Anger leads to hatred, hostility, irritation, and corruption. Pride, slander, envy, and aggression all follow in its wake. There is a saying that "the fires of anger burn away all the roots of goodness," for anger is capable of destroying the good and decent nature of the mind.

P

### 3. The Poison of Ignorance（愚痴）

The poison of ignorance arises from wrong view. "Wrong views" encompass all views in which one is ignorant of true reality and attached to falsehood. Examples of wrong views include an improper understanding of cause and effect, and the way things are.

Ignorance leads us to mistake falsehood for truth, and makes our thoughts jumbled and confused. Ignorance makes us say what we should not, think what we should not, and do what we should not. An ignorant person does not know good and bad, cause and effect, karma and its effect, and the nature of the world. The harm caused by ignorance is great indeed.

Ignorance leads to prejudice, doubt, wrongheadedness, and fabrication. Disbelief, confusion, and mental dullness follow in its wake. There is a saying that, "Delusion and ignorance produce all suffering," for ignorance shrouds our radiant intrinsic nature in darkness.

## Practice, Four Stages of
## 信解行證

*See also: Nirvana.*

The Buddhist sutras contain the following parable: A traveler on a long journey is suffering from hunger and thirst. Finally, after much difficulty, the traveler manages to find a lake. But upon arriving, the traveler only gazes upon the lake and does not drink, for he considers that the lake is too big, and that there is no way he will be able to drink all of it. Instead, he doesn't drink any of it.

This parable is satirizing those Buddhists who believe that their own spiritual foundation is too shallow, and so when facing the vastness of the Buddhist path they do not feel up to completing the task and instead make no progress at all. In actuality, each of Buddhism's eighty-four thousand methods of practice can bring one to liberation. Even though the Dharma is vast and extensive, once the beginning student of Buddhism has a taste of its profound insights, he or she can practice the Dharma by following the sequence of "faith, understanding, practice, and realization." As long as one follows this ordered sequence, progress will be made.

### 1. Faith（信）

Faith is the basic motivational force in all matters. Only faith can produce the strength to advance forward with courage. Faith is the source we draw upon to achieve our goals and concentrate our energy. Only faith in each other can bring unity and success to a group; only faith in each other can bring harmony and joy to a family; and only faith in each other can bring depth to a friendship. Only faith in oneself can lead to success and accomplishment. In addition, learning Buddhism in particular requires faith, for it is only with faith that one can obtain the benefits of the Dharma. There is a Buddhist saying that, "The great Dharma ocean can only be entered through faith." Therefore, the first step to learn Buddhism is to take refuge in the Triple Gem. This expresses the conviction of one's faith.

### 2. Understanding（解）

Buddhism is a religion of both wisdom and faith and it has no place for blind faith. Therefore, the second step in learning Buddhism is to understand the sutras. That is, one must understand what the Buddha taught, why we should have faith, and how faith is beneficial to us. In order to understand the teachings, one must read the sutras and listen to Dharma talks. One must also have the correct attitude when receiving the teachings, and receive them as a field is seeded or a cup filled with water, to avoid the three kinds of error: inattentiveness, arrogance, and wrong views. One should maintain an attitude of devotion, sincerity, respect, humility, gentleness, and purity. In this way the field of the mind can readily receive the seeds of enlightenment.

### 3. Practice（行）

There is a Buddhist saying that, "Ten feet of talk is not as good as one foot of practice." Buddhists must practice; only talking about Buddhism will bring no benefit, just as the talk of food does not fill one's stomach. Practice entails correcting one's conduct according to the teachings of the Buddha. For example, the greed, anger, and ignorance of the past is transformed into giving, loving-kindness, and wisdom. That is why it is said in Buddhism that "the diligent cultivation of morality, meditation, and wisdom will extinguish greed, anger, and delusion." Important practices include observing the five precepts and the ten wholesome actions, performing the many practices associated with the six perfections, and developing other aspects of the Dharma such as compassion, generosity, discernment, gratitude, determination, contentment, and freedom in one's everyday life. In this way, one can attain the benefits of the Dharma. This is why, when learning Buddhism, equal emphasis should be placed on both understanding and practice.

### 4. Realization（證）

The liberation of *nirvana* is the ultimate goal of Buddhist practice, and it is also the state in which one realizes enlightenment. *Nirvana* is not something that is attained only after death. If we can remain unaffected when dealing with sorrow and suffering, if we

P

can remain free according to conditions and undisturbed by gain or loss, if we can abide with trouble without feeling troubled, and abide with suffering without feeling suffering, and if we can discover the true nature of the cycle of birth and death and act freely, then we have realized, right here and now, the enlightened state of liberation. Therefore, to realize the state of enlightenment means: to be unaffected by sorrow and suffering, to be undisturbed by success or failure, to be untroubled by hindrances and constraints, and to be untouched by birth, old age, sickness, and death.

This realization is the ultimate goal of Buddhist practice. To reach this goal, one must believe in, understand, and practice the Dharma. However, faith, understanding, practice, and realization should not be understood as a linear sequence, but rather as a cycle. First comes correct faith which generates a pure mind that strives to attain wisdom and understanding. This is followed next by practice which serves to realize and confirm the truth. Finally, this further enhances one's faith as one delves deeper and deeper into understanding and practice. Such repeated cycles will slowly advance one along the Buddhist path, and one eventually realizes enlightenment.

Whether this should be considered "sudden enlightenment" or "gradual enlightenment," the realization of enlightenment is the state of liberation that is attained over the course of "minor enlightenments" in everyday life. Therefore, students of Buddhism need not entrust the realization of enlightenment to some future time. It is more important to experience some small enlightenment every day, and most especially, whether or not one can remain committed and never backslide. There is a Buddhist saying that "It is easy to develop a mind of goodness, but much harder to remain

P

committed." Buddhists can persevere with courage by remembering their initial motivation to the path, for it is only in this way that they can defeat the armies of affliction and realize the liberation of enlightenment.

## Prajna
般若空性

*See also*: Mountain gate; omniscience of the Buddha; perfections, six; wisdom, four kinds of; wisdom, three kinds of.

Among all Buddhist sutras, the *Flower Adornment Sutra* is known as the "king of sutras," in part because of its importance, but also because of its great length: one translation is 60 fascicles long, while another is 80 fascicles. The *Mahaprajnaparamita Sutra* is even larger, and is made up of 600 fascicles. The *Heart Sutra*, though it is only 260 Chinese characters, captures the essence of the *Mahaprajnaparamita Sutra*. The *Heart Sutra* describes the *prajna* of the "inherent emptiness of dependent origination." It teaches how we can use *prajna* to contemplate the emptiness of all phenomena, so we can come to know our true selves.

*Prajna*, transliterated in Chinese as *bore* (般若), means "wisdom." However, *prajna* implies something much more extensive and transcendent than our normal concept of wisdom. Worldly wisdom can be either good or bad, correct or mistaken, but *prajna* is pure goodness and beauty, for it is truly undefiled. That is why the word *prajna* is so often transliterated as *bore* (般若), rather than being given the full translated as *zhihui* (智慧).

There is nothing in this world that remains constant and unchanging, and exists independent of other things. But sentient beings do not understand this on a deep level. Only the development of *prajna* can penetrate the impermanence and non-self nature of all phenomena. *Prajna* is what allows us to see all phenomena as nothing more than a temporary combination of causes and conditions. *Prajna* is what can know the inherent emptiness of dependent origination, from which we can learn the truth of life and follow the Buddhist path to its completion. That is why the sutras say, "*prajna* is the mother of all Buddhas of the past, present, and future."

*Prajna* is traditionally separated into three types:

1. *Prajna* of true reality (實相般若)
2. *Prajna* of contemplation (觀照般若)
3. *Prajna* of skillful means (方便般若)

The *prajna* of skillful means refers to logically judging the characteristics and distinctions of phenomena. The *prajna* of contemplation means to see into the true reality of such phenomena. The power of the latter two kinds of *prajna* is projected from the *prajna* of true reality. In this sense, the *prajna* of true reality is the intrinsic nature of *prajna*, which all beings inherently possess.

The term *prajna* (transliterated as *bore*) has become popular in Chinese, but even though many use the term, few understand what it means. *Prajna* is a heightened state of awareness; and there are many different levels of *prajna*, from the *prajna* of an ordinary person to the *prajna* of a Buddha. For ordinary people, *prajna* is holding right view. For *sravakas* and *pratyekabuddhas*, *prajna* is understanding dependent origination. For bodhisattvas, *prajna* is the wisdom of emptiness. Only the *prajna* of the Buddha is true, complete *prajna*. In this sense, while an ordinary person can develop some *prajna*-wisdom by having the correct knowledge and view, only by attaining awakening and becoming a Buddha can one be truly said to have developed *prajna*.

*Prajna* is our intrinsic nature, it is the same as the Buddha nature which we all posses. *Prajna* is like the light that shines forth from our intrinsic nature and helps us to attain awakening and free ourselves from the cycle of birth and death. The quality that leads us from this shore of the cycle of birth and death to the other shore of *nirvana* is the perfection of *prajna* (*prajnaparamita*). This is the goal of Buddhist practice.

Of the Buddha's forty-nine year teaching career, he spent twenty-two of those years giving teachings on *prajna*. Such teachings are collected in the six hundred fascicles of the *Mahaprajnaparamita Sutra*, and can guide sentient beings to be free of the cycle of birth and death by realizing true reality.

*Prajna* is not something that can be explained in words. Anything that could be explained in words would simply be worldly knowledge, and not truly *prajna*. But one way to approach an understanding of *prajna* is to see it as a mirror. A perfect mirror truly reflects whatever is before it: whether a person is fat or thin, beautiful or ugly, the mirror reflects someone just as they are. In the same way, the mirror of *prajna* reflects the true nature of reality, just as it is. The problem is that the mirror of our *prajna* has been covered by the dust of our afflictions. When we engage in spiritual practice such as chanting sutras, paying homage to the Buddha, or listening to the Dharma, we progressively wipe clean the mirror of the mind. Once the mind is clear, *prajna* will manifest within.

Even if we are slandered, cursed, or criticized for no reason, *prajna*-wisdom will allow us to look upon these instances as helpful learning experiences to avert future troubles; even others'

P

reneging on our loans to them can be treated as the repayment of a karmic debt. *Prajna*-wisdom can change our lives. There is a Chinese couplet that reads:

> That same old moon before the window
> Is now transformed by the plum blossoms.

## Pratyekabuddha
緣覺
*See:* Dharma realms, ten; Mahayana and Hinayana.

## Precepts
戒
*See:* Ordination; precepts, five; precepts, eight; spiritual wealth, seven kinds of; training, threefold.

## Precepts, Eight
八關齋戒
*See also:* Precepts, five.

The *Nirvana Sutra* says, "The lay life at home is narrow and constrained like a prison, and gives rise to all affliction. The monastic life away from home is as vast as space, and strengthens all wholesome teachings." The merit of joining the monastic order is extraordinary, but not all people are equipped with the causes and conditions to do so. For this reason the Buddha implemented as a skillful means the practice of the "eight precepts," to give laypeople an opportunity to experience monastic life. Those who undertake the eight precepts gain a positive experience of renunciation and can plant the seed for undertaking the monastic life in the future.

**P**

In Chinese, the eight precepts are called *baguan zhaijie* (八關 齋戒), "eight sealed fasting precepts." *Ba* (八), "eight," simply refers to the number of precepts, while *guan* (關), "seal" refers to the act of "sealing away" eight kinds of wrongdoing to ensure that the body, speech, and mind are without fault. *Zhai* (齋), "fast," means to fast from doing anything non-virtuous, so that one only engages in virtuous conduct. *Jie* (戒), "precept," are those rules which guard against wrongdoing. The eight precepts are as follows:

### 1. Refrain from killing (不殺生)
This precept means to not violate the life of others. "Killing" includes both grave acts of killing such as taking human life, and lesser acts such as killing mice, cockroaches, ants, and the like. Wasting time or material resources is also a form of killing. However, it is important to remember that Buddhism is a religion based upon human beings, and as such the precept to refrain from killing primarily refers to the killing of human beings.

### 2. Refrain from stealing (不偷盜)
This precept means to not violate the property of others. Stealing can be defined simply as taking anything which was not given. According to the monastic rules, taking anything that is valued at more than five coins (based upon the currency of the kingdom of Magadha during the Buddha's time) is a violation of the precept. Taking minor articles in public places like paper, envelopes, and pens or borrowing things without returning them are considered lesser offenses.

### 3. Refrain from sexual conduct (不淫)
In the five precepts, the third precept is to refrain from sexual misconduct, which refers to any carnal act between a man and a

P

woman outside of marriage. However, within the eight precepts, the third precept is not to refrain from sexual *misconduct*, but from sexual conduct of any kind. This is why those who are participating in an eight precept retreat are called "celibate *upasakas* and *upasikas.*"

### 4. Refrain from lying（不妄語）

This precept not only includes not speaking words that are false, but also includes not speaking words that are divisive, harsh, or idle. Even knowing something but failing to speak up is considered lying. However, among these the worst offense is to lie about one's spiritual attainment. Additionally, criticizing others, particularly members of the monastic order, is a serious violation of the precepts.

### 5. Refrain from consuming intoxicants（不飲酒）

This precept means to refrain from any drug that causes one to lose rationality and damage one's moral character. In addition to alcohol this includes marijuana, narcotics, barbiturates, and hallucinogens.

### 6. Refrain from wearing personal adornments
（不著華鬘香油塗身）

This precept means to wear clothing that is very simple. Not wearing clothing that is dazzling or beautiful and not applying perfume or makeup is conducive to concentrating the mind and establishing mindfulness. By turning away from greed and attachment in this way, one will progress along the path of purity.

### 7. Refrain from partaking in music and dancing（不歌舞觀聽）

This precept means to not enter places of sensual entertainment, to protect our physical, verbal, and mental karma from causing trouble. The scent of perfume can bewitch the mind, and the pleasures of song and dance can sap the will. Such things are not suitable for spiritual practice.

### 8. Refrain from sleeping in fine beds （不坐臥高廣大牀）

This precept means to refrain from a rich material life. "Not sleeping in fine beds" is one example of striving for material simplicity, and not craving after material enjoyment. By practicing this and persevering, one will become aligned with the noble path.

Another additional stipulation of the eight precepts is to not eat out of the prescribed hours for monastics, which means not eating after noontime.

The eight precepts are typically observed for a day and a night. Although the time is short, if one practices well, it can bring infinite, limitless merit. Since undertaking the eight precepts often requires leaving one's home to stay at a temple, it is also sometimes called *jinzhu lüyi* (近住律儀), "living in observance."

## Precepts, Five
## 五戒

The five precepts are fundamental to being human and are the basis for attaining Buddhahood. What are the five precepts?

### 1. Refrain from killing （不殺）

This means to do no harm to sentient beings, and not to violate the lives of others.

P

*2. Refrain from stealing*（不盜）
This means not to take things that are not yours, and not to steal from others.

*3. Refrain from sexual misconduct*（不邪淫）
This means not to upset family harmony, and not to break the moral standards of ethical relationships.

*4. Refrain from lying*（不妄語）
This means not to falsify or distort the truth when speaking, and not to say things that hurt others.

*5. Refrain from consuming intoxicants*（不飲酒）
This means not to crave stimulating foods, and not to consume alcohol or tobacco that impairs judgment.

All the criminals in jail have, by in large, broken one of the five precepts. Those who have committed such acts as murder, assault, battery, and poisoning, have broken the precept against killing. Those who have committed such acts as robbery, stealing, extortion, fraud, and bribery, have broken the precept against stealing. Those who have done such things as breaking up families, upsetting social morality, breaking up marriages, polygamy, and rape, have broken the precept against sexual misconduct. Those who have committed such acts as fraud, instigating criminal activity, libel, defamation of character, and spreading rumors to confound the public, have broken the precept against lying. Those who traffic in opium, inject morphine, illegally manufacture alcohol and tobacco products, and other such illicit substances, have broken the precept against intoxicants.

Those who are new to Buddhism often approach the precepts with a sense of fear. They think that upholding the precepts means that they can't do this, or they can't do that, and that their lives will become constrained. But the precepts are there simply to prevent us from doing wrong. Not only are they not restrictive, but they carry with them a sense of freedom. This freedom comes from not interfering with or disturbing others. To uphold the precepts we must regulate the body and mind so that we do not violate the lives of others.

Buddhism's five precepts are similar to the five cardinal virtues of Confucianism: "benevolence" comes from not killing, "righteousness" comes from not stealing, "propriety" comes from not committing sexual misconduct, "honesty" comes from not lying, and "wisdom" comes from not consuming intoxicants. Observing the precepts can put an end to our faults and increase our blessings, and will help us to become better people and advance upon the spiritual path.

## Pure Land
## 淨土
*See*: Maitreya Bodhisattva; namo amitofo; noble ones of the West, three; om mani padme hum; schools of Chinese Buddhism, eight; supports, three.

## Pure Land School
## 淨土宗
*See*: Schools of Chinese Buddhism, eight; supports, three.

## Purna
## 富樓那
*See*: Disciples, ten great.

# Purva-videha
## 東勝身洲

*See*: Continents, four great.

# Q

## Qualities, Ten
## 十如是

The Skillful Means chapter in the *Lotus Sutra* states: "The Dharma which the Buddha has awakened to is the preeminent and unprecedented Dharma that is difficult to understand. Only another Buddha can fathom the true reality of all phenomena, given that all phenomena are endowed with such a form, such a nature, such an entity, such ability, such activity, such a cause, such conditions, such direct effects, such indirect effects, and is as such complete from beginning to end."

As stated in the above passage, those who wish to understand the true nature of phenomena should master the ten qualities of form, nature, entity, ability, activity, cause, condition, direct effect, indirect effect, and completion from beginning to end. In Chinese these ten are known as the "ten qualities of suchness" (十如是). All phenomena are endowed with these ten qualities. They are:

### 1. Form（相）

"Form" refers to the outward, visible appearance of an object. For example, every human being has his or her own form and animals all have their forms as well. All wholesome and unwholesome conduct as it manifests externally also has a given form.

### 2. Nature（性）

"Nature" refers to a thing's internal, fundamental principle which is not outwardly visible. All phenomena differ from one another in terms of their nature. For example, wood has the nature of combustibility, metal has the nature of hardness, water has the nature of wetness, wind has the nature of circulation, and so on.

### 3. Entity（體）

This quality refers to the substance of sentient beings. All phenomena in the universe have mind as their entity, and it is from this entity that everything arises from and exists upon.

### 4. Ability（力）

"Ability" refers to how a given thing's powers can be applied to carry out some function. For example, sand, gravel, and cement have the ability to be used to make walls.

### 5. Activity（作）

"Activity" refers to the generation of the karma of body, speech, and mind.

### 6. Cause（因）

"Cause" refers to karmic causes generated by body, speech, and mind that will result in karmic effects.

## 7. Condition（緣）

"Condition" refers to those minor causes that support the major causes during the operation of causation. For example, for the growth of a flower, the seed is the cause, while the soil, nutrients, fertilizer, air, human effort, and so on would all be considered conditions. A flower can bloom and generate more seeds only when these supporting conditions are in place.

## 8. Direct Effect（果）

This quality refers to karmic effects based on past habitual tendencies such as which of the six realms of existence one is reborn into.

## 9. Indirect Effect（報）

This quality refers to karmic effects that result in pleasure or pain incurred in future lifetimes.

## 10. Complete from Beginning to End（本末究竟等）

This quality encompasses the previous nine from the quality of form to the quality of indirect effect, and shows that each is produced through a combination of causes and conditions. As this entire process is composed of causes and conditions, each quality is empty. Since all phenomena are completely empty from beginning to end, this allows for the universal equality of all phenomena.

The significance of the ten qualities of suchness is to show the connection between each of the qualities: if a given phenomena's form is unwholesome, then its indirect effects will also be unwholesome; whereas if the form is wholesome the indirect effect will also be wholesome. In this way the ten qualities are consistent, and can be applied to the ten dharma realms. Not only can these ten qualities account for the Buddha with his perfected merit and wisdom, but they can account for the suffering of those beings in hell. Each of the ten dharma realms features these ten qualities, resulting in one hundred such combinations. Additionally, since each of the ten dharma realms is contained within the ten dharma realms, this results in one thousand such combinations. This structure provides the basis for the important Tiantai doctrine of the "hundred dharma realms with their one thousand qualities."

## Questions of the Buddha, Four
## 四問

Just as when the sun is setting in the west its light is most beautiful, before a Buddha enters final *nirvana* he radiates a light that is even more rare than usual.

On the 15th day of the second lunar month in his eightieth year, the Buddha's compassionate countenance manifested an unimaginable radiance; one that was ever more perfect, pure, and magnificent than usual. The gathered disciples wept silently as the Buddha was about to enter final *nirvana*. Wishing to preserve the true Dharma into the future, the disciples agreed that the Venerable Ananda would ask the Buddha four questions.

Ananda respectfully knelt beside the Buddha and asked, "Lord Buddha, during your time on earth, all of us relied upon you as our teacher. After your final *nirvana*, who should we rely on as our teacher?"

The Buddha replied compassionately, "After my final *nirvana*, you should all rely upon the monastic precepts as your teacher."

Q

Ananda then asked his second question, "Lord Buddha, during your time on earth, all of us relied upon you for our abiding. After your final *nirvana*, where should we abide?"

"Ananda, after my final *nirvana*, you all should abide in the four bases of mindfulness. The four bases of mindfulness are: contemplate the impurities of the body, contemplate the suffering of feeling, contemplate the impermanence of the mind, and contemplate the non-selfhood of phenomena."

Ananda asked his next question, "Lord Buddha, during your time on earth, you were the one who pacified vicious individuals. After your final *nirvana*, how should we deal with vicious people?"

"Ananda, the best was to pacify vicious people is to not associate with them. Just disregard them; that is all."

Feeling extreme gratitude for the Buddha's compassion, Ananda asked his last question, "Lord Buddha, during your time on earth, it has been easy for all of us to believe the teachings that you spoke. After your final *nirvana*, how can we ensure that people will have faith in your teachings?"

"When recounting my teachings, remember to state, 'thus have I heard,' to show that you, Ananda, heard what I said."

The great, exalted Buddha then quietly entered final *nirvana*, but the Buddha's Dharmakaya will remain in this world forever.

# R

## Rahula
羅睺羅

*See also:* Arhats, eighteen; disciples, ten great.

## Realization
證

*See also: Nirvana;* practice, four stages of.

## Realms of Existence, Six
六道輪迴

*See also:* Dharma realms, ten; heaven; hell; human realm.

Where do we come from when we are born? Where do we go after we die? These are some of the great mysteries of life, and only the Buddha can solve these mysteries.

Some people believe that one becomes a ghost upon death, while others believe that after one dies there is nothing. Both of these are mistaken views, for after death one does not necessarily become a ghost, nor is there nothing at all. Whether one is a man

**R**

or a woman, enjoys high or low status, is a human or non-human being, all are trapped in the cycle of birth and death. There are some beings who will dwell for some time in heaven, while others will live for some time in the hells. Some may be reborn as humans, and others are reborn as animals. No matter who you are, as long as you are part of the cycle of birth and death, you are within what are called the "six realms of existence." These six realms are the heavenly realm, the human realm, the *asura* realm, the animal realm, the hungry ghost realm, and the hell realm.

### 1. Heavenly Realm（天道）

Those being reborn in this realm have the greatest merit of the six. The physical bodies of heavenly beings are also extremely large, with the shortest being nine hundred feet high and the tallest being some 256,000 kilometers in height. They also live extraordinarily long lives, with the shortest being equivalent to 900 years and the longest being 80,000 *kalpas*. Heavenly beings enjoy extraordinary pleasure, with some enjoying sense pleasures and others the joys of meditation. There is no chaos or disorder, nor is there sorrow or pain. Heavenly beings have high levels of meditative concentration, but when their lives come to an end, their meditative concentration is exhausted. The heavenly realm is the most magnificent among the six realms of existence.

### 2. Human Realm（人道）

In the human realm, some people are happy and some people suffer. Some people are wholesome and some are unwholesome. The human realm has both pleasure and pain, for it is an intermediary place where life has its ups and downs. However, the human realm is also the best place among the six realms of existence for cultivation. This is why the Buddha arose in the human realm and attained awakening in the human realm. For this reason, the human realm is the most praiseworthy.

### 3. Asura Realm (阿修羅道)

The *asura* realm is for those sentient beings who love war. *Asuras* are beings who have similar blessings to heavenly beings, but lack their virtue. One can certainly find beings with such a warlike disposition among the other five realms.

### 4. Animal Realm (畜生道)

There is the greatest variety of beings within the animal realm. Some fly in the sky, some walk on the land, some live in the water, and some bury themselves beneath the earth. Another way to classify animals is by how many legs they have: some animals are legless like earthworms, some have two legs like fowl, some have four legs like beasts of burden, and some have many legs like insects. The lives are animals are usually short, and their intelligence is typically meager. They brutally kill one another as they gobble each other up; the big fish eat the little fish and the large insects eat the smaller ones. There are some animals that are even raised by human beings for slaughter, such as cattle and horses, who are driven around by the whip and the lash. Such is truly a fate worth pitying.

### 5. Hungry Ghost Realm (餓鬼道)

There are three different kinds of beings that live in the hungry ghost realm: hungry ghosts without wealth, hungry ghosts with some wealth, and hungry ghosts with much wealth. In terms of their physical qualities, there are ghosts with flaming mouths, those with needle-like mouths, those with odorous mouths, those with needle-like hair, those with odorous hair, those with goiters, those that subsist on what is discarded, those that subsist on what is lost, and those that are powerful. Hungry ghosts suffer from hunger and thirst, and as such they are deserving of our pity.

### 6. Hell Realm (地獄道)

The hell realm is the most painful of the six realms of existence. Some of the beings who are reborn here suffer from the intense burning infernos of the eight hot hells, while others suffer from the freezing cold of the eight cold hells. Some experience the suffering of the isolated hells, while others go through the miseries of the adjacent hells.

Within the six realms of existence, we reside in the human realm, and are able to see those beings in the animal realm. We cannot see beings in the heavenly realm, *asura* realm, hell realm, or hungry ghost realm. *Asuras* also reside in the heavenly realm, and hungry ghosts also reside in the hell realm—so one might ask, where is heaven and where is hell?

One way to answer that question is to say that heaven is in heaven and hell is in hell. That is certainly one way to put it. However, we can also see that heaven and hell exist in the human realm. Just look at how many people in the world are enjoying heaven-like happiness. And when one sees fresh fish and meat at the market, is this not the same as the suffering of hell? In a very real way, the six realms of existence exist within our own minds.

# Rebirth in the Pure Land, Nine Grades of
# 九品往生

Pure Land can be practiced at many different levels. Whether you are a great sage well-versed in the Tripitaka or just an ordinary person, as long as you concentrate on reciting Amitabha Buddha's name with pure devotion then you will be welcomed by Amitabha Buddha and his noble assembly and be reborn in the Pure Land. However, due to difference in the level of cultivation, there are different levels of rebirth in the Pure Land. According to the *Contemplation Sutra*, there are nine levels of rebirth in the Pure Land, known as the "nine grades of rebirth":

*1. The Top of the Highest Grade* (上品上生)
To be reborn here requires generating true sincerity, profound mind, and the dedicatory vow (the "three states of mind"). One must also observe all the precepts and rules, read and recite Mahayana sutras, and practice the six objects of mindfulness. If one can do so with perseverance and courage, then upon death, one will be greeted by Amitabha Buddha, Avalokitesvara Bodhisattva, and Mahasthamaprapta Bodhisattva, an infinite number of manifested Buddhas, thousands of *bhiksus,* and boundless heavenly beings bearing a *vajra* throne to welcome one to the Pure Land.

*2. The Middle of the Highest Grade* (上品中生)
One who is reborn at this grade has developed the three states of mind described above, but does not read and recite the Mahayana sutras. However, one does understand the supreme truth and has deep faith in cause and effect. Upon death, one will be greeted by Amitabha Buddha, Avalokitesvara Bodhisattva, Mahasthamaprapta

Bodhisattva, one thousand manifested Buddhas, and a boundless retinue bearing a golden throne, reaching out in welcome.

### 3. The Bottom of the Highest Grade (上品下生)

One reborn at this grade is able to develop the three states of mind, but does not read and recite Mahayana sutras, nor understand their meaning, and only believes in cause and effect. Upon death, one will be greeted by Amitabha Buddha, Avalokitesvara Bodhisattva, Mahasthamaprapta Bodhisattva, and five hundred manifested Buddhas and bodhisattvas bearing golden lotus flowers to welcome one to the Pure Land.

### 4. The Top of the Intermediary Grade (中品上生)

One reborn at this grade observes the five precepts and the eight precepts. In addition to practicing all precepts, he does not commit the five great violations and is free from all unwholesomeness. Upon death, one is surrounded by Amitabha Buddha and his retinue of *bhiksus*, who will project a golden light. Upon seeing such light, one will feel great happiness, and will see oneself sitting on a lotus flower throne.

### 5. The Middle of the Intermediary Grade (中品中生)

One reborn at this grade has upheld the eight precepts for one day and one night, the *sramanera* precepts for one day and one night, or the full *bhiksu* precepts for one day and one night, and has maintained proper comportment. Upon death, one will see the golden light projected by Amitabha Buddha and his retinue as they come in welcome, bearing lotus flowers of the seven treasures.

## 6. The Bottom of the Intermediary Grade（中品下生）

One reborn at this grade has given loving care to their parents and practiced benevolence and righteousness. As death approaches, they encounter good Dharma friends who will teach them about the joys of Amitabha Buddha's Pure Land and the forty-eight vows of Dharmakara Bodhisattva. With perfect faith and joy, they will obtain rebirth in the Pure Land.

R

## 7. The Top of the Lowest Grade（下品下生）

One reborn of this grade is a sentient beings who commits all manner of negative karma, slanders the *vaipulya* sutras, and engages in wrongdoing with no sense of remorse. As death approaches, if such people encounter good Dharma friends who read them the Mahayana sutras, it shall drive away the negative karma of a thousand *kalpas*. If they teach them how to join their palms and chant "Namo Amitofo," it will drive away the negative karma equal to five billion lifetimes in the cycle of birth and death. Upon death, Amitabha Buddha will send manifestations of Buddhas, Avalokitesvara Bodhisattva, and Mahasthamaprapta Bodhisattva to greet them.

## 8. The Middle of the Lowest Grade（下品中生）

One reborn of this grade violates the five precepts, eight precepts, and the *bhiksu* precepts. Such people steal the property of the temple and speak of the Dharma with impure intentions. All of this is done with no remorse; rather they adorn themselves with wrongdoing. As death approaches, such people will surely face the fires of hell, but if they meet good Dharma friends who praise the ten powers of Amitabha Buddha's moral influence, they can be freed of their serious wrongdoing that would lead to eight billion *kalpas* in the cycle of birth and death. Thereafter the first of hell will be transformed into a cool breeze that carries a cascade of heavenly flowers, with the manifestations of Buddhas and bodhisattvas upon these flowers to greet them.

### 9. The Bottom of the Lowest Grade (下品下生)

One reborn of this grade commits the five great violations and the ten unwholesome actions, and involves themselves in all manner of unvirtuous behavior. As death approaches, if such people meet with good Dharma friends they can receive various forms of comfort. Through the teaching of the wondrous Dharma, they can learn how to recite Amitabha Buddha's name. By taking these lessons to heart and reciting the name continuously to fulfill the ten recitations of "Namo Amitofo," each recitation will remove the wrongdoing of eight billion *kalpas* in the cycle of birth and death. Thereafter, they will see golden lotus flowers like the sun discs that now appear before them, welcoming them to the Pure Land.

The lowest grade mentioned above shows that even people who have done wrong during their lifetime can still obtain rebirth in the Western Pure Land, as long as they receive guidance from good Dharma friends as death approaches, so that they can perform ten recitations of Amitabha Buddha's name. However, those who try to rely upon this method and do not cultivate positive karma in their everyday lives will face all manner of danger. People can die in a million different ways and there is no way to guarantee that one will have the clarity of right mindfulness. The presence of good Dharma friends is even harder to come by. Therefore, engaging in Pure Land cultivation is the most reliable form of practice, which can only be perfected by accumulating merit on a daily basis and making the vow with profound faith.

## Refuge
## 南無

*See also*: Gem, triple.

R

When chanting the name of a Buddha, the expression *namo* often precedes the name of the Buddha. For example, someone may chant "Namo Amitofo." Some non-Buddhists misinterpret this, thinking that they hear the Buddhists chanting "No more Amitofo" or some other similar misconception. Some even mistakenly think that *namo* is the name of a Buddha. Each of these mistakes stems from a lack of understanding.

There is a Buddhist saying that, "If one is confused, go to a temple. One 'Namo Fo,' and you will attain the Buddha way." *Namo* is a Sanskrit word meaning "to show respect" or "to take refuge." Thus "Namo Amitofo" means "to respectfully take refuge in Amitabha Buddha." Taking refuge is the first step to officially becoming a Buddhist, and involves undergoing a particular ceremony.

To take "refuge" means to return, to take what has been stained and return it to its original purity. Before coming to Buddhism one may deal with worldly things with a worldly attitude, but after coming to Buddhism one deals with the matters of truth, goodness, and beauty with an attitude of truth, goodness, and beauty. The purpose of taking refuge is to direct the human mind towards the good in this way.

Taking refuge means believing in the Triple Gem of the Buddha, Dharma, and Sangha with all one's body and mind. The unsurpassed morality and wisdom of the Buddha and the

**R**

Sangha serve as our model for how to be human, while the principles revealed by the Dharma represent our standards for how to live. We rely upon the Triple Gem just as a child relies upon its mother, how the people rely upon the ruler, how the weak rely upon the strong, how the lame rely upon the staff, and how those drowning in water rely upon a boat. When our body and mind find that refuge, our life will have its support and our spirit can be uplifted.

Taking refuge is a lifelong process, and is not something that only occurs during a certain period of time. Taking refuge also involves taking refuge in all three components of the Triple Gem: the Buddha, Dharma, and Sangha. There are some people who have incorrect views about taking refuge, and thus take refuge incompletely. Some people only take refuge in one thing, such that they only venerate the Buddha, only listen to teachings, or only show respect to monastic teachers. Some people only take refuge in the first two gems, for they venerate the Buddha and chant the sutras, but they do not honor the sangha. There are still others who venerate the Buddha and listen to the Dharma, but they only honor their own teacher rather than the monastic order as a whole.

The Buddha is like a skilled physician who can cure the various different illnesses of sentient beings. The Dharma is like miraculous medicine that can reveal the correct path and show us how to free ourselves from suffering and attain happiness. The sangha is like a nurse, who can guide us to correct faith. Only the triple refuge can assure that we will be happy and peaceful in body and mind. When we take refuge, none of these elements can be missing.

After taking refuge in the Triple Gem as described above, one then takes refuge in the Triple Gem of one's intrinsic nature. They are as follows:

1. The Buddha Gem of Intrinsic Nature: Maintaining awakened awareness with every thought so that confusion does not arise.

2. The Dharma Gem of Intrinsic Nature: Holding onto correct principles in every thought so that wrong views do not arise.

3. The Sangha Gem of Intrinsic Nature: Purifying the mind with every thought so that desire for things or states does not arise.

After recognizing the Triple Gem, one's beliefs become steadfast, so that one will not practice blindly nor stray from the path.

## Reliances, Four
四依止

*See also: Prajna;* wisdom, four kinds of; wisdom, three kinds of.

Life is like a great ocean. On this shore there is pain and suffering, while on the other shore there is joy and happiness. To cross over to the other shore, one must rely on the Dharma's boat of compassion to make the trip of liberation. All those who learn Buddhism wish to be free from pain and suffering, though we come to Buddhism with different sets of causes and conditions. Though our circumstances are not the same, there should be unanimity regarding the attitude with which one learns Buddhism. There is a Buddhist teaching regarding how one should approach learning the Dharma called the "four reliances." They are:

R

## 1. Rely on the Dharma, not on individual teachers (依法不依人)

"Dharma" refers to what is true and when learning Buddhism, one should rely upon and act according to the truth. We cannot rely upon individual teachers, because each differs in their thinking and understanding. People suffer from birth, old age, sickness, and death, and thus their comings and goings and impermanent. The Dharma, on the other hand, has remained unchanged from the past to the present, and is forever renewing itself throughout time. When learning the path we must rely upon the Dharma rather than any individual. Do not be one of those people who likes to socialize with their friends by going to various temples, for such people are enveloped in a web of social ties and in the end cannot choose any real faith. The Buddha shows that we should rely on the Dharma through pursuing faith, understanding, practice, and realization. We must not lose faith because of the good or bad qualities of individual teachers, nor should we follow only a certain temple or monastic group, while ignoring the whole Dharma.

## 2. Rely on wisdom, not on knowledge (依智不依識)

In this context, "wisdom" refers to pure *prajna*-wisdom, while "knowledge" refers to the learning that arises from distinctions made by the six sense consciousnesses. Because of the illusory nature of worldly phenomena, all that is recognized and distinguished by the eye, ear, nose, tongue, body, and mind changes from moment to moment. Therefore it is ultimately not very thorough to use knowledge based upon our consciousnesses' ability to make distinctions about phenomena among the vast multiplicity of form and shape.

On the other hand, *prajna*-wisdom is undefiled, and functions like a perfect mirror, able to reflect all worldly phenomena just as they are. Like a shining bright light, *prajna*-wisdom allows us to see our own original nature. Therefore, not only should we be sure to "rely on wisdom, not on knowledge," but also endeavor to transform our consciousness into wisdom. In this way, we will not be confused by the illusions of the world.

### 3. Rely on the meaning, not on the words (依義不依語)

Language and writing are convenient means for us to obtain knowledge and ascertain the truth. Such things are like labels; they are tools we use to explain principles, but they are not the essence of the truth itself. In our daily lives, language and writing can serve as a bridge for people to communicate with one another, but they also make it very possible for misunderstandings to arise due to misinterpretation, loss of context, or differences in language or expression. If this is true even for mundane things, it is certainly true when applied to something sublime and profound like the Dharma.

That is why the Chan School says of itself that it is "not based upon the written word." Huineng (638-713 CE), the Sixth Patriarch of the Chan School, even said, "The wondrous teachings of the Buddhas are not within words." Such sublime truths and practices cannot be communicated solely through relying on written words. Therefore, in learning Buddhism we should understand the Dharma in terms of its meaning, rather than becoming involved in conjecture, disputation, or attachment over the language. Otherwise language becomes an obstacle, and we will drift farther and farther away from the path.

*4. Rely on the ultimate truth, not on relative truth*（依了義不依不了義）

There is a distinction within the Dharma between relative truth and ultimate truth. Relative truths are known as "skillful means," while ultimate truth is absolute. The Buddha used skillful means in order to adapt his teaching to the spiritual capacity of his audience, but it is important that we do not treat these skillful means as ultimate truth. Ultimate truth is that which corresponds to the Buddha mind. Therefore, when learning Buddhism we should rely on the ultimate truth of the Buddha mind, rather than the relative truth of skillful means.

These four reliances are principles that Buddhists should know and put into practice. The *Diamond Sutra* says, "My teachings should be understood to be like a raft. If even the Dharma must be let go of [upon reaching the other shore], what about what is not the Dharma?" The Buddha gave various teachings to help sentient beings find their Buddha nature, just as a pointing finger can help us to see the moon in the night sky. In practicing Buddhism, we remember to see the moon that the finger is pointing at, rather than becoming attached to the finger that points the way. If we were to become attached to the finger it would block our vision, such that we would no longer be able to see the moon.

# Retreat
# 結夏安居

*See also:* Precepts, eight.

Within orthodox Buddhist monastic traditions, there are rules set in place to encourage isolation, restrict movement, and create a

R

quiet atmosphere so that members of the monastic order can focus on their practice. Such rules are adapted from the monastic retreat system instituted by the Buddha.

During the time of the Buddha, the rainy season in India lasted for three months. The Buddha set aside that period from the sixteenth day of the fourth lunar month to the fifteenth day of the seventh lunar month as a retreat period. During this three month period, members of the monastic order were not permitted to travel, and would instead stay in one place to practice diligently. In Chinese, the first day of the retreat period is called *jiexia* (結夏), and the concluding day is called *xiexia* (解夏). This retreat period is also called *zuoxia*, (坐夏) "summer meditation."

Retreat periods were most commonly held during the summer, but a similar period of retreat is sometimes held from the sixteenth day of the tenth lunar month through the fifteenth day of the first lunar month, known as the "winter retreat." There is no set location where such retreats must take place: a small room, the foot of a tree, a cave, or a remote hermitage will do. However, according to the *Five-Part Vinaya*, one should not observe the retreat period in a place lacking emergency help, due to the possibility of attacks from wild animals like poisonous snakes, tigers, and other such dangerous animals.

The monastic retreat is a period of restricted movement, and those monastics who are on retreat are strictly forbidden from leaving the monastery. The reasoning is that during the rainy season, most plants, trees, and insects are undergoing the reproductive process, and that travel beyond the monastery may lead to harming these living beings by mistakenly stepping on them and thereby bring ridicule to the monastic order. At the same time, the retreat period is a time for for practice, so travel is forbidden.

If a monastic needs to leave in the middle of a retreat, he or she must ask for leave and obtain permission before doing so. Among Buddhist monasteries, those of the Vinaya School give special attention to the retreat period.

At the end of the retreat, the community performs four rituals: repentance, dispersing the sacred boundaries (*sima*), renewing the sacred boundaries, and the bestowing of robe cloth. The repentance ritual is conducted after the monastic retreat has been completed; participants reflect upon their conduct during the retreat. If anyone has broken the rules, they confess their faults to the community, as each repents to the other. The day this ritual is performed is known as *zizi* (自恣), "day of repentance." As all the members of the monastic community have newly purified bodies and minds, many have attained awakening during the period following the day of repentance. This made the Buddha joyful, and as such the day is also known as *fo huanxi ri* (佛歡喜日), "day of the Buddha's joy."

It was also at the time following the summer retreat that the Buddha directed Maudgalyayana to prepare all manner of food and drink to be offered to the monastic community, so that the merit of this act could help Maudgalyayana ease his mother's suffering in the realm of hungry ghosts where she had been reborn. This was the origin of the Ullambana Dharma service.

The system of monastic retreat has been observed in China since the Latter Qin dynasty (384-417 CE). Though the system was adopted, not every aspect of it has been practiced as it was in India due to the differences in physical locale and social custom. For example, one reason for the prohibition against unnecessary travel during the retreat period is to protect the mind from distraction. The monastic retreat in China has thus become a more solitary affair, in which one practices on one's own to attain awakening, and cultivates to ever greater depths to quiet the self. Today, most Buddhist colleges operate year-round as if it were a retreat period.

## Right Dharma, Age of
## 正法
*See:* Ages of the Dharma, three.

R

## Right Effort
## 四正勤
*See also:* Path, noble eightfold.

To have a positive spirit and strive for improvement is what is meant by "right effort" in Buddhism. There are four kinds of right effort, and these are called the "four right efforts."

*1. Prevent Unwholesome States (未生的惡法，使它不生)*
We should prevent thoughts from arising that would violate the precepts, much less any action that may violate them. We must apply effort to removing our afflictions, purifying our desire, abandoning wrong views, and ridding ourselves of attachment.

"Unwholesome states" refers to unwholesome thoughts, unwholesome words, and unwholesome deeds. We should apply effort to prevent unwholesome thoughts of greed, anger, and ignorance from arising; unwholesome words like lies, harsh words, divisive words, and idle chatter from being spoken; and unwholesome actions like killing, stealing, and sexual misconduct from being committed. This is the first right effort: preventing unwholesome states that have not yet arisen from arising.

## 2. End Unwholesome States (已生的惡法，使它斷除)

People are not perfect sages, and there is no one among us who is without fault. We are all ordinary people, and who among us can forget their feelings? The distractions of our feelings, thoughts, and perceptions and the provocations of greed, anger, and ignorance cause us to do all kinds of wrong and create negative karma every day, such that our unwholesomeness grows more and more. This is like an elephant stuck in the mud; the more it thrashes, the deeper it sinks.

At times like these, we must keep a cool head, and apply our effort to remove such unwholesome states by the root. If we are diligent, we can cut away all unwholesome thoughts, unwholesome words, and unwholesome deeds with the sword of wisdom. This is the second right effort: ending unwholesome states that have already arisen.

## 3. Develop Wholesome States (未生的善法，令它生起)

Even the best of fields will not yield a harvest if not planted; and even the wisest sage is unfit if he is lacking in virtue. We should apply our effort to develop faith and commitment which has yet to be developed, and generate compassion that has yet to be generated.

What are wholesome states? Not killing, but having benevolence. Not committing sexual misconduct, but acting with propriety. Not stealing, but being righteous. Not lying, but being honest. Not consuming intoxicants, but having wisdom. Giving what brings joy to others and offering assistance to those in need. When we plant the seeds of goodness in the world's field of merit, though there is no expectation of gain, there will naturally be a fruitful harvest. This is the third right effort: developing wholesome states that have not yet arisen.

## 4. *Strengthen Wholesome States* (已生的善法，令它增長)

We should apply effort to strengthen the sprouts of faith and commitment, expand our feelings of compassion, and purify our practice and virtue. By not expecting anything in return, one will not regret any act of generosity. By not expecting any praise, one can endure any slander or attack. By not expecting to be free from illness, one will develop constitution that comes from enduring the hardship of illness. By acting in this way, our wholesome qualities will grow stronger. This is the fourth right effort: strengthening wholesome states that have already arisen.

There is a saying, "Even if some gold washed in with the tide, one will still need to rise early to get it." We should not allow ourselves to do the wrong thing because the consequences will only be minor, for even drops of water can cut through a stone in time. Nor should we fail to do the right thing when the reward is very small, for even a tall oak grows from a tiny acorn. One must be diligent to achieve victory over unwholesomeness, for only then can what is wholesome flourish. There is no shorter path to attaining Buddhahood than the path of right effort.

# Robe and Bowl
# 三衣一缽

The earliest members of the Buddhist monastic order were represented by their "three robes and one bowl." No matter where they wandered, they always kept their three robes and bowl with them. Each of the three robes has a different name and purpose, and they include the *sanghati*, the *uttarasanga*, and the *anatarvasaka*. Collectively the three robes are known as the *kasaya*, which is Sanskrit for "mute color," "off color," or "dyed color." The uses for the three robes are as follows:

### 1. Sanghati (僧伽梨)

Also called the "monastic robe," "great robe," "doubled robe," "mottled robe," "outer robe," and "robe for going to palaces and villages." The *sanghati* is worn when leaving the monastery or during solemn ceremonies. Examples of such events include visiting the royal palace, entering a village, gathering alms, ascending the dais to teach the Dharma, or debating non-Buddhists. The *sanghati* is made by sewing together between nine to twenty-five strips of cloth, and is thus also known as the "robe of nine strips."

### 2. Uttarasanga (鬱多羅僧)

Also known as the "upper robe," "robe of seven strips," "intermediate robe," and "assembly robe," the *uttarasanga* is worn when attending lectures and during chanting ceremonies, as well as fortnightly recitations of the monastic precepts. It is stitched together from seven pieces of cloth.

### 3. Anatarvasaka (安陀會)

Also known as the "inner robe," "robe of five strips," and "nighttime robe," the *anatarvasaka* is worn all day and when going to sleep. It is made by stitching together five strips of cloth.

After Buddhism was introduced to China, due to factors relating to customs and climate, monastics began to wear the three robes only during Dharma services and other related Buddhist activities. The Chinese monastics opted for the more utilitarian Chinese-style long gown for everyday wear.

Each of the three robes is made by first cutting cloth into patches and then later stitching them together. This custom originated during the time of the Buddha when the Buddha remarked to Ananda upon passing some rice paddy fields that the Buddhas of the past wore robes that resembled the patchwork pattern of the rice paddies. Thus, the monastics' robes were made to feature the pattern, as well.

R

The three robes are made by sewing the cloth patches into squares of four patches each to resemble rice fields, and are also called "field of merit" robes because they offer the faithful the opportunity to plant merit. The patchwork design on the three robes provides additional advantages: 1) it designates the robes as religious garments that are not to be used for other purposes, 2) it prevents monastics from coveting the robes, and 3) it prevents the robes from being stolen by others.

According to the *Treasury of Meanings Sutra*, the monastic robes grant ten benefits to those who wear them:

1. You will be guided toward *bodhi*.
2. You will only reside in the heavenly or human realms.
3. Your parents will pay homage to you.
4. *Nagas* will sacrifice themselves for you.
5. *Nagas* will wrap themselves in it to protect themselves from danger.
6. Kings will honor you and give rise to faith.
7. Sentient beings will worship you.
8. *Raksas* will venerate you.
9. Heavenly beings and *nagas* will protect you.
10. You will be able to attain Buddhahood.

R

In his *Ritual for the Preface to the Brahma Net Sutra's Bodhisattva Precepts*, Chan Master Yongming Yanshou (904-975 CE) tells of how Utpalavarna Bhikkuni, before she was ordained, once draped some monastic robes over her shoulders in jest, and owing to these causes and conditions she was able to happen upon where the Buddha was dwelling. There she joined the monastic order and became an arhat. This gives some indication of how venerable the monastic robes are.

The bowl is the eating implement of the monastic order, and it is carried while gathering alms. In the same way that monastics are known for being worthy of the support of heavenly and human beings, the bowl, too, represents a "field of merit." The bowl is also called the "proper vessel," for it is proper in three ways: 1) it is the proper color, in that a bowl must be a dark color that does not give rise to attachment, 2) it is the proper material, in that it is constructed from a coarse material that does give rise to desire, and 3) it holds the proper amount, in that one may eat the right amount of food such that one can be content and not covetous.

The three robes and bowl symbolize the purity and moral character of the monastic community. Emperor Shunzhi of the Qing dynasty (r. 1664-1661 CE) composed a verse praising monastic life as follows:

> Food for all the monasteries in the world is piled
> > as high as a mountain,
> Whenever you go with your alms bowl there is
> > food to eat.
> Gold and jade are not dear,
> Only the monastic's robe is hard to wear.

# S

## Saha World
五濁惡世

*See also*: Human realm.

The sutras say, "Only excessive desire leads to birth in this Saha world; only a firm vow can lead to birth in the Pure Land." *Saha* in Sanskrit, or *suopo* (娑婆) in Chinese refers to our world; the world in which Sakyamuni Buddha, the founder of Buddhism, teaches the Dharma. *Saha* means "endurance," for although this world is tormented by suffering, human beings have the power to endure it. According to the *Amitabha Sutra*, the Saha world degenerates in five ways:

### 1. Kalpa Degeneration （劫濁）
At one time, human beings could live for 84,000 years. But as the human mind became increasingly brutish and morality declined, every hundred years or so the average human life span became shorter and shorter. As this *kalpa* continues, the average human life span will eventually reduce to thirty years, and the world will

be beset by a calamity of famine. When the average human life span is twenty years, there will be a calamity of pestilence, and when it has reduced to ten years there will be a calamity of war which will bring harm to all sentient beings.

### 2. View Degeneration（見濁）
The Age of Right Dharma and the Age of Semblance Dharma have already passed. The world has degenerated into the Age of Declining Dharma, in which sentient beings increasingly hold wrong views, such that they do not know how to follow the wholesome path.

### 3. Affliction Degeneration（煩惱濁）
As sentient beings pursue the five desires and the six sense objects, they continue to build the afflictions of greed, anger, ignorance, pride, and doubt, which trouble the body and mind.

### 4. Sentient Being Degeneration（眾生濁）
As the understanding of sentient beings has degenerated, their minds have become dominated by affliction such that they no longer honor their parents, do not cultivate virtue, do not cut off nonvirtue, and do not fear the effects of negative karma. Because of this their positive karmic effects decrease and their negative karmic effects increase.

### 5. Life-span Degeneration（命濁）
As mentioned above, due to the their increasingly negative karma, the average life span of sentient beings has degenerated from 84,000 years in the ancient past to today, when it is rare for one to live to be 100.

As recorded in the *Vimalakirti Sutra*, at one time Sariputra asked the Buddha, "All the other Buddha lands are of such incomparable purity. Why is the realm that you teach in so foul and polluted?"

The Buddha then pressed his toe into the earth, and in a moment the four great continents manifested before their eyes, but now there were beautiful golden rivers, burgeoning trees, blooming flowers, and soft grass. The Buddha said, "This is my land. The unbearably polluted and base realm that you see is a manifestation of the karma of sentient beings."

The Buddha manifested that Saha world to bring liberation to sentient beings, while sentient beings are reborn here due to the pull of their karma. Due to the differences in the karma of each individual their share of suffering or happiness, fortune or misfortune will also vary. Each being's appearance, intelligence, life span, and talents are also unique, depending on their built up positive and negative karma.

During the Buddha's time, King Bimbisara of Magadha was usurped by his wicked son Ajatasatru. The prince imprisoned and tortured his father. King Bimbisara was deeply affected by the blight of the Saha world, and at the apex of his pain and hopelessness, he prayed to the Buddha with great devotion. In response the Buddha taught the Pure Land method to the king and queen, and opened up a new window of hope for the sentient beings of this Saha world.

The Buddha said that the sentient beings of the Saha world have a great propensity for listening, and that all learning proceeds from listening and memorizing. Buddhists must enter *samadhi* by hearing, thinking, and practice. That is why there is a Buddhist saying: "the more one hears, the more it becomes ingrained."

The Saha world is full of suffering, but this does not mean there is no happiness whatsoever. Suffering is just more plentiful than happiness. To live means one will bear the suffering of birth, old age, sickness, death, separation from loved ones, being near loathsome people, not getting what one wants, and the five aggregates. One must also bear hunger, thirst, cold, heat, slander, condemnation, false accusation, injustice, humiliation, frustration, and even natural and man-made disasters.

In this human journey so full of hardship, if one can be at peace with the realization that living means bearing all sorts of pain and suffering, then one has the "patience for life." The next step is to live according to the Dharma, so that one can be amidst suffering but be able to transform it through wisdom, this is called the "patience for phenomena." Ultimately, if one is able to apply dependent origination and know that all phenomena lack an independent nature, that they are empty, such that one transcends patience itself, this is called the "patience for the non-arising of phenomena." When one has the supreme, perfect wisdom of this level of patience, one can transform this Saha world here and now into the Pure Land.

## Samadhi
三摩地

*See also*: Heaven; path, noble eightfold; perfections, six; stopping and seeing meditation.

Buddhism is a religion of wisdom, and wisdom comes from listening to the teachings, thinking about their meaning, and practicing according to the principles. Similarly, there is a saying in Buddhism that "one enters *samadhi* by means of listening, thinking, and practicing."

*Samadhi,* transliterated in Chinese as *sanmodi* (三摩地) or *san-mei* (三昧), is a Sanskrit word meaning "holding oneself in equanimity" or "right meditative concentration." "Equanimity" refers to the peace and harmony one attains beyond the ups and downs of one's mind; and "holding" refers to concentrating the mind in one state. This condition of keeping the mind focused in a single state without distraction is also called "one-pointedness of the mind."

There are two types of meditative concentration: meditative concentration that is innate and meditative concentration obtained through cultivation. Innate meditative concentration refers to the meditative concentration obtained by heavenly beings born into the form and formless realms due to their wholesome karma accumulated during previous lives. For those born in our realm (also called the "desire realm"), meditative concentration must be obtained through diligent practice.

Cultivating meditative concentration generally involves concentrating the mind on one point, free from distraction, while maintaining a peaceful state of mind. This is *samadhi.*

In addition to the type of *samadhi* practice described in the Tiantai teaching of stopping and seeing meditation, there is an additional categorization of *samadhi* called the "four types of *samadhi.*" They are as follows:

### 1. Constant Sitting Samadhi (常坐三昧)

A typical session consists of ninety days of devoting oneself entirely to sitting meditation and reciting a Buddha's name. As one's thoughts become concentrated in one place, one can contemplate the absolute nature of the Dharma. By practicing towards *samadhi* in this way, one will realize the non-duality of ignorance and awakening, and the oneness of the sagely and the ordinary. Since one only undertakes the single practice of constant sitting, this form of practice is also sometimes called "single-practice *samadhi.*"

## 2. Constant Walking Samadhi (常行三昧)

Like constant sitting *samadhi,* this is typically practiced over the course of a ninety day session. During a ninety day session one cannot sit nor lie down. One is only allowed to stand or move around. During the twenty-four hours of each day one walks around a room without stopping; there are no breaks. This kind of *samadhi* is also called the "presence *samadhi,*" because it is based on the *Presence Samadhi Sutra.* According to this *sutra,* practicing this form of *samadhi* can allow the practitioner to see all Buddhas of the ten directions appearing before the practitioner.

## 3. Half Walking, Half Sitting Samadhi (半行半坐三昧)

This is also known as the "universal *samadhi,*" or the "*Lotus Sutra Samadhi.*" This type of practice is not associated for any specific unit of time, but sessions may last between seven to twenty-one days or more. This form of practice is also associated with groups of ten or more people practicing together. This type of practice includes the following phases:

- Purifying the temple.
- Purifying the body.
- Making offerings of the body, speech, and mind.
- Invoking the Buddhas.
- Worshipping the Buddhas.
- Repenting the faults of the six sense organs.
- Circumambulating the shrine.
- Chanting the sutras.

- Performing sitting meditation.
- Realization of reality.

## 4. Non-Walking and Non-Sitting Samadhi（非行非坐三昧）

This category includes all varieties of *samadhi* outside of the three kinds described above. This kind of *samadhi* is not limited to any particular body position, be that walking, standing, sitting, or lying down, and can be sustained by any method. At all times and during any activity without restriction, one can contemplate and realize *samadhi* in each thought. Of the four, this *samadhi* is the most important.

S

A sutra states, "Concentrating the mind in one place is a meritorious achievement, while a moment of distraction is affliction." Meditative concentration is an inquiry into the mind that turns away from the profane desires produced when the mind is seduced by external objects. By calming the mind and quieting thoughts, one can end desire. The *Dharmapada* states, "If I do not think of you, then you will not arise." By eliminating craving and overcoming confusion, one is able to achieve a calm and peaceful mental state.

Meditative concentration naturally produces wisdom. Buddhist meditation methods and non-Buddhist meditation methods are not different, yet the practices of non-Buddhist schools emphasize obtaining supernatural powers, while Buddhist meditation focuses on the cultivation of wisdom. This is one way that Buddhism is different from other religions.

This shows that attaining meditative concentration in and of itself is not the goal; it is the attainment of wisdom through concentration that is the goal of Buddhist meditation. If one wishes to attain meditative concentration, one must first eliminate concern for success or failure and not be worried by gain or loss. In this way, the mind will not be swayed by external circumstances and will naturally become focused.

## Samantabhadra
## 普賢
*See:* Mountains, four great.

## Sangha
## 僧
*See:* Assembly, sevenfold; gem, triple; harmony, six points of reverent.

## Sariputra
## 舍利弗
*See:* Disciples, ten great.

## Schools of Chinese Buddhism, Eight
## 八大宗派

> Chan is poor, the Esoteric rich, Pure Land is a
> skillful means.
> Faxiang is patient, Three Treatise speaks of
> emptiness,
> Huayan has its lineage, Vinaya cultivates conduct.
> Tiantai organizes the doctrine and its meaning.

This verse explains the unique characteristics of eight schools of Chinese Mahayana Buddhism. Among these eight some emphasize doctrine, such as the Tiantai, Huayan, Faxiang, and Three Treatise schools, and some emphasize practice, such as the Chan, Pure Land, Vinaya, and Esoteric schools.

### 1. Tiantai School (天台宗)

The school was named after its founder, Zhiyi (538-579 CE), who lived on Mount Tiantai. The school derives many of its teachings from the *Lotus Sutra*, and is thus also known as the *Lotus Sutra School*.

Zhiyi divided all of the Buddha's teachings into five periods, culminating in the teachings on the *Lotus Sutra*. Zhiyi specified four methods of instruction: the sudden method, the gradual method, the secret method, and the indeterminate method. Zhiyi also defined four objects of instruction: the canonical teachings, the common teachings, the particular teachings, and the complete teachings. Using these schemes he classified the many sutras of the Tripitaka according to the differing spiritual capacities of their intended audiences. He then analyzed and compared each and every method of practice and stage of realization. As a result, the doctrines within the Tiantai School are very rigorous and systematic.

Formalized doctrines of the Tiantai School include "one thought containing the three thousandfold world system," "one thought, three contemplations," and the "doctrine of the integration of the three truths." The main methods of practice include the "three kinds of stopping and seeing," the "four kinds of *samadhi*," and the "five repentances." Even though its doctrine is complex and its teachings profound, the school has managed to survive into modern times because there were those in every generation who carried on its tradition.

## 2. Huayan School (華嚴宗)

This school is named after the Chinese title of the *Flower Adornment Sutra*, which is its principle text. It is also sometimes called the "Xianshou School," because the vision of the school was primarily established by National Master Fazang Xianshou (643-712 CE).

The *Flower Adornment Sutra* is honored as the "king of sutras," for it is the greatest and most profound among the Buddha's teachings. The *Flower Adornment Sutra* originated in India. After being transmitted to China, it became fully integrated into Chinese Buddhism, which developed the doctrine of "dependent origination of the dharma realm." Many great teachers also developed methods to encode the school's philosophical principles into real practices. This allowed the philosophy of the *Flower Adornment Sutra* to reach its apex in Chinese Buddhism.

The Huayan School primarily extols the concept of the absolute "dharma realm," from which such doctrines as the "four dharma realms," the "ten gates of profundity," and the "interpenetration of the six characteristics" were developed. The Huayan School's main methods of practice include making the four universal vows, cultivating the ten vows of Samantabhadra Bodhisattva, and sitting meditation.

## 3. Faxiang School (法相宗)

This school specializes in delineating the nature and characteristics of all phenomena, which is why it is called the *faxiang* (法相), "phenomenal characteristic," School. The Faxiang School is also closely aligned with "consciousness-only" thought. It is also known as the Cien School, because the school's main architect, Kuiji (632-683 CE), lived at Cien Monastery.

The school values a number of texts, but most especially the *Esoteric Meaning Sutra*, the *Lankavatara Sutra*, the *Treatise on the Stages of Yogacara Practitioners*, and the *Compendium of the Mahayana*. The main doctrines of the school include "all phenomena are consciousness-only," the "five categories and one hundred *dharmas*," the "eight kinds of consciousness and four wisdoms," and the "five natures." As the Faxiang School uses an elaborate terminology to articulate many complex layers of doctrine, those who wish to learn its teachings require a great deal of patience.

### 4. Three Treatise School（三論宗）

This school is so named because it is principally focused on three texts: the *Treatise on the Middle Way*, the *Treatise in a Hundred Verses*, and the *Treatise of the Twelve Aspects*. These three texts focus on *prajna*-wisdom, and the inherent emptiness of dependent origination, and as such the school is sometimes called the *"Prajna*-wisdom School" or the "Emptiness School." It is also sometimes known as the Jiaxiang School, because it became strongest under Jiaxiang Jizang (549-623 CE).

The chief aim of the Three Treatise School is subdue wrong views and promote right views, for it believes that the principle of the inherent emptiness of dependent origination can remove all delusion and attachment. The Three Treatise School also holds that sentient beings are fundamentally Buddhas and originally awakened; thus there is no question about whether one can or cannot become a Buddha, and this distinction is only a label. While doctrines like "inherent emptiness" and "name only" are quite profound, the number of great sages who study under the Three Treatise School are dwindling, and the school seems to be in decline.

## 5. Chan School (禪宗)

This school is named after the Chinese word *chan* (禪), "meditation" because meditation is its main form of practice. It is also known as the "Buddha Mind School," because it is based upon the wordless transmission of the Buddha mind seal.

The Chan School was brought to China by the Patriarch Bodhidharma. After introducing the principles in China the lineage continued to be transmitted through a series of patriarchs: Huike (487-593 CE), Sengcan (d. 606 CE), Daoxin (580-651 CE), Hongren (602-675 CE), and Huineng. After the Sixth Patriarch Huineng, the Chan School blossomed like a flower into "five houses" and flourished throughout China, becoming one of the most important schools in Chinese Buddhism. Almost all the Buddhist sects in Taiwan today are connected to the heritage of the Chan School, showing what a profound influence the Chan School exerts upon modern Buddhism.

The Chan School emphasizes a separate transmission beyond the teachings that is not based upon the written word, and as a consequence, the school is not based upon any particular text. The Chan School has venerated various texts throughout its history with no consistent pattern. For example, before the time of Hongren, the *Lankavatara Sutra* was widely studied, while Huineng himself relied upon the *Diamond Sutra*. After the time of Huineng, it was the *Platform Sutra* that was used most often.

The goal of practice in the Chan School is to directly see one's nature by illuminating the mind, so that one can see intrinsic nature in its simple and undefiled state.

## 6. Pure Land School (淨土宗)

The Pure Land School is a collection of the various practices to seek rebirth in one of the many pure, magnificent Buddha Lands.

Since the teachings on Amitabha Buddha's Western Pure Land became very well-known, this Pure Land became synonymous with the school. Beings are reborn in Amitabha Buddha's Pure Land in lotus flowers, and thus this school is also sometimes known as the "Lotus School." It is also sometimes called the "Mount Lu School," because of its founder Huiyuan (334-416 CE) who lived on Mount Lu.

The fundamental texts of the Pure Land School are represented by three scriptures and one treatise: the *Infinite Life Sutra*, the *Contemplation Sutra*, the *Amitabha Sutra*, and the *Treatise on Rebirth*. In accordance with the original vow of Amitabha Buddha, this school believes that as long as one has faith in Amitabha Buddha's Pure Land, vows to be reborn there, and recites Amitabha Buddha's name with single-minded effort, one will be reborn in the Pure Land.

Since the practice is convenient and easy to do, many Pure Land organizations have arisen, such as Amitabha Buddha recitation organizations, lotus societies, and lay groups that focus on the practice.

## 7. *Vinaya School* (律宗)

This school is named after the *vinaya*, the collection of Buddhist monastic precepts. It is also called the "Mount Nan School," because Daoxuan (596-667 CE), the founder and compiler of the *Four-Part Vinaya* taught at Mount Zhongnan.

The Vinaya School venerates the "four vinayas and five treatises": the *Four-Part Vinaya*, the *Five-Part Vinaya*, the *Ten Recitations Vinaya*, the *Mahasamghika Vinaya*, the *Root Treatise on the Vinaya*, the *Root Treatise*, the *Treatise on the Samantapasakika*, the *Treatise on the Sarvastivadins*, and the *Treatise which Clarifies*.

The school is chiefly concerned with the clarification of the *vinaya* or monastic rules, which are divided into "precepts of proper conduct" and "precepts of wholesome deeds." Precepts of proper conduct are intended to prevent the mind and body from committing all manner of negative action; while the precepts of wholesome deeds are intended to encourage all positive physical, verbal, and mental actions.

Master Daoxuan was the culmination of the *Four-Part Vinaya* in China, and the masters Yunkan and Yuanzhao (1048-1116 CE) revived this tradition during the Song period. The Vinaya School was transmitted to Japan by Master Jianzhen (687-763 CE). During the late Ming dynasty, the Master Jinling Guxin (1541-1615 CE) reestablished the school, while his disciple and grand-disciple, the masters Sanmei (1580-1645 CE) and Jianyue (1601-1679 CE) respectively, continued his work, establishing an ordination platform at Mount Baohua. Even today, all the Chinese Monasteries still observe the ordination practice of Mount Baohua.

## 8. Esoteric School（密宗）

The Esoteric School is based upon Vairocana Buddha's self-realized state of esoteric mystery depicted in the *Vairocana Sutra* and the *Susiddhikara Tantra*. It is also known as the Mantra School, since the recitation of sacred formula called "mantras" is one of the school's main practices.

The Esoteric School is generally considered to be extraordinarily mysterious, for it is contrasted with the non-esoteric traditions. In reality, except for some mantras and sacred formulas that are not accorded any explanation, everything in the Esoteric School can be transmitted to others. It is just that the ceremonial practices of the Esoteric School are extraordinarily complex, for every performance of its spiritual practices requires a considerable amount of time; and one must also provide rich offerings to the guru. Those wishing to become genuine students of the Esoteric School must be quite well-off financially, and have a considerable amount of free time on their hands.

Additionally, for a person to become a formal Buddhist follower in the non-esoteric traditions, one must take refuge in the Triple Gem, what is known as the "three refuges." In the Esoteric School, one must take a fourth refuge; besides taking refuge in the Buddha, Dharma, and Sangha, one must also take refuge in the guru.

**S**

Each of the eight schools described above has its own unique characteristics, but they also share something in common: they all rose to prominence between the Sui dynasty and the Tang dynasty (581-907 CE). These schools benefitted from and added to the prosperity of that time in Chinese history.

## Semblance Dharma, Age of
## 像法
*See:* Ages of the Dharma, three.

## Sense Objects
## 六塵
*See also*: Consciousness, eight kinds of; dependent origination.

A common metaphor used in Buddhist writing is to describe our Buddha nature as a "bright pearl covered in dust." This describes how our Buddha nature is obscured by the five desires and six sense objects, or *liuchen* (六塵), "six dusts." The term "six sense objects" refers to those objects which are cognizable by the six sense organs: the eye, ear, nose, tongue, body, and mind. When the six sense organs contact the six sense objects, they give rise to the six kinds of consciousness.

### 1. Sight （色塵）

Sight is everything the eyes can see, including colors like blue, yellow, red, and white, as well as features like clouds, smoke, dust, and mist, qualities such as shadow, light, brightness, and darkness, and physical features like long, short, square, round, high, low, straight, and curved.

### 2. Sound （聲塵）

Sound is everything the ears hear. This encompasses pleasant sounds like chanting, music, song, and applause, unpleasant sounds like sounds of crying, swearing, cursing, arguing, and other irritating noises, as well as natural sounds like the sound of wind, rain, and thunder.

### 3. Smell （香塵）

Smell is everything the nose can smell. This includes nice smells like the scent of sandalwood, bad smells like onions and leeks, moderate smells, and pungent odors.

### 4. Taste （味塵）

Taste is everything that the tongue can taste. This includes all the flavors of food and drink such as sourness, sweetness, bitterness, spiciness, saltiness, pungency, pleasantness, and plainness.

## 5. Touch （觸塵）

Touch is everything that the body feels. This includes sensations such as firmness, dampness, softness, hardness, slipperiness, roughness, lightness, heaviness, coldness, and warmness.

## 6. Dharmas （法塵）

"Dharmas," or mental sensory data, are everything the mind thinks, which can include all the things in the universe.

We have afflictions because our six sense organs are constantly seeking out the six sense objects and the five desires. The five sense organs want to eat the best, use the best, hear the best, and see the best; and our minds do not wish us to be unfavorably compared to others. Selfishness, attachment, and ignorance arise as a result. The six sense objects are just like dust that can pollute our true intrinsic nature, which is why they are also called the "six dusts." The six sense objects can generate the afflictions of greed, anger, and ignorance,

The six sense objects can also lead us to create greed, anger, and ignorance. These cause us to ruin our good minds, and can steal away our good deeds. For this reason the six sense objects are also called the "six delusions," the "six ruinous things," and the "six thieves."

Though the six sense objects can pollute the mind, they must first be apprehended by the six sense organs to arise. That is why the Buddha once warned his disciples, "Hide the six sense organs like a turtle withdrawing into its shell, and enclose the mind within a defensive wall." We should lock up the doors to our six sense organs just like a turtle hides its head and legs within its shell, so that there is no fear of being attacked by sea otters.

Cultivation does not mean the complete and total eradication of external conditions, but rather, it should begin with not being distracted by the external world. This means not pursuing power and status or craving life's enjoyments, nor enjoying a life of wine, women, and song. In this way, the six sense organs do not grasp at the six sense objects, and evil has no way to gain access. The *Platform Sutra* says, "Purify the inherent mind and allow the six consciousnesses to exit through the six sense organs onto the six sense objects without attachment or integration. Come and go freely, and circulate without obstruction; this is *prajna samadhi*, liberating and carefree."

Normally, our life is lived amid the troubles caused by the five desires. It is rare for one to stand apart from the ebb and flow of ordinary life, but it is even more precious if one can engage in ordinary life and remain unhindered by it. To leave the world behind and retreat to the mountains and forests to practice is hardly the ultimate path. Only living along the busy streets and remaining unperturbed by the outside world is the Mahayana path. There is a Chinese saying that captures this idea well: "The true hermit retreats to the city."

## Sex
### 色
*See:* Desires, five.

## Shrine, Main
### 大雄寶殿
*See also*: Structures and buildings.

The main hall within a Buddhist monastery or temple in which Buddha images are venerated is called the "treasure hall of the great hero." No monastery or temple, regardless of size, is without one, for it is the place set aside for monastics to perform morning and evening services and for lay people to venerate the Buddha and chant sutras. It is also where Dharma services for both monastics and lay people are held.

*Daxiong* (大雄), "Great hero" is one of the epithets of respect for the Buddha. He is called the "great hero" because his great wisdom allows him to subdue all harmful obstructions. In most temples the treasure hall of the great hero contains an image of Sakyamuni Buddha, the founder of Buddhism, as the main object of veneration. Some halls include the "three treasured Buddhas," where Sakyamuni Buddha is joined by Amitabha Buddha and the Medicine Buddha. An image of Sakyamuni Buddha is also sometimes flanked by his attendant Ananda and the disciple Mahakasyapa, who symbolizes the dual emphasis upon understanding and practice. Other halls feature the Huayan trinity with Mahavairocana Buddha, Manjusri Bodhisattva, and Samantabhadra Bodhisattva, or the trinity of the Western Pure Land with Amitabha Buddha, Avaolkitesvara Bodhisattva, and Mahasthamaprapta Bodhisattva. The main shrine may also venerate the eighteen arhats, the twelve *yaksas,* the eight vajra deities, or other Buddhist figures.

Buddha images are made through a variety of methods, including wood carving, copper casting, clay molding, painting on paper, and jade carving. Buddha images are also made with unconventional materials like cement and fiberglass. In the minds of Buddhist followers, however, the significance and value of these images is the same, for they are symbols of faith rather than idols to be worshipped.

The various positions the Buddha is depicted in indicate the different roles of the Buddha. Images of a standing Buddha are

S

meant to evoke the Buddha as teacher, while images of a sitting Buddha show the Buddha in meditation, and images of a reclining Buddha are indicative of his completion of merit and wisdom.

Buddha images are usually placed in a shrine in one of two positions: wall-niche or island-dais. The island-dais placement includes a connecting corridor behind the image that permits circumambulation of the Buddha image. How the circumambulation is performed depends upon the layout of the hall. In the case of wide, horizontal spaces, the left and right sides of the assembly will often circumambulate in separate lines traveling in opposite directions. In more narrow, long spaces the left and right sides of the hall will often join into a single line to circumambulate the image.

The roof of the treasure hall of the great hero in a Chinese temple will either feature an upward curling roof-line, typical of northern Chinese temples, or a flat roof-line, more common in southern China. Main halls are predominately constructed from timber, in imitation of ancient building styles, or from cement. Timber is less fire-resistant, and is thus less safe, while cement halls appear too modern. Today some main halls use steel-frame construction. This has the advantage of being able to offer a wide open interior without the need for supporting columns, making the hall available for many additional possible uses.

The most common design for the interior walls of the treasure hall of the great hero in a Chinese temple is to lay out row upon row of small Buddha images. Another design is to adorn the walls with colorful paintings of stories from the Buddhist sutras. Some older Buddhist monasteries make use of floor-to-ceiling windows along the entirety of their wall space.

In some main halls, it is asked that one's shoes be removed before entering, while in others there is no such requirement.

Generally, this is determined based upon the materials used for the flooring. Commonly used materials include carpet, marble, vinyl flooring, and red brick, with each having advantages and disadvantages. Carpet easily attracts dirt and grime while marble flooring, though easier to clean, can be quite cold and hard. Wood flooring can more easily become bug-infested and grows loose over time as the wood contracts when cold and expands when hot. Wood is also particularly sensitive to moisture, which can darken it over time.

The treasure hall of the great hero also contains various offerings to the Buddha. Besides the ten kinds of offerings mentioned in the sutras (incense, flowers, lamps, perfume, fruit, tea, food, treasure, pearls, and clothing), offerings include bells, drums, and banners that are hung to the left and right of the main altar. Generally speaking, it is not considered proper to clutter up the main Buddha hall, particularly the offering table in front of the Buddha image, for emphasis should be placed on keeping things orderly and clean. An appropriately sparse setup could include a pair of lamps placed before the Buddha, three sticks of incense, two vases of fresh flowers, four plates of fruit offerings, and an offering of three cups of tea. It is not even necessary to offer fresh flowers every day, for leaving out the offering of flowers both reduces a temple's expenses while creating less waste. Rather than allowing the incense burner to become filled with incense sticks, keeping three sticks of incense burning at any given time allows the wafting smoke to highlight the quiet solemnity and peaceful tranquility of the great hall. Even the Buddha image itself should not be too large, so that as one gazes up at it from a distance, the Buddha image appears to sparkle amid the dappled haze. In this way, visitors become even more impressed with the august greatness of the Buddha, and will come to feel admiration and devotion.

The treasure hall of the great hero should be moderately well-lit, quiet, orderly, and clean. There should be no laughing or playing in the hall, no loud noises, and no lounging about or eating. In short, the treasure hall of the great hero should be maintained in a state of dignified respect and peaceful tranquility, so that anyone entering the hall can feel a sense of sincere devotion and be moved to express their admiration. There is a verse that describes this feeling of admiration well:

> In heaven above and earth below there is no
>     one like the Buddha;
> Nor can a comparison be made to anyone in
>     the worlds of the ten directions.
> I have seen all that this world has to offer;
> But there is absolutely no one like the
>     Buddha.

## Sickness
### 疾病
*See:* Field of merit; offerings, four; parables of the *Lotus Sutra*.

## Siksamana
### 式叉摩那
*See:* Assembly, sevenfold.

## Skillful Means
### 方便
*See:* Mountain gate; teaching, four modes of; parables of the *Lotus Sutra*.

# Sleep
# 睡

*See:* Desires, five.

# Small Things Not to Be Taken Lightly, Four
# 四小不可輕

A hundred years after the Buddha's final *nirvana*, King Asoka (3rd cent. BCE) unified India and became the most powerful patron of Buddhism. On one occasion King Asoka had pledged to make offerings to the monastic community, when a young novice monk approached him. King Asoka was unsure as to whether or not he should bow before the young novice. Later this young novice manifested his supernatural powers to awaken the king. From then on, King Asoka would always treat all members of the monastic community with respect without any thought of pride, regardless of their age or level of intelligence.

While in the world, the Buddha often exhorted his disciples by pointing out that younger students were not to be taken lightly; and on one occasion even, the Buddha personally instructed King Prasenajit on the principle of "four small things not to be taken lightly." As explained by the Buddha, there are four things in the world that appear to be quite small, but are not to be taken lightly:

## 1. Small Little Sparks（小小火苗）
A little spark can start a great fire. Seemingly small and insignificant sparks can develop into an uncontrollable disaster once they get going, and thus should not be taken lightly.

### 2. Small Young Water Nagas（幼小之龍）

Small *nagas* will grow up to become great *nagas* that can stir up wind blown waves and overturn rivers and oceans. Therefore, they are not to be taken lightly.

### 3. Small Young Princes（年少王子）

Princes will grow up to be kings who will command the world, for they alone can either confer benefits upon their people, or lose their country with a single word as a ruinous legacy upon the land. Therefore, they are not to be taken lightly.

### 4. Small Young Novices（年幼沙彌）

Novice monastics may be few in years, but all they need is to cultivate the path with devotion and they will certainly be transformed over time to become model teachers for heavenly and human beings and bring liberation to all sentient beings. This is a power in the world that must not be ignored to any degree whatsoever.

The *Dharmapada* says, "Do not fail to do what is only a little wholesome, do not do what is only a little unwholesome. Though drops of water are small, they will gradually fill a large container." Things that are small have limitless potential. Throughout our lives, there are many people, activities, and things that do not attract our attention because they are small and insignificant, but end up playing a large role in our futures. For example, small though a seed may be, it can grow into a large tree that can provide shelter to people. A small, insignificant good thought might lead to some great undertaking that will benefit the country and its people. A small, insignificant crack may cause a dam to break, resulting in a major disaster; and even a small, insignificant act of generosity can save someone in a dire emergency. A simple, little smile can give someone limitless confidence; and the small, insignificant good deed we do every day can create wholesome karmic connections for a positive future.

In particular, though novice monks may be young, they are the future. Lay Buddhists may look up to those eminent monks and sages of high character and prestige with great respect, but they must not treat lightly those small, young novices who have just begun the Buddhist path. That is why Venerable Master Hsing Yun teaches that, "In looking after the old, we must look after the young all the more."

## Spiritual Wealth, Seven Kinds of
## 七聖財

*See also*: Giving; practice, four stages of; *prajna*; precepts, five; *samadhi*.

We all like the wealth of gold and silver, but Buddhism considers this kind of wealth to be easily destroyed by the five causes of loss: floods, fires, thieves, corrupt officials, and wayward children. Thus there is a Buddhist saying that "You can't take anything with you except your karma." No matter how much wealth of this world you have, you cannot take anything with you once your life comes to an end. Therefore it is only the wealth of the Dharma that is worth pursuing, for it is what assists us in progressing along the Buddhist path.

The *Dharmapada* describes seven kinds of Dharma wealth:

### 1. Faith (信仰)
The *Flower Adornment Sutra* says, "Faith is the mother of merit and the source of awakening which nourishes the roots of all virtue."

Faith is the basis of all good works. If we can generate faith in the Dharma, we will naturally be able to do what is right according to the Dharma and align ourselves with the proper goal and realize its benefits. That is why the sutras liken faith to a hand, a staff, a root, a boat, one's power, and one's wealth.

### 2. Listening and Learning（聽聞）

Learning Buddhism requires listening to the true Dharma before one can come into accord with the Buddhist path. This is what is meant by the saying, "one enters *samadhi* by means of listening, thinking, and practicing." To learn Buddhism it is necessary that one be well-informed. One should listen to the Dharma like a field ready to be planted, or an empty cup ready to be filled to avoid inattentiveness, preconceptions, and delusion. Only by listening to the Dharma with an attitude of devotion, sincerity, respect, humility, pliancy, purity, and gratitude will one then be able to receive any benefit.

### 3. Perseverance（精進）

One should endeavor to do whatever is proper and beneficial for oneself. This is perseverance. A sutra states: "If lay practitioners are lazy, they will lose out on ordinary benefits; if monastics are slothful, they will lose the Dharma Gem." Laziness and sloth are major defects in human life, and so one should constantly apply perseverance to correct them.

### 4. Morality（持戒）

Buddhist morality is most commonly codified as adherence to the precepts. The precepts are a set of standards and rules that serve as guidelines to regulate one's conduct. Like a set of train tracks, they lead the mind and body down the correct moral path and advance us towards the liberation of *nirvana*. The fundamental spirit of the precepts is to not violate the rights of others, for as long as we do not violate the rights of others and be of benefit to them, we are keeping the precepts. Doing what is wholesome and refraining from what is unwholesome constitutes the basic spirit of Buddhism.

## 5. Conscience（慚愧）

A conscience will spare one from committing all manner of bad deeds, for one will feel shame from doing what is unwholesome. The *Sutra of the Teachings Bequeathed by the Buddha* says, "Being clothed with a sense of shame is an unsurpassable adornment." One's morality and character can only be improved by developing a sense of shame for what one does not know, has not yet done, had not done enough, or what one has not purified.

## 6. Giving（布施）

Giving is sharing what one has with others. For example, the giving of food, drink, clothing, medicine, and money to those who are poor, sick, or indigent, is known as "giving wealth." Sharing of one's skills, talents, and experience with others so that they might understand and gain wisdom, is known as "giving Dharma." Additionally, not adding to the pain, suffering, and fears of others and helping them turn away all worry and panic is "giving fearlessness."

## 7. Meditative Wisdom（定慧）

Meditative wisdom means to focus the mind so that it does not scatter, and thereby attain insight into all phenomena. Meditative concentration is the essence of wisdom, and the development of wisdom is a function of establishing meditative concentration. The two are like a lamp and its light, or a body of water and its waves:

the two complement one another, neither being identical nor entirely different. By maintaining a lucid and pure mind, one will generate wisdom from meditative concentration, and maintain meditative concentration within wisdom. Only through meditative wisdom can one attain liberation from the cycle of birth and death. Studying Buddhism involves cultivating both wisdom and virtue, as well as practicing meditative concentration and wisdom.

Having faith in the Dharma is itself a form of wealth. Worldly wealth is limited, finite, and defiled, and in the end it will one day disappear. Only noble wealth cannot be destroyed.

## Sramanera
沙彌
*See:* Assembly, sevenfold.

## Sramanerika
沙彌尼
*See:* Assembly, sevenfold.

## Sravaka
聲聞
*See:* Dharma realms, ten; Mahayana and Hinayana.

## Stopping and Seeing Meditation
止觀雙修
*See also:* Samadhi.

The *Essential Points for Practicing Stopping and Seeing Meditation* states: "There are many ways of attaining *nirvana*, but the most important of these is none other than the dual practice of stopping and seeing." *Zhi* (止), "stopping," and *guan* (觀), "seeing" are two methods for cultivating meditative concentration and wisdom, and are the most important methods of practice in the Tiantai School. The Tiantai teachings cannot possibly be understood without including a discussion of stopping and seeing meditation.

"Stopping" refers to putting to rest all thoughts and remaining in a state of non-thought. In this way one can remove deluded thinking to allow for the wisdom that arises from meditative concentration. Once the confusion of deluded thinking has been eliminated, "seeing" is applied to contemplate all phenomena and attain the wisdom of knowing the fundamental essence of all phenomena.

In other words, "stopping" means to stop the mind from generating illusory thoughts, such that unwholesome states cannot arise. This is the development of meditative concentration. "Seeing" means to see mental objects, such that one diligently investigates the nature of all phenomena. This is the development of wisdom. These are the ways that practitioners develop meditative concentration and wisdom, and the two depend upon one another. That is why *Essential Points for Practicing Stopping and Seeing Meditation* states: "The dual practice of meditative concentration and wisdom are like the two wheels of a cart or the two wings of a bird. If either one of these is practiced to the exclusion of the other, then one will fall into error."

The practice of meditative concentration must be in accord with wisdom, and they both can be developed through the dual practice of stopping and seeing. When stopping and seeing are practiced together, meditative concentration and wisdom are cultivated equally. This practice can produce extraordinary results, and begins with a three-part method:

## 1. Gradual Stopping and Seeing（漸次止觀）

"Gradual" in this instance means being guided through different stages of meditative concentration, from the simple to the profound. In general there are five such stages:

1. Taking refuge and upholding the five precepts.
2. Learning meditative concentration.
3. Entering the undefiled path.
4. Attaining liberation from the cycle of birth and death.
5. Cultivating the compassion of the bodhisattva.

During this process one must not neglect to practice seeing meditation so that one may eliminate the attachments to both emptiness and mundane existence, and to realize the path of non-action in absolute reality.

## 2. Indeterminate Stopping and Seeing（不定止觀）

This level is called "indeterminate" because there is no longer any stated sequence of stages. Some may advance suddenly, some may advance gradually, and some may even go backwards. Sometimes one may practice according to provisional truth, and at other times practice according to ultimate truth. This approach combines the simple with the profound, unites all phenomena with their principles, and is established to meet the spiritual needs and capacities of sentient beings. That being said, mindfulness of breathing is still the most important method of practice.

## 3. Complete Stopping and Seeing（圓頓止觀）

One begins by taking true reality as the object of stopping and seeing meditation, but after one has understood and practiced, one will reach the state of non-duality. It differs from the previous modes of practice and includes the following stages:

1. Generating a great aspiration.
2. Cultivating great practice.
3. Producing great results.
4. Transcending the sutras.
5. Returning to emptiness.

Of these stages the second stage, "cultivating great practice," refers to the cultivation of *samadhi*, namely the four kinds of *samadhi*, which is another major doctrinal category within the Tiantai tradition.

The text *Explanation on the Stages of the Perfection of Meditative Concentration* states those who wish to practice stopping and seeing meditation must pay close attention to the following four matters:

1. Prepare the five external conditions: observe the precepts, have adequate food and clothing, dwell in a quiet place, clear away worldly obligations, and be close to a teacher.
2. Turn away from the five desires of wealth, sex, fame, food, and sleep.
3. Abandon the five hindrances of desire, anger, sleepiness, agitation, and doubt.
4. Be balanced in four aspects: balanced in meals, balanced in sleep, balanced in breathing, and balanced in mind.

The dual practice of stopping and seeing meditation is a practice to develop meditative concentration and wisdom; this does not mean they can only be practiced by sitting in a meditation hall. Even in the midst of a normal, busy life one can set aside five minutes every day to quiet the mind and relax. It is even possible to set aside a whole day or even half of a day each month to be alone and retire from the clamor of everyday existence, to calm the mind and still one's thoughts, and find peace and quiet. This can allow one to become re-energized. In this way, there is nothing of greater benefit than the ability to practice stopping and seeing meditation.

## Structures and Buildings
## 寺院庵堂

*See also*: Shrine, main.

There are many names for various religious buildings and structures in Chinese. The terms *miao* (廟), *gong* (宮), *guan* (觀), *dian* (殿), and *tan* (壇) are typically associated with Daoist buildings, while the following terms are used to describe Buddhist buildings and structures:

| Chinese | Pinyin | Translation |
|---------|--------|-------------|
| 寺 | *si* | Hall |
| 院 | *yuan* | Court |
| 庵 | *an* | Hermitage |
| 堂 | *tang* | Shrine |
| 道場 | *daochang* | Dharma center |
| 精舍 | *jingshe* | Archaic term for monastery |
| 講堂 | *jiangtang* | Lecture hall |
| 伽藍 | *qielan* | Monastic park |
| 蘭若 | *lanre* | Rural temple |
| 叢林 | *conglin* | Monastery |

| 蓮社 | *lianshe* | Lotus society |
|---|---|---|
| 佛剎 | *focha* | Buddhist pillar |
| 學舍 | *xueshe* | Buddhist learning center |
| 念佛會 | *nianfohu* | Buddha's name recitation center |
| 佈教所 | *bujiaosuo* | Buddhist teaching center |
| 居士林等 | *jushilin deng* | Lay Buddhist Association |

Most names for Buddhist sites are encompassed by the Chinese characters *si* (寺), *yuan* (院), *an* (庵), and *tang* (堂). However, there are people who refer to Buddhist temples as *simiao* (寺廟), though the character *miao* is more associated with Daoist temples. This demonstrates how Chinese folk beliefs often make no distinction between Buddhism and Daoism and are quite deeply rooted.

In ancient times the character *si* originally referred to a government office, such as the *honglu si* (鴻臚寺), and the *taichang si* (太常寺). When the first two Buddhist monks to come to China, Kasyapa-matanga and Dharmaraksa, first arrived they were temporarily housed in the office of the minister of heralds. Later, a site outside the capital was selected to construct the first Buddhist monastery, called *baima si* (白馬寺), "white horse monastery," and the two monks settled there. This site became the first Buddhist monastery in the history of Chinese Buddhism.

The character *yuan* means an enclosing wall, and it came to refer to any building with a surrounding wall or corridor, such as those used for imperial residences. Emperor Taizong of the Tang dynasty (r. 626-649 CE) ordered that a place be constructed to house Xuanzang's sutra translation work within Dacien Monastery, and the structure was named *yijing yuan* (譯經院), "Sutra Translation Court." From then on, *yuan* has been used to refer to many different Buddhist buildings, including sutra translation courts, ordination platform courts (戒壇院), and sutra teaching courts (講經院). Typically, Buddhist buildings referred to as *yuan* have a greater emphasis on education.

The character *an* has been incorporated into the terms *caoan* (草庵), *pengan* (蓬庵), *anshi* (庵室), *maoan* (茅庵), and *chanan* (禪庵), which all refer to various small, simple dwellings where monastics and hermits live far away from villages. Later generations used this character as well as the compound *ansi* (庵寺) to refer to Buddhist nunneries. However, the term *ansi* originally referred to structures that housed either male or female monastics, not only to nuns' housing.

*Tang*, which is also incorporated in the compound *diantang* (殿堂), refers to places where Buddha images are housed and venerated, or buildings which serve as locations for practice and the learning of sutras. *Tang*, along with *tasi* (塔寺), "stupas" are one type of structure that make up the main monastery complex. These structures are named depending on which Buddha or bodhisattva image is installed within, such as the Samantabhadra Hall (普賢殿) and the Ksitigarbha Hall (地藏殿). Other examples of these structures include founders' halls (開山堂), which house images of founding patriarchs, and reliquary halls (舍利殿), which intern cremated remains. Other structures are simply named for the functions that they perform, such as dining halls (齋堂), reception halls (客堂), and tea halls (茶堂).

As Buddhism has continued to reach out into society venues for spreading the Dharma have expanded, with places as small as an open square in a village to large college auditoriums and even national theaters becoming places where one can hear the Dharma. However, the Buddhist monastery will forever remain the center of faith and a source of strength. A monastery is a gathering place for good Dharma friends on the path together, a place to refuel on the road of life, and a vacation retreat for cultivating one's spirit. It is a place of purity where we can wash away our affliction, bring ourselves close to the jewel of the Dharma, and learn about compassion, wisdom, vows, and practice. As Buddhist practitioners, we should spend more time at Buddhist monasteries and take care of Dharma centers.

## Subhuti
須菩提
*See:* Disciples, ten great.

## Subinda
托塔羅漢
*See:* Arhats, eighteen.

## Suffering, Eight Kinds of
八苦
*See also*: Aggregates, five.

Laozi said that "The greatest trouble for human beings is having a body." It is only because we have a human body that we create karma in delusion, and thereby experience all the afflictions of suffering that prey upon the mind and body. That is why Buddhism teaches that suffering is one of the realities of life.

The Buddhist sutras mention many different groupings of suffering: two kinds of suffering, three kinds of suffering, eight kinds of suffering, one hundred and eight kinds of suffering, and even up to innumerable and limitless sufferings. One of the most common categorizations is the eight kinds of suffering:

### 1. Birth（生苦）

For the fetus in a mother's womb being surrounded by amniotic fluid, with its head down and feet up, is not unlike being in a prison. The process of childbirth itself endangers both the child and the mother, and after birth the child is subject to the cold, biting wind upon its body, unable to express its suffering in words. This is the suffering of birth.

### 2. Old Age（老苦）

One goes from childhood to the prime of life and then into decline. One's vim and vigor drain away and one becomes anxious all the time. As fullness departs and decline sets in, one's physical strength weakens. One's life grows shorter with each passing day until one becomes decrepit and worn down. This is the suffering of old age.

### 3. Sickness（病苦）

When the four great elements become imbalanced, one becomes infected with disease. It becomes difficult to drink and digest food, one can become bed-ridden, gasping for breath and moaning in pain. This is the suffering of sickness.

### 4. Death（死苦）

As death approaches, one's spirit leaves the body like a tortoise being pulled from its shell, for such is the unbearable suffering and pain of death.

### 5. Separation from Loved Ones（愛別離苦）

There are times when one becomes separated from those so loved and dear, such that it is impossible to be together any longer. This is the suffering of separation from loved ones.

## 6. Closeness to Loathsome People (怨憎會苦)

There are other times when it becomes impossible to escape the company of those one hates and despises. This is the suffering of being close to loathsome people.

## 7. Not Getting What One Wants (求不得苦)

Such effort is placed into getting desirable and enjoyable things, yet one cannot have it all. This is the suffering of not getting what we want.

## 8. The Five Aggregates (五陰熾盛苦)

Sentient beings produce pain and suffering because, due to their delusion, they create karma. The body and mind are made up of the five aggregates of form, feelings, perception, mental formations, and consciousness, and the actions of the five aggregates produce karmic effects that oppress the mind and the body again and again in endless succession, like the spreading of a raging fire. This is the suffering of the five aggregates, and it includes the previous seven forms of suffering.

Suffering is a fact of life, but the Buddhist analysis of suffering is not a goal in and of itself; it is to help us recognize the source of suffering so that we can realize the goal of abandoning suffering and obtaining happiness. For those who wish to eliminate pain and suffering, faith in the Triple Gem of Buddhism is a way out: the Buddha is like a good physician who excels in treating the sickness of sentient beings; the Dharma is like good medicine that can eliminate our suffering, and the Sangha, the monastic community, is like a nurse who is constantly attentive in relieving our afflictions. In the vast ocean of the Dharma, sentient beings are able to obtain comfort, faith, wisdom, joy, and freedom. In this way, the Dharma is a light for humanity, and a shining star capable of liberating the world.

## Sumeru, Mount
## 須彌山

*See:* Continents, four great; world system.

## Supernatural Powers, Six
## 六神通

"Supernatural power" refers to phenomena such as mind reading, heavenly vision, teleportation, the ability to manifest in whatever form one wishes, the ability to live or to die as one wishes, and live free and unencumbered.

What may be a coincidence is sometimes called a miracle, and when something unpredictable happens it is sometimes called a mystery. A good plan might be called a "supernatural" scheme, and a good doctor may be called a "supernatural" healer. Some people may pray to the "supernatural" in the form of gods and deities, or chase after "supernatural" power by reciting magic spells. Many seek control of the supernatural through different means. Buddhism too speaks of different kinds of supernatural power, with the most common categorization being a list of six kinds of supernatural power:

*1. Heavenly Vision*（天眼通）
Heavenly vision means that one can see what is obstructed and unobstructed. One is able to see what is near and what is far. One can see that which is illuminated, but also see in

darkness. One can see things that are large, as well as extremely minute. One can see the surface of things as well as the interior. One is capable of seeing the present physical form of sentient beings, and whether they will attain future rebirth in heaven or hell. With heavenly vision, there is nothing that one cannot see.

### 2. Heavenly Hearing（天耳通）

With heavenly hearing, one is able to hear voices that are near as well as far. One can understand all human languages, as well as the languages of animals. With heavenly hearing, there is nothing that one cannot hear.

### 3. Mind Reading（他心通）

Mind reading is the ability to know one's own mind and the minds of others. One can know the mind of the past and the mind of the future. One can discern the thoughts of an ordinary person and a sage, as well as distinguish deluded thoughts from true thoughts. Mind reading is the power to know all the thoughts of sentient beings.

### 4. Teleportation（神足通）

With the power of teleportation one can penetrate mountains, enter oceans, ascend to the heavens, or dive into the earth. One can transform oneself into many, and return many manifestation into one. One can grow to an incredible size, or shrink down so small that one cannot be seen. One can appear or disappear at will and can also go wherever one pleases. The power of teleportation means that nothing can hinder or obstruct one.

## 5. Knowledge of Past Lives （宿命通）

With the knowledge of past lives one knows the location and manner of one's past, present, and future rebirths. One can know the karmic causes that lead to previous lives, as well as the karma that was created during those lives. By knowing the karma of previous lives, one can understand the location of present and future rebirths. The knowledge of past lives means that one knows all about the past, and all about the future.

## 6. Destruction of All Affliction （漏盡通）

Have you subdued the bandits of affliction? Have you eliminated habitual tendencies? Have you cured the illnesses of affliction? Have you removed the obstacles of affliction? With the power of destroying all affliction, one has eliminated all afflictions with outflow and all afflictions without outflow. The power to destroy all afflictions means that one can put an end to affliction and attain liberation.

The supernatural powers described above are indeed incredible, but attaining them is not the goal of true Buddhists. Developing a mind of equality and compassion is the Way; the Buddha did not encourage his followers to develop supernatural powers. The Venerable Maudgalyayana, known as the foremost disciple in supernatural powers, was still ranked below the Venerable Sariputra, who was considered the foremost in wisdom. Additionally, the Venerable Pindola once demonstrated his supernatural powers to the laity and was severely reprimanded by the Buddha and not permitted to enter *nirvana*. Supernatural powers cannot overcome karma, nor can they purify our afflictions. Only by eliminating negative karma and purifying the mind is one in constant pursuit of the Way. This is the approach of Humanistic Buddhism.

# Supports, Three
三資糧

*See also*: Namo amitofo; schools of Chinese Buddhism, eight.

To go on a long journey, one must prepare appropriate traveling expenses and provisions before proceeding. The journey into Buddhism is the same, for if one wishes to attain Buddhahood, one must ensure that there is sufficient support in order to reach the goal.

What supports Buddhism? The Pure Land School teaches the "three supports" of faith, vows, and practice in order to attain rebirth in the Pure Land of the West.

## 1. Faith（信）

Faith allows the mind to purify itself. It is important to note that the faith discussed here is informed faith, not blind faith. Only faith based in wisdom can purify the mind and wash away defilements so that we can manifest our Buddhahood. On the other hand, blind faith and superstitious beliefs create nothing but trouble and impede wisdom. Blind faith makes us more confused each day, and obstructs the path to liberation.

Faith can also be true faith and wrong faith. True faith is true in its details and its principles. True faith is not some empty legend, but can be used as a model for the people of the world. A true faith comes with some sort of religious teaching, and can be traced to a historical figure. The historical founder should be morally upright, and the teachings should be able to relieve the suffering of those who follow them. The founder of Buddhism, for example, Sakyamuni Buddha, was the prince of the ancient Indian kingdom of Kapilavastu. Moral purity, as possessed by the Buddha, has unimaginable power to liberate sentient beings, and is therefore worthy of faith.

Religion begins and ends with faith and is also the first step to attaining Buddhahood. The *Flower Adornment Sutra* says that "Faith is the mother of merit and the source of awakening. It nourishes the roots of all virtue." The sutras also say "The great ocean of the Dharma can only be entered through faith."

Faith is the source of both self-power and other-power. Those wishing to be reborn in the Pure Land of the West must have faith that such a place exists and believe in the wondrous virtue of reciting Amitabha's name. Only through faith can one establish a goal and only then will one be able to be reborn there.

## 2. Vows （願）

Vows are based in faith, for only after one's faith has become strong can one generate a vow to attain awakening. Only by reciting the name of Amitabha Buddha with the vow to become a Buddha and liberate sentient beings can one respond to Amitabha Buddha's forty-eight great vows. Even better is to make a vow to focus all of one's merit and wisdom to be reborn in the Pure Land of the West, and dedicate one's merit so that all sentient beings can be reborn in the Pure Land.

## 3. Practice （行）

Faith, vows, and practice are like the three legs of a tripod, for the structure to stand none can be lacking. When faith has allowed one to generate a vow, one can then engage in practice, namely, doing good deeds and reciting Amitabha Buddha's name. When one can recite the name with single-minded concentration, all that is left is to await the ripening of causes and conditions to find rebirth in the Pure Land.

Not only does seeking rebirth in the Pure Land of the West require faith, vows, and practice, but cultivation of other forms of Buddhism requires the same sort of commitments. In the same way, one must hold incorruptible faith in the Triple Gem. A practitioner generates the same four universal vows to liberate limitless sentient beings, eradicate endless afflictions, learn infinite teachings, and attain supreme Buddhahood. Furthermore, there are many Buddhist practices including undertaking the five precepts and ten wholesome actions, applying the six perfections, engaging in the threefold training, cultivating the four immeasurable minds, and so forth. Only with these three will the goal be reached, which is why faith, vows, and practice are called the "three great supports" for attaining Buddhahood.

S

## Sutra
契經

*See:* Gem, triple; sutras, twelve divisions of; translators, four great Chinese; Tripitaka.

## Sutras, Twelve Divisions of
十二部經

*See also*: Gem, triple; teachings, four modes of; Tripitaka.

The Buddha's teachings are great, profound, and extremely subtle. The Buddhist sutras are made up of numerous texts and many volumes, amounting to more than nine thousand fascicles. Together these texts are known as the "twelve divisions of the sutras." There are some who do not understand and think that this means that the Buddhist teachings are made up of only twelve texts. However, the twelve divisions are actually twelve different genres of narrative form and content that are present throughout the sutras. They are as follows, with Sanskrit names given first:

### 1. Sutra（長行）

Technically, a "sutra" is a prose narrative, and directly records the teachings of the Buddha without any restrictions as to sentence length. The *Amitabha Sutra* and *Heart Sutra* are examples of this category.

### 2. Geya（重頌）

Geya writings repeat in verse form the contents of a prose text immediately preceding it. An example of this would be the verses in the Universal Gate chapter of the *Lotus Sutra*.

### 3. Gatha（孤起）

Gatha writings record the teachings of the Buddha entirely in verse form. The *Dharmapada* and *Buddhacarita* are examples of gatha.

### 4. Avadana（譬喻）

Avadana are allegorical stories or parables to explain the meaning of the Dharma. Examples include the *Sutra of One Hundred Parables*, as well as the Parables chapter in the *Lotus Sutra*, among others.

### 5. Nidana（因緣）

Nidana writings describe the causes and conditions under which the Buddha gives his teaching and instruction. The introductory chapters in the various sutras are examples of this.

## 6. Udana （無問自說）

Udana writings are teachings given by Buddha that are not prompted by any question. The *Amitabha Sutra* is an example of this.

## 7. Jataka （本生）

Jataka writings record what the Buddha said about the causes and conditions of his own past lives. Examples of this are the *Jataka Sutra*, the *Six Perfections Sutra*, and the *Miscellaneous Treasures Sutra*.

## 8. Itivrttaka （本事）

Itivrttaka writings record what the Buddha said about the causes and conditions of his disciples' past lives. One such example is the Medicine King Bodhisattva chapter in the *Lotus Sutra*.

## 9. Abdhutadharma （未曾有）

Abdhutadharma writings record the unique and fantastic attributes of the Buddha. One such text is the *Sutra on the Causes and Conditions of Miracles*.

## 10. Vaipulya （方廣）

Vaipulya writings proclaim the universal and profound meaning of the teachings, like the *Flower Adornment Sutra*.

## 11. Upadesa （論議）

Upadesa writings contain discussion and debate. This refers to texts which are largely in question-and-answer format, like the *Vimalakirti Sutra*.

## 12. *Vyakarana*（授記）

Vyakarana writings contain the Buddha's predictions of when various disciples or bodhisattvas will attain awakening. One such text is the Five Hundred Receive Predictions chapter of the *Lotus Sutra*.

The twelve divisions of the sutras described above are also called *shier fenjiao*（十二分教）, "twelve divisions of the teaching," and *shier shengjiao*（十二聖教）, "twelvefold noble teaching." The twelve divisions are actually twelve teaching methods used by the Buddha, and show the expediency of his teaching methodology as well as his wisdom in tailoring his message to suit the needs of his audience. The twelve divisions of the sutras are also a useful methodology for modern educators.

# Swastika
# 卍字

All world religions have their various symbols, signs, and ritual objects to represent their core ideas. The most commonly seen symbols used to represent Buddhism include: the swastika (卍) sign, the Dharma wheel, the lotus flower, the *stupa*, the halo of light, Buddhist beads, the bodhi tree, the *mandala*, and the Buddhist flag. Among these symbols, Buddhists and non-Buddhists alike are often curious about Buddhism's association with the swastika, and what it really means.

The swastika is one of the Buddha's "eighty noble characteristics," a set of physical features which manifest on the Buddha as a result of previous wholesome karma. The swastika in particular appears on such places as the breast of Buddhas and tenth-stage bodhisattvas. The sign symbolizes the coming together of good fortune and all virtues. It has been used in India since ancient times as a symbol for good fortune, purity, and perfection. Later, both the swastika and the Dharma wheel became symbols to represent Buddhism, and both are commonly seen on Buddhist structures, ritual objects, and even on such Buddhist souvenirs as necklaces, pins, and stickers.

In Mandarin Chinese the swastika symbol (卍) is treated as a Chinese character and pronounced as *wan* (萬), but this pronunciation is not present in any early texts or records. It was not until 638 CE that Empress Wu Zetian set the pronunciation as *wan*. *Wan* means "the coming together of good fortune and virtue," signifying fortune, sacred purity, and the perfection of merit.

However, since the Nazis in Germany used the swastika as their party emblem, people have come to associate the sign as a symbol of struggle. Actually, the Nazi swastika is drawn on a slant, and thus differs from the Buddhist swastika (卍), but in order to avoiding creating any impediment to the development of Buddhism, Buddhist circles in Germany still try to avoid using the swastika as much as possible. Actually, the Nazi usage of the swastika as their symbol, though resembling the Buddhist sign, was really an attempt to employ a false image of peace as a cover for their acts of war!

The swastika was originally just a symbol and not considered a Chinese character. But after its use for generations it is not considered different from any other character. This reflects the customary practice of using the symbol, but also shows some of the misunderstandings that arise when Sanskrit texts are translated into Chinese.

Additionally, there are two variants of the swastika symbol used throughout Buddhist writings: the right-facing swastika ( 卍) and the left-facing swastika (卐). There are various conceptions of which variant is the "correct" variant, mostly derived from which more completely depicts the clockwise circumambulation of stupas and the clockwise turning of the Dharma wheel. Each variant has its staunch advocates who believe that only their method for drawing the sign is consistent with the clockwise motion. Even during the 1960s, many senior monks within Buddhist circles in Taiwan still held opposing views over which swastika variant was correct. However, in June of 1963, Venerable Master Hsing Yun led a pilgrimage to the sacred Buddhist sites of India where they discovered an ancient circular stupa at the Deer Park, around which were rows filled with right-facing swastikas (卍). The stupa was built during the time of King Asoka around 300 BCE, to commemorate the spot where the Buddha in the past had entered deep meditation. From this, Venerable Master Hsing Yun became even more convinced that the view he had previously advocated was correct. How the swastika depicts the direction it is turning cannot be determined from our point of view, but only by how the swastika itself is constructed. Thus, the right-facing swastika (卍) best represents the sacred clockwise direction.

Since the beginning, the symbols representing Buddhism have taken many forms, like the swastika, the Dharma wheel, the lotus flower, the stupa, the halo of light, Buddhist beads, the bodhi tree, the mandala, and the Buddhist flag; it is hard to establish one as definitively representative. Therefore, although Buddhism is a religion that believes in freedom and democracy, in the future it would seem best for all Buddhists to come together and select a single symbol from among these, so that there could be a single Buddhist symbol with a degree of authority.

S

# T

## Teachers
## 教師

*See also*: Field of merit; reliance, four kinds of.

## Teaching, Four Modes of
## 四悉檀

*See also*: Mountain gate; parables of the *Lotus Sutra*; sutras,
   twelve divisions of.

There is a saying that, "The Buddha teaches the Dharma with one
voice, and sentient beings each understand according to their level." This is because the Buddha excels at adapting his teachings to
his audience by applying the four teaching modes.

   In Chinese the four are called *xitan* (悉檀), which is a transliteration of the Sanskrit *siddhanta*, "accomplishment." They describe the
four methods that the Buddha used to liberate sentient beings. Since
these methods are employed according to the spiritual capacity of
sentient beings, they are able to accomplish the task of liberating all
sentient beings; that is why they are called "accomplishments."

## 1. Worldly Method (世界悉檀)

This method utilizes explanations of causes and conditions using mundane phenomena. It uses mundane thinking, language, and concepts to explain the truth of dependent origination. For example, sentient beings are a combination of the five aggregates, and are therefore empty. But non-Buddhists generally see the "self" as real and concrete. The Buddha thus teaches in accordance with everyday phenomena so that most people will understand, be pleased with the teaching, and gain some wisdom. For this reason the method is also known as the "method that pleases."

## 2. Individual Method (各各為人悉檀)

This is the method used by the Buddha to teach various supramundane practices in accordance with the spiritual capacity and ability of each individual sentient being, so that in doing so they would be able to generate wholesome roots. The Buddha would do this by observing each individual beings superior and inferior faculties, seeing the depth of their wholesome roots, and providing them the appropriate teaching. In this way the Buddha established their faith and fostered their wholesome roots. Therefore it is also known as the "method for generating wholesomeness."

## 3. Specific Method (對治悉檀)

This method provides certain Dharma teachings to correspond to sentient beings' specific afflictions, such as greed, anger, and ignorance. For example, for those beings with much greed, the Buddha would teach them the contemplation of impurity. For those beings with much anger he would teach the contemplation of compassion. For beings with distracted minds he would teach the contemplation of counting the breath. For beings who are ignorant he would teach the contemplation of causes and conditions. For sentient beings with many obstacles, he would teach contemplation through reciting Amitabha Buddha's name. This "specific" method is a means to eliminate the afflictions and negative karma of sentient beings. For this reason it is known as the "method for eliminating negativity."

### 4. Ultimate Method（第一義悉檀）

With this method the Buddha employs skillful means to teach the principles of the Middle Way as the one reality, according to the ultimate truth as understood by the Buddha, so that sentient beings can eliminate delusion and attain awakening. To overcome all discursive language, the Buddha teaches the ultimate truth directly to show the principles behind the true reality of all phenomena. This allows sentient beings to accord with the teachings, and is as such known as the "method through principles."

These four modes of teaching are what underpin the Tripitaka, the twelve divisions of the sutras, and their associated 84,000 practices. Only the Buddha can master all of these methods and use them to respond to the spiritual capacity of sentient beings with unimpeded freedom. Because the Buddha is able to apply the four modes of teaching to such great effect, and since he can perfectly modify the teachings based on the audience's capacity, the Buddha is the greatest of all educators. It is for this reason that the Buddha's teachings act as a light for the world that shall never be extinguished.

# Temporary Monastic Lodging
## 掛單

*See also*: Wandering mendicant.

In order to travel in search of teachers and to learn the way, the Chan masters of the past would live temporarily in various different temples and monasteries.

The term used to describe requesting temporary residence in Chinese is *guadan* (掛單), "hang up the name," referring to a small card with a monastic's ordination name that is hung above his room in a monastery. This process is also sometimes called *guaxi* (掛錫), "hang up the staff," or *guabo* (掛鉢), "hang up the bowl," referring to hanging up one's walking staff and travel bag, with the three robes and bowl on a peg within the monastic dormitory.

According to the Chan temple rules, any traveling monastic who is fully ordained and is equipped with monastic robes, an alms bowl, and an ordination certificate, can go to any monastery and register for temporary lodging at the "hall of clouds and water," named after the image of a monastic wandering as freely as clouds that float through the sky,

The traditional process for requesting such temporary lodgings included a certain set of procedures: One must first wait in the reception hall where the steward makes the initial inquiry and passes on the information obtained to the receptionist. Once the receptionist arrives, the visitor quickly says, "I bow to the receptionist," and if the receptionist says "Only a half bow," then the visitor should follow the instructions and make a half bow.

At this time, the receptionist will ask, "What is your Dharma name and in which temple do you reside?" The guest answers the question in the form of, "My name is ... and my temple is ...."

The receptionist will then ask, "Where have you come from and what do you intend to do?" If the guest is traveling and only intends to stay for one or two nights, the guest then answers, "My presence will just be a temporary bother to the temple." Upon hearing this, the receptionist generally makes no further inquiries and calls for someone to lead the guest to his lodgings. If the guest wishes to stay for a while and study he says, "I would like to learn from the temple," at which point the receptionist will ask a few more questions, such as: "How old are you and where have you studied in the past?" In this way the receptionist gains a better understanding of the situation so that arrangements can be made to give the guest access to the meditation hall, the Amitabha chanting hall, the Buddhist seminary, and to assign the guest work duty. The guest should answer the questions in a comfortable and unhurried manner, speaking neither too fast nor too slow, and be sure to answer properly and correctly.

After the interview, the guest's ordination certificate and belongings will be inspected and then arrangements for the guest's lodging will be made. By this time, the receptionist has already sent someone to inform the head of the dormitory. Upon meeting the head of the dorm, the guest will bow to him, and he will say to the guest, "See the receptionist off." The receptionist will then say to the guest, "There is no need to do so. Stay and chat with the head of the dorm." The head of the dorm will then ask another guest who has been living there for some time: "Lead this new visitor to our hall and show him his lodgings." It is only at this point that the guest can take his belongings and settle in to his temporary lodgings.

After a monastic takes up temporary monastic lodging, he must observe the rules. If he wishes to ask for instruction from a senior teacher, an appointment must be made in advance. He must also observe the following five rules:

1. One must be polite and circumspect.
2. One must know the seating order; that is, one must appreciate how juniors and seniors interact and know where one is situated in the order of seniority.
3. One must refrain from idle conversation; that is, one must not talk about trivialities unrelated to study and practice.
4. One must listen carefully, and master what one has learned by committing it to memory.
5. One must be able to receive the teachings and then truly practice them.

After a monastic has registered, he is led to his lodging. After he settles in and is accepted into the community, it is said that he has *andan* (安單), "settled his name," and eventually *jindan* (進單), "joined his name," to the monastery. To visit other monastics is called to *kandan* (看單), "see their name," and to be allowed to remain at the monastery is to *liudan* (留單), "remain in name." If a visiting monastic breaks the rules he is said to *qiandan* (遷單). "remove his name," and if he departs without requesting leave he is said to *liudan* (溜單), "slip one's name away."

In the past, the "travel bag" carried by monastics when registering for temporary lodging contained only the following eighteen items: willow branch, washing powder, three robes, water bottle, alms bowl, sitting mat, walking staff, incense burner, incense box, water strainer, hand towel, knife, fire making gear, tweezers, rope bed, a copy of the sutras and the vinaya, Buddha statue, and bodhisattva statue. A monastic carried nothing more than these eighteen items, such that there is a saying in Chinese that "a monastic's bag weighs two and a half pounds." This clearly shows the simplicity of the monastic life, for they are not driven by or burdened with things. This is why they can wander the world like drifting clouds and flowing water, making their home anywhere. Hence, in Chinese it is said of monastics that, "Having left home, they are as clouds and water."

Today, not only can members of the monastic order register for temporary lodging at most Buddhist temples and monasteries, but there are quite a few temples who accept lay Buddhists to stay for several days at a time. In doing so, lay Buddhists can remove themselves from the hustle and bustle of mundane life and partake of the serene harmony of the monastery or temple. They can cleanse their mind of the grime of mundane concerns before setting sail once more with renewed spirits. A Buddhist monastery is a place to refuel.

Whoever goes to a monastery or temple today, whether they are monastics or lay Buddhists, they will find the process of registering for temporary monastic lodgings to be simple, easy, and conducted in a gracious and courteous manner. This is a far cry from the past, when monastics wishing to register for temporary lodging had to undergo interrogations and examination at layer upon layer of check points, and in some case were even subject to humiliation and abuse before they could fulfill their wish. In order to seek the teachings and learn the Dharma, the etiquette surrounding registration for temporary lodging required respectfulness, piety, perseverance, and patience. Only those able to grind away all attachment to the self and material things would be successful, clearly showing how difficult it is to seek the Dharma.

# Three Treatise School
## 三論宗
*See also*: Schools of Chinese Buddhism, eight.

# Thus Have I Heard
## 如是我聞

When the Buddha was about to enter final *nirvana*, the Venerable Ananda, on behalf of all there assembled, asked the Buddha four questions. Among these, the following question was posed: "Lord Buddha, during your time on earth, it has been easy for all of us to believe the teachings that you spoke. After your final *nirvana*, how can we ensure that people will have faith in your teachings?"

The Buddha replied, "When recounting my teachings, remember to state, 'thus have I heard,' to show that you, Ananda, heard what I said." This is the origin of the phrase "Thus have I heard," which can be found at the beginning of the Buddhist sutras today.

The phrase "Thus have I heard" has three functions:

### 1. To Remove the Three Doubts (斷三種疑惑)
The Venerable Ananda was the Buddha's attendant; he possessed the thirty-two marks of excellence and resembled the Buddha in appearance. During the council to compile the Buddhist canon held after the Buddha's final *nirvana*, it was the general consensus of those assembled to have Ananda lead reciting the verbal teachings of the Buddha. When Ananda ascended the dais to speak the Dharma, a series of misunderstandings broke out among the assembly. Some people thought that the Buddha had not really entered final *nirvana*, but had returned once more to give teachings. Some thought Ananda was a Buddha from some other world

system who had come to give teachings. And there were still others who thought that Ananda himself had become a Buddha. In order to remove these three doubts, the phrase "Thus have I heard" shows that the "I," Ananda, has heard the teachings that were given by the Buddha. Every word and every sentence spoken by Ananda in this context are indeed the teachings proclaimed by the Buddha. It is not the case that Ananda himself has become a Buddha, nor has a Buddha from some other place come to give teachings.

### 2. *To Quell Disputes* (息諍)

There is a saying that, "The Buddha teaches the Dharma with one voice, and sentient beings each understand according to their level." Sentient beings vary in spiritual capacity, and they each differ in terms of how they understand and comprehend the Buddha's teachings. In order to avoid any future disagreements regarding the Buddhist sutras, the phrase "Thus have I heard" stands for the verbal teachings of the Buddha. In this way, disputes regarding personal opinions can be avoided.

### 3. *To Distinguish Buddhism* (異邪)

How can we differentiate between Buddhist sutras and non-Buddhist texts? The phrase "Thus have I heard" clearly indicates that this is a Buddhist sutra, and differentiates it from the texts of all other religions. This allows Buddhists to know which teachings to follow.

"Thus have I heard" explains how Buddhists should read the sutras and listen to the true Dharma. But, it is important to remember that, in Buddhism, a greater emphasis is placed on actual practice. This is why sutras end with the phrase, "Believed it, received it, and practiced it." This shows that understanding and practice are equally important. Understanding and practice are like the two wings of a bird or the two wheels or a cart, for neither can be lacking.

## Tiantai School
## 天台宗
*See:* Schools of Chinese Buddhism, eight.

## Training, Threefold
## 三學
*See also:* Mountain gate; ordination; *prajna*; precepts, five; precepts, eight; *samadhi*; wisdom, four kinds of; wisdom, three kinds of.

To cultivate the Buddhist path we must eliminate the three poisons of greed, anger, and ignorance. To do this we can cultivate the "three trainings" of morality, meditative concentration, and wisdom.

### 1. Training on Morality (戒學)
This is also known as *sila* and *vinaya*, which refer to the Buddhist precepts. The precepts show the norms and standards for cultivating our bodies and minds; following them can prevent all negative karma and generate all positive karma. In life we should not only adhere to the rules and keep from transgressions, but we should engage in good works to purify the body and mind, allowing for meditative concentration.

There are three kinds of precepts. The first kind is called "precepts for proper conduct," which include the five precepts, ten precepts, and monastic precepts that prevent wrongdoing and negative karma. The second kind are "precepts for wholesome deeds," which means applying the precepts in one's own life to perform wholesome deeds. The third kind are "precepts for benefiting sentient beings," which means having compassion for all beings as one's precepts and providing benefit to them. These three kinds of precepts can be seen in the famous Buddhist verse "Do nothing that is unwholesome, do all that is wholesome, purify the mind. This is the teaching of all Buddhas."

### 2. Training on Meditative Concentration (定學)

Meditation means to bring cessation to one's karmic conditions and purify the mind. Mediation is also the process of concentrating the mind and cultivating awareness, and is a method to settle the mind. During meditation practice, we watch the six sense organs to turn away delusional thought and eliminate affliction. By fixing the mind in one-pointed concentration the mind and body become calm and settled, and wisdom will arise.

There are three levels of meditative concentration: mundane meditation, supramundane meditation, and highest supramundane meditation. Mundane meditation is practiced by ordinary people and non-Buddhists; it uses the method of mindfulness of breathing to achieve extraordinary spiritual attainments. Supramundane meditation is practiced by *sravakas* and *pratyekabuddhas,* and uses the method of observing form to achieve the highest Hinayana attainments. The highest supramundane meditation is practiced by Mahayana bodhisattvas, and uses the method of observing the mind to achieve supreme awakening.

### 3. Training on Wisdom (慧學)

This refers to *prajna*-wisdom. This is the ultimate truth, the wisdom that is capable of perceiving reality and eliminating confusion. When developing this wisdom, we must cultivate meditative concentration and eliminate ignorance and delusion so that we can remove our afflictions and directly awaken to the truth. This is the attainment of Buddhahood, and brings freedom to the body and mind.

There are also three levels of wisdom: mundane wisdom, supramundane wisdom, and the highest supramundane wisdom. Mundane wisdom is the wisdom of ordinary people and outsiders; it does not bring freedom nor does it remove delusion or karma. Supramundane wisdom is the wisdom of *sravakas* and *pratyeka-buddhas*, also known as "wisdom of all phenomena," though it is not the highest wisdom. The highest supramundane wisdom is the wisdom of Buddhas and bodhisattvas, also known as "complete wisdom of all phenomena," and is an unsurpassable form of wisdom.

The threefold training of morality, meditative concentration, and wisdom is also known as the "three undefiled trainings." They are the factors that sentient beings practice to attain Buddhahood. They are to be cultivated in order: By relying on morality, one achieves meditative concentration, by relying on meditative concentration one develops wisdom, and by relying on wisdom one attains Buddhahood.

## Translators, Four Great Chinese
## 四大譯師

*See also*: Untranslatable terms, five kinds of.

After Buddhism came to China, the task of translating the sutras stirred a wave of enthusiasm for research into Buddhist study and thought. This facilitated the successive establishment of the various schools and sects and gave rise to new perspectives that allowed for the fervent development of Chinese Buddhism.

The four sutra translators who were the most prolific and influential in the history of Chinese Buddhism are: Kumarajiva, Xuanzang, Paramartha, and Yijing. The Esoteric School additionally venerates the translator Amoghavajra, who they recognize as the Sixth Patriarch of their school.

### 1. Kumarajiva (鳩摩羅什)

Kumarajiva (344-413 CE) came from the kingdom of Qiuci (now Shule in Xinjiang Province). Kumarajiva's father, Kumarayana, was the son of the prime minister in an Indian kingdom, but he left for Qiuci because he did not want to succeed his father as prime minister. Kumarayana married the king's sister, and they had a son, Kumarajiva. When Kumarajiva was seven, his mother went on a hunger strike, demanding that her husband allow her to join the monastic order. The father assented and, thereupon, mother and son lived a life together as wandering monastics.

Kumarajiva had been bright from an early age. As he followed his mother in her pursuit of the Way, he later studied abroad in India, learning from all the famous scholars as his reputation spread far and wide across the five regions of India. Fu Jian (r. 357-85 CE) of the Former Qin dynasty heard of his virtue and sent his general Lü Guang (337-399 CE) to receive Kumarajiva with numerous soldiers. But it was not until 401 CE that Kumarajiva arrived in Chang'an. The ruler Yao Xing (r. 393-416) honored him as National Master and installed him in the Xiaoyao Garden, where he began his work translating the sutras along with such individuals as Sengzhao (384-414 CE) and Sengyan (4th-5th cent. CE), becoming quite famous for a time. Kumarajiva translated more than three hundred fascicles of Buddhist texts, and among these, the *Lotus Sutra*, the *Vimalakirti Sutra*, the *Diamond Sutra*, and the *Amitabha Sutra* are still widely chanted and memorized by people today.

Beyond this, Kumarajiva translated in succession the *Treatise on the Middle Way*, the *Treatise in a Hundred Verses*, and the *Treatise on the Perfection of Great Wisdom*, among others there texts systematically introduced the theories of Nagarjuna's (150-250 CE) Madhyamaka and had a tremendous impact upon the development of Chinese Buddhism. Kumarajiva has many disciples, with some of his prominent disciples later founding the Three Treatise School and the Establishing the Truth School.

Since he first joined the monastic order under Bandhudatta, Kumarajiva studied the Hinayana, yet later on he also studied the Mahayana teachings. When Bandhudatta learned about this, he actually honored Kumarajiva as his teacher, thereby leaving to posterity this celebrated story of how the Mahayana Buddhist and the Hinayana Buddhist served as one another's teacher.

## 2. Xuanzang (玄奘)

Xuangzang (600-664 CE) was born in Chenliu in Henan Province in the year 600 CE. He joined the monastic order as a youth and studied widely from such sutras and treatises as the *Nirvana Sutra*, the *Treatise on the Great Compendium of the Abhidharma*, the *Compendium of the Mahayana*, the *Treatise on Establishing the Truth*, and the *Treatise on the Treasury of the Abhidharma*. Because the various teachers at the time were inconsistent in their understanding of the Buddhist scriptures with many wide and differing opinions, Xuanzang decided to journey to India and bring back the original texts of the Consciousness-Only philosophy.

In 629 CE, Xuanzang crossed more than several hundred miles of desert all by himself with the determination to seek the Dharma. It was said that he "prefered to take one more step towards death in the West rather than take one step back towards life in the East."

After experiencing hardships and difficulties, and surviving several brushes with death, Xuanzang finally arrived at Nalanda Monastery in India, where he came to know Silabhadra (ca. 6th cent. CE), the leading authority on Consciousness-Only philosophy. Xuanzang studied such texts as the *Treatise on the Stages of the Yogacara Practitioner*, the *Acclamation of Sutras*, and the *Treatise on the Great Compendium of the Abhidharma*, and gained a deep understanding and connection with the profound meaning of the Consciousness-Only doctrines.

In the nineteenth year of the Zhenguan reign (645 CE), Xuanzang returned to Chang'an bringing with him more than six hundred texts from the Hinayana and Mahayana canons. The most important of these were the precious texts of the Consciousness-Only School, such as the *Thirty Verses on the Consciousness-Only Treatise*, the *Twenty Verses on the Consciousness-Only Treatise*, the *Compendium of the Mahayana*, the *Treatise on Establishing Consciousness Only*, and the *Treatise on the Stages of the Yogacara Practitioner*. Xuangzang's reputation spread throughout the land.

Upon his return to Chang'an, Xuanzang spent the next twenty years training his disciples and carrying on his sutra translation work. In total, Xuanzang translated over a thousand fascicles of texts, over a quarter of all the Buddhist texts translated into Chinese. He laid the foundation for the rise of the Consciousness-Only School of Chinese Buddhism and was treated by Emperor Gaozong as a national treasure.

### 3. Paramartha（真諦）

Paramartha (499-569 CE) came from Udyana in northwestern India. He was well-versed in the Tripitaka and the five vinaya texts, and had gained an understanding of the profound principles of the Mahayana through extensive study and research. In 546 CE, Paramartha arrived at China's southern coast with many Buddhist sutras, and gained the deep respect of Emperor Wu of the Liang dynasty (r. 502-549 CE).

Despite having to wander from place to place during the Hou Jing rebellion (549 CE), Paramartha continued his translation work, producing nearly three hundred fascicles of Buddhist texts. His major translations include such Consciousness-Only texts as the *Treatise on the Transformation of Consciousness* and the *Treatise on Consciousness-Only in the Mahayana*, as well as the *Sutra of Golden Light*, the *Compendium of the Mahayana*, the *Explanation on the Compendium of the Mahayana*, and the *Awakening of Faith in Mahayana*. Additionally he produced an incredible corpus of commentaries and notes with which he endeavored to make his meaning perfectly clear. With the breadth of his understanding and the excellence of his methodology, he is rightly known as a leading figure in the history of Chinese Buddhism.

### 4. Yijing（義淨）

Yijing (635-713 CE) came from Fanyang in Hebei Province. At the age of twelve and owing to his admiration of Xuanzang, Yijing decided to join the monastic order to follow Xuanzang's example of going to India to seek the Dharma.

After he requested and received full ordination at the age of twenty, Yijing was concerned over how incomplete the vinaya canon for *bhiksus* had remained, which further strengthened his determination to go to India and explore vinaya studies. Having prepared himself and raised funds for seventeen years, Yijing invited a group of a dozen like-minded companions, including Chuyi, Hongwei, Xuanda, and Shanxing, to accompany him on the journey. However, when this impressive group arrived in Guangzhou, concerns over the dangers of the ocean voyage arose in everyone's mind, and one after the other, the members of the group decided to proceed no further. Only Yijing remained faithful to his original intent and courageously went on by himself. Along the way, Yijing fell ill and was also once robbed by bandits, but none of this caused him to waver in his mission to seek the Dharma. Finally, he arrived at the great Buddhist university, Nalanda Monastery, where he studied for ten years. Later, he also studied abroad in Sumatra for seven years. In his travels, Yijing visited more than thirty countries.

When he returned to China, he brought with him about four hundred sutras and works of Abhidharma in Sanskrit, and subsequently devoted his energies to translating them. Over the next twelve years, Yijing translated more than two hundred fascicles of sutras and treatises, with the majority of his work coming from the vinaya canon. The various texts on the monastic rules and precepts from the Sarvastivadin Vinaya preserved today are mostly his work.

## 5. Amoghavajra (不空)

Amoghavajra (705-774 CE) came from Sri Lanka, and possessed an innate intelligence. During his early years, he accompanied his uncle on journeys to the countries of Southeast Asia and later joined the monastic order. In his early years, he studied with Vajrabodhi (671-741 CE) and received a complete education in the "five parts" and "three secrets." He also honored his teacher's dying wish and returned once more to India to seek the Dharma.

Upon his return to China, Amoghavajra bestowed an empowerment upon Emperor Xuanzong (r. 712-756), and came to reside in Jingying Monastery. Since his prayers for rain were miraculously effective, he was given the imperial title "Wisdom Treasure" and given a purple robe. He was revered by the emperors Xuanzong, Suzong (r. 756-762 CE) and Daizong (r. 762-779 CE) during their reigns. Amoghavajra translated more than one hundred and twenty fascicles of Buddhist texts, and became the Sixth Patriarch in the Esoteric School.

Each of these five great translators discussed above had to leave their hometowns and overcome difficulty and hardship, only achieving success after much hard work and diligent practice. They left behind a rich treasury of sutras. Therefore, when Buddhists read the sutras today, one should feel gratitude and keep in mind a sense of utmost sincerity and devout respect for the great achievements of these exalted figures.

## Tripitaka
三藏

*See also:* Sutras, twelve divisions of; translators, four great
    Chinese.

After the Buddha's final *nirvana*, his disciples wished to preserve the Buddha's teachings. Over a number of Buddhist councils the teachings were compiled, edited, and eventually divided into three divisions: the collection of discourses, the collection of monastic rules, and the collection of treatises. This became known as the *tripitaka* in Sanskrit, or *sancang* (三藏) in Chinese, meaning "three collections," encompassing the threefold division of the sacred texts of Indian Buddhism.

### 1. Collection of Discourses (經藏)

In Sanskrit this collection is called *sutra*, meaning "concordant scriptures." The basic meaning here is that the teachings of the sutras are mutually in accord with one another, just as all the flowers on a stringed garland are interconnected.

The sutras contain all that accords with the principles of the Buddhas above, and all the teachings of the Buddha that accord with the spiritual capacity of sentient beings below. There is a verse that describes the various types of teachings the Buddha delivered across his forty-nine year teaching career:

> *Flower Adornment* the first three weeks.
> *Agamas*, twelve years; *vaipulya*, eight years.
> Twenty-two years teaching *prajna*,
> *Lotus* and *Nirvana* totaled eight years.

Among these, the *vaipulya* scriptures include various Mahayana scriptures beyond those listed above, such as the *Vimalakirti Sutra*, the *Queen Srimala Sutra*, and the *Sutra of Golden Light*.

### 2. Collection of Monastic Rules (律藏)

In Sanskrit this collection is called *vinaya*, which means "discipline and restraint." This is the body of monastic rules the Buddha instituted to discipline the minds of his disciples and correct their bad habits. In Chinese the *vinaya* is also called *mie* (滅), "extinguish," for the Buddhist precepts can extinguish the faults and wrongdoings of physical, verbal, and mental karma.

There are three types of vinaya texts: expansive vinaya, precept texts, and vinaya commentaries. Expansive vinaya, like the *Ten Recitation Vinaya*, the *Four-Part Vinaya*, the *Mahasamghika Vinaya*, and the *Five-Part Vinaya*, explain the origins of how the Buddha formulated the monastic precepts and their finer details. Precept texts, like the *Bhiksu Precepts* and *Bhiksuni Precepts*, only contain a list of monastic rules, and are for the purpose of recitation. Vinaya commentaries, like the *Treatise on the Sarvastivadin Vinaya* and others, comment upon the monastic rules.

### 3. Collection of Treatises （論藏）

In Sanskrit, this collection is called *abhidharma*, which means "analysis of the Dharma," and showcases the wisdom to be gained from explicating the Dharma. The abhidharma is a collection of texts by disciples of the Buddha to discuss, explain, and organize the doctrines of the sutras. Some such texts that many people are familiar with include the *Treatise on the Middle Way*, the *Treatise of the Twelve Aspects*, the *Treatise on the Perfection of Great Wisdom*, the *Treatise in a Hundred Verses*, the *Treatise on the Stages of Yogacara Practitioners*, the *Treatise on the Awakening of Faith in Mahayana*, and the *Treatise on the Ten Stages Sutra*.

The texts of the Tripitaka constitute the teachings and doctrines of the Buddha, and Buddhists rely upon them to guide their cultivation. Monastics who are well versed in the collection of discourses are called "sutra masters." Those who are well versed in the collection of monastic rules are called "vinaya masters." And those well versed in the collection of treatises are called "abhidharma masters" or "treatise masters." Monastics well versed in all three collections are called "tripitaka masters." Monastics like Xuanzang (600-664 CE), Kumarajiva (344-413 CE), Paramartha (499-569 CE), Yijing (635-713 CE), Faxian (b. 340 ce), and even Zhu Shixing, among others, were well versed in the sutra, vinaya, and abhidharma texts of the tripitaka, and known as "tripitaka masters."

Consider the Triple Gem: It was because of the Dharma that the Buddha was able to attain awakening, and the Sangha is able to teach us because it maintains the true Dharma. Thus, among the Triple Gem, the Dharma is the most revered.

The *Diamond Sutra* states, "Wherever this sutra can be found, there also is the Buddha; and it should be honored as if it were one of his disciples." This shows how we should revere the Dharma.

## Truths, Four Noble
四聖諦

*See also: Nirvana;* path, noble eightfold; suffering, eight kinds of.

The Four Noble Truths were realized by the Buddha in his awakening, and constitute a general outline of the Dharma. What are the Four Noble Truths?

1. The truth of suffering (苦諦)
2. The truth of the cause of suffering (集諦)
3. The truth of the cessation of suffering (滅諦)
4. The truth of the path leading to the cessation of suffering (道諦)

The first noble truth, "suffering," describes human life in this world. The body experiences the pain and suffering of old age, sickness, and death while the mind experiences the pain and suffering of greed, anger, and ignorance. The natural world undergoes the pain and suffering of floods and fires. Our relationships are strained by the pain and suffering of being near loathsome people and being separated from loved ones. Society experiences pain and suffering in the form of broken dreams and hardship. Suffering is a fundamental characteristic of life.

The second noble truth identifies the causes of this suffering: ignorance and delusion, as well as karma from past lives. This includes physical karma of killing, stealing, and sexual misconduct; verbal karma of lying and argument; and mental karma of greed, anger, and wrong views. The suffering of life is simply the effect of all of these causes.

The third noble truth, the cessation of these causes, describes the state of the Buddha. This is the cessation of the accumulation of karma; a wonderful state where one can be liberated from the impermanence of the cycle of birth and death—the tranquility of *nirvana*. In the state of *nirvana* differences are replaced by equality and turmoil is replaced by tranquility. Attachment no longer arises, and a brilliant and infinite light shines throughout the world system.

The fourth noble truth is the path or process that can lead to cessation. Without cultivating the path, how can one expect to be like a Buddha? Without practice, one's faith and vows cannot be fulfilled. The path is made up of eight factors: right view, right thought, right speech, right action, right livelihood, right effort, right mindfulness, and right meditative concentration. Following this path leads to liberation.

The Four Noble Truths operate on both a mundane and supramundane level. The Venerable Aniruddha, one of the ten great disciples of the Buddha, once said, "The sun could grow cold and the moon could grow hot, but the Four Noble Truths spoken by the Buddha will never change."

T

# U

## Untranslatable Terms, Five Kinds of
五種不翻

*See also*: Translators, four great Chinese.

Buddhism began in India and flourished in China. Buddhism's growth in China was assisted by the translation of Buddhist sutras into Chinese, for only then was it possible for Buddhism to flourish in China and bear fruit to dazzle the world with its splendor.

The task of translating the Buddhist sutras into Chinese began during the Eastern Han period (25-220 CE) and reached its height during the Six Dynasties (420-581 CE), Sui (581-618 CE), and Tang (618-907 CE) periods. Translations of the Buddhist sutras not only formed the basis for spreading the Dharma, but have also provided scholars with source material for researching the histories of India, Central Asia, and the countries of the South China Sea. The translations expanded the vocabulary of Chinese literature, enriching the breadth of the culture.

The three highest principles to consider when translating are fidelity, elegance, and readability. A translation must be faithful to the original, as well as elegant in literary diction and comprehensible in meaning. According to biographies of eminent monks, over the centuries there have been more than one hundred monastic translators who have left their name to posterity, but among these, Kumarajiva, Xuanzang, Yijing, and Paramartha have been singled out as the four greatest translators in the history of Chinese Buddhism.

Kumarajiva took readability as his guiding principle for scriptural translation, believing it was more important to rely on the meaning rather than textual structure. The fluency of his translations and the polish of his verse have always entranced his readers. On the other hand, Xuanzang emphasized fidelity to the original text, and further advocated a system known as the "five categories of terms not translated." Later scholars have treated Xuanzang's work as a watershed, and have come to refer to the sutras translated before Xuanzang as the "old translations," and those that came after Xuanzang as the "new translations."

The "five categories of terms not translated" refers to five situations in which a word or passage from a source text is not given a semantic translation, but rather is transliterated in order to preserve the original pronunciation. The five categories of terms not translated are as follows:

### 1. Terms with Multiple Meanings（多含不翻）

Terms with multiple meanings are transliterated rather than translated. For example, the term *arhat* has the three meanings of "slayer of the enemy," "not reborn," and "worthy of respect," and is thus transliterated in Chinese as *luohan* (羅漢) The term *bhagavat* has the six meanings of "carefree," "flourishing," "dignified," "renowned reputation," "auspicious," and "revered," and is thus transliterated in

Chinese as *bojiefan* (薄伽梵). It would not be possible to translate these terms and choose only one of their meanings.

## 2. Terms with Esoteric Meanings (祕密不翻)

Terms with esoteric meanings, like the *dharani* and *mantras* found in the sutras, are sounds which resonate with all the Buddhas. Being so profound and inconceivable, they are not given a word for word translation of their meaning.

## 3. Terms of Reverence (尊貴不翻)

Terms that are subject to great reverence or respect are not translated. For example, *prajna* could be translated as *zhihui* (智慧), "wisdom," but "wisdom" can also mean a worldly cleverness and sophistication that stems from the defiled consciousness of discrimination. Wisdom can be virtuous or non-virtuous, beneficial or harmful. *Prajna* on the other hand is perfectly true, perfectly virtuous, and perfectly beautiful, and constitutes the unafflicted and undefiled nature of suchness. There is no word that is more honored or respected than *prajna*, hence it is not translated as "wisdom."

## 4. Terms Traditionally Transliterated (順古不翻)

For example, *anuttarasamyak-sambodhi* means "supreme, perfect awakening;" however since the Eastern Han (25-220 CE), generations of translators have always transliterated the term, and so in order to be consistent with time-honored practice, such terms are not translated.

## 5. Terms without Local Equivalent (此方無不翻)

Terms with no local equivalent in China are transliterated. For example, the fruit of the *amala* tree is native to India, though no such fruit exists in China. Thus when the fruit is mentioned it is transliterated as *anmoluo* (菴摩羅).

Observing these "five categories of terms not translated" has become standard practice in the sutra translations of later generations.

## Upali
優婆離
*See:* Disciples, ten great.

## Upasaka
優婆塞
*See:* Assembly, sevenfold.

## Upasika
優婆夷
*See:* Assembly, sevenfold.

## Uttara-kuru
北俱盧洲
*See:* Continents, four great; difficulties, eight.

# V

## Vajraputra
笑獅羅漢
*See:* Arhats, eighteen.

## Vanavasin
芭蕉羅漢
*See:* Arhats, eighteen.

## Vehicles, Five
五乘佛法
*See also:* Dharma realms, ten; heaven.

The Sanskrit word *yana*, "vehicle," can refer to any means of conveyance such as a road, a boat, or a cart. In his career of teaching the Dharma to liberate sentient beings, the Buddha divided the Dharma into five methods of practice called "vehicles," based upon the spiritual capacity of his followers. Following these five methods of practice can convey sentient beings from the cycle of birth and death on this shore to the *nirvana* of the other shore. The five vehicles are the human vehicle, the heavenly vehicle, the *sravaka* vehicle, the *pratyekabuddha* vehicle, and the bodhisattva vehicle.

## 1. The Human Vehicle （人乘）

The human vehicle emphasizes taking the three refuges and upholding the five precepts so that one can avoid the three lower realms of rebirth and instead be born as a human being. To undertake the three refuges means to take refuge in and rely upon the Triple Gem, with the Buddha as your guide, the Dharma as your truth, and the Sangha as your spiritual friends.

By relying upon the merit of the Triple Gem to empower and protect us, we can transcend the limitless suffering of cyclic existence, be free from fear, and liberate ourselves from all sorrow. There is a sutra that says, "By taking refuge in the Buddha, one will not fall into the hells; by taking refuge in the Dharma, one will not be reborn as a hungry ghost; and by taking refuge in the Sangha, one will not be reborn as an animal."

The five precepts are: to refrain from killing, which is not to violate the lives of others; to refrain from stealing, which is not to violate the property of others; to refrain from sexual misconduct, which is not to violate the honor or body of others; to refrain from lying, which is not to violate the reputation or trust of others; and to refrain from consuming intoxicants, which is not to consume any substance that would impair one's health or judgment and lead to harm.

## 2. The Heavenly Vehicle （天乘）

The heavenly vehicle involved practicing the ten wholesome actions and the eight *dhyana* meditation states, which can propel sentient beings into the heavenly realms. The ten wholesome actions are an extension and expansion of the five precepts, and correspond to the three types of karma: physical, verbal, and mental. Refraining from killing, stealing, and sexual misconduct constitutes physical karma. Refraining from dishonest speech, harsh speech, divisive speech, and idle speech constitutes verbal karma. Refraining from greed, anger, and wrong views constitutes mental karma.

Training in meditative concentration must be practiced as well. There are eight levels of meditative concentration which correspond to the four form heavens and the four formless heavens.

### 3. The Sravaka Vehicle（聲聞乘）

The *sravaka* vehicle is founded in the teaching of the Four Noble Truths, and can transport sentient beings beyond the three realms, to become arhats and attain *nirvana* without remainder. The Four Noble Truths are: the truth of suffering, which explains how the world is characterized by suffering; the truth of the cause of suffering, which shows how greed, anger, and ignorance lead to the cycle of birth and death; the truth of the cessation of suffering, which describes the pure state of *nirvana* that is the absence of all suffering; and the truth of the path leading to the cessation of suffering, which includes teachings such as the threefold training, the Noble Eightfold Path, and the thirty-seven aspects of awakening.

These four truths describe the true reality of human life and the universe, which only sages are able to profoundly realize with certainty. The *Sutra of the Teachings Bequeathed by the Buddha* says, "The Buddha's explanation of the truth of suffering means that suffering is true and real, for it cannot be turned into happiness; the cause of suffering is the real cause, for there is no other. If suffering is to cease, it must be that its cause ceases, for when its cause ceases, so does its effect. The path that leads to the cessation of suffering is the true and real path, for there is no other."

### 4. The Pratyekabuddha Vehicle（緣覺乘）

The *pratyekabuddha* vehicle has the twelve links of dependent origination as its basis, which can transport sentient beings beyond the three realms into *nirvana* without remainder by becoming *pratyekabuddhas*. Dependent origination is the process by which all mundane phenomena arise. It is the simple formula that "When there is this, then there is that. When this arises, then that arises. When there is no this, then there is no that. When this ceases, then that ceases." The teaching of dependent origination describes an interdependent relationship of cause and effect that ties together the existence of all phenomena. All sentient beings are subject to dependent origination as they travel through the cycle of birth and death.

*Pratyekabuddhas* attain awakening by contemplating the twelve links of dependent origination. The twelve links are: mental formations depend upon ignorance, consciousness depends upon mental formations, name and form depend upon consciousness, the six sense organs depend upon name and form, contact depends upon the six sense organs, feeling depends upon contact, craving depends upon feeling, clinging depends upon craving, becoming depends upon clinging, birth depends upon becoming, aging and death depends upon birth.

### 5. The Bodhisattva Vehicle（菩薩乘）

The bodhisattva vehicle is founded upon compassion, wisdom, and the six perfections, such that it can transport sentient beings beyond the three realms to the other shore of great *nirvana* of unsurpassed awakening. The six perfections, called *paramita* in

V

means that which allows us to cross over and reach the other shore. The six perfections are giving, morality, patience, diligence, meditative concentration, and wisdom.

The human and heavenly vehicles are focused on improving the mind by accumulating merit in this world, so that we can find fulfillment and happiness in this life and the next. This is the aspect of the Dharma that is held in common with the whole world. For example Confucianism is similar to the human vehicle of Buddhism, and Christianity and Islam are more similar to the heavenly vehicle. The *sravaka* vehicle and *pratyekabuddha* vehicle emphasize renunciation and liberation, where the bliss of *nirvana* is considered the ultimate goal. This is similar to the Daoist concept of *wuwei* (無為), "non-action" that renounces the world with pure freedom. The bodhisattva vehicle is founded upon developing *bodhicitta*, the mind that aspires to awakening, and wishes to benefit others and liberate the world. The ultimate practice of the bodhisattva vehicle is the bliss of wisdom and compassion, while the more practical goals are represented by the six perfections and other such practices.

**V**

# Vimalakirti
維摩
*See:* Non-duality.

# Vinaya
毗奈耶
*See:* Gem, triple; schools of Chinese Buddhism, eight; Tripitaka; translators, four great Chinese.

# Vinaya School
## 律宗

*See:* Schools of Chinese Buddhism, eight.

# Violations, Five Great
## 五逆

The kindness of fathers, the filial piety of sons, and respect between brothers are all excellent virtues of traditional Chinese relationships. But as times have changed, obedience towards one's parents is no longer common. Instead it is now commonplace for unruly sons and daughters to be violent towards their parents, because they cannot accept their parents' supervision or their refusal of some demand. Some even go so far as to kill their mother and father. This clearly shows how our behavior has changed and our morals have declined.

This kind of extreme impropriety is a great violation against the norms of society. In the Buddhist world, there are five heinous crimes which are known as the "five great violations," such that those who commit these violations are surely bound to be reborn in hell. The five great violations are: killing one's father, killing one's mother, killing an arhat, shedding the blood of a Buddha, and creating a schism in the monastic community.

The kindness with which parents themselves raise their children is as high as the mountains and as deep as the ocean. Even if children exerted all their energy in serving and caring for their parents, they still would not be able to repay even one ten-thousandth of their parents' kindness. Thus we can see what a great violation it would be to kill them, for the karma of such an extremely serious crime would mean falling into Avici Hell after death.

Arhat is a Sanskrit word meaning "worthy of offerings," for an arhat is a noble person who has realized the fruit of sagehood and is worthy of offerings from human and heavenly beings. As such wise and noble beings are deserving of our reverence and respect, it would be a great violation to kill one, for such a crime would be a heinous act against heaven and unpardonable.

The Buddha is an awakened being, and it is only the Buddha's appearance on earth that can bring light to the world. The Buddha is like the sun and the moon which shines upon all things without distinction. Causing the Buddha to bleed is a great violation and a grave act of negative karma far more serious than even killing one's father, mother, or an arhat.

Members of the sangha, or monastic community, are the messengers who carry on the true Dharma. They are able to shoulder this great responsibility because of the sangha's harmonious, dispute-free environment. If one were to sow discord through gossip and destroy the harmony of the monastic community, such that it cannot carry on the true Dharma, causing it to decline, it is an extremely serious crime. Among the five great violations, this one is the most grave.

At present there are some Buddhists who have unintentionally created schisms within the monastic community. There are some people who visit a number of temples, spreading gossip to each of them, leading to conflict and misunderstandings between temples. There are some people who criticize members of the monastic community, thus ruining their image. There are even those who congratulate themselves for taking in monastics who have left their temples, thinking that they are furthering Buddhism by looking after these homeless monastics, and that they are doing some good deed to protect the Dharma. But such actions damage temple regulations,

V

and keep the monastic community from being what it should be. Not only is taking in such monastics not meritorious; it is actually a grave error. The principle is not unlike children who run away from home: the proper thing to do in such a situation would be to help the child return home, rather than providing them shelter; this hurts the other family. Such behavior does not even conform to basic human morality, and even less so to the Buddhist path.

## Virtues of the Buddha, Three
## 三德

*See also*: *Prajna;* wisdom, four kinds of; gratitude; means of embracing, four; truths, four noble; *nirvana*.

The three virtues of the Buddha are some of the more celebrated meritorious qualities of the Buddha and his Dharma:

### 1. Wisdom (智德)

The Buddha has attained wisdom, and the Dharma he teaches can overcome all ignorance. In regards to time, the Buddha knows the past, present, and future. In regards to space, the Buddha can perceive all places in the world. In regards to sentient beings, the Buddha knows all their various shapes and forms. The Buddha is the embodiment of truth, has personally attained *prajna*-wisdom, and is radiant and bright. To the Buddha, there is no darkness, no ignorance, and no unknown, for the Buddha is the one who has achieved the wisdom of supreme awareness.

### 2. Kindness (恩德)

The Buddha is the great compassionate one, and the Dharma he teaches can liberate all sentient beings. All beings within the six realms of existence, from heaven to hell, are subject to the Buddha's liberation. All beings, whether born from the womb, from an egg, from moisture, or from transformation, are subject to the Buddha's compassion. All beings of the highest heavens and formless realms are subject to the Buddha's guidance. The Buddha is the great teacher and liberator of the three realms, who extends his compassion across an ocean of suffering. No matter who you are, you can be liberated by the Buddha, end your suffering, and be happy. The Buddha is our compassionate benefactor.

### 3. Eliminating Afflictions（斷德）

The Buddha is the great liberator, and the Dharma he teaches can eliminate all affliction. The Buddha has taken all the various practices to their completion; his work is done. The Buddha has removed all obstacles and no longer has any habitual tendencies or afflictions. The Buddha has already attained the Dharmakaya of absolute reality, and perfected his merit and virtue. The Buddha is the liberator of the universe, who knows the fundamental essence of reality. No matter who you are, the Buddha can eliminate obstacles, remove afflictions, and free you from suffering. The Buddha is courageous, and fears nothing.

The Buddha's virtue of wisdom is *prajna*-wisdom, his virtue of kindness is compassion, and his virtue of eliminating affliction is liberation. The three virtues of the Buddha are comparable to the three Confucian virtues of wisdom, benevolence, and courage, though they in no way reach the limitless depths of the Buddha's virtues.

As for the three virtues of the Buddha, the virtue of wisdom belongs to rationality, the virtue of kindness belongs to the emotions, and the virtue of eliminating affliction belongs to the will. The Buddha awakened rationality, purified the emotions, and transformed the will. The Buddha became who he is by fulfilling the highest moral perfection in human life.

## Visakha
## 毘舍佉

*See*: Offerings, four.

## Vows, Four Universal
## 四弘誓願

When cultivating the Mahayana bodhisattva path, we must first generate the four universal vows:

*1. Sentient beings are limitless, I vow to liberate them.*
（眾生無邊誓願度）

Within the six realms of existence beings are born in four ways. Some are born from eggs, like chicken, geese, and other fowl. Some are born from the womb, like cattle, horses, and human beings. Some are born in moisture, like mosquitoes, gnats, and other insects. Some simply become manifest, like deities, immortals, and other supernatural beings. All these innumerable and limitless beings are drowning in the ocean of suffering, where they endure the suffering and pain of birth, old age, sickness, and death, hoping to be set free by someone powerful. It is said of being a bodhisattva: "It is only for the sake of freeing sentient beings from suffering, and not for the sake of seeking one's own peace and joy." The vow to liberate all sentient beings is the Mahayana spirit of benefiting others.

## 2. Afflictions are endless, I vow to eradicate them.
（煩惱無盡誓願斷）

Since the beginning, sentient beings have been beset by ignorance and have forgotten their intrinsic nature and been lost in delusion. Acts of killing, stealing, and sexual misconduct, along with greed, anger, ignorance, sadness, jealousy, and wrong views produce negative karma which results in suffering. Because of this, beings continue to be reborn in the cycle of birth and death without pause. There is a saying that one must, "Forge resolve even in the face of death, so that the Dharmakaya may live." The vow to end all afflictions is the wisdom of realization that can end all unwholesome qualities.

## 3. Teachings are infinite, I vow to learn them.
（法門無量誓願學）

After the Buddha attained awakening he taught the Dharma for forty-nine years in over three hundred assemblies. His teachings including both the Mahayana and Hinayana, the essence and characteristics, and both emptiness and existence. In China, eight schools of Buddhism developed: Chan, Pure Land, Vinaya, Esoteric, Tiantai, Huayan, Faxiang, and Three Treatise. Regardless of which of these teachings is followed, their purpose is the same: elucidate the truth of the universe and human life, and reveal, proclaim, realize, and attain the wisdom of the Buddha. A profound understanding of the sutras leads to developing wisdom as vast as the ocean. To liberate sentient beings a bodhisattva must first liberate himself. The vow to learn the infinite teachings of Buddhism supplies us with the power to benefit both ourselves and others.

V

*4. Buddhahood is supreme, I vow to attain it.*
（佛道無上誓願成）

Sakyamuni Buddha practiced over many lifetimes for three great *kalpas* to perfect his virtue and wisdom and one hundred small *kalpas* to perfect the thirty-two marks of excellence and eighty notable characteristics. In his final rebirth, the Buddha attained awakening under the bodhi tree while staring at the bright stars of the night; he realized the five eyes and six supernatural powers, and came to understand the past, present, and future. We should learn how the Buddha brought an end to the cycle of birth and death, attained the Dharmakaya, and came to abide always within the liberated state of *nirvana*. There is a saying that, "In heaven and earth, there is nothing like the Buddha. Throughout the worlds of the ten directions, nothing can compare to him." The vow to attain Buddhahood means to awaken oneself, awaken others, and complete the mission of awakening.

## Vulture Peak and Jeta Grove
## 靈山祇園

It was at one particular assembly on Vulture Peak that the Buddha held forth a flower and Mahakasyapa smiled, leaving this famous anecdote to the ages and marking the beginning of the Chan School's lineage.

The "Vulture Peak" mentioned in the story refers to a particular peak on Spirit Mountain outside Rajagrha, the capital city of the Magadha Kingdom of ancient India. Throughout his life, the Buddha held countless Dharma assemblies there: the wide-ranging teachings included such sutras as the *Lotus Sutra*, the *Perfection of Great Wisdom Sutra*, the *Sutra on the Buddha of Immeasurable Life*, and the *Lotus Samadhi Sutra*, among others. In particular, when the Buddha was teaching the *Lotus Sutra*, a host of a million human and heavenly beings participated in the gathering, and this event became known and celebrated as the "magnificent assembly on Vulture Peak."

While the Buddha was staying at Vulture Peak, Magadha's King Bimbisara undertook an extensive construction project that spanned valleys and skirted cliffs, as stones were set in a stairway that led all the way to the top of the mountain. In addition to the dais upon which the Buddha once gave teachings, there are also many other ancient Buddhist sites on the mountain, including the spot where Devadatta threw rocks at the Buddha, the cave where the Buddha and such disciples as Sariputra entered deep meditation, and the place where Ananda was tormented by Mara. In addition, below Vulture Peak is where King Bimbisara was imprisoned by his son, Prince Ajatasatru. It was on this occasion that the Buddha proclaimed the Pure Land of the West, and thus it was from Bimbisara's prison that Pure Land thought spread throughout the Saha world. Today Buddhists place Vulture Peak on their list of must-see sacred sites.

Jetavana Monastery, also known as "Jeta Grove" or "Jeta Garden," was donated by the elder Sudatta of Sravasti, in the kingdom of Kausala. The elder Sudatta took joy in good works and charitable acts, and he happily assisted the weak and supported orphans on a regular basis; thus he was called *anathapindaka*, "benefactor of the poor and orphaned." It was his sincere faith in the Buddha that inspired Prince Jeta to donate his garden, and later to supply funds to construct a monastery. In order to commemorate these two for jointly accomplishing this meritorious task, the site was named the "Jetavana Anathapindaka Grove," also known as the "Jeta Forest Monastery."

In addition to Jetavana Monastery, another early monastery was the Bamboo Grove Monastery. Both are celebrated as two of the earliest and greatest Buddhist monasteries. It was due to the establishment of these two great monasteries that the Buddhist monastic order was thus able to develop a position of greater strength. These two monasteries represent an enduring contribution to the later development of Buddhism. However, Jetavana Monastery, unlike Bamboo Grove Monastery, contained magnificent buildings and complete facilities that were impressive and beautiful. The Buddha stayed at this monastery over countless rainy seasons and gave the teachings recorded in many sutras. For example, the famous *Amitabha Sutra* was proclaimed at Jetavana Monastery.

Although Buddhism began in India, today its influence has greatly diminished. Not only do its various sacred sites appear forlorn and neglected, but it is unlikely that we will ever see a reoccurrence of a grand assembly of a million human and heavenly beings as when the Buddha proclaimed the *Flower Adornment Sutra* on Vulture Peak so long ago. Master Taixu's (1889-1947) description is quite apropos:

> The bodhi tree has flourished and declined many
>     times;
> And Vulture Peak is silent, awaiting some later
>     revival;
> But now one need not agonize over being late,
> For spreading the Dharma has always been the
>     monastic order's calling.

When recalling the past and reflecting upon the bounty bestowed by the Buddha, Buddhist followers know that they are duty-bound to see to the revitalization of Buddhism and ensure its long prosperity, in hopes that the great assembly on Vulture Peak will occur again and the light of Jetavana Monastery will shine forth once more. This indeed is our great mission.

V

# W

## Wandering Mendicant
### 行腳雲遊

*See also*: Temporary monastic lodging.

> A single alms bowl holds food from a thousand
>     families,
> A solitary monk wanders over ten thousand
>     miles;
> All for the liberation of birth and death,
> As he begs and teaches year after year.

The poem above describes the untrammeled spirit of the Chan master who remains devoted to the spiritual path while living contentedly in poverty. Since ancient times, monastics have wandered with their three robes, alms bowl, bamboo staff, and straw sandals, bringing liberation wherever they go. They do not wander to enjoy the scenery, for they are instead seeking something of great importance: the spiritual path. This search for the way is how they conduct themselves: they wander the ten directions, teaching as they go. They have no set abode, but they drift free and contented like wandering clouds or flowing water. Thus they are called *yun-shui seng* (雲水僧), "cloud and water monks," *youfang seng* (遊方僧), "wandering monks," and *xingjiao seng* (行腳僧), "mendicant monks."

Those Chan masters who are wandering mendicants possess their own unique, free-spirited style. They come and go unhindered, for they are unencumbered and unattached. They do not long for their hometowns, nor do they become enamored with a beautiful vista should they come upon one. They look upon the vast universe and all its phenomena like birds passing through the sky, leaving no trace.

One such example is the famous Chan Master Mazu Daoyi (709-788 CE). On one occasion he returned to his hometown for a visit, where he met an old woman washing clothes on the riverbank who recognized and called out to him, "Little boy!"

> In practicing the Way, one better not return
>     home,
> Returning home, one does not achieve the Way.
> Just now that old lady on the riverbank,
> Called me by my old name.

Chan Master Mazu Daoyi lived in Jiangxi Province. Students would come in droves from great distances to travel to Jiangxi to learn Chan from him. At the same time, another prominent Chan master named Shitou Xiqian lived in Hunan Province. All monks of that era would travel to either learn from Mazu Daoyi in Jiangxi or Shitou Xiqian in Hunan, and thus Chan practitioners became known as *zoujianghu* (走江湖), "travelers to Jiang and Hu." While this term was originally an abbreviation of the provinces of these two great masters, *zoujianghu* later came to describe traveling theater troops. However, the term originally referred to Chan practitioners who wandered about visiting teachers.

Wandering in search of teachers is the finest form of practice for monastics to benefit both themselves and others. Visiting teachers improves the body and mind, and traveling allows monastics to spread the Dharma to benefit sentient beings. As they wander they gather alms and teach Buddhism wherever they go. In receiving the generous support from the devoted laity, they serve as fields of merit for sentient beings, who are rewarded with teachings on the Dharma. In this way, wandering not only advances the monastic's own spiritual work, but allows them to advance the cause of teaching the Dharma to benefit others. This explains the Buddhist saying that monastics, "Request the truth from the Buddhas above to nourish wisdom, and request food from sentient beings below to sustain the body."

The *Diamond Sutra* opens with the following passage:

> Thus have I heard. At one time, the Buddha was in the city of Sravasti at the Jeta Grove Monastery with a gathering of monks numbering 1,250. At mealtime, the World-honored One put on his robe, picked up his bowl, and went into the city of Sravasti to beg for food. After he had gone from house to house, he returned to the grove. When he had finished eating, he put away his robe and bowl, washed his feet, straightened his mat, and sat down.

This clearly shows that the beginnings of Buddhist monastic life involved gathering alms, and that wandering with an alms bowl in hand is a Buddhist tradition.

In the past, the Buddha wandered from south to north with alms bowl in hand, teaching the Dharma as he went. It was only in this way that the Dharma was spread throughout the five regions of India. While times have changed and monastics no longer depend upon alms, Fo Guang Shan has created several programs to preserve the mendicant tradition with the goal of preserving tradition while advancing towards modernity. The hope is that teaching the Dharma with alms bowl in hand will purify the minds of people and spread the light of Buddhism to all corners of the world. These efforts strive to bring strength and prosperity to the nation, light to humanity, renewal to Buddhism, and true faith to Buddhists. In this way the legacy of the Buddha's teachings will be glorified.

## Water
水
*See:* Elements, four great.

## Wealth
財
*See:* Desires, five.

## Wind
風
*See:* Elements, four great; winds, eight.

# Winds, Eight
八風吹不動

The lay Buddhist Su Shi of the Song dynasty once composed a poem and instructed his attendant to sail across the Yangtze River from Guazhou on its northern bank to Jinshan Monastery on its southern bank. The attendant was to present the poem to Chan Master Foyin and hear his remarks. The poem read:

> Bowing, heaven within heaven,
> A light that illuminates the boundless universe,
> The eight winds cannot move me,
> Sitting mindfully upon the purple golden lotus.

Chan Master Foyin read the poem, and wrote down one word in response: "fart." He then gave his reply to the servant to take back. Su Shi read the Chan master's reply and became extremely angry. He immediately made the journey across the river to upbraid Chan Master Foyin. The Chan master said to him, "I read your poem and could tell your practice has reached a high level, but if you say that 'the eight winds cannot move me,' how did a little fart blow you across the river?"

Su Shi was speechless. He then knew he was not even close to the Chan master's level of cultivation.

What are these "eight winds"?

## 1. Praise （稱）
Praise refers to all the various kind words are spread about on one's behalf. Praise occurs at any time or place that such expressions bring support and joy.

## 2. Ridicule（譏）

Ridicule encompasses taunts and jeers, disgust and revulsion, and all manner of blame for things that may never have even happened. Such careless criticisms make one angry and worried.

## 3. Defamation（毀）

Defamation includes baseless gossip and malicious smears that damage one's trustworthiness. Defamation makes one appear worthless, and causes disappointment and embarrassment.

## 4. Honor（譽）

Honor means praising one's achievements and contributions. One may be proclaimed a bodhisattva on earth or a great sage who has returned to the world once more. Such words are pleasing and build one's popularity.

## 5. Gain（利）

Gain can be money, property, all manner of benefits, and even gifts.

## 6. Loss（衰）

Loss includes those things which are misplaced or ruined. Such things as a successful business which is suddenly bankrupt or the sudden disappearance of wealth. Loss leads to poverty and decline.

## 7. Sorrow（苦）

Sorrow is when the body is harmed or the mind is vexed. Negative causes and conditions make life hard, while negative surroundings torment the body and mind. Sorrow brings hardship and oppression.

W

*8. Joy*（樂）
Joy is attaining one's heart's desire and easily finding peace and joy. Joy can be material enjoyment or emotional satisfaction; whatever makes one joyful and happy.

The eight states discussed above are like winds blowing from eight different directions that can disturb and shake up the body and mind. When things go well we may be joyful and happy, but when things go badly, we become miserable and sad. This is because we are not able to withstand these eight "winds."

All eight winds are destructive. One's character can be harmed by praise and honor, just as one's accomplishments can be undone by ridicule and defamation. Gain and pleasure can take away one's dignity just as loss and sorrow can bring one down. The eight winds are truly terrible. But if one can remain unshaken and unagitated by these eight states, then one can be free and stand tall without fear or shame.

# Wisdom
## 智慧

*See:* Merit and wisdom; mountain gate; omniscience of the Buddha; perfections, six; *prajna*; reliance, four kinds of; training, threefold; virtues of the Buddha, three; wisdom, four kinds of; wisdom, three kinds of.

# Wisdom, Four Kinds of
## 轉識成智

*See also*: Consciousness, eight kinds of; *prajna*.

All phenomena in the universe exist just as they are until our consciousness begins to discriminate. Then all the mountains, rivers, and land appear different because of the changing projections of our different forms of consciousness. The Consciousness-Only School of Buddhism has a saying that, "the three realms are mind-only and all phenomena are consciousness-only." In this instance, "consciousness" means the mind that discriminates, which is defiled and impure. This is the mind that is the root cause of the cycle of birth and death within the six realms of existence, but this same mind can be the medium that moves us from the mundane to the supramundane.

In order to change the defiled world projected by our consciousness into a world of purity, we must change the discriminating consciousness that we have as ordinary beings into the wisdom of the Buddha. This process, which is the central practice of the Consciousness-Only School, is called "transforming consciousness into wisdom," and describes transforming our different levels of consciousness into four kinds of supramundane wisdom:

### 1. Wisdom of Perfect Conduct（成所作智）

In Consciousness-Only thought, the first five kinds of consciousness correspond to the five sense organs of the eyes, ears, nose, tongue, and body. These five consciousnesses arise from the discrimination generated by the five sense organs in response to craving for sights, sounds, smells, tastes, and touch. Craving for sense objects creates delusion and karma, and obscures our true mind like dust covering a mirror. These fives kinds of craving are like five bandits who occupy our body as if it were a village and plunder the wealth of our merit.

To transform our sensory consciousness into the "wisdom of perfect conduct" one must transform the destructive elements of consciousness into wisdom that can work to fulfill worldly tasks.

With the wisdom of perfect conduct, one's words and deeds are constructive, undefiled, and of benefit to others.

### 2. Wisdom of Profound Insight (妙觀察智)

Among the eight kinds of consciousness described by the Consciousness-Only School it is the sixth consciousness, the mind consciousness, that has the strongest power of discrimination. When an object is judged by the mind consciousness its degree of worth, beauty, and correctness will immediately be determined.

Since the mind consciousness performs this function of discrimination upon all phenomena, it is also sometimes called the "discriminating consciousness." The mind consciousness works in conjunction with the five sensory consciousnesses described above to generate thoughts regarding what is good or bad. Typically the mind consciousness is superficial, simplistic, narrowly focused, and conceptual in nature. By transforming the mind consciousness into the wisdom of profound insight one can ponder deeply and perceive directly the principle of things without being confused by their outer appearance.

### 3. Wisdom of Universal Equality (平等性智)

The seventh or *manas* consciousness is grounded upon the notion of an independent self. It grasps at the elements that are stored in the *alaya* consciousness as constituting an enduring or unchanging self. As a consequence come the afflictions of self, including views of the self, self-pride, self-ignorance, self-desire, and attachment to the self. Deluded attachments are formed that separate phenomena that are "me" and "mine" from the rest. This discrimination leads to comparisons, score-keeping, inequality, and categorizing things as good or bad, wholesome and unwholesome, and mine and yours, such that the body and mind cannot find peace.

By transforming the *manas* consciousness into the wisdom of universal equality one eliminates the notion of an independent self and the discrimination of phenomena. One can then contemplate how all phenomena, regardless of whether they are wholesome or unwholesome, good or bad, friend or foe, or yours and mine, are all equal just as they are. Simply put, this is the process of transforming the "small self" that is self-centered and self-absorbed into a "larger self" that is all-inclusive.

### 4. Perfect Mirrorlike Wisdom （大圓鏡智）

The eighth or *alaya* consciousness is the source of life. It functions as a storehouse, and stores up all of our positive and negative karmic seeds. These seeds do not disappear with the death of the body, but are passed on to a new living entity in the next life. In this sense, the *alaya* consciousness is the basic essence of the cycle of birth and death. It is not unlike a "soul," but in Buddhism it is more properly thought of as karmic consciousness.

By transforming the *alaya* consciousness from something defiled into perfect mirrorlike wisdom, we have truly "transformed consciousness into wisdom." Perfect mirrorlike wisdom allows the pure seeds of the *alaya* consciousness to manifest as the wondrous state of Buddhahood and, just like a mirror can reflect all things, it can genuinely reflect back the true reality of all phenomena.

Transforming consciousness into wisdom is the final goal for students of the Consciousness-Only School. However, for many the doctrine of the Consciousness-Only School seems overly specialized, complex, and arcane. Those lacking sufficient patience will find its study a daunting task.

Even so, one need not study Consciousness-Only doctrine in order to transform consciousness into wisdom. Being able to recognize dependent origination in the face of people and things one dislikes and suffering injustice, false accusation, and abuse without becoming resentful or angry, and being able to maintain a calm and peaceful attitude also transforms consciousness into wisdom. Even in the face of adversity, if one is able to weather suffering and hardship without thinking about it, one can be successful and develop an open, generous outlook on life. It is this optimistic and positive attitude that allows one to elevate the value of life.

## Wisdom, Three Kinds of
## 三慧
*See also: Prajna.*

Buddhism is a religion that emphasizes wisdom. Only with wisdom are we able to distinguish good from bad, and right from wrong. Wisdom is what allows us to eliminate afflictions and attain Buddhahood. Without wisdom, one cannot attain ultimate liberation, no matter how blessed one may be. Therefore, in addition to cultivating merit, one must develop wisdom.

"Wisdom" as described in the Buddhist teachings is different from ordinary wisdom. Ordinary wisdom is simply knowledge and cleverness, which at times can be used for unwholesome purposes. Buddhist wisdom is called *prajna*-wisdom. *Prajna*-wisdom is the ability to comprehend the truth of all phenomena; it is the light of the Dharma that indicates the correct path. To attain this kind of wisdom, one must be diligent in learning and practicing the

Buddhist teachings, and progress through their stages from simple to profound. There are three methods for developing Buddhist wisdom:

## 1. Wisdom from Hearing (聞慧)
This is learning about Buddhism from the twelve divisions of the sutras or from good Dharma friends. One is introduced to awakening through what is read or heard, whether that is hearing the teachings or reading the sutras. This generates a profound faith in and understanding of the Dharma, thus generating undefiled, noble wisdom.

## 2. Wisdom from Thinking (思慧)
With the wisdom from hearing as a foundation, the next step is to deeply contemplate the meaning of the Dharma and to investigate the nature of all phenomena along with the causes and conditions so that one has an even more direct and immediate experience of realization. This is the undefiled wisdom that comes from the process of contemplating the hows and whys of what has been heard and read.

## 3. Wisdom from Practice (修慧)
With the realization from the wisdom from hearing and thinking, one proceeds to develop meditative concentration to see the true reality of all phenomena and the truth of dependent origination. This wisdom comes from the meditative practice known as "stopping the illusory mind and seeing the truth."

W

In Buddhism there is the saying, *duowen xunxi* (多聞薰習), "to permeate through hearing much." This means that, to learn

Buddhism, one must always listen to the teachings and read the sutras, contemplate their meaning, and most importantly, practice according to their principles. By developing the wisdom from hearing, thinking, and pratice, one can perceive one's intrinsic nature, the Buddha nature which we all inherently have.

## World System, Three Thousandfold
## 三千大千世界
*See Also*: Continents, Four Great

The *Diamond Sutra* says that if someone were to make an offering of the seven treasures so great that it could fill the three thousandfold world system, they would generate less merit than one who has faith in the *Diamond Sutra's* four-line verse and explained its meaning to others. In this instance, the term "three thousandfold world system" refers to the entire universe.

According to Buddhist cosmology, there are many, many worlds. A group of one thousand such worlds is called a "small world system." One thousand small world systems equals a "medium world system." One thousand medium world systems is called a "large world system." A "three thousandfold world system" is a combination of these three types of world systems; the term does not literally refer to 3,000 large world systems. One "three thousandfold world system" is the area in which a Buddha teaches the Dharma, and as such is also referred to as one "Buddha land."

Every minor world in a three thousandfold world system is made up of a Mount Sumeru at its center which is surrounded by nine mountains, eight oceans, four continents, sun, moon, and stars. When taken together, they are similar in scale to a "solar system." At the lowest level of each world is a layer of air, called the

W

wind wheel; above the wind wheel is a layer of water known as the water wheel; and above the water wheel is a layer of metal known as the metal wheel; and above the metal wheel is the great earth itself made up of mountains, oceans, the four continents, and so forth.

Within each world are the six realms of existence, including the hell realm, the hungry ghost realm, the animal realm, the *asura* realm, the human realm, and the heavenly realm. The first five realms make up what is known as the "desire realm," while the heavenly realm can be differentiated between the "form realm" and the "formless realm." We can see that the Saha world in which we live is but a small part of the universe which contains countless three thousandfold world systems. The sutras say that "the worlds of the ten directions are as numerous as sands along the Ganges River," and that "the worlds of the ten directions are as numerous as particles of dust." Considering the vast expanse of the universe, our existence is infinitesimally small in comparison.

In short, Buddhism refers to a large expanse of space as a "Buddha land," or simply as "the vastness of space," while the smallest unit of space is often referred to as a "particle of dust." These units of space are distinguished by different names, but each of them can be a three thousandfold world system. In Buddhism, the "three thousandfold world system" is a general reference to the universe, which can be so large that nothing exists outside of it, or so small that nothing exists within it. In Buddhism, the universe is seen as infinite and limitless, without border or boundary.

The *Amitabha Sutra* says that the distance between our world and the Western Pure Land is ten trillion Buddha lands. Since one Buddha land is the equivalent of one three thousandfold world system, that means that there are ten trillion three thousandfold world systems separating this Saha world from the Western Pure Land. This is an immensely large astronomical number, upon which we would seemingly look with regret. But the sutra also says that we can be reborn in the Western Pure Land with a single thought. Even the *Flower Adornment Sutra* says, "A single particle of dust can manifest a three thousandfold world system, and a three thousandfold world system can be completely contained within a single particle of dust."

For an awakened person, each flower is a world and each leaf is a Buddha. One can see a three thousandfold world system within a rock or a single grain of sand. In the same way, a three thousandfold world system can be contained within one's heart. Buddhism's perspective on the perfect integration of the dharma realm that transcends time and space without obstruction is contained within the phrase, "from one, many; and from many, one."

The former chair of the Buddhist Association of China, the layman Zhao Puchu (1907-2000), once said of Master Hsing Yun, "He is as noble as a teacher of heavenly and human beings, and is enriched by containing the three thousandfold world system."

Each of us can expand and broaden the mind to encompass the vastness of the universe, with its worlds as numerous as grains of sand. Not everyone will be as noble as a teacher of human and heavenly beings, but each of us can be enriched by containing within us the three thousandfold world system.

# X

## Xuanzang
玄奘
*See:* Translators, four great Chinese.

# Y

## Yanqi School
楊岐派
*See:* Chan schools

## Yijing
義淨
*See:* Translators, four great Chinese.

## Yunmen School
雲門宗
*See:* Chan schools.

# Z

## Zibo, Master
## 紫柏大師
See: Masters of the Ming dynasty, four.

# List of Articles by Chinese Title

A TOR
DOUBLE
ACTION
WESTERN

# Max Brand

## OUTLAW CREW

## THE BEST BANDIT

**TOR**

A TOM DOHERTY ASSOCIATES BOOK
NEW YORK

OUTLAW CREW

Copyright © 1932 by Street & Smith Publications, Inc. Copyright renewed (c) 1960 by Dorothy Faust. First appeared in *Western Story Magazine*.

THE BEST BANDIT

Copyright © 1932 by Street & Smith Publications, Inc. Copyright renewed (c) by Dorothy Faust. First published in *Western Story Magazine* as by David Manning.

A Tor Book
Published by Tom Doherty Associates, Inc.
49 West 24th Street
New York, N.Y. 10010

ISBN: 0-812-51317-7

First edition: May 1991

Printed in the United States of America

0 9 8 7 6 5 4 3 2 1

# OUTLAW CREW

## · 1 ·

TRENT AND WAYLAND, WHEN THEY DEVELOPED THEIR MINE a little, knew perfectly well that there was a fortune for them if they could find many hands to work in it. There was plenty of the ore, but the grade was not high; the pair of them, grinding away at the coffee mill the rest of their lives, would just about make good day's wages, and little more. They had now made the experiment thoroughly, and they had been thoroughly beaten.

Twenty miles from them as the bird flies, thirty as the mustang runs, forty as wheels must go, was the town of Sunnydale.

In spite of its name, it was not sunny. It was the center of a mining rush. For six months it had been growing wilder and more crowded, more lawless, more confident that Sunnydale did not need to pay the slightest attention to the rest of the world.

There were thousands of men in Sunnydale. The majority of them were the sharpsters, gamblers, crooks of all sorts, who came to exploit the honest prosperity of others. But there were laborers, also; a limitless supply of them. The trouble was that they were only willing to work for bonanza prices.

3

And bonanza prices were exactly what Wayland and Trent could not afford to pay. They could offer two dollars a day and found, but that was all. And how could those excited men in the gorge of Sunnydale be tempted away from a spot where every one of them hoped to find his individual fortune sooner or later? The laborers in that valley were willing to work in the rich, easy placer diggings for from six to ten dollars a day. But how could they be induced to come up the forty-mile trail and there, in the midst of the naked cliffs, break the hard face of granite at two dollars a day?

It seemed an insuperable problem. And as Trent and Wayland sat in front of their lean-to, which was built conveniently near the dump of the mine, they were deciding, on this evening, that it was better to give up the game for the present.

Trent, as usual, made the downright decision. He was a big, fierce man of fifty, with an unshaven gray beard straggling like a stormy mist over his face. It was he who had prospected and found the claim; it was Wayland who had grubstaked the expedition out of his savings as a country doctor. His slender hands and narrow shoulders were not of much use in handling a drill; his spectacled eyes could not look so sharply into this kind of a future, either.

Wayland had risked much in leaving his home and coming up here with his daughter. A younger man had moved in and was taking his practice. And it was toward his daughter that he was continually glancing with troubled eyes on this evening. The scheme was that Harriet Wayland should do the cooking for the required gang of miners until the proceeds from the mine began to stack up and a regular cook and cook's roustabout could be hired. They had attempted to work the mine on a shoestring, and Harriet was a necessary part of the string.

Now she worked quietly, scrubbing up the pans after supper and making all orderly, never speaking, pretending that she did not hear the gloomy words of her father and his partner.

All the day had been blistering hot, for the mountain shoulder on which they had opened the shaft faced south and west, and the mountain itself was a series of naked rocky steps that reflected the brilliance of that clear sun. There were no trees for shade, but only a scattering of tough shrubbery good enough for firewood, but little use for anything else. They had constructed a winding footpath that led down a quarter of a mile to a point where the mountain shelved out toward the valley. That was the highest point possible for freighting in by wheels, and there the buckboard was standing, covered with tarpaulin. There, also, the two mules were hobbled for grazing.

There was only one blessing of a practical sort in this situation, and that was the meager trickle of water that broke from the rock above and ran down onto the shoulder where the mine was opened; there it gathered in a shallow pool, and then ran on toward the valley.

There was another blessing in the way of beauty, for the eye leaped from this high place across gigantic distances to other ranges, green and brown and blue, and some darkened by a growth of pines, and others offering the clear sheen of naked rocks, and some, about the summits, offering to the eye cool bits of snow like little white clouds blowing up the sky.

However, neither of the men had any interest in the scenery just now.

Trent, as he tamped the coal of his hot pipe with a horny forefinger and dusted off the finger against his sweat-marked overalls, was saying: "You take it this way: The pair of us, we work like the deuce, and we break enough ground and work enough of it to clear up about five dollars a day apiece. There's not much to be said for that. But suppose that we had twenty men working here. They would get out enough for us to pay them two dollars a day and three or four dollars more for our profit. Even more than that, maybe. We could make a lot of saving in extras. There'd be one gent traveling all the time to town and back with supplies; there'd be a cook; there'd be a hunter and general roustabout. There'd be you and me to keep the gang working.

"And the gang would have nothing to do but break ground for us. Maybe that way we'd begin to clear seven or eight dollars a head for every doggone one of them. That way we

5

could have something like a hundred or two hundred dollars a day coming in. And it would come in steady. It would come in regular as a clock. That vein is gunna go right on down to China. It ain't high-grade, but it's steady.

"After a while we could get some machinery out here and an engineer to handle it, and then we'd rip into things and make a fortune fast. But the way it is now, you and me just about make enough to break even. We gotta quit and leave the thing to stand for a while. And after a while, when the Sunnydale rush settles down, in six months, or a year, or maybe two years, we can get men out here willing and glad to work for the right kind of wages. That's the only way to tackle the game."

He spoke grimly, almost brutally, for he knew how much pain this decision was giving to the doctor. The latter's business in his home town was now practically destroyed. If he returned to his house, he would be going back as a failure. And failures are rarely trusted by clients.

However, Wayland met the future with a set jaw and a determined eye.

"If it has to be this way," said he, "it has to be. I'll take my medicine and we'll wait. Only"—here he lowered his voice—"Harriet, yonder, is—" He paused.

"I know," muttered Trent. "It's hard on her. She's come out here and slaved. All she's got out of it has been sunburn—and the knowing that she's done her duty by you, Wayland."

"Her duty by me! Her duty by me!" murmured the doctor sadly. "She's always done that. It looks as though she will keep on doing it. And in the meantime she pays no attention to men of her age. Boys, I mean to say. She won't go to dances because she won't spend the money on clothes. She won't go to boy-and-girl parties because she's been busy with housework. *She's* the one, Trent, who did most of the work for the last two years to save the money we needed for this experiment. And now the money's thrown away. I don't mind. I'm not thinking of myself, for once in my life. But I'm thinking of her wasted time. The young years are the time for a girl to be lighthearted. And she's not lighthearted, Trent. Sad labor and very few hopes have been her share!"

Trent said nothing. He felt the truth of these things, but he also felt the impossibility of offering comfort through words, and words were all he had to offer.

The girl herself, in the meantime, had finished her work, and now she walked out to the edge of the little plateau to look over the sunset light that filled the great valley with russet dust. There was no comfort to the men in that beauty, but for her it made life possible. The weariness of the day fell away from her, and out of the blue twilight always there was an assurance that no matter what success or failure had marked the day, the end of it was all that was profoundly worth while.

From the darkening mountains she looked down at last to the darker valley. There was still dull gold on the heights, and like old gilt along the faces of the cliffs, but the valley beneath was blue as water, and through this mist of thin color she saw a man coming, not on a horse, but walking swiftly. It seemed a very extraordinary thing indeed that he was on foot; no one traveled in this country without a mule, or a burro, at the least.

He, however, came straight on, and while he was still in the distance she could see that he was a very big man, and as wiry as he was large, for he carried his poundage swiftly up the slope, and then turned and came striding with unabated strength up the winding trail toward the mine.

"There's some one coming," she said over her shoulder.

"Who?"

"Man on foot—a great big fellow—alone on foot!"

"Who'd be coming on foot through this kind of a country?" demanded Trent, standing up.

The girl did not answer that reflection. She was too intent on the pedestrian; the exhaustless strength of him lifted her own heart. She began to smile long before she clearly made out his face.

Trent joined her on the edge of the plateau.

"I've seen that fellow before," said he. "I've seen him somewhere—it's somebody that I ain't got any kindness for, I guess. Them shoulders, and that head—by thunder, it's Little Minny Trent. It's my own nephew! It's that same worthless scatterhead and vagabond! Works harder than any man in the world to get out of work!''

Harriet Wayland moved back toward the lean-to as the big fellow gained the level of the plateau. Her pleasure in him disappeared, partly because of what his uncle had said, and more because of his ugliness. She never had seen such a face before; she hoped that she should never have to see one again! For he had black hair, black eyes, a swarthy skin, and over it the growth of four or five days of beard was as solidly black as a painted mask. It was a face not modeled by the hand, but hewed with a blunt edge. The lines of brow and nose and jaw had been knocked out rudely, and never finished. It was a drawing, blocked out, but never completed. And she felt, as she looked at him, an uneasy sense of alarm.

## · 2 ·

"This is Minder Paul Trent," said his uncle to the Waylands. "But you don't have to call him that. Nobody does. You talk of Minder Trent and there ain't a soul, hardly, that'll know who you mean. But talk of Little Minny, and you'll see a whole lot of gents reaching for their guns, or anything in the line of a club that's handy. Minny, this is Miss Harriet Wayland; this is Doctor Wayland, her father and my partner. Now what the deuce are you here for?"

"I was at Crow Creek yesterday," said Little Minny, after he had acknowledged the introductions. "And over there I heard about you and your mine, so I came over to take a look at it."

His uncle snorted.

"Yesterday? Crow Creek is seventy-five mile away. You mean that you walked it, eh?"

"I'm hungry," said the big man. "Got any hardtack and coffee around here? Yes, I walked over from Crow Creek. It's not so very far."

"You were broke, eh, and you came over here for a hand-out. That's the truth, ain't it?" demanded the harsh uncle.

"I'm not broke," said the giant.

9

"No, you got a whole quarter left, maybe?"

"*And* a dollar," said the other.

"We don't feed tramps in this camp," said Trent savagely. "We need workingmen, and we pay 'em good, too. Two dollars a day. You lazy fellow, how long is it since you done any work?"

"I'm working all the time, Uncle Jim," said the other. "Touring the world and completing my education. Have you got any fresh meat in the camp? I could eat a few steaks, between you and me."

"We have some bacon," said the girl. "I'll have something ready for you in a minute or two."

"Thanks," said Little Minny, and sat down upon a rock.

"Look at you!" exclaimed Jim Trent. "Setting down to let a lady that's already tired go and wait on you, eh?"

"Why don't you have fresh meat?" asked the giant, pointing. "There's a couple of hundred pounds of it waiting to be snagged."

Through the blue and golden dimness of the evening, a hundred yards or so above them, a mountain goat appeared among the rocks, standing on the edge of a cliff and reaching for a tuft of grass.

"You can't shoot that goat," said Jim Trent. "I've used up twenty bullets on it. The doggone thing, it comes up and wags its beard in your face, as you might say, but the minute that it sees a rifle it jumps for cover, and it always gets there. I've hankered after that goat for days and days. And—"

"I'm going to eat goat meat, roasted, tonight," said Little Minny, and from beneath his coat he pulled out a revolver that was bigger than any Harriet Wayland had ever seen before. The barrel of that Colt was built three inches longer than the ordinary pattern, and it seemed of a heavier frame throughout.

The mountain goat had seen the flash of the steel; it turned with the uncanny agility of its kind and leaped for cover as the gun spoke.

It leaped, struck a root, and then fell limply back, making a long, blurred streak of white as it slid down the smooth

10

face of the rock and landed on the plateau with a thump not a dozen strides away.

Little Minny went to it, leaned above it, then he raised it from the ground.

"I was wrong by a hundred pounds," said the giant. "Three hundred pounds of bone and eating in this thing. Now, Uncle Jim, are you glad that Little Minny came for supper?"

"If you could shoot your way to money," said Jim Trent, "you'd do pretty good. But you ain't even got the nerve to be a bandit. You're too bad to be good, and too darn lazy to be bad enough to count."

"A good, fat young goat," said Little Minny. "Shall I dress him here?"

"That's all right," said the uncle. "How long since you ate?"

"Haven't had a thing but a couple of rabbits all day long," said the other.

"Yeah, you must be starved, then," agreed Jim Trent.

His nephew already had tied the heels of the dead goat together, and now he hung the bulk by the legs from a projecting point of a great boulder. He produced a great, wicked-looking knife with a scimitar-like curve in it, and with long, dexterous, powerful strokes he dressed the kill. In a few moments the thing was done, and by the time the fire was right for cookery, the meat was at hand.

Little Minny went to wash; he began to sing as he splashed.

"This is a pretty good place, Uncle Jim," he said. "I might stay a while. Don't let that fire get too hot, Harry," he advised. "You have to cook grown-up goat with care. Otherwise it's like chewing rubber."

"Her name's Harriet, not Harry," corrected Jim Trent. "Don't be making a fresh mug of yourself, Minny."

"Spoil the manners and save the meat, is my motto," answered the giant. "Harriet's a long name to say, even if it means a lot. But I know a buckaroo by the name of Harry that was a good skate and fine company. I'm complimenting the lady, I'd have her know."

The girl flushed a little.

11

The speech was not exactly insulting, but she tingled and grew misty-eyed with anger. Her father, sitting stiffly apart from the rest, just on the verge of the circle of the firelight, looked coldly upon the big stranger.

Jim Trent went back to the speech before the last one.

"If you stay here, you stay alone," he said. "We're moving along."

"Why?" asked Little Minny.

"Because we haven't got enough hands here to break this ground," answered the prospector.

"There's Sunnydale just over the hill," said Little Minny. "Lots of men down there."

"Yeah. Six-dollar, ten-dollar-a-day men. This is a two-dollar job, and a hard one, at that."

"Where there's a will there's a way," said Little Minny. "I'd have some of those boys up here if I were you."

"If I got 'em up here they wouldn't stay. I've tried it," said the other.

"If I got 'em up here, I'd *make* 'em stay," declared Little Minny.

"How would you make 'em?"

"Where there's a will there's a way," said Little Minny with annoying complacence.

"Shut up, will you?" said his uncle. "You got a smart way of talking about you. To hear you talk, anybody might think that you amounted to something."

"I've got an appetite that amounts to something," said Little Minny.

He sat down close to the fire, regardless of the heat of the flames, and the light shone over the surface of his growth of black beard. He began to toast gobbets of meat at the fire, turning them with a careful attention. And when they were cooked to his satisfaction, he offered the wooden spits to the others, after sprinkling a little salt on the roast. Both the other men refused the titbits; the girl, forced on by a sort of angry curiosity, made an attempt to eat a morsel, but shuddered at the taste and the rubbery toughness.

"How can you eat such stuff?" she asked.

"With a pair of real jaws," said Little Minny. "The trouble with you, Harry, is that you've used you jaw muscles chiefly on cake and candy, and small talk, and singing hymns. But you take me—I've used my teeth the way God intended me to. A little gristle here and there in my friend, the goat, but gristle gives a substance to the meat. Gives you something that stays with you a while. I need something like that, because I can see that I've got to round up some of those crooks in Sunnydale and bring them up here to the mine. How much do you pay me a head for 'em, Uncle Jim?''

''You're gunna go down and persuade 'em up here—for two dollars a day?'' demanded his uncle.

''That's the idea. For a crop of ten, twenty, thirty of 'em, how much do you pay a head?''

''I pay,'' said Jim Trent, ''a dollar a day for every working day that you make 'em put in up here.''

''I'm going to be rich,'' said Little Minny. ''What do you say, Harry? A month or two of savings like that—How many men can you use?''

''Fifty!'' said Jim Trent. ''As many as you can get for me!''

''Fifty dollars a day,'' said Little Minny, ''is fifteen hundred dollars a month of anybody's money. I'll be on the way to being rich. Is there that much gold in your diggings, Uncle Jim?''

''There's enough pay dirt here,'' said Jim Trent firmly, ''to keep a hundred men busy working every day for a thousand years.''

''The first fifty years is all that I care about,'' answered Little Minny. ''How about you, Harry? That would do for us, wouldn't it?''

She said nothing.

Jim Trent broke in: ''Are you gunna try to make a fool of Miss Wayland? All that you can do is to make a fool of yourself, Minny.''

The girl filled the emptied coffee cup of the giant in a disdainful silence.

''Thanks, Harry,'' said he. ''You don't mind me thinking out loud, do you? I never had enough money to think of marrying before. But now that I see I'm going to be a rich

13

man before long, why, I naturally look at the first girl, and there you are, Harry. Look me over!''

As he spoke, he did not glance at her, but continued to eat busily, saying around his mouthfuls: ''You'll see that I've been around the world long enough, and rubbed up against things hard enough to thicken my skin. I'm old enough to shave, and I'm young enough to eat goat meat. What more do you want in a husband? Easy man to have around the house, too. You'd have lots of my company. Never would be dashing off to an office. Handy man around a garden, too, if it's not too big, and handy at patching things around the house, too. Keep burglars away better than a bulldog, and never criticize the cook as long as there are plenty of beans in the pot.''

''You've driven her away into the house,'' said Jim Trent furiously. ''You're an insulting young fellow, Minny!''

''Every girl to her own fancy,'' said the giant. ''If she's gone inside, just reach me that coffeepot, Uncle Jim, will you?''

# · 3 ·

Little Minny went to Sunnydale the next day. When he came over the rim of the hills to the north of it, striding long and fast as usual, he paused just long enough to make out the long and sinuous windings of the narrow valley. And just at that moment, it being about the end of the day for most of the mines, the gunshots began to go off up and down the length of the ravine. And down the trails that led from the holes to the town he could see men walking, or riding, or driving; and far away over the hills toward the southern side of the valleys he looked at the white windings of the road, and saw no fewer than three freighters coming in, with three white clouds of dust about them; while another long outfit climbed the slope to leave Sunnydale. Day and night these outfits must be coming and going.

And still, as the big man stepped forward once more, he heard the explosions of the mines, sometimes distant, and sometimes seeming to shake the very earth about his feet.

"The salute," said he, grinning. "They know the king's coming to town!"

He had shaved from his face the black shadow of his

15

gleaming beard, so that without it one was able to see his face and his smile more clearly.

He looked much younger, so viewed; but also, in a sense, he looked more grim.

One could see his mouth that was smiling, for instance, more clearly than when the shining black shadow had covered it. It was a mouth too large even on that face, and the wrinkles on the sides of the smile extended far into cheeks that appeared hollow, perhaps because of the size of the cheekbones, and the bulge of the jaw muscles. It was a crooked smile and a crooked mouth, and one could hardly tell whether the expression of it were sneering or openly amused.

This was a man who would draw the eye, but the judgment about him might remain distinctly divided.

When he got to the town, it was what he expected—but a little more so.

There was the same single main length of the ravine. And down the creek. There was the same gathering of shacks, big and small, made of board, of canvas, even pieced out with tin cans straightened out in thin sheets.

A blast of heat reflected from it, though the strength of the sun was now diminishing. It was hotter indoors than out. People had poured out to "take the air."

And what people!

He knew them of old—the thugs, the thieves, the confidence men who smiled upon the world, the sedate gamblers, the active businessmen, the honest laborers of the mines. He had seen them all before, and the mixture pleased him. The air, for him, became loaded with excitement.

He saw other signs of excitement, signs which were obvious to his eye. He passed half a dozen blackened sites where the destruction caused by fire was hardly allowed to cool before the new buildings began to arise on the ground. He passed under a saloon sign on which was painted: "Ned Kimbal, Honest Whisky."

But the "Ned Kimbal" part of the sign was obviously new.

In darker paint, beneath that name, appeared another, with a single brush stroke through it. "Denny Rourke" was the name of the former proprietor.

It had a meaning to Mr. Minder Trent. He turned in through the swinging doors beneath that sign.

Inside he expected to see few people, there were so many in the streets; but he saw that he was wrong. At least fifty people were in the long and narrow room.

He stopped a man who was leaving the place.

"You know Denny Rourke?" he asked.

"No, but I've seen him," said the stranger.

"Lately?"

"He's using his last ten bucks on faro," said the other.

"This Rourke, what sort of a looking fellow is he?"

"He looks about your size," replied the other.

Big Minder Trent went on into the back room and saw Rourke readily. He was a red man, red of skin, red of hair, and fierce blue of eye. He was, in fact, as big as Little Minny. And now he stood coatless, in a blue flannel shirt, before the faro table, biting at a cigar and snarling to himself as he played.

Little Minny waited until he had lost and then won. He waited until the winning was greater than the loss. Then he stepped through the choking wreaths of pipe and cigar and cigarette smoke and tapped the bulging, hard shoulder of the Irishman.

Rourke turned his big head and glared. The glare turned into a smile so vast that the cigar was suddenly no larger than a toothpick in the vast stretch of his mouth.

"Little Minny," he said, "blast my eyes, but it's you!"

He turned all about and shook hands.

"How are you?" asked Little Minny.

"Worse than I was when you last raised a lump on the side of my jaw," said the frank Irishman. "How's yourself?"

"Broke," said Little Minny.

"That's nothing—for you," said the other. "But I got about a hundred left; here's fifty, if you want it."

"I don't want it," said Little Minny. "I want five minutes of talk. Tell me about this town."

"It's a good town for a crook; it's no good for you and me," said the red man. "I tried to buck the game here, and I made thousands. Then they got to me. The thieves cracked

**17**

my safe. The gunmen shot up my place. I was pretty rich, one day. The next day I was on my uppers. I had to sell. I cleared five hundred. I've got a hundred left, and faro has the rest. That's Sunnydale. It's sunny, all right. You don't mind this kind of sun if you got an asbestos overcoat.''

"I thought it looked that way," Little Minny said. "Looks as though Sunnydale needed some law and order.''

"It don't need nothing else but law and order," said the red man. "What's your game here?''

"Law and order is my game," said Little Minny. "Where would that kind of a game stand?''

"Clean off the boards," said the other. "They shoot a deputy sheriff every three or four days, and they got the sheriff himself laid up in bed. They got a judge here, but everybody that he sends to jail breaks out the next night. The boys don't mind the jail here. It just gives them a rest.''

"The strong-arm boys friends of yours?" asked Little Minny.

"Friends of mine?" snarled Denny Rourke. "I could eat their hearts. Some time I'm gunna do it, too. I know the skunks that have sunk their teeth in me. I was framed. They frame everybody that don't play their side of the game.''

"Maybe I'll be calling in on you again," said Little Minny. "So long.''

He left the saloon and inquired his way to the house of the sheriff. It was a little shack on the rim of the town, near the creek. It was distinguished by having, in its front yard, the only tree which had not yet been cut down for building purposes. When he knocked at the front door a growling voice told him to enter. He stepped in and found himself looking at the double mouth of a riot gun.

Behind the gun was a man in bed, with a cigarette pressed flat between hard lips—a middle-aged man with black circles of suffering beneath his eyes.

"Who are you, brother?" asked the man in the bed. "And what's your gag?''

"Just stepped in to call," answered Little Minny. "Will this chair stand my weight? I don't know yet what I am to you.''

"Take the stool over there under the window," said the sheriff, "and don't try to maneuver around behind me. From this time on I start shooting first and do my thinking afterward."

Little Minny drew out the stool and sat down.

"This is nice and cozy," said he. "What's the matter with this town?"

"Why nothing much," said the sheriff. "Just a big Western play town is what it is. Just a lot of fine, upstanding fellows here in Sunnydale, as long as you ask. You wouldn't want to see anything better. Now and then they crack a safe, or dynamite a shack or two, or shoot a few of the gents through the back, but they got a whole lot of style, you can take it from me. They're quick. Just a little quick-tempered, if you could call that a fault."

"Me? No, no, no," said Little Minny hastily. "I wouldn't ever accuse anybody of being quick-tempered. What's your name, brother? Mine is Little Minny."

"I've heard that moniker before," said the sheriff. "I'm Anton Breen. What's your game here, Little Minny?"

"I don't know exactly," said Little Minny. "But it looks to me as though I've got to stand for once on the side of law and order."

"You can't stand on that side," said the sheriff. "There's nothing to stand on. There was me, but now there's nothing left."

"I thought you had a judge and a jail and all that?" suggested the big man.

"We got a jail that's just like a sieve," said the sheriff. "And we got the best judge you ever saw. He's real worked up, too. He'd put a sparrow in jail for flying between his window and the sun. He'd give you fifty days for coughing in church. But what good is that when there's nobody to arrest any crooks and when the jail won't hold 'em when they're arrested?"

"Well, look at me," said Little Minny.

"There's a lot of you to see," said the sheriff, "if all that ain't beef is brains."

"You think you're talking to a hobo, partner," protested

**19**

Mr. Minder Trent. "But you're not. You're talking to a statesman."

"All the statesmen I ever seen," commented the sheriff, "were hobos, outside of the newspapers. So that's all right. I don't see your graft yet, though."

"I'm leading you to it step by step," answered Little Minny. "I'm going to clean up Sunnydale."

"You're going to which?"

"I'll say it another way," said Little Minny. "I'm going to do so much that you'll buy a pair of crutches and come out to watch. You're going to cry with joy when you see what I'll do to this town."

The sheriff looked at him.

"I dunno why it is," said he. "I've heard gents talk like you do before this. But it's always kind of soothing to me."

"Open your heart, brother," said Little Minny. "I've come to you with a message."

"Go right ahead," answered the sheriff. "I like you, the way you talk. You've got style."

"I'll have more style when I've dressed up with a steel shield. I'd feel safer behind it, too," declared Little Minny.

"Maybe you're crying to be a deputy sheriff?" asked Anton Breen.

"You guessed that right away the tenth time," said Little Minny. "You're wonderful. You're a statesman yourself, perhaps."

The sheriff pointed to a table.

"Open that drawer," he said, "and you'll find a lot of shields. There's been so many of them shot all to pieces lately that I had to send in a wholesale order. Take a couple of handfuls; you'll find that they wear thin pretty fast in this air."

"Thanks," said Little Minny, and stepping to the table, he helped himself.

"You got plenty of guns?" asked the sheriff. "Gimme that Bible, will you, and I'll swear you in. Got plenty of guns?"

"I've got a club and a gun together, a sort of a private combination. I always have thought that a steel nightstick with a bullet inside it would do pretty well in this sort of town. But I'm not through yet. I want to ask you some questions. I want to find out about the honest men. I've seen one already—Rourke.''

"What's the way you define an honest man?'' asked the sheriff.

"Anybody,'' said Little Minny, "who stands behind you and me is honest. Anybody who stands on the other side is a crook.''

"That's simple,'' said the sheriff. "That's good enough for me. What are you going to do about it?''

"I'm going to put all of the crooks in jail,'' declared Little Minny.

"The jail won't hold 'em. The jail leaks,'' said the sheriff.

"The pouring of it full,'' said Little Minny, "will be a lot more fun for me than for those who are dropped into the cooler.''

"Brother,'' said the sheriff, "it seems to me that I ought to have met you long ago. Maybe you're my long-lost brother.''

"I thought so from the first,'' said Little Minny, "but by nature I'm modest. It's only education that gave me my brass.''

"I don't know exactly what you're after,'' said the sheriff. "But you can catch all the rabbits in this town that you're fast enough to grab. I only hope that you're made of tool-proof steel, is all I hope.''

"That stuff was named after me,'' declared Little Minny. "Where do I find the judge?''

"In the courthouse,'' said the sheriff. "That was one of the first things that they built in this town. The early comers, they come in with a whole flock of illusions, and all the tough birds west of the Mississippi have been laughing ever since.''

## · 4 ·

LITTLE MINNY WENT TO THE COURTHOUSE. THE HOUR WAS
wearing late, but he found a one-legged janitor pretending to
sweep the main hall.

"Where's the judge?" he asked.

"Who are you?" demanded the cripple without enthusiasm.

"You're minus a leg, but you've got two eyes," said Little
Minny. "Can't you recognize a deputy sheriff when you see
one?"

"Sure I can. I just wasn't thinking," said the janitor. "I've
seen just your style and fashion before, only you're cut a little
bigger and fuller in the sleeves. That's the judge's office, down
there, but it's after hours. He don't see nobody this time of
the day."

"I have an appointment to meet him," answered the big
man, and went down the hall.

He knocked on the door.

"Keep out!" roared a hoarse voice within.

Little Minny opened the door and stepped in.

The light inside was rather dusky; a white-headed man sat

22

by a window reading a book. His face was as red as his hair was white; it turned redder still when he saw Little Minny.

"I have a mind to give you fifty days!" he said. "What do you mean by breaking in here on me?"

"You're Judge Herbert Loring," declared Little Minny.

"I'm Herbert Loring," said the other, "and I'd be a judge if anybody ever were brought into my court. I'd like to have you there, and I've got an idea that I may, before long. Get out and stay out."

"You can't give me the run," said Little Minny. "I'm here on duty."

"You're here on—get out and stay out!" shouted the judge.

"If you can't get on with your own deputy sheriffs," said Little Minny, "you can't get on with anybody."

"Are you half-wit enough to take that job?" said the judge. "The bigger they are the harder they fall in Sunnydale."

"I always get up again," said Little Minny. "I wear shoulder springs."

"I think I've seen you before," said Judge Loring. "Sit down, my boy. Where did I see you before, and how many months did I give you?"

"It must have been a cousin of mine," said Little Minny.

"Maybe it was," said the judge. "How much time have you done?"

"I'm not that kind of a crook," answered Little Minny. "I'm not on the bench yet, but I'm on my way to it."

"I ought to give you ninety days for that," said the judge. "But I won't. After all, this is a democracy, and a deputy sheriff today may be a dead man tomorrow. Promotion like that comes quickly in Sunnydale. What do you want?"

"A free hand," said Little Minny.

"Your hands are not tied," said the other. "What do you want to do with them?"

"Plug up the holes in the jail and then fill it to the brim."

"I see," said the judge, "that if age is a disease of the body, youth is a disease of the brain. That jail is a sieve."

"I'll plaster up the holes."

"There's no money to pay for the repairs," said the judge.

"Why not? Aren't there any taxes in this town?"

"There are," said the judge, "and the tax money always goes to the first man who shoots the tax collectors. In Sunnydale they never close the season on tax collectors—and deputy sheriffs. I hope I'm not discouraging you."

"Not a bit," replied Little Minny. "My system pays its own way. It lives on the prisoners it arrests."

"Suppose you manage to hold some prisoners for a while," said the judge, "there's no money to pay for their food."

"I've got a cistern all arranged," said Little Minny, "that will hold the overflow from the Sunnydale jail. It will pay for the chance to hold them."

"Go on," said the judge. "Here, have a cigar."

"I've smelled the one that you're smoking," said Little Minny. "That'll do me, thank you."

"All right," said the judge. "Keep on talking. What can I do for you?"

"Everybody that I bring into your court is guilty," said Little Minny.

"That's not law," said Judge Loring. "Before I condemn and pass sentence, I've got to have proofs of guilt."

"What sort of proof?"

"Proof that you made the arrest in Sunnydale," said the judge with a glint like that of polished steel in his eyes.

"I see," said Little Minny, "that there's only one mind between us."

"I see that you're a flatterer," said the ironic judge. "What will you do to keep your prisoners in jail?"

"I'll use men to wall them in."

"What sort of men?"

"I have a list ready," said Little Minny, "of fellows who'll do the work for the love of it."

"I'm sorry that Anton Breen is confined to his bed," said the judge. "He'd like to be up and about in these stirring times. But how will you support your prisoners?"

"They fast on bread and water for a day or two," said Little Minny. "That's a health measure."

"And when the jail's full?"

"I forgot to tell you what you sentence them to," said Little Minny.

"Yes, you forgot to tell me that," answered the judge soberly. "But it's not too late. Tell me now."

"You sentence them to hard labor, and no sentence under a month."

"Labor on what?" asked the judge.

"An uncle of mine has a hole in the rocks twenty miles from here as the crow flies and forty miles by foot."

"Friend," said the judge, "I begin to see that I am talking to a distinguished man."

"You're slow, but you're sure," said Little Minny. "My uncle pays two dollars a day and found for every head of convict labor. The two dollars goes to the town of Sunnydale, of course. It'll help to repair the jail, and it'll pay the back salaries of the judge and the sheriff. Is there a mayor?"

"He was shot last week," replied Judge Loring. "What sort of a salary does this deputy sheriff get?"

"Nothing but affectionate praise," said Little Minny. "Not a blame cent from the treasury of Sunnydale."

"Not only a great man, but a good man. I hope you last for a day or two; and I promise to attend your funeral."

"Thanks," said Little Minny. "And I want to know that the law is behind me till I rob a bank."

"There are no banks left to rob," said the judge. "So go as far as you like."

## · 5 ·

Little Minny went calling. He hunted up several gentlemen named by the sheriff, and found three of them.

The first was a gambler; a tall, lean, sallow-faced man with a look of pain about the eyes and a look of mirth about the mouth.

He was sitting on the veranda of the hotel, and Little Minny asked him to come down to the sidewalk.

"I'm a friend of the sheriff," he said.

"Then you're no friend of mine," said Lew Eastern.

"You're wrong," Little Minny said. "I'm practically a cousin of yours. Don't you remember my face?"

"No, I'm darned if I do."

"I'm the new deputy sheriff," said Little Minny.

"I'll do this much for you," said Lew Eastern. "I'll put some flowers on your grave tomorrow."

"Thanks," said Little Minny. "I knew that blood would tell in the end. I wanted to ask you if you know the boys that burned down your joint last week."

"What good does it do to know them?"

"So I can put them in jail."

"You couldn't put them in jail," said Eastern, "and if you did, you'd see 'em walk out again."

"They won't walk past the new jailer," said Little Minny.

"Wouldn't they?"

"No, they wouldn't."

"Who's the new jailer?" asked the gambler.

"You are."

"Is this a joke, or who are you?" demanded Eastern.

"I'm the uncle of the sheriff and the favorite grandfather of Judge Loring," replied Little Minny.

"I begin to think that I saw you somewhere before," said Eastern.

"Any good memory is worth refreshing," replied Little Minny. "Do you take the job?"

"What's all this guff about?"

"This guff is worth thirty dollars a week to you," said the deputy.

"Paid in advance?"

"No, you work for your cash and your bonus."

"Ain't you a little rash?" asked Lew Eastern.

"No, I'm only farsighted," replied Little Minny. "Do you want the job?"

"If I can slam those crooks," said Lew Eastern, "I'll take all the lead that can be salted away in my hide the very next day."

"Can you lead me to them?"

"Sure I can. They always hang out in one dump."

"Got any proof on 'em?"

"I haven't got any proof. But there's plenty of proof on them just the same. Let me fan any one of those boys and I'll turn up some of my own on 'em!"

"This way, brother," said Little Minny. "Right down the street with me. We have a couple of calls to make first."

And Lew Eastern, stepping long and soft, followed Little Minny.

They found a short, wide-shouldered man in the room of the Oasis Bar. Little Minny tapped that solid shoulder and motioned him back to the wall. He came as though he intended to walk straight on through the giant.

27

"You," he said, "whatcha want?"

"Both your hands and both your guns, Jack," said Little Minny.

"You can have all four if you got the nerve to collect 'em," said the other.

"Don't be rough," answered Little Minny. "I was raised with tender care, and my feelings are easily hurt. You'd be surprised to know how easily they're hurt."

"You may know yourself, but you don't know me," said the short man, looking more and more like a bulldog.

"I know that you're Jumping Jack Story," said the deputy sheriff, "and I know some of the safes that you've cracked. Is that enough?"

"That's enough to get you a sock on the chin," declared Jack Story. "Your chatter ain't funny to me."

"That's because you don't know me," said Little Minny cheerfully.

"I'm not gunna know you," said the Jumping Jack. "I don't like the looks of you, you big stiff!"

"Do you like the looks of this?" asked Little Minny.

The Jumping Jack saw the flashing move, and his own hand was almost as fast—almost, but a vital degree too slow. And now the length of the largest revolver that Jack Story had ever seen was leveled at the third button of his coat.

Except for tall Lew Eastern, they were unnoticed by any other man in the room, for they were standing in a dim corner. Jack Story drew his hand from beneath his coat. There was no revolver in it.

"I think I've seen you before," said he.

The long gun disappeared from the hand of Little Minny.

"I knew that you'd remember me pretty soon," he said pleasantly. "The next thing you'll be remembering will be the names of your pals who rolled you after you and they split up a big melon here in town."

"I know their names," admitted Jack Story. "And I'm gonna get 'em one by one, all for myself. I'm gonna taste the marrow in 'em after I've cracked 'em up!"

"You'll never get 'em," suggested Little Minny, "because

they all work together. You've waited, and they still keep in a herd. Isn't that true?"

"You read the mind all right," admitted Jack Story. "What's your game?"

"I'm the new deputy sheriff."

"You oughta be seeing the undertaker, not me," said the Jumping Jack.

"That's funny, too," answered the big man, "but not as bright as I've seen you before. Before they bury me, I'll be worn so small that a shovelful will be enough to cover my bones. Jack, you're going to lead me to the hangout where your friends are playing pinochle."

"And then what?"

"Then you can join the party, or just watch me and Lew Eastern, here, collect the fun."

"Are you on this bandwagon, Lew?" asked Jack with interest.

"I'm on the driver's seat," answered Lew Eastern.

"Well," said the Jumping Jack, "I'll get aboard and help make noise, I guess. Where did you get that rod, brother?" he demanded of Little Minny.

"It was tailor-made to fit my chest," said Little Minny. "Come on, boys. We've still got a couple of calls to make."

They found a small shack farther down the street, and when the door was opened to their knock, a man in overalls and a coat of the same material appeared. He was of middle age, a little gray about the temples, and his clothes bulged significantly here and there. He had a wide face, as sour as cider vinegar.

"Hello, brother," said Little Minny.

The other slammed the door and turned the lock. The large boot of Little Minny arose, and smashed the lock, and cast the door wide.

The householder waited in the gloom of the hall, with a gun in each hand.

"Put up your guns," said Little Minny, "or I'll eat 'em and spit 'em back in your face in hunks."

"I know you," said the other. 'You and your crooked

29

friends, what in blazes d'you want here? I'm gunna slam you, is what I'm gunna do!''

''You don't know me, but I know you,'' said Little Minny. ''You're Buck Penrose, and you had a mine up the valley once upon a time.''

The other cursed.

''You know my name, but you don't know me. You're gunna pay for that busted lock with a busted head,'' said Buck Penrose.

''I'm Minder Trent,'' said the big man. ''Better known as Little Minny. I've come to give Sunnydale law and order, and I thought you might know where to start. You know the boys that jumped your claim for you. They're still around the town.''

''I'll find 'em one by one,'' said Buck Penrose.

''Let me take them for you, brother,'' said Little Minny. ''I'm the deputy sheriff now.''

''It's a good thing your ma don't know it,'' said Buck Penrose. ''Just what sort of a deal is this, anyway?''

''The sheriff is holding the cards,'' said Little Minny, ''and Judge Loring is handling the bank.''

Buck Penrose stepped out through the doorway.

''I kind of take some stock in you, kid,'' he said. ''What's the deal?''

''Lead us to where your old chums are hanging out. We'll do the rest, unless you want to warm your hands on 'em, too.''

''I'll warm a knife and a couple of slugs of lead in 'em,'' said Buck Penrose. ''You boys follow me.''

''We've got one last call to make,'' answered Little Minny. ''This way, boys. Buck, this is Lew Eastern, and this is Jumping Jack Story. We've all seen the dogs eating grass, and so we know that there's a change of weather ahead for Sunnydale. Come along!''

At the saloon of Ned Kimbal he paused and went through the swinging doors.

It was not hard to find Denny Rourke. He had lost every penny at faro, and was consoling himself with liquor which his friends were buying him.

30

"You know me, Denny?" asked Little Minny.

"I don't know you," answered Denny, "and what's more, I don't wanta know you. Get out."

"Not till I hear a real man tell me to budge," said Little Minny.

"You want a man? I'll be the man for you!" yelled the Irishman.

He turned, and struck in wheeling. Little Minny brushed the blow aside with an arm of iron, and with a hand of iron, not too heavily, he tapped the wide jaw of the other.

Then he picked up the sagging body of Denny Rourke in his arms and carried him to the outer air.

"What happened?" groaned Denny, opening his eyes and glaring about him as the other settled him carefully on his feet.

"A thug slugged you on the back of the head," said Little Minny.

"Is that all?" gasped the Irishman. 'I thought that a sledge hammer had socked me on the jaw. Hello, Little Minny, where'd you drop from?"

"Out of the sky," said Little Minny. "Are you with us, Denny?"

"Who else would I be with?" asked Denny Rourke. "I'm with anybody, but I gotta have action, Minny. I simply gotta have action. My doctor, he went and put me on an action diet, Minny, and I gotta have action every day. Where's there some action in this little old town?"

"There's no action except where we're going," answered the giant. "So that's the right street for you, Denny, I guess."

"Good old Minny," said Denny Rourke, rubbing his jaw. "It's sort of like old days to see you ag'in. I gotta lay my hands on something. If you don't show me where to put 'em, I'm gunna put 'em on you, you big lump!"

"I'll show you some places to work yourself out," said the other. "Have you got a gun?"

"No."

"Buck, give him a gun, will you? You've got plenty! Listen to me, Denny. Are you sober?"

**31**

"Sober?" exclaimed Denny Rourke. "I'm so dry that you could set me on fire with one touch of a match. But go on, man! Are we going to stand here all day and get our minds rusty?"

# · 6 ·

THEY DID NOT STAND THERE ALL DAY. THEY PROCEEDED down the street, while Little Minny said to long-striding Lew Eastern beside him: "What's the lid on this town, brother? What's the head of the government, and the chief of the crooks?"

"You mean Fatty Orcutt, I guess," said Lew Eastern.

"It sounds as though I mean Fatty," said the deputy sheriff. "Who is he?"

"He runs the biggest saloon and gambling house and dance hall in the town. He's young, but he's so bright that he shines, I tell you."

"He sounds better and better," said Little Minny. "Has he got a big gang around him?"

"He's got everybody," said Lew Eastern. "You can't fool with him. No thug dares to stay in town unless Fatty Orcutt has O.K.'d him."

"He's the man I want. *I'll* do something to Fatty that'll take some of the fat off him. Is he a fighting man?"

"Nobody knows. He might be, and then again he might not. You never can tell about Fatty. He's a whole box of tricks."

"So am I," answered Little Minny. "Which is his hang-out?"

"Why, right down there, with the big lanterns on top of the sign and underneath it. That's Orcutt's place. Can't you spell his name clear up here?"

"It's always easy to see what you know is there," answered Little Minny. "Stop a minute, boys. We're going to drop in on Fatty Orcutt. This is the idea—guns ready, but no shooting until I give the signal, and the only signal I'll give will be to send a bullet smash into Fatty Orcutt's fat face."

"Lemme have that job," said Buck Penrose in an almost trembling tone of entreaty. "I been dreaming about Fatty for weeks. I been dreaming of spoiling his face for him!"

"I like the way you talk, Buck," said Little Minny. "I can see that you're a man to be depended on. But plenty will happen to Fatty later on. Understand? You'll be on hand to overlook some of the things that are going to happen to him. Now follow me."

When they got to the brightly lighted entrance, two gate-keepers, flanked by two bouncers, demanded admission fees.

"Boys," Little Minny addressed them, "you think that we've come here for fun. You're wrong. We're here on business. We're here because Fatty Orcutt needs us. Take us straight in to him."

The two bouncers looked at one another.

"It's all right," said one of them. "Come on, pals, and I'll show you the way. What's the racket now?"

He conducted them down a narrow corridor made of canvas tent material only, until they came to a door at the end of the alley.

On this the bouncer knocked, and it was presently opened a trifle.

"Five-six fellows out here that wanta see Fatty pretty bad," said the bouncer.

"Wait a minute," came the answer as the door closed.

"It'll be all right, I guess," said the bouncer cheerfully as he turned on the others. "He's got a big conference or something on, but he always manages to see the boys. What's the game, anyway?"

34

"It's the biggest game in town that we're after," said Little Minny confidently.

"Is it?" asked the other earnestly. "I wouldn't mind a cut in a deal like that. Look here—ain't I seen you before, brother?"

"Sure you have," replied Little Minny, "and you're going to see a lot more of me, too, I think."

The door of Mr. Orcutt's room opened, and out came a man with great shoulders and a face which seemed to be darkly imprinted with all the sins.

"Fatty's all tied up, boys," he said. "He can't see you. But I'll take any message that you've got. I'm Tolliver. You know me, I guess?"

"Why, I've seen you before, Tolliver, haven't I?" said Little Minny.

The other looked him over suddenly, but with rather a side glance. Then his ugly face brightened.

"Sure, and I've seen you; I disrecollect where," said he.

"Let's go on in," said Little Minny, "and I'll refresh your mind for you."

"Hey, don't be a fool!" exclaimed Mr. Tolliver. "I told you that the chief's all tied up in there."

"That's the way I want to find him," said Little Minny, and laid the muzzle of his revolver on the place where Mr. Tolliver's stomach projected like a little shelf.

"What's this gag?" whispered Mr. Tolliver from the side of his mouth.

"This is poison, brother," said Little Minny. "Just stick up your hands for a minute, will you? You boys take any weights you can find off of our bouncer friend, will you?" he asked without turning his head.

In the meantime he was taking a single, very beautifully decorated revolver from the person of Tolliver. Then he heard the muttering voice of Buck Penrose enumerating:

"Three guns, a knife, a set of knuckles, and a sling shot. That's all this gent needed to keep himself warm. Look how chilly he is right away. He's all trembling with the cold!"

"You lead the way in," said Little Minny, "and step smiling, Mr. Tolliver. If you remember me at all, you won't try any of your little tricks now."

"Nobody'll ever believe it," said Tolliver. "Nobody'll ever believe that anybody ever tried a gag like this right under the nose of the chief."

But he led the way as commanded, the prodding muzzle of the revolver helping him to make up his mind with greater speed.

And so they stepped through the doorway into a little room which was so occupied by a big desk that it seemed a miracle that there should be room for the five people who were seated here and there around the wall—a precious collection of rascals by their looks, and above all Mr. Fatty Orcutt shone. He was young, big, soft, smooth, and smiling. He looked like some rich old woman's favorite son. And yet again, as had been said, he shone. There were other men in that room who might have been considered far more formidable, but none had in their eyes the light which adorned the eyes of Fatty Orcutt.

It was not remarkable that he ruled in Sunnydale. It was only wonderful that he had not chosen a much larger field.

He began, "Tolliver, you know better than to bring in—"

Then, before he saw the guns, he saw something in the face of his lieutenant that made him reach for the lamp.

He would have caught it, too, and washed that room into solid blackness in another moment had it not been for the length of Little Minny's arm and the extra inches on the barrel of his gun. As it was, he was just able to flick the gambler across the forearm with the rim of the muzzle of that great Colt.

The arm of Fatty Orcutt jumped away and was caressed by the other hand.

In the meantime, the four friends, or business associates, of Orcutt were out of their chairs, but the game was too hard for them, hardy fellows though they were. Faces like Lew Eastern's and Buck Penrose's, looking down gun barrels, were too disheartening. Two of them half drew weapons, but they all thought better of it.

Fatty Orcutt asked: "What sort of a gag is this, brothers?

And who are you?'' he went on, looking at Little Minny. ''Haven't I seen you before?''

''Most people have seen me before; nearly everybody that's ever had a good nightmare has seen me before,'' said Little Minny, his broadest smile on his crooked mouth. ''Jumping Jack, will you fan these gentlemen for me? And if any one of 'em tries a funny move, don't waste time talking or warning. Just bash in his skull with a butt end, or else ram a couple of bullets through his spine.

''You don't have to be delicate in handling this cargo,'' he went on. ''Anyway, it won't be shipped in a refrigerator car, and some of it is bound to spoil before the shipment arrives. That's all right. There's plenty more of these melons growing in the same fields. That's right; take the wallets, too, Jack. You've got a set of useful fingers on those hands of yours. I wouldn't be without them and you. Now a few bits of this twine wrapped around their wrists and put their hands behind their backs. Thanks very much, boys, but I'll do the tying myself. I know the job, and I like it.''

## · 7 ·

THERE WERE THREE HEAVILY ARMED MEN STILL AT THE ENtrance to Orcutt's place, but they gave no trouble. The sight of their chief's bulky form—their chief, with his hands tied behind him—seemed to paralyze their bodies and their brains. They allowed themselves to be stuck up, fanned, and taken in tow.

And rapidly the procession moved by back alleys to the jail. And not so rapidly that they failed to hear a murmur and then a humming that began to pass through the trembling air that overhung the town of Sunnydale.

Mr. Orcutt was calm and coldly indignant. He said to Little Minny: "This is a good bluff. You boys can't do anything with me. I'm too big. There's too much of me. Know that? You can't throw me away, brother. This is only going to be trouble for you!"

"I'm only doing this for your own good, Fatty," said Little Minny.

"Are you?" murmured the other.

"Yeah. Only for your own good. The way that you've been putting on weight is pitiful, Fatty. And think of the days when you used to be so slim and so slender that you could dance all night long! Gone are those days, Fatty, but they'll return again. And remember when your skin was a fine, healthful brown? Now see how pale and pink it is! Not a manly color, old fellow. But we'll change that. In about sixty days we'll bring you back a perfect picture of all that a young man ought to be. You won't have to pay a tailor so much when that time comes, old son."

"Sixty days?" said Orcutt. "What in blazes are you talking about, partner?"

"I'm talking about a little summer resort that I know of. An uncle of mine is one of the proprietors. And it's a funny sort of a resort, at that. Mighty funny. You see, they actually pay the guests instead of the guests having to pay the resort. It's a simple life, but it will do great things for you, Fatty. Any good doctor in the world would advise the course for you. And the delightful part of it is that you will be surrounded by your best friends. You see, we've thought of everything. We're simply doing you good by force!"

So they arrived at the jail, where Little Minny climbed the steps and knocked on the door.

A voice inside drawled: "Open that door, boy. Doggone me if it don't sound like somebody wanted to get inside!"

A key grated in the lock. The door opened, and a grinning black man stood before them; at a little distance, lolling in a comfortable chair with legs extended before him, was the sallow-faced jailer, yawning prodigiously.

"You can step right outside, George," said Little Minny, walking inside. "You won't be needed any more here."

The black man took one look at the bared guns of that strange posse, and then leaped into the outer darkness with a gurgling cry.

Inside, the jailer looked up with amazement at the giant who advanced upon him.

"Hey, what's this gang want?" he demanded.

"More room," said Little Minny. "We want all the space you're occupying in this jail, brother. You've been the hole in the cask that a lot of good liquor has run out through. You'll be the easy exit no more, friend. This way, please. This way!"

With his left hand he took the other literally by the ear while he rammed the portentous length of his Colt against the ribs of the unlucky jailer. A twist of his iron fingers made the jailer howl and prance. In this manner they came to the door of the building, and from that point Little Minny started the other into the world with the longest first step he had ever made. For he was buoyed up and assisted from behind with such a mighty impact that as he shot upward and outward into darkness his yell went like a sword of fire before him.

Little Minny turned back into the building. Already the cell room had been opened by Buck Penrose, and the prisoners were being herded inside.

Little Minny made a brief inspection. Then he said:

"Gentlemen, I've already explained to Mr. Orcutt that our chief idea in arranging this little surprise party is to give you a healthful time of exercise and rest, on good, simple food and plenty of the freshest air in the world. Only one thing we insist upon. That is discipline. We believe, in fact, that discipline is a thing which we can teach better than you have ever been taught it before. We are going to do our best, humbly and patiently, to keep you in strictly good order. Where humility and patience have no effect we will use the whip. Where the whip is not sufficient, we'll use the riot gun.

"Lew, you'll be in charge of this first installment. We won't leave you alone with them very long. Others will be joining them, I'm sure, to fill out our little mission. But while you're here alone, I call your attention to the row of riot guns hanging along that wall. See if they're loaded, Buck."

"Every doggone one is loaded," said Buck Penrose. "Double charges of Number One buckshot, Minny!"

"The very thing! The very thing to encourage discipline. I'm delighted," said Little Minny.

"Listen, Mr.—" began Fatty Orcutt in a hoarse voice.

"Always pleased to hear a man of your intelligence speak," said Little Minny. "Mind the whip, Lew. That quirt ought to do pretty well."

Lew Eastern picked up the quirt with an avid hand.

Fatty Orcutt snarled, "You think, blast you, that you've pulled a pretty good trick here, don't you? But lemme tell you that I'm going to break this jail to bits, and when I get through with the jail I'm going to start in on you. You write that down in red, you—''

Mr. Minder Trent raised one finger, and Lew Eastern struck through the bars of steel and slashed the quirt across the shoulders of Fatty Orcutt.

A gasping oath was the answer, and then silence. Fatty Orcutt showed his teeth, but he dared not speak again. He merely writhed and rubbed the weals which the lashes had raised upon his tender flesh.

His adherents and advisers stood dumbly glowering behind their bars. They stared not at one another, but at this strange giant who had stepped so suddenly and so violently out of nowhere into their lives.

''This is a good little jail, a snug little jail, a tight little jail,'' said Little Minny to Eastern. ''Now, while we're gone, I want you to sit here with a riot gun across your knees, and two more, one on each side of your chair. That gives you six charges to pay off any trouble that starts inside of this place.

''No matter what happens, don't let that front door be opened until you hear my voice outside of it. And if there's any trouble inside, I don't want you to hesitate. Just turn loose the buckshot and let them talk for you. If I come back and find seven dead men in the cells, I'll be hurt, but not surprised. Is all that clear?''

''Brother,'' said Lew Eastern, fondling one of the double-barrelled, sawed-off shotguns, ''nothing ever pleased me any more than this here job. I never was so tickled in my life as I am to be right in here with these boys. I'm seeing some faces that mean a whole lot to me, Minny.

''Look at that man with the one eye and the patch over the other. That's Dan Binney. Curse his black heart, he's cut more throats than anyone in this town. He's a butcher, is what he is. And there's Mr. Greengoods Walters. I'm glad to see him, too. And they're glad to see me, too—they are not! They'd rather be throwed into a pit filled with snakes than be left here alone with me. Why, Minny, there won't be a sound out of them. There won't even be a whisper while you're away. They're just going to sit around like so many little mice and wait for the cat to come back and eat 'em up!''

Still, as he spoke, he chuckled, and the sound of his laughter was very like the low growling of a bulldog.

Little Minny turned to his other adherents.

''Boys,'' he said, ''the next part of our program is really pretty simple, though it seems complicated. Follow me and do as I do. First you take your coats off.''

It was done.

''Then you rip out the lining. You make the lining into a hood that comes over your head and shoulders, with holes for the eyes—look, Lew, how these boys seem to know exactly how to make masks; every one of them! I wonder where they all learned the trick? Oh, I have a talented posse with me!''

In fact, hardly five minutes were needed before there stood before the leader three masked men.

It seemed to Little Minny that he could see the smiles of that trio behind the black cloth of the masks.

''Which way this time?'' asked Jumping Jack Story.

''This time back to the same place,'' said Minder Trent.

''Back to the same place!'' exclaimed Story.

''Look here, chief,'' protested Denny Rourke. ''You may get past the wasps once, but not when they're all buzzing in the air and ready for trouble.''

''It's throwin' ourselves away,'' said Buck Penrose. ''A long pull and a strong pull and a pull altogether may turn a big trick, but not a trick as big as that!''

''I have an idea, partners,'' Little Minny answered. ''Ideas are better than numbers, and they're better than guns. You come with me and take your chances, and there won't be a gun fired except if one of you gets too nervous.''

He could see their heads nodding in agreement. They had seen something done, and they were willing to follow him quite blindly this time. So it was that they marched out of the jail behind him and down the steps, and into the darkness across the field, and so by a back alley they came again to the gambler's stronghold.

Even then Little Minny did not try to get in by a back

entrance; but around the side of the big, sprawling shack, now seething with the noise of excited voices, they came to the front of the building again, and found at the entrance half a dozen angry men, armed, and apparently waiting for them.

# · 8 ·

When Little Minny started to enter, before any other question, a rifle barrel flashed, and the muzzle of the gun was pressed against his broad chest.

"What are *you*?" asked the angry guard.

"I'm this," answered Little Minny, and from under his arm he produced a double-barreled, sawed-off shotgun.

"That may be your first name, but it ain't your last name," said the guard. "Lookit here. What are you doing here with masks on?"

"What fool wants to go up to the jail wearing his right face?" asked Little Minny. "The rest of you are yelling your heads off about Fatty Orcutt, but I'm going to *do* something about him. But you just back up, brother, and don't waste your time bothering me. I'll just tell you this, that Fatty knows that I'm here right now. You pass the word around. Say that I want to see some armed men wearing masks in the big game room, will you?"

"You'll see me one of 'em, as soon as I can get a hood over my head," said the guard. "Doggone me, but I think that you mean business."

He stood back, and Little Minny, with his three solemn

followers, marched into the game room of the Orcutt establishment.

There was room enough in that place for a hundred men to lose their money all at the same time, and now it was swirling with a tumult of excited men, not one of whom was seated at the tables. Guns were everywhere. It was a mob that simply wanted leading.

All heads turned toward that grim procession which now entered in single file, four solemn forms.

Three of them, obeying muttered instructions, moved to the right and the left of the entrance. Little Minny went on until he stood upon the raised dais where the roulette wheel was mounted, a sort of eminence which Fatty Orcutt's most crooked device deserved.

By the time the giant had reached that post he had the attention of every man in the room. Then he raised a great arm, at the end of which the heavy riot gun looked no more than a mere clumsy revolver.

"You boys are talking about Fatty Orcutt in the jail," he said. "You're talking, but you're doing nothing about it. I intend to take you there—as many of you as are sorry to see Fatty in trouble. I don't want a man that wouldn't go through thick and thin for Fatty. I don't want a man who doesn't think that Fatty Orcutt is the best fellow in this town. Fatty and six of his partners are in the jail, tied and helpless. I'm going to lead some of you who have enough courage and grit to go to that jail. I want to see you, but I don't want to see your faces. You may have to do some things that you won't be talking about tomorrow. There may be some blood shed tonight. Or it may just amount to a few necks being squeezed by sliding nooses. Now lemme see how many of you put on masks to follow me into the Sunnydale jail!"

The talking ended.

On the spot there was a sudden bustling. Some men followed the obvious device of Little Minny himself and ripped the linings out of their coats to make hoods for their heads. Others declared that they would have to get cloth elsewhere for that purpose; still others said that they had not with them the right sort of weapons; and all of those who left the building under these pretexts never returned. Of the original crowd, hardly twenty remained. But others sifted in through the doorway, all armed to the teeth, and all masked.

The noise throughout Sunnydale began to die down. It was plain that the rumor that something important was about to happen had quelled the lesser spirits and sent scampering home all of those men who were more willing to talk than to act.

And now, when no more newcomers entered the place, and when there were present a full fifty masked men, someone jumped on a table and called out: "Let's get together now, boys. We wanta find out the best plan. We wanta—"

The thunderous roll of Little Minny's voice broke in upon this harangue and stopped it. "What we want to do is to get into the jail. Am I wrong?"

Story, Rourke, and Buck Penrose shouted heartily: "Aye! That's it! We want to get into the jail!"

"That's it!" called other voices.

The man who had climbed to the top of the table stood unmarked.

Little Minny continued: "I'll get you all in there in a jiffy. Look this way, all of you, and listen to me! D'you hear? Listen to me and try to understand that I mean what I say!"

Every head turned toward him. Crowds of men are like crowds of sheep. Not the best, but the first, leader is usually followed. So these men attended patiently on Little Minny. He went on: "Buck, Jack, and Denny, cover this gang; and the first hand that tries to lift a gun, open up with those riot guns and blow them to blazes!"

As he spoke the gasp of the crowd seemed a single voice exclaiming, sharp and high, as the trick began to be apparent. And hardly a man there refrained from reaching for a weapon.

Every man reached for one, but none was drawn, for now, in the massive fists of Little Minny, appeared two sawed-off shotguns which he handled with absurd ease. The great muzzles swung slowly in a semicircle, covering the assembly; and it seemed to every man that he was picked out for the particular attention of that masked giant on the dais of the roulette-wheel table.

For there was hardly a man there who was not deserving of particular attention. It was a handpicked group, containing all of the most hardy spirits in the town.

They were such men as would readily have taken their chances against revolvers, but chances against sawed-off shotguns do not exist. In the hands of Little Minny and his three assistants there was enough of a hailstorm of lead to sweep the cheap pine boards of that floor with blood and death. And those grim figures very well knew it.

"Move over against the wall!" commanded Little Minny. "The whole lot of you, crowd over there against the wall. Start in. Move, blast you, or we'll wash you out!"

And suddenly he loosed the barrel of his left-hand gun. He fired down toward the floor, and when the sudden roar of the barking explosion was ended, those who were curious could see how the floor had been mangled by the sweeping effects of the heavy leaden shot.

There was no hanging back.

One man groaned, "We're sold, boys, and that's all there is to it!"

"We've been taken in. It's a low trick," protested another.

The hardiest of men, or wild cats, may be caught in a trap, and these fellows knew that they were trapped. They moved; they sidled and backed until they stood in what averaged a closely ordered double rank against the wall.

When they reached that position it was plain that their case was infinitely worse than before.

Straight before them stood the giant, with a gun in each hand. At the one end of their line was a masked man kneeling, his riot gun pressed close to his shoulder, studying that line with the steady muzzles of his weapon. And at the other end two more, in the same position, regarded them.

Little Minny said: "Denny, you wade through those boys and collect their hardware. Jack and Buck, if trouble starts, just turn loose. It doesn't matter if you have to shoot Denny along with the rest of 'em. He'll be glad to go out in that sort of company. Step along, Denny!"

And Denny stepped along.

He was cursed by voices that quivered with rage. But no

**47**

man attempted to harm him. The watch was too close. The chances against them were too great. Who would try to dodge at close range from the spray of a garden hose? And here were three steel hoses, and the drops they were ready to spray were of lead!

Denny Rourke was not nice. He plucked weapons right and left. He dropped rifles and revolvers to the floor and slid them out into the center of it. One of them exploded and knocked a little hole in the wall.

That was all that happened. Even the cursing began to die out.

Every one of these fellows had gambled heavily and lost before this evening. It was not exactly strange to them to lose again.

Presently a great heap of weapons appeared in the center of the floor.

There were rifles, shotguns, revolvers predominantly, knives of all sorts and sizes. And finally Denny Rourke stepped back with a nod and a grunt.

"They're a lot cleaner now than they were, chief," said he. "I ain't gleaned 'em to the skin. But I've got all the cream."

"Go back and take a gun," said the leader. "Watch those boys steady and sure. Now, Jack and Buck, take those lengths of twine and tie their hands. Tie 'em hard and fast. Take plenty of time. Nobody in Sunnydale will come to help 'em, because there's nobody left in Sunnydale. We've got the whole town here, and we're going to take it along with us."

Heavy groans arose from the unlucky ones. But what could they do save submit?

There are well-witnessed tales of how one desperado with a single revolver has stuck up a room filled with twenty armed men. And here were four against fifty, and the four carried riot guns!

Step by step that hardy gang had been backed against the wall. Every step had made its position worse. And now there remained nothing except blank submission!

Their hands were tied. Then long ropes were passed from arm to arm, secured by half hitches.

And so the procession was started through the doors of the gaming house, with Little Minny, standing at the door, snatching off the hoods that masked them one by one.

Three abreast they entered the principal street of Sunnydale, and three abreast, closely huddled, they marched down its length, while nearly every man, woman, and child of the rest of the population lined the street and looked on with murmurs.

It was plain that a change had come to the town. Upon the spot certain of the wilder spirits who had escaped that rope gang determined to leave for other places, for any place that was far away from this sort of trouble!

## · 9 ·

Wʜᴇɴ ᴛʜᴇʏ ʀᴇᴀᴄʜᴇᴅ ᴛʜᴇ ᴊᴀɪʟ, Lɪᴛᴛʟᴇ Mɪɴɴʏ ᴍᴏᴜɴᴛᴇᴅ the steps of the building and made a speech. It was not a long speech, but the words of it sank deep.

He had taken off his mask by this time; but his face and his smile were not pleasant to those who looked up to him from the lower darkness.

"Boys," he said, "you all wanted to do something about Fatty Orcutt. He was your friend. You knew that he was in the jail, and you wanted to break the jail open. You won't have to do that. You can see that the doors of the jail are open for you. You all like Fatty a lot, and I don't blame you. Fatty's a pleasant fellow. He's taken some crooked money now and then and here and there, but never out of your pockets. A few people have been tapped over the head in his place, and some of them never opened their eyes again. But he never rolled any of you.

"He's spent a lot of money on thugs and gunmen, and a good many of you have that money in your pockets. No wonder you care about Fatty, and now you're going to be able to do something for him. You'll be able to keep him company where he's going. And he's going to a summer resort where

50

he won't have to pay for board and lodging. Partly for his sake and partly for your own, you're all going to have the same opportunity. Jack, start them up the steps. We'll bed them down in here for tonight!''

It was a tight fit, but it was managed. Into the little jail the mob was brought and turned into the cells by three. There were only a dozen cells, and therefore some of the men had to sleep in the corridors, their hands manacled to the bars.

They were amazingly quiet. Lew Eastern, striding up and down all night with a lantern, kept guard over them, and Jumping Jack Story, who had found his particular enemies in the throng, and who had to go and see them now and then, burst into loud and long laughter.

But as for the others, Little Minny, and Rourke, and Buck Penrose, they slept rolled in blankets in the jailer's room. And soundly they slept, and long, until the dawn turned from gray to red and the sun came up.

Then Little Minny arose, and he said in his loud voice to the prisoners: "I'm going to get the court ready for you boys. This is a just country, and we want you to have nothing but justice. That summer resort wouldn't take any of you without a recommendation from a judge!''

Then he left the jail and went to find Judge Herbert Loring. He found that gentleman taking a breakfast of ham and eggs in the little shack that served him as a home, and the judge made him sit down at the same table. He paused long enough to pump a washbasin full of water. When he had soaped and washed his hands and face, he sat down opposite the judge. A one-legged veteran came stumping in with a new supply of food and coffee.

"You don't look as though you've been up all night, Mr. Trent, alias Little Minny,'' said the judge.

"I haven't,'' said Little Minny. "I've had a good long sleep.''

The judge nodded. "When you got through, I hear that there was no one left in Sunnydale to keep people awake. It's the quietest night the town has ever had since the gold rush started. But what are we to do with that collection of beauties that you've gathered in the jail?''

"Where did you hear about 'em?" asked Little Minny.

"You can't keep people from talking," answered the judge. "They'll talk whenever they get a fair excuse. And you gave them more than a fair excuse, I take it. I hear that Jud Biddle is in that gang?"

"Who's Jud Biddle?" asked Little Minny.

"Why," said the judge, "he's a fellow who's wanted for murder in Arizona, and for arson in Nevada, and for pushing the queer in California. There are enough charges against him to hang him three times and put him in prison for seven lifetimes. Then I understand that you picked up the gentleman called Dagger Jim."

"That sounds interesting," said Little Minny, "but I don't know Dagger Jim, either."

"Dagger Jim is a great artist," said the judge. "Murder is his special talent, and he uses it overtime. It's hard to keep an artist from using his hands, you know. And Dagger Jim uses his. He draws his pictures with a knife, and some of them have been very interesting. They've attracted world-wide attention. He's wanted for only one crime. But he's wanted in seven States, and always for murder. A lot of sheriffs in this country will almost cry for joy when it's known that Dagger Jim has been caught."

"Any more that have been spotted?" asked the captor, frowning.

"A lot more," said the judge. "Enough to keep me busy for six months giving sentences. But there'll be a great deal of extradition. Lawyers are going to rub their hands when they hear about all of this!"

"Judge Loring, I'm sorry."

"Why?" asked the judge.

"Because," said the giant, "I don't like lawyers."

"No?"

"Except in their own place."

"And what is their own place?"

"In a jail, or near it."

The judge grinned; his eyes sparkled with a sudden brightness.

"Go on," he said.

"About these murderers and such," said Little Minny.

"Yes, I've just been talking about them."

"We're going to have a new kind of justice in Sunnydale," said Little Minny.

"I believe that," answered the judge. "We already have a new kind of justice. You got most of the foremost crooks in one sweep, and the others, the smaller fry, suddenly find the air of Sunnydale is bad for what ails them. All night long there have been buckboards and horses and mules starting out of town, all bound out for parts unknown, all carrying a freight of things of one sort or another. I haven't closed my eyes since the first reports came in!"

"Good," said Little Minny. "And it's too bad, too. Pretty soon it won't be possible to raise enough crooks to make a poker game, not with a sheriff's posse to help collect 'em!"

"Would that be hard on you, Trent?" asked the judge.

"I wouldn't stay in that kind of a town."

"*This* town would like to have a mayor again; it would like to have you, man," said the judge. "A handful of the leading citizens—citizens, I mean to say, who will lead now that Fatty Orcutt is out of the way—left my house just at dawn this morning. They all decided that you were the man for the job."

"I'm sorry," said Little Minny. "But I've got to help my uncle run his summer resort for fifty days. And after that I'll be outward bound."

"Fifty days?"

"Fifty days," said the other, "is what I hear all those thugs are going to get from you by way of a sentence."

Herbert Loring bowed his head a little and looked up at the big man from under darkened brows.

"Those murderers, safecrackers, counterfeiters, cut-throats, you think that they all will receive fifty days?" he demanded.

"Yes," said the other.

"Who told you that?"

"A still, small voice," answered the big man, grinning.

The judge did not smile in return.

"You've done a great thing, a wonderful thing, Trent,"

said he. "You've broken up a hotbed of corruption. You've washed the poison out of Sunnydale's gold. But you can't interfere with justice."

The other shrugged his shoulders.

"What's your answer?" said the judge. "Some of those men are blackened by every crime in the calendar, and yet you want to let them off with sentences of fifty days apiece?"

"I'm blackened by a good many crimes myself," answered the giant slowly. "The only reason I was able to make this roundup is because I know a lot of roughs and know how to handle 'em. This was partly business for me, but it was chiefly a game. I'm not going to turn it into more than fifty days of business. After that they go free. There may be murderers and such in that gang. But I went after laborers, not thugs."

The judge struck the table with his fist, but he struck it lightly.

"Things have gone so far that you can't interfere," said he.

"Suppose," said the giant more slowly than ever, "that I go over to that jail and turn loose the whole hive of wasps on Sunnydale?"

"You can't do it!" exclaimed Judge Loring.

The big, craglike jaw of the giant thrust forward.

"I'll take some stopping," he said.

"Confound it, man," said Loring, "are you going to turn your invaluable contribution into a joke?"

"I'm going to turn my joke into fifty days of sweat for 'em," said Little Minny. "I won't have their blood. I don't want their blood. I'd rather cut off my right hand than have it on my head!"

"Are you afraid of 'em?" asked the judge suddenly.

"Afraid of them?" repeated Little Minny, amazed. "Why, before they've finished raising blisters and headaches in my uncle's mine, every one of those thugs will be ready to starve for ten years to have one shot at me. If I get them hanged, I can't get them to hate me any more than they will!"

"Then, under heaven," exclaimed Loring, "I don't understand why you want to let them off with paltry sentences."

The other thought for a moment.

"It's an instinct with me, not a reason," he said. "But I suppose that I'd rather have the hatred of men and stand in their danger than have them dead and be haunted by the thought of them."

Then he added: "I've broken enough laws myself. Who am I to bring other people to justice?"

Judge Herbert Loring actually rose from his chair, and then he made a swift turn up and down the room. At last he said: "Partner Trent, you confound me!"

"I'm sorry," said Trent.

"But," continued the man of the law, "whatever it may be, justice or foolishness, I'm going to let you have your way. But let's get it over with quickly. Bring those rascals into my court at once, and I'll be there waiting. It's not law. It may mean that I'll be thrown off the bench, but I'll do what you want."

"Judge Loring," said the other, "I've an idea that after this morning any one who tries to throw you off the bench will have to face every gun that Sunnydale can pull to keep you seated."

"From what I've heard," said Loring, grinning suddenly, "there are no guns left in the town!"

# · 10 ·

Since the French Revolution there never was such a trial. On the prisoner's bench, or, rather, grouped closely in front of it, stood fifty-seven men, their hands bound, long ropes holding them together. Nearby stood the formidable forms of Jumping Jack Story, crook; Lew Eastern, crooked gambler; Denny Rourke, saloonkeeper and general man of all trouble; and Buck Penrose, whose single love was a hard fight.

The judge sat behind his desk on the raised platform. The clerk sat at the table below it. The old sergeant at arms was by the door, his eyes as big and round as apples. The only other man in the room was the giant, Little Minny.

The newspapers were not represented.

The people of Sunnydale were not represented.

The district attorney was not there.

No lawyer attached to the court was on hand.

The sheriff was not appearing.

But in the street was a crowd of three or four thousand, humming as ten million bees might hum.

The judge said: "Mr. Deputy Sheriff, what is all this about?"

Mr. Minder Trent, deputy sheriff extraordinary, answered: "Your honor, here are fifty-seven fellows whose names don't matter, all charged with breaking the peace."

"Are you standing in the witness stand, Mr. Deputy Sheriff?" asked the judge, rubbing his knuckles across his chin.

"I'm standing in my boots," said the giant, grinning.

"How did they break the peace?" asked the judge.

"Most of them wore masks," said the giant. "And those who didn't wear a mask wore concealed weapons, all the way from knives of illegal length to Colt revolvers."

"This is a serious charge," said the judge, still faintly smiling. "What have you to substantiate it?"

"I have there," said the deputy sheriff, "one half gross of revolvers, and eighteen rifles, and twelve shotguns, and three dozen of the knives that I talk about. There are also certain other illegal weapons, such as brass knuckles, sling shots, lead-pipe sections in hose, and other devices. There are burglar sets, and several packages of counterfeit money. But the worst charge against the prisoners is the faces they wear. Look at those beauties!"

The judge looked, and he did not smile. Few people, other than Minder Trent, could have smiled at the glowering hatred and malice that darkened fifty-seven faces!

"A serious charge," said the judge. "I feel that I must proceed to sentence."

A loud, gasping voice, the voice of Fatty Orcutt, exclaimed: "Your honor, what does this mean? I appeal to law and justice. I want my due rights as a citizen of the United States. I demand a chance to consult a lawyer. I protest against this mock trial of fifty men on one charge. I protest against evidence that—"

"There's other evidence, Mr. Orcutt," said the judge very dryly. "There are scores of men in the street who are aching to give evidence almost as much as they are aching to tie a rope around your fat neck. And if you are held for a week, there will be sheriffs and their deputies from half the States in the country to lay charges against you. Perhaps this is not a trial. Perhaps it is a mockery. But the mockery is of the law and the rights of the law, not of you and most of the other reptiles who are gathered around you.

"You, Orcutt, have serious charges of fraud pending against you. Five separate times officers of the law, to my certain knowledge, have come to Sunnydale to arrest you, with legal warrants. One of those men was found dead in the street. Another disappeared mysteriously. Another now lies recovering from wounds. Two more were able to leave the town alive, but not unhurt. Orcutt, do you seriously challenge full justice for yourself, or do you prefer to have me hand you over to Mr. Trent for fifty days?"

"Blast him; and you, too!" muttered the fat man, but his voice was barely audible.

"I would have held you for the full operation of the law," said the judge. "Legally or illegally, I would have held you all. But in this uncertain time, the power of Mr. Trent is greater than mine, and he has refused to permit a single major charge to be offered against a single one of you. Such generosity is, in my opinion, more extraordinary than sensible. But some of you, in my belief, can thank him for your lives, and others that the rest of your days are not spent in prison. But I proceed to sentence, unless," he added, lifting his head and grimly glaring along the rows of faces, "unless there are other voices raised to demand particular justice in each case?"

Not a voice answered, though the judge purposely maintained that grim silence for the whole of a long minute.

He said, at last: "Since everyone is satisfied, I now deliver you into the hands of Mr. Minder Trent, deputy sheriff of this county.

"Each and every one of you is sentenced to fifty days of penal servitude—hard labor. Mr. Deputy Sheriff, remove the prisoners. Mr. Clerk of the court, write nothing in your book. Sergeant at arms, attend the prisoners to the street and keep the mob from lynching them if you can!"

That was the end of the most singular trial ever held west of the Mississippi.

Perhaps there were trials for witchcraft in certain dark old days that might have matched it for freakishness.

But though the trial had ended, the troubles of the prisoners, in a sense, and certainly their danger, had just begun.

For when they were ushered down the steps to the street, a murmur, a groan, a shouting, and then one long, wild howl arose from the crowd gathered there.

A singular process went on in the mob at the same time. Women and children, as though by magic, were sifted to the rear of it. There remained in front only men. And rough men they were, and angry.

They had seen murder done almost wholesale in their town. They had been robbed, tricked, cheated in a thousand ways. They had seen rascality walk barefaced through the streets, and still there had seemed no way of organizing to put down crime. Now they saw crime itself gathered in ranks before them, helpless, hands tied. And the temptation was too great.

Single voices began to break through that general hymn of hatred.

"There's Fatty Orcutt! There he goes. Where's the rope to hang him?"

"Here's the rope for Orcutt. Here's another for Bill Levine, the gunman. He killed Pete Thomas! I saw him kill Pete Thomas!"

"There's Gonzales, that murdered Steve Hampshire on a bet. Get him!"

And now, as the crowd began to rush, the thundering voice of Mr. Minder Trent arose and boomed down that street and put every man back on his heels.

"Gentlemen, keep back! If you start to make trouble, I'll turn the prisoners loose, and then handle 'em if you can! Keep back or we'll turn loose on you with the riot guns! March on, there in front. Jack and Buck, clear the street. Use your gun butts if you have to. If that won't do, shoot, and I'll take the responsibility. Gentlemen of Sunnydale, we're giving you a safe town for the first time since it was built. But I won't see helpless men murdered, no matter what they've done before! March ahead! Fall back, you!"

He was everywhere. Those enormous strides carried him to the front and to the back. And wherever angry townsmen began to draw close and prepare to gather head, the looming bulk of the deputy sheriff discouraged them before they could act.

So, down the main street to the first break in the houses moved that troop, the prisoners holding closely packed together. More than one lost both coat and shirt sleeves, as fingers hard with rage plucked at them. Such was the temper of the crowd that once a man had been detached from the general mass there would have been no questions asked. Death on the spot would have been the order of the day.

But now, down a side lane, they were marched into the open country behind the town, and as though the clean, open spaces banished murder from their minds, the townsmen fell back and let the procession go forward.

There was talk of pursuit. There was even arming, and the saddling of horses, but no sufficiently large group could draw to a head. The mighty form of Little Minny remained looming too formidably in the memories of these men.

In the meantime the guard of the prisoners had mounted on mustangs. Six dozen confiscated revolvers and eighteen rifles and various sundry other weapons had been exchanged for the horses and for the solid and heavy packs of provisions that helped to weigh down the saddles.

So Little Minny and his four men herded the captives quickly across the plain, and up the slope and over the ridge.

By that time the sun was beating with great force upon them, and more than one was without a hat! Moreover, though some of these men were as tough as bands of iron and leather, yet many others were, like *Falstaff,* larding the lean earth they walked upon. Fatty Orcutt began to groan and roll his eyes. Plenty of food and little exercise had been very bad for the condition of Fatty. He was cut loose. He was allowed to march at the rear of the procession, and when he lagged, a quirt snapped near his ears taught him to hurry forward once more.

Presently every man in the lot was permitted to have free hands, and the controlling ropes that grouped them all together were dispensed with. For they were not needed. Beaten, staggering, groaning, cursing, that mob of desperadoes of many kinds climbed the long slopes toward the mine.

It was forty miles that they had to cover, very nearly. And the pace they were able to maintain was not more than two and a half miles an hour, even at the first. It grew less and less as the day progressed.

Thrice in the day they came to water. But there was no food.

"An empty belly makes a bright dog," said Mr. Minder Trent.

The day ended as they started on the last long pull. The darkness closed, with the guards riding busily here and there to make sure that no one of the herd dared to try to slip behind a bush or a rock and so escape.

Then the moon rose, and just above them it gilded the rocky face of the mountain where stood the mine of Tom Wayland and Jim Trent.

# · 11 ·

JIM TRENT, AFTER SUPPER, USUALLY SMOKED ONE PIPE, rolled in his blankets, and went to sleep. On this night he had smoked the pipe, rolled himself in his blankets, but sleep he could not. Between him and repose slid a thought of trouble that kept his eyes wide open. They began to ache and burn as he stared up into the darkness.

Finally he got up and went striding out across the little plateau that extended before the mine.

He and Wayland, he knew, had reached the end of their tether. They really had reached it a long time before. The ground they were breaking was just as hard as ever; there was neither softening of the strain in which they labored, nor did the vein become richer as they explored it farther. They would have to give it up. Just as he had said, it seemed to extend clear down to China, but two men simply could not exploit it. They could make a day's wages—hardly that, considering the overhead and the labor that the girl was forced to do. They would have to give up now.

He must press the issue upon Wayland at once. For himself he hardly minded. He had prospected for twenty years; he had labored in a thousand holes of his own discovery; he could return to the maddening and fascinating business once more. But it was a tragedy for Wayland. He would have to return to find his clients gone to other physicians. He would return so poor that his daughter would have to make her own living however she might manage it—as a camp cook, perhaps, or a slavey in a crossroads boarding house.

These thoughts darkened the mind of Jim Trent as he stood and stared at the moonlight that stepped across the mountaintops and dropped vainly into the blue deeps of the gorges. He was not a lover of beautiful pictures, but he was a lover of spaces; and some harmony in this gigantic composition entered his soul unknown to him.

Then it seemed to him that he heard from the valley beneath a murmuring like the humming of bees when they are swarming not very far away upon the wind.

He had never heard such a sound as this in such a setting. So he shaded his eyes with a frown and peered into the deeps beneath him.

Gradually he could make out something that moved close up under the rock. It seemed one unshaped monster, flowing slowly over the ground, reaching the cliff, entering upon the windings of the upper trail.

But then, his eyes clearing with a start, he made out riders, five of them, and a multitude of men.

The murmur was the scraping of their feet upon the ground, and the groaning breaths which they drew, and the oaths which they gasped out. They walked like drunkards, staggering. Sometimes a man went down. He was kicked to his feet by his companions and forced on.

For who dared to drop by the wayside in this march and thereby prolong the agony of the entire group?

The riders had dismounted. One of them held the horses of the others and started to unsaddle them. Three more made a rear guard, with the faint sheen of guns in their hands. But the fourth man strode straight through the compact throng.

He seemed to step over the men, as well as among them. He came swiftly to the front, and then the bulky outlines of him were suddenly familiar to the eye of Trent. He shouted: "Little Minny, is that you, you rascal?"

"Here I am!" thundered Little Minny.

"What are you up to? What have you got there?" called Trent.

"Men to work the Wayland-Trent Mine!" shouted Little Minny.

A swirling of dizzy hope mounted into the brain of Jim Trent. He would not believe what his eyes beheld—the steady upward flooding of these men, come, as his nephew said, to work in the mine. Why, with as many hands as that they would simply be able to crack the mountain open like a nut and get at the rich kernel, if kernel there were!

The call of Trent brought out Wayland and the girl from the shack. The great voice of Little Minny began to give orders before he had scaled the last of the steep trail.

"Get the coffeepot boiling. Slice some bacon. Stir up some bread. Here are fifty men that have to eat before they sleep, and sleep before they work. Uncle Jim, get the guns together and out of the way, where no hands but your own can work them. There may be gun work to do on this gang before they're ready to turn into honest miners."

Now the form of the giant loomed above the edge of the rim rock, looking huger than ever with the moon behind his head and the great shadow streaming before him.

"Uncle Jim," he said, "and you, Wayland—I've brought a little present for Harry Wayland. Harry, where are your pretty manners and your thank yous? Here are fifty-seven thugs that I gathered here and there in Sunnydale. Sunnydale didn't want them. It was glad to get rid of them. And the judge sentenced them to fifty days of hard labor in this summer resort. You keep them busy and feed them, and you pay me a dollar a day for bringing them here and keeping them at work. I have four sheep dogs along with me that'll help to herd the sheep. Here they come, Harry. Look these fellows over. Some of them aren't pretty, and some of them never handled a double jack before, but we'll teach them the rudiments of how to make an honest living."

As he spoke, the forward ranks of the prisoners staggered, groaning, over the rim of the plateau, swaying and lurching.

"This is home, boys. This is the little old summer resort

that'll make you fit and hard! This is the end of the journey, boys!''

When they heard this, many of them simply pitched forward and lay still, some on their faces, some turned on their backs in utter exhaustion, arms flung wide, heedless of the boots that stumbled about them and kicked and mauled them. Very nearly all that can be drained from the strength of human bodies had been drained from theirs.

Harriet Trent, who had made no answer at all to the extravagances of the giant, was busily working at her fire for cookery purposes; and as the last of the prisoners came groaning into the camp, big Minder Trent introduced the three rear guards to his uncle and to Wayland.

''They get five dollars a day from me,'' he explained, ''and the best found that you can supply to 'em. There's another fellow down there in the hollow. He'll be up before long.''

Then Trent and the worried Wayland drew him to the side. Wayland, shuddering, pointed to the faces, grotesquely ugly in the firelight. Not many of them were handsome by nature; nearly all had been handmarked by crime, and the exhaustion of this day's work had completed the grim pictures.

''What are these men?'' demanded Wayland.

''Fellows who would murder you for five cents,'' answered Little Minny, with a look of the greatest content as he ran his eyes over them. ''That one with the gray hair—prematurely gray—is a smuggler. Used to run the Chinese over the river. That one close to the fire, stretching out his hands to it, is a dope peddler. The fellow beside him, with his head hanging down, is a well-known safe-cracker. He's taken a fortune out of banks, but not by writing checks. The little pale man with the sad and poetic face—that's Charley Legrange, the murderer.''

''Murder, drugs, smuggling, robbery—'' exclaimed Wayland. ''Great heavens, man, why have you brought these scoundrels up here? Is this your idea of a joke?''

''That's the beauty of 'em,'' answered the big man. ''Every man has his own story. Every doggone one of 'em. If you get tired of looking at 'em, you can just start in thinking about 'em. A smart fellow could write fifty-seven biographies about that bunch of fifty-seven clever gentlemen. But they'll work in the mine, believe me, and they'll work for two dollars a day a head. I'll see that they work, all right."

"It means that our throats will all be cut," declared Wayland. "It means that we'll all be destroyed. I never saw so many villainous creatures in my life to call men! Besides, I've no doubt that we'll be liable to the law for this."

"I'm a deputy sheriff," said Little Minny, and opened his coat so that the firelight flashed upon his steel badge.

Jim Trent stared, then he burst into shattering laughter.

"Oh, he's a lamb, this boy," he said to Wayland. "He's started this game, and we've got to let him try to finish it. Maybe we'll all be dead men in three days—or maybe he'll rip the mountain open for us with all these workers, and we'll be so far ahead that we can afford to turn them all loose. That's a possibility. Anyway, they're here."

Little Minny stepped forward and stood close to the fire. The great shadow of him flared and flickered up the rocky face of the mountain behind him.

"Boys," he said, "I've got to talk to you for a minute. Now we've come to the summer resort, and tonight you get bread and coffee and a strip of fried bacon apiece. But beginning with tomorrow, nobody eats unless he's worked. Every man who works is going to have plenty. Those that only do a half day's job get a half ration. Those that try to run away will be chased. We're going to have guards posted night and day. If you slip past the guard, you'll be spotted on your way up or down the cliff, and then you're going to be tagged with bullets. I shoot fairly straight, and so do the rest of us. We have riot guns to shoot you down if you try mob action. We have plenty of rifles to pick you off if you try to sneak away one by one. And every one of us will shoot to kill.

"This is a bad game for you, and you're cornered. Play the game with the cards you hold and you'll be well enough treated. Try to soldier on the job and you'll catch it.

"That's all I have to say."

He turned to where the girl was busied with her cookery,

and without a word he took up a side of bacon and began to cut slices from it rapidly.

Then, as the food was made ready, he was the chief hand in distributing it among the exhausted prisoners who had marched so far.

And that was only a beginning.

All night long he worked, tearing up brush to make into the foundations for beds, and distributing spare coats and saddle blankets, and even slickers, for covering. He was tireless. But many of the weary rose neither for food nor for a more comfortable bed. They slept where they had fallen.

# · 12 ·

Morning showed, rising in the blare of the early sun, a haggard lot of rascals drawing together in groups, sullenly murmuring, and looking about them with grimly calculating eyes.

Plainly, it was one thing to have brought them here, but it might be quite another to keep them!

They were roused up by the loud voice of Little Minny, which called: "All hands for the creek, boys. Here's soap, and there's water. We like to see clean faces for breakfast at the mine. Clean faces make bigger appetites, and the more you eat, the harder you can work. No washing, no eating."

They came, but slowly.

The calm voice of Little Minny reminded them: "The grub may be used up before the last men come in!"

That roused them more than whip and spurs, and they swarmed rapidly to the waiting soap, and the clean run of the water. Still, as they washed, they talked with one another. Fatty Orcutt was the chief center of the most considerable group, and the others constantly watched him, as though they did not feel that so important a man could possibly have gone down unless there were a formidable plan in his mind.

Then they were marshaled for the breakfast.

There were now three cooks, and all three were very busy. The head cook, as a matter of course, was the girl; her father assisted, and one "Mississippi Slim," tramp royal, and man of many parts, had proffered to do his work by the fire rather than in the mine. His services were accepted, and he was proving his genius, practiced in many a tramp jungle throughout the land, at the cooking fire in front of the Wayland shack.

Jim Trent would handle the business of packing out supplies from the town, and Little Minny would see that the gangs were kept working in the mine. There were to be two shifts, so after the breakfast, which was eked out clumsily because of the lack of eating utensils, the men were drawn by lot, divided into two sets, and the first was taken into the shaft by Buck Penrose. He and Denny Rourke had both worked more than once in mines, and they knew how to direct labors.

Lew Eastern and Jumping Jack Story acted as general outside guards and lookouts. For it was not beyond credence that some of the adherents of Fatty Orcutt who remained in Sunnydale might sally out and strike a heavy blow to effect his delivery.

In the meantime, Wayland, after breakfast, was directing all the work in the mine, and Jim Trent already had departed with the mustangs on the long trek toward Sunnydale.

Little Minny, when the day was fairly started, and when the cursing and raging of the impressed miners had died down under the direct threats of leveled rifles, so that they were now sullenly moiling and toiling at the drills and the sledge hammers and at the shovels, and the hoisting of the loaded buckets of ore or debris to the mouth of the shaft—Little Minny now stretched himself in the shady side of the shack and went fast asleep with the bare rock for a bed and his rolled-up coat for a pillow. He slept till mid-morning, and then sat up quickly.

Near by him was the girl, peeling potatoes with skilled hands, and dropping them one after the other into the capacious bucket at her side.

She kept on working by mere dexterous touch, while she looked askance at the giant.

"Lie down and sleep again, Minder," she said. "You haven't had enough rest."

"I've done enough sleeping lately to last me," said he. "That's where I have it over a camel. He can store up food and water; I can do that, too, and store up sleep besides."

He rolled a cigarette, hunched about until his shoulders were pressing against the side of the house, and then began to smoke.

His looks were not entirely for her, but also for the men who were lolling about in the shade of shrubs, or of projecting fragments of rock. But there was no coolness anywhere. The sun was brilliant, and shone with a steady, tyrannical force. Even where its direct rays did not fall, its strength was reflected in part from the surface of the plateau. All of these men of Sunnydale were gathered in significant groups, and all of their talking was in low voices. Now and again a head turned toward the big man and regarded him with a wolfish steadiness and malice.

"How long have you ever done without food and water?" asked the girl.

"Five days," said Little Minny.

"I thought that three days was the limit of human life."

"That's what books say," he replied. "Books weren't written about me. They may be later on, a few!"

He grinned as he said this. And she looked askance at him again. The beard he had shaved off in Sunnydale was growing, and the thick gloss covering his face like paint, bluish, now, but soon to be the sleek black. There was an outcropping ugliness in this man that would not remain hidden.

"Yes, books might be written about you," she admitted. "How did you happen to be that long without food and water?"

"Oh, it's a long yarn," he said. "Some friends of mine decided that they'd be friends no longer."

"Why?"

"Because I got away with the fat part of a big poker game."

"How much?"

"I had about twelve thousand bucks in my pockets."

"So they did what?"

"They cornered me in a shack—eight of 'em. But the quarters were too close for their guns. I threw them out. Five of them got into the rocks around the shack and began to shoot into it."

"What had happened to the other three?" she asked.

He looked at her for a moment before he answered. Then he said: "They stayed behind with me in the shack."

"Were they dead?" she asked.

"No, but they were hurt. One of them was killed later on by the bullets that the five outside were shooting into the shack. Then I sent the other two out crawling; and they got off that way. No advantage to me to have 'em there in the house, starving."

She nodded; she kept her eyes to the potatoes then. "How did you get away?" she asked. "Posse come to help you?"

"I tunneled out under a side of the house," he said. "It was loose ground. I made frames for the tunnel with timbers from the inside of the shack."

"Did they try to rush the house, ever?" she asked.

"No, they didn't try that. Now and then I came out from the tunnel and took a shot at 'em. They kept discouraged and downhearted. There was a patch of shrubbery twenty yards from the house; they always kept a man posted there, but on the fifth night the ground caved away under him and I came up through the dust. He thought I was a ghost, and ran and yelled. I took his horse and rode away. That was all there was to it."

"Was that all?" she asked.

"Yes."

"You were weak, I suppose?"

"Yes, I was pretty weak. But I managed to get into a house and find myself a meal. They didn't follow me after the first day."

"And you've been a long time without sleep?" she asked him.

"Never more than a hundred hours."

"Let's see. That's more than four days?" she murmured.

"Yes, more than four days."

"How did *that* happen?"

"Why, I was stopping one night with an old friend of mine, a trapper, and a fellow who didn't like me came in and shot me through both legs. I got his guns and things away from him before he could shoot again. And then I sent the trapper for help."

"I don't exactly understand that," said she.

"It was like this," he answered. "That trapper was seventy years old—tough as shoe leather, but too old. And I wanted to put the thug who shot me in jail. It's no fun to be shot. So I sent the trapper for help after I'd tied up the thug. It was only fifty miles to a town. I expected a doctor and the police inside of twenty-four hours. But the trapper didn't show up.

"After a while I had to have the bandages changed, and I had to have food, too. And the fire had to be kept up, because it was freezing weather. And I couldn't move around to take care of myself. So I reached over and cut the ropes that held the thug. That was the second day. The pain kept me awake the first day. I held a gun on the crook and made him cook and work around for me, but I had to be on the watch every minute because if I closed my eyes, he'd beat me. He took his sleep when he wanted it, but I never knew when he'd open an eye and see that *I* was asleep. So I had to be on the job all the time."

"Was it very bad?" she asked.

"After about eighty hours it got bad," he said. "I'd been leading a busy life, and I was tired to begin with—dead tired. Loss of blood and pain make you tired, too. Along in the fourth day I had to tie a knot in the bandage over one of the wounds. When I felt myself getting sleepier, I tied another and a bigger knot. It was pretty bad. It was worse than the five days without food or drink. Finally they came."

"What had happened?" she asked.

"Why, the old trapper had been thrown from his mustang and broke his leg, and the horse ran away. He dragged himself on that spoiled leg for days. Finally he got to the town."

The girl gasped. "How frightful!"

"He was dead game," said Little Minny. "His leg was never any good after that."

"How did he manage to live then?" she asked.

"He kept house for me for a year, and then he died. He couldn't stand living inside when he heard the wind in the trees outside. That's what killed him."

"And you had a house?" she went on.

"Yes, to make a place for him. I wasn't glad that he died, but I was glad to be on the road again."

"You'll never take to the road again as long as you live."

"Oh, won't I? What'll keep me from it, then?"

"These fellows," said she, and indicated the dark-faced men who lounged in the shade.

## · 13 ·

He followed her glance and shrugged his vast shoulders. "You mean that I'd be apt to meet them and that they'd have the knife out for me?" he asked.

"I mean that," she answered.

"They'd only be added spice along the trail. But that's not why I'm leaving the open road."

"What's the other reason?" she asked.

"I'm going to make a home and get married," said Little Minny.

"Is that it?"

"Yes, I'm thinking of marrying you, Harry."

At this she laughed pleasantly and looked him in the face.

"I was angry the first time," said she. "But now I see that you're always having your joke on the world."

"I'm not joking."

Her laughter turned into a quizzical smile.

"You're going to pass some time telling me that you fell in love the first moment your eyes found me, is that it?" she asked.

"Not the first time. You had a smudge of soot on your nose that evening," said he, "and that was as bad as a black

**74**

mask. I couldn't see you, even though I knew that I'd have to marry you.''

"What made you know that?'' she asked.

"I'd made a promise to myself. A vow, you might call it.''

"Go on,'' she said. "What was the vow?''

"I was beginning to see that some day I'd be too old for the road. Have to settle down. So I swore to myself that I'd marry the first girl I met who could talk clean English and cook at a camp fire. You're the first girl, Harry.''

She smiled again, turning her head slowly, meeting his glance without difficulty. She said nothing.

"I haven't found the way to get you on my side yet,'' he admitted. "But I've opened the way.''

"Have you?''

"Yes. You like big things. You're cut that way. And I'm big. Big enough to fill your eye, even if not big enough to fill your mind. I'm ugly enough to keep you looking, too.''

"I like big things,'' she admitted. "This country, for instance. But I—''

She waited for him to speak again.

"Go on,'' he said. "Finish off. What don't you like about me? I want to know. Tell me how high the ladder is so that I can climb it.''

"Talking is no good, Minder,'' she answered.

"I know what you want,'' he told her. "You want a fellow with a college education leaking out all over him, and good connections, a shave every day, trousers pressed, a traveled man who speaks the languages, a man who is known. Isn't that what you want?''

She looked up at the sky, frowning a little.

"Yes, that's what I want,'' she said.

"All right,'' answered Little Minny. "You can't have him, because you're going to have me.''

"Tell me why I'm going to have you, Minder.''

"A lot of reasons will work all together,'' said he. "Outside of my size, which you like, you'll be grateful when I push this thing through and crack open the mountain and make your father rich. You're fond of him. You pity him.''

"Why do I pity him?''

"Because he's one of those nice fellows who generally need help or luck to get to the end of the trail. He wouldn't do a wrong thing, but sometimes he finds the right thing too hard for him to swing. Otherwise he wouldn't have brought you out here."

"He didn't bring me. I came."

"That was Fate," answered Little Minny. "It brought you my way. Every minute I see that I'm going to get you. I think you're weakening right now."

She laughed aloud again.

"Go on," she said. "You like to have your joke, and I don't mind how you talk!"

Then she grew serious. "Don't you suppose I see what will come out of all of this?" she demanded, her lips compressing as she anxiously waited for an answer.

"Go on," he advised. "I want to know what's going to come out of it."

"I'll tell you, then," she said. "My father and Jim Trent won't see it because they simply don't want to look on the black side of things. But I can see what will be the result of your enormous kindergarten game."

"I'm waiting to know," said he.

"You have three-score of criminals here," she said. "And you have four other criminals, beside yourself, to guard them. My father doesn't count, and Jim Trent can't shoot fast and straight enough to count very much, either."

"I'm fighting fire with fire," said the giant.

"You're fighting fire with foolishness," said the girl sternly. "Before three days are out, those people will have agreed. I can almost pick out the projecting rock that they'll hang you from and build a fire at your feet!"

"Have you got second sight?" The giant grinned.

"I have common sense," said she.

"Will you bet on your common sense?" he asked her.

"Money?"

"No. Yourself."

Suddenly she flushed, and her eyes widened. She stared at him.

"Don't you think that it's time to play another game?"

"Game?" murmured Little Minny.

Then he held out both his hands in a gesture of unexpressed power that yearned to be free.

"You'll see how dead serious I am," said he.

He stood up and looked calmly down at her.

"You're young and cool and sure of yourself," he told her. "You know what you know, all right, and most of it was learned in school. I've offered you a bet. I'll keep these crooks working for the whole fifty days. If I fail, I'll be a dead man. If I win, you marry me."

"You want me to think that you mean that?" she asked. "You want me to think that without caring I—"

"You can learn to care about me later on," he answered with brutal abruptness. "You're sure of yourself. I'm sure of myself. Now, come across and take the bet or admit that you're a short sport."

She was quivering with intense anger.

"I have half a mind to!"

"You have the mind, but not the courage," said he. "You can sit still and calmly foresee things, but you won't back your judgment. I'm backing mine. I'm staking my life on it, Harry. What do you stake?"

She could not speak for another moment, because of rage rather than hesitation.

"I'll take that bet!" she snapped at last. "But not if I can first persuade my father and Jim Trent to give up this crazy business!"

Suddenly men began to pour out of the mouth of the mine.

"What's that?" she asked.

"They've drilled the holes and planted the first charges," he replied. "Now we'll hear the shots."

It was an odd thing to see the laborers as they issued from the mouth of the shaft, most of them looking like condemned souls redeemed. Some of them threw themselves down without waiting to find shade, and others sat down on rocks here and there and looked woefully at their blistered hands. But a considerable portion of the men instantly drew into close groups, talking with fierce faces, their voices low.

"That's the real beginning," said Little Minny to the girl.

"They've had a taste of the work now, and they hate it like the devil. I don't blame 'em. Soft-handed gamblers and confidence men hate the rough grip of a sledge hammer. So do I! And yet my hands are not soft! Now they're talking, and they want to find a way to do the business. Your business it is now, Harry—of smashing me to bits!"

His great jaw thrust out.

"But that's where the fun begins for me, too."

And as he spoke, almost as though in answer, the plateau trembled, and the muffled, prolonged roaring of the shots came hollowly from the mouth of the shaft, sounding, through that thin mountain air, strangely dim and far away. To the girl that roaring was as the opening guns of a great battle; but Little Minny was laughing, with his teeth set hard.

# · 14 ·

IN SPITE OF THAT OMINOUS BEGINNING, TEN DAYS WENT BY before a shot was fired, and that shot drew no blood. It was simply that Dick Flinders, trying to escape by worming his way upward among the rocks, was overseen by Buck Penrose, and a rifle bullet clipping the rocks above the head of that celebrated second-story man instantly made him surrender and come back.

His punishment for this attempted escape was very gentle. It consisted, very simply, in twenty-four hours without rations; but twenty-four hours of labor in that sharp, bracing mountain air was enough to torment Dick Flinders severely. He made this attempt on the third day after the prisoners started their work; and ten days went by before a really serious event occurred.

In the meantime, interesting news was brought back from the town of Sunnydale on every trip that Jim Trent made to the place for supplies of food, and for powder, hammers, shovels, stamps, drills. It seemed that Sunnydale had passed at one stride from a state of black evil to one of almost whitewashed purity. The gunmen and thugs were thoroughly in hand. The crooked gamblers had been run out of town, and all at the expense of not a single lynching; there had been merely a few rides on a rail!

But there was a new mayor in the town; the sheriff was again limping about his work; and the amiable judge, Herbert Loring, had little to do except to pass judgment upon minor offenses, such as breaking the peace.

This condition was attributed by all hands to the efficient cleaning up of the leaders of crime of every kind, which Little Minny had performed.

"You don't need to work no more, you lazy fellow," said Jim Trent to his nephew. "You could go over there to Sunnydale and they'd give you an income for life! And that's where you'll wind up, sitting pretty, with your face in the sun and your back to a wall!"

This might be the opinion of Jim Trent, but at the end of a fortnight two important things happened on one and the same day. The first happening was very pleasant; the second was just as unpleasant.

The first chance was that in the opening round of shots which blasted down farther along the vein, a chunk of rock was tossed up and lay on the floor of the shaft with a yellow gleam across its face—wire gold!

When they cleared out the debris and examined the face of the vein, Jim Trent saw that it had widened suddenly, and in one place there was a pocket of this pure gold—not a great deal, but where it occurs once, it may occur again.

There was no question any longer of barely scraping together from each man's labor a few dollars more than his pay. It was a totally different affair. Jim Trent, after a few calculations, estimated that they were now able to take well over a thousand dollars' worth of metal from the rock every twenty-four hours. And at that rate, before many weeks they would have enough capital dug out of the ground to install the proper machinery and handle the diggings in the best modern manner. What profits they would make then staggered even the free and easy imagination of Jim Trent!

It was the happiest day they had put in at the mine, until three o'clock that afternoon, when four men rode up the valley to the foot of the trail, dismounted, tethered their horses, and climbed up the trail to the plateau. Jack Story stood at the top of that trail and covered them with a riot gun as they stepped onto the level.

Lean as greyhounds, hard as rawhide, with gray-blue eyes gleaming beneath sun-faded brows, they looked enough alike to pass for brothers; but it was very plain that they were not brothers.

One of them stood forth before the others. "I wanta see the big man here," said he. "I wanta see that fellow Little Minny, as they call him at Sunnydale."

"Whatcha wanta see him about?" demanded Jumping Jack.

"About business," said the other. "Where is he? I'm Sheriff Lacey; and I've got sheriffs of three other counties along with me."

Jack Story grew a little green about the gills. He shouted, and presently Little Minny came striding from the mouth of the mine.

He stood before the four strangers, looking bigger than ever because he looked more gaunt, and the spareness of flesh brought out the adamantine frame of the man. Constantly for a fortnight he had been watching his mob of laborers, moving among them, studying their faces, keeping them in check, and silencing their muttered conversations by his very presence. His sleep consisted entirely of an hour taken here and ten minutes of dozing there. His eyes were sunk far in his head, and his cheeks were hollow; but there remained in him, still untapped, what seemed an exhaustless well of nervous and muscular energy.

"I'm Minder Trent. Glad to see you fellows."

"You oughta be glad," said Sheriff Lacey. "We've come up here to take a lot of responsibility off your hands."

"What responsibility?" asked the other.

"A good many of these crooks that you've herded here from Sunnydale."

"You're going to take 'em off my hands, are you?" asked Little Minny gently.

"I'm going to take that cutthroat, Dan Binney, for one," exclaimed one of Lacey's companions. "I see him yonder.

See him, Jack? I eyewitnessed one of his killings, and I've been hankering after him ever since.''

"There's Doc Bogue, too," said another of the quartet. "I want Bogue more'n I want money. I've got enough on him to keep him in jail for the rest of his life!''

Said Sheriff Lacey: "But there's the real man of the lot. There's the brains. There's the brains that I can hang! There's Fatty Orcutt. Hello, Fatty!''

Fatty Orcutt had lost a pound a day with great steadiness under the régime at the mine. He had proved himself an exemplary laborer, keeping at his task even when his raw hands left blood on the handle of the sledge hammer. Now, as his hands had hardened, he was able to keep pace with all except old and experienced miners. He appeared far less plump now, and he smiled far less; and even when he smiled his broadest, the wrinkles of fat no longer tried to hide his eyes. Those eyes appeared bright and clear and keen.

They were fixed now upon Sheriff Lacey, and Orcutt waved a hand to him.

"Hello, Lacey," said he.

"You're going home with me," said the sheriff.

"Glad to go anywhere with an old friend like you," said Fatty Orcutt. "But you can't get me away from Little Minny. Not four like you. You can't handle him, Lacey. He's too much for you, and he means to sweat us for five more weeks in the mine."

"No matter what he means, I'm going to have you," said Lacey.

He turned back to Little Minny.

"Trent," he said, "you've done a grand job down there in Sunnydale. It was a grand bluff, and it worked. You had brains, and you had a pile of luck, too. Everybody gives you a lot of credit. But now the real law has gotta take a hand in the business."

"What'll the real law do?" asked Little Minny.

"It'll take the prisoners that it recognizes. I see six men lounging around here that I want. When I look over the gang that's working in the mine now I'll probably want six more. And the rest of these fellows are gunna want just as many, most likely. That won't leave you many of the crooks to weigh down your hands and keep you awake at night, Little Minny! You'll have all the glory, mind you, but we gotta have the men. It's our business, and the law besides.''

"The law's a grand thing," said Little Minny. "I've got a lot of respect for it, particularly when I see it in the distance. But I don't like to have it bothering me at close hand. You can have all the law in the world, Lacey. But I've got the men, and I'm going to keep them here for thirty-six more days.''

The head of Lacey lowered a little.

"I hope you don't mean that, Trent," he said.

"I mean it," answered the giant.

"I can arrest you on the spot," said Lacey. "I hate to do it, but I can arrest you for interfering with the execution of the law. It's a serious charge, Trent.''

"Arrest me?" asked Little Minny with great good nature.

"We'll have to take you by force if there's no other way," said Lacey.

"That's all right," answered Minder Trent. "You blaze away and take me if you can. Buck," he called in a louder tone, "keep this fellow Lacey covered first. Lew, keep your rifle on the rest of 'em.''

From the shadows beside the shack those four sheriffs now made out the gleam of two rifles held at the shoulder by men who reclined at their ease upon the ground. Besides, Jack Story himself was still at hand, with his rifle at the ready.

"You mean it?" exclaimed Lacey. "You mean that you're gunna play the fool and make a fight out of it?''

"Why, Lacey," said Little Minny, "if you wanted any of these fellows, why didn't you get 'em before? They were running loose in Sunnydale. Nobody was keeping you from getting in there to catch them like rats in your trap!''

"You know darn well," exclaimed the sheriff, "that Sunnydale used to be a solid army of thugs. If you touched one of 'em, you got a shock from the whole battery and were knocked stiff. You know that, Trent.''

"I know that I broke up the combination," said Little Minny. "And I brought it out here, and I'm going to keep it going till the fifty days are up. I've got the judge's sentence behind me.''

''That sentence means no more'n the barking of a dog,'' answered Lacey angrily. ''Herb Loring wasn't acting the judge then. He didn't follow any three of the forms of law. It was simply a joke, except that he hoped that it would help to clear up that town of Sunnydale for a while. It was nothing but a joke, man. If you try to play it out seriously, it'll land you in jail; and believe me, I'm the fellow to put you there if you stand in the way. I'm going to take Fatty Orcutt back with me today or know the reason why. Are you ready, boys?'' he muttered in a lower voice.

But a long-barreled revolver, a longer one than Sheriff Lacey ever had seen before, seemed to fall into the fingers of the giant. It was a gun, in fact, proportioned to his size. And he waved the muzzle of it toward the four men of the law.

''Partners,'' he said, ''this has been a fine little chat. But I'm a busy man, and now I've got to get back to work. I'm sorry to have seen the cards that you were so ready to play. You see that I've got a few up my own sleeve. Lacey, so long.''

Sheriff Lacey for a moment gritted his teeth as though he were feeding on his own wrath.

Then he nodded.

''You've got to have it, man. I see that. You won't stop till you've had it! You're dug in here, and you've got the jump on us, but don't think that this is the finish. We'll be back, and when we come the second time we'll come with enough men to pull the mountain down around your ears!''

He turned on his heel, paused, and then pointed a quick finger, like a gun, at Jumping Jack Story.

''That's Story, too,'' said he. ''I recognize him now. And he's another that I want. You know what for, Jack!''

Jack Story blinked like an owl. He said nothing, but the rifle shook in his hands.

And now the four men of the law, slowly, with deliberate strides, as though to sustain the weight of their defeated dignity, passed down the trail to their horses, mounted them, and rode at a trot back across the valley.

"They'll come back, too," said Jack Story, glaring after them. "They'll come back, and bring plenty more. It's time to break camp, Little Minny."

"If they come back, they'll only break their faces on the rock," answered Little Minny. "Let me do the worrying."

But he had a distinct feeling that the end was not far off.

# · 15 ·

THERE WAS EAGER DISCUSSION THAT DAY. THE GIRL WAS insistent that the criminal gang should be discharged. Her father wavered, but Jim Trent was equally insistent that the work should be kept going every possible day. They were in bonanza. They were richly in it. And who could tell what the future would deal to them? As for the return of a powerful posse—well, that was the business of Little Minny. He could take care of that situation.

So the work went on. And bonanza it was, deeper and richer than dreams. For still the vein widened, and the percentage of the gold increased. There was richer ore, and more of it, and more easily worked, and so many hands to perform the labor.

The very crooks who had been swept in from Sunnydale seemed to join in the excitement. Sometimes a few of them raised a song. There were jokes in the evening, and yarning about the fire. And always Fatty was the center of the fun.

"Fatty's changed his mind. He may go straight," said Little Minny.

Both Wayland and Jim Trent agreed, but the girl said: "Orcutt will never change. The more he smiles, the more devil there is in him. I've watched his sleek face."

Anxiety had preyed upon her in the last days, and her eyes were shadowed with purple. They looked gloomily now toward the giant, but Little Minny merely said: "You're the pessimist, Harry. Things always go better than you suspect that they will!"

"I hope with all my might that you're right," said the girl. And she said it with such a fervor that he lifted his great head and looked rather grimly back at her.

That very evening the blow fell.

It was the rose and golden time of the day, when the sun was down, but the night still seemed far away, that big Minder Trent, in striding through a lounging group of the off shift, saw something gleam and sparkle like mica in rock. It had shone in the hand of one of the men, and was instantly extinguished under a flap of the fellow's coat.

But Little Minny, though he had seen the thing merely from a corner of his eye, knew what it meant. It was death, perhaps, for all of them.

For that sparkle of light had been from the barrel of a Colt six-gun!

If one of them was armed, others were sure to be. And if they were armed, they were only waiting for the change of shifts at the end of the day to make the outbreak.

He finished his inspection tour of the plateau beside the cook's fire near the shack, and standing there with his feet spread and his hands toward the fire, he seized a moment when Mississippi Slim was off gathering brushwood for the fire to say to the girl: "You were right, and trouble is about to pop. They've got guns. Somebody's been crooked, and they've got guns—I don't know how many."

She looked up in his face and saw his calmness. Her own heart stood still.

He went on: "Your father's inside?"

"Yes," she gasped.

"You and he have to slip away at once. Get down the trail, find the horses, and then ride like the wind—for help," he added as an afterthought.

He turned and went into the house. There he found Wayland lolling at ease, reading an old newspaper for the tenth time. He passed him and opened the old empty powder box at the side of the room where all the weapons, rifles, revolvers, and riot guns were kept.

On top he saw a solid mass of rifles and revolvers, and he sighed with relief. They could not have taken many weapons, then. Only, it was strange that the shotguns, which, of course, were the most necessary weapons for the handling of a crowd, were not on top of the rest.

He lifted two or three guns, and a chill sank through him. Beneath that topmost layer was a tarpaulin, and under the black tarpaulin was simply brushwood.

That was not all. For when he looked carefully at the locks of the weapons which remained, he saw that every one of them had been ruined dexterously.

What weapons remained? His own revolver and the six bullets which it contained! Jim Trent and Wayland were not in the habit of carrying guns when they mixed among the prisoners for fear lest they might be overpowered and their weapons fall into the hands of that mob.

That revolver and the guns of the four guards remained.

He went to the door and glanced out. Yonder, near the group of the loungers, he saw Jack Story leaning against a rock, his rifle hung carelessly behind his shoulders, while Story joked with the thugs. Lew Eastern was not far away, sitting on a rock, arguing intently with Fatty Orcutt, and Buck Penrose was nearby, listening and nodding.

Denny Rourke?

Aye, there was Denny, striding up and down along the edge of the plateau, on guard. They never could budge that honest Irish heart, but it was perfectly clear that the others had thrown in with the mob—almost openly they had thrown in.

He heard the voice of Jim Trent coming from the mine. And he waited for the arrival of his uncle.

The latter came in, cursing.

"They got something on their minds," said he. "The whole gang of 'em are muttering and whispering and laughing down there in the shaft. I told Dan Binney to stir along and he said that he'd stir fast enough to suit me before long!"

"They've got our guns," said Little Minny. "Eastern and Story and the rest have the guns. That's where I was a fool— to trust crooks to guard crooks! Anyway, there are only six guns left in that box, and every one of those is spoiled. And there's not one round of ammunition left except what Denny and I have in our guns. This evening or tonight's the time they'll do it! It's Fatty Orcutt's brain that managed the thing. Harry was right."

Neither Wayland nor Jim Trent was capable of speech.

"Wayland," said Little Minny, "you go and take Harry off the plateau and down the trail. They won't think much about that. Go down to the horses and ride like the wind to find help! Uncle Jim and I stay here and hold the fort, along with Denny Rourke."

"I can't leave," said Wayland huskily. "My place is beside the rest of you."

"You can't help here," said the giant. "Go get Harry. Think of her, if you can't think of yourself!"

Wayland, without an answering word, went to the girl; she had risen from beside the fire and met him as he stepped through the door.

"Harriet," he said, "we have to go to—"

She shook her head and came on into the shack.

"I made a bet of it," she said, looking at Little Minny. "And now I'll stay and see it through. I won't leave."

"What good will you be to us?" demanded Little Minny harshly. "What good, if you're murdered along with us, when you might be riding for help?"

"You know it'll be over hours and hours before help could come," she answered. "I'm not arguing. I'm staying!"

"And I," said Wayland.

Jim Trent began to swear, but his nephew stopped him abruptly, saying:

"It's no good arguing with 'em. People like that can't be budged when what they call their consciences are stirred up. They'll only serve to make the mess a little bigger and bloodier. But that can't be helped. The next thing is to get Denny in here.''

He went to the door and called, ''Hey, Denny! Come in here a minute, will you?''

A sudden volley out of the red of the evening answered him.

Half a dozen shots whistled by the door or crashed into the woodwork. And big Denny Rourke, as he turned to answer the call, staggered, fell upon his side, strove to rise, and then toppled back and lay motionless.

Wayland, at that sight, which he could see through the doorway, screamed suddenly in a thin voice, pinched and high, like the cry of a woman.

But his daughter ran to Little Minny and caught his arm, murmuring, ''Did they strike you, Minder? Are you hurt?''

He looked down at her with agony on his face, but it was only pain of mind. Dumbly he shook his head.

And now they saw through the doorway how Lew Eastern—lately a guard—ran across to where the fallen man lay and deliberately kicked him in the face!

The long-barreled revolver flashed out into the hand of Little Minny. He poised the weapon, but he did not shoot.

''Shoot him, Minder!'' snarled Jim Trent. ''Kill that dog!''

Little Minny shook his head again. His great chest was heaving with emotion, but he answered, ''Every bullet in this gun we save for the time when they're sure to rush the house. They know that, too. We have six bullets in one gun. They have sixty men.''

''We'd better charge and break through!'' exclaimed Wayland.

''You know as well as I do,'' said Little Minny, ''that there's only one way off the plateau, and that's down the trail. Even a mountain goat couldn't get down the other cliffs. That's why you spent so much work building the trail. And they've got half a dozen men already there at the head of the trail. You see?''

A cluster, in fact, already had formed there, every man armed with a rifle or a shotgun. The exit was effectively blocked! And now, as the night wind began to blow up cold, and the sky went suddenly dark, a great bonfire was built in the center of the plateau, and around it gathered the men of Sunnydale. They seemed drunk with joy at their liberty. Their shouting, their roars of laughter, were punctuated by two other sounds—the clang of a rifle from time to time, fired maliciously into the shack where the late tyrants now lay prone upon the floor; and, still more awful to the ears of those four, in intervals of the uproar and celebration, they could hear the groans of big Denny Rourke, left to die on the wind-swept rock!

# · 16 ·

LITTLE MINNY, HIS FACE PRESSED CLOSE TO A CRACK BE-
tween two boards, watched with care the proceedings about
the fire. It was plain, through the midst of the general celebration, that Fatty Orcutt was the hero of the moment. His
brains must have planned and directed the whole event, the
corruption of the guards, and the stealing of the guns and
ammunition, and the time fixed for the uprising. Now and
again closely packed groups gathered around him, and his
back was slapped and his hand shaken in congratulation. Even
in the distance the firelight shone brightly upon the sleekness
of his face.

However, mere noise and laughter were not entirely to the
mind of Fatty Orcutt. No doubt he was now deliberating the
best means of putting an end to the four lives of those who
remained in the shack, still unharmed. There were various
methods that might commend themselves to him. For instance, a steady rifle fire would probably kill all four in time.
Or again, there were such interesting possibilities as that of
throwing a stick of dynamite into the place, or even better,
letting the wind roll a fire ball against the flimsy little build-

ing, then shooting down the inhabitants as they scooted for dear life.

Perhaps these and other devices were forming in the clever brain of Fatty Orcutt as he withdrew from the brightly lighted circle and walked slowly up and down in the more thoughtful gloom beyond the immediate range of the firelight.

Most of all, how his soul would be warmed if he could devise a scheme whereby he could get Little Minny alive into his hands!

A similar scheme formed suddenly in the mind of the giant, and he set about its execution.

To leave the house, it was hopeless to try to crawl out of the door; the riflemen at the head of the trail would cover that point efficiently.

There remained almost as simple a way. It was not hard to work loose two boards at the back of the shack, and through this he crawled. The muttered questions of the others he hushed, and crept slowly out into the darkness.

But it was far from as dark as he could have wished, for now and again the wind tossed up a gigantic arm of flame that sent a shuddering wave of illumination far up the face of the cliffs and all across the plateau. He could only hope that most of the thugs would be so close to the fire that the glare of it would blind them to dimmer objects far away.

He moved first straight to the back of the plateau. Under the wall of broken rocks that fenced it in he changed his direction, rose to his hands and then to his feet. People would not be expecting trouble from this angle of approach; and as for his bulk, he could mask that in this light by sagging his knees as he walked.

So he made straight for the place where Fatty Orcutt walked up and down with his hands clasped behind his back, head bowed in thought—in deep thought.

That head raised with a jerk and turned toward the bulky shadow that was approaching when a strong voice, the voice of Jack Story, called from near the fire, "Hey, Fatty! Hey!"

Orcutt turned his head toward the speaker.

"Come here," yelled Jack Story, "and we'll tell you a

scheme that'll squirt 'em out of that shack like watermelon seeds out of your fingers.''

"Shut up, Jack," answered the leader. "Let me alone while I do my own thinking."

"Leave him alone, Story," said another voice. "Fatty can think for himself, and for us, too!"

And then, as Fatty Orcutt turned to resume his striding, a shadow leaped at him. He reached for a gun; he parted his lips to shout for help. But the blow that reached the base of his jaw benumbed brain and throat and hand. A loose weight, he fell into the arms of the giant, and lightly the latter raised that welcome burden and bore it away.

All had been lucky so far; but very strange it seemed, as he made one prodigious stride after another, that those men about the camp fire had not seen what was taking place to their chief.

No, not until he was within six steps of the shack did a sudden shouting rise, and then a clanging of guns.

"Who's that by the shack? Where's Orcutt? What in blazes has happened?" cried the outlaws.

But Little Minny was running like a deer in spite of the freight that he carried.

He came to the place from which the boards had been broken away, and through it he cast the bulk of Orcutt's senseless body; he himself dived after.

What did it mean? Even Little Minny could not tell as yet. He only knew that they had secured one hostage against destruction. How great a hostage, how immensely the crooks valued the man whose cleverness had set them free from this shameful life, they could guess a moment later, when, as bullets began to crash through the little house, emphatic voices yelled to stop firing or Orcutt might be hurt.

Orcutt himself now sat groaning in the dark. His two guns had gone to arm Wayland and Jim Trent; and certainly if a fight had to come, there was more of a ghost of a chance for the besieged.

Through the door, which they left open, they now saw a delegation of three men approach, bearing a white rag in token of the flag of truce.

The smooth voice of Lew Eastern said: "Little Minny, the game is all tied up now. We've got you fellows, and you've got Orcutt. You give us Orcutt and we'll let any one of the four of you go. Yeah, any two, except you, Minny. We all want to see a little more of you!"

And suddenly the girl's voice answered: "Lew Eastern, we've determined to live or die together. You can have Orcutt; but only if the four of us go free—and if we have a chance to take care of poor Denny Rourke!"

"Rourke's as good as dead," said the gambler calmly. "But all right. You give us Fatty and then we'll let you all go."

"If we give you Fatty, you'll change your mind," she said. "We'll keep him until you've cleared out altogether. Then we'll turn him loose."

"D'you think," exclaimed Lew Eastern, "that we're fools enough to do that?"

Orcutt himself cut in, still groaning, and his voice was changed by the effects of the blow which had twisted his jaw to the side.

"Do what they say, Lew," said he. "I can trust 'em if they give their word. Little Minny, give me your hand and your oath."

"Here's the hand," said Minder Trent. "And my promise."

"That's enough for me," said Orcutt. And he called loudly, "Boys, it's time for you to march. Get out of here, and get fast. You know what Lacey is. He said that he'd come back, and he will. He'll come with an army. About Little Minny—there's plenty of time to cook his goose for him later on. But if you stay here, you're wasting time; and you'll kill me while you're killing them. Besides, they've got more guns, now—the ones they took from me. Boys, take my word—the best thing is to vamoose!"

There was no long discussion. They dreaded the return of Sheriff Lacey; and so in five minutes they were trekking down the trail, shouting back their last insults, their last promises of revenge to Minder Trent.

He waited until the last of them was gone, then out they went with a rush. One armed man at the head of the trail was enough to secure it from any surprise attack. They turned Orcutt free to follow his herd. And Little Minny rushed to the side of Denny Rourke.

To his amazement, the latter sat up suddenly and rubbed his face.

"Denny, Denny," said his friend, "Lie back, man. Everything's going to be done for you to—"

"Do nothin' for me but gimme a chance to bust in the face of Lew Eastern," exclaimed Denny. "Did ye think that I was dead, or dyin', Minny? No, but when the guns went off I played hurt to keep from getting my finish. My throat's sore from groaning, and my face from where that dog Eastern kicked me. But that's all!"

Sheriff Lacey and his men did not come back to the mine after all. More interesting to them, by far, was a certain troop of fugitives which they intercepted on the march toward Sunnydale. They caught many; they caught enough to gladden their hearts and fill the newspapers for a week. But Fatty Orcutt evaded them.

These were strenuous days that followed at the mine, for there was money now to buy machinery, and all was installation of engines and steel monsters that baffled the mind of Little Minny. He had been on the center of the stage for a long time. He had started the machine working, but now it ran beyond his guidance.

Gloomily he sat and watched, on this day, with his chin resting on his clenched fist, and did not look up even when Harriet Wayland stopped by him.

"Minder," she said, "what trail are you thinking of now?"

"The out trail," said he, without looking at her.

"When do you start?" she asked.

"In about half an hour."

"All right," she answered. "I can pack my things in that time."

"Now, what do you mean by that?" he asked her, looking up at last.

"If you were more than a great hulk," said she, "if you were even half a man, you could guess."

He rose and towered over her.

"Don't try to bully me, Minder," she cried.

"Bully you?" he exclaimed. "Great Scott, I can see which one of us is going to need help. But tell me, Harry, when you made up your mind to burden yourself with me?"

"The very first day," she answered. "I saw you needed teaching, because your manners were so very bad."

# THE BEST BANDIT

# ·1·

In THE DAYS OF THE CHISHOLM TRAIL, GREENSVILLE WAS
betwixt and between. On the map it was nothing that you
could put your finger on, because it was neither Mexican nor
American. You see, at that time, where Greensville stood,
the Rio Grande had the wobbles. Part of the year it hooked
an arm around Greensville, leaving a strip of dry land which
connected it with Mexican soil. The rest of the time it washed
across this strip, and the town was then linked up with the
American side.

It would have taken the work of three investigating com-
mittees from the United States Senate, and half a dozen emissaries from Mexico, to settle the rights of ownership, but
no senators, no emissaries were ever dispatched. The reason
was, neither the United States nor Mexico wanted Greensville. Who will go clamoring for a nest of wasps?

To be sure, the inhabitants of Greensville were nearly all
fair women and brave men. Yet neither the Mexican rurales
nor the Texas Rangers desired to have dealings with them.

Three brave marshals and five equally brave sheriffs had
died in that no-man's-land. As for Mexican officials, they
were not counted and, since the river was the favorite cem-

101

etery of the town, how could history keep tabs or run up reckonings at a later time?

As a matter of fact, there was nothing to be said in favor of owning Greensville. For one thing, nobody in the town wanted to be owned. They all preferred, while they were in the place, to be people without a country. Many a cutthroat, many a thief, forger, counterfeiter, gunman hurried to Greensville and heaved a sigh of relief when they walked those dusty, narrow, winding streets. If valiant officers of the law dared to venture into the town in pursuit, their careers were glorious, perhaps, but exceedingly brief.

It was never a large town; but the cost per capita of life in that place was higher than in any spot on the globe. Faro and roulette wheels soaked up a great part of the coin. Then there were the saloons, one for every other sort of building in the place. There were, also, eating houses where French wines could be had. They were good wines, too, good and almost priceless.

Small though it was, no one could have put Greensville under a hat. There was such eruptive force in the place, it had burned itself to the ground half a dozen times from sheer excess of the joy of life. For fear lest it should burn again, it had been built the last time, about three years before, chiefly of canvas and tin and boxwood. Those three fiery years had weathered and aged it so that it looked like a gypsy camp, and an old one, at that.

Into that town, one day, rode Randal Dale, fair and young, tall and straight, with an engaging smile, a gentle manner, and the look of one who loves and trusts the world because the world never has deceived him or done him harm. He was clad in clothes that smacked of the East. He spoke in a voice and in language that announced him to be one of the educated few. Greensville drowsily opened one eye and looked at the youth, calmly winked that one eye shut again and continued to sleep until the evening.

In the meantime, Randal Dale had found a hotel, had put his pack in his room, and looked to the lodging of his horse, which was a handsome, gentle creature, tall and straight and reliable.

After this, he had walked back into the hotel and talked to the proprietor. The latter had only one eye because, some cruel people said, he had seen too much evil to retain both optics.

He sat behind his desk, with a pair of greasy hands stretched out idly upon his knees.

"Can you tell me the name of the best man in town?" asked Randal Dale, with that gentle, trusting smile.

The proprietor raised both brows, then lowered one brow over his good eye and squinted at the questioner.

"What might you call a good man?" he asked.

"A good man?" asked Randal Dale, apparently amazed.

"Yeah," said the other, "there's gents that are good at faro and some that are better at poker. There's good drinkers, good hunters, good wrestlers, good boxers, good sleight-of-hand artists, pickpockets, thugs of all kinds, gunmen. Then, on the other hand, you might be meaning the best church-goers, or the best preachers, or the ones that pray the best. I dunno what you mean."

"I dare say that I mean what you would mean by a good man," said Randal Dale. "I believe that all humanity agrees about certain of the fundamentals of life. I'm sure that you could name the best man in Greensville."

The hotel proprietor hooked a thumb under the single band of the suspenders that kept his trousers up to the hips.

Then he said: "All right, you go up to your room, and I'll send you the best man in Greensville, to my thinking!"

Randal Dale thanked him and straightway mounted to his room, having left with the proprietor, for safekeeping, a roll of greenbacks. And Tubby Graham, the hotel man, sent for the "best man in Greensville according to his thinking." In the interval of waiting, he made a careful estimate of that roll of greenbacks.

Jeemy, or plain Jeems Loring, if one stopped to think about it, was the best man in Greensville in many ways.

He was the best poker player.

He was the best shot.

He was the best horse wrangler.

He was the best spinner of long yarns.

**103**

He was the best plain liar.

He was the best fancy liar.

He was the best idler.

He was the best gunman and general all-round killer.

Having all these "bests" to his credit, it was hardly strange that Tubby had picked him out as the best man in the town of Greensville.

Jeems Loring came in presently, in response to the message from his friend, Tubby Graham.

Mr. Jeems Loring was neither tall nor short, neither old nor young. He had very wide shoulders, a very wrinkled forehead, and a very long, outthrusting jaw. Moreover, he wore continually the smile of one who knows more than he ought to know.

He rested a hand on the desk, and said in a confidential tone which was habitual with him: "Look here, Tubby, what's the deal going on now?"

"Easy money," said Tubby. "Have a cigar?"

"I don't use that kind of poison," declared the other. "Not when I'm talking with a two-headed wolf like you. Whatcha want?"

"The best man in town," said Tubby.

"Yeah? Take it from me, that might cost you some money," said the other.

Tubby chuckled.

"You dunno what I mean," said he.

"No, because you won't talk," declared Mr. Jeems Loring. "What's brewing in you?"

"Easy money!" said Tubby tantalizingly.

"How much?"

"Scads."

"How much is a scad?"

Tubby looked doubtfully about him, as one tempted to do evil, but wishing to do it in private. Then he reached back of him, jerked open the door of the hotel safe, and pulled out a well-filled chamois bag. In this there was a paper package containing a closely packed stack of greenbacks, which he now held up for inspection. Then he cast an eye around the lobby and, with haste, returned the money to the safe and slammed the door after it.

He was panting a little when he faced Jeems Loring again and, drawing out a big bandanna, he mopped his face.

"Well," said Jeems, "you had the coin in your hand. Is it real?"

The other opened his eyes. Then he sneered.

"Is it real!" said he.

His friend shrugged his shoulders.

"Go on," said he. "Explain."

"There's a poor simp, a tenderfoot," said Tubby, "that's just come to town and asked if I could find him the best man in Greensville."

He laughed before he was able to end his sentence. Then he continued: "So I asked what did he mean by 'best,' and he said undoubtedly the same sort of 'best' that I would have in mind. And he smiled at me, the poor boob. And I said that I'd get ahold of the best man in Greensville for him, all right, according to my way of thinking. So here you are, brother. All I want is a split."

"You had the dough in your hands," said Jeems.

"I can't do that," said the other. "I got a reputation. I don't rob people."

"No, not that way. You don't take their coin out of your safe," said Jeems. "But suppose that I stick you up, right now, and clean out the safe?"

"It wouldn't work," said the other regretfully. "Because everybody knows that I'm your friend. They'd smell the plant, right away."

"Are you gonna go and get all complicated?" asked Jeems sadly.

"It ain't complicated at all," said the other. "Go up and have a look at 'it.' It's in Room 17. You don't need no letter of introduction. Just you go on up, and have a look, and say that I sent you."

"It sounds like a phony deal," said the best man in Greensville, "but I'll go and waste a little time on your idea, anyway."

## · 2 ·

Wʜᴇɴ Jᴇᴇᴍs Lᴏʀɪɴɢ ᴡᴀs ɪɴᴠɪᴛᴇᴅ, ɪɴ ᴀɴsᴡᴇʀ ᴛᴏ ʜɪs knock, to enter Room 17, he saw the bright face of Randal Dale bowed over a large sheet of paper on which the boy was making rapid notations with a fluidly moving pencil. The bright face looked up and smiled at Jeems.

"Tubby, down yonder, sent me," said Loring and waited.

"Ah! I'm glad to see you," said Randal Dale.

He got up, as he spoke, and shook hands heartily, showing Jeems to a chair. The latter remembered to take off his hat, which he dropped on the floor.

"I asked the proprietor who was the best man in town," said Randal Dale, "and he's sent you to me. It's a pleasure to have you with me, Mr.—"

"Jeems Loring," said the manslayer.

"Mr. Loring," said Randal, "I've determined to go into the cattle business."

"The which?" says Loring, somewhat startled.

"The cattle business," says Dale, "because, obviously, it's the best business in the world."

"Is it?" says Jeems.

"Why, of course it is," said Dale, bright and surprised.

**106**

"Look at this. Just take it over a ten-year period. You have a hundred cows, say, and in the first year they have a hundred calves, and in the second year, a hundred calves. That gives you a herd of three hundred in two years. Then, in the third year, the first lot of calves have calves of their own, so the herd increases to five hundred. And there you are!"

"Where are you?" said Jeems Loring.

"Why, at five hundred. Every three years, the herd will increase fivefold. Take a nine-year period, to make it come out even. There is a fivefold increase three times. Or, from one hundred to five hundred, from five hundred to twenty-five hundred, from twenty-five hundred to twelve thousand five hundred. Why, think of a vast army of cattle like that produced in nine years from a hundred cows."

"Yeah, it's a lot of noise to think about," said Jeems Loring.

"Nine years seems a long time," says the boy cheerfully. "But I have patience. And I can make a bigger beginning, by a great deal more than by a hundred cows. A thousand cows, say, or even more. Think of it! That would be a hundred and twenty-five thousand head of cattle in the course of the nine years!"

"Yeah, it's something to think about," said Jeems Loring.

"There's only one wonderful thing about it all," says the boy.

"Is there?" says Jeems. "You go on and tell me what it is, will you?"

"Why, it's this. I only wonder that everybody else in the world doesn't get the facts as I do, and immediately begin to raise cattle. Why don't you do it yourself, for instance?"

"Why, I dunno," says Jeems, honestly enough, "but maybe I never thought about it. And maybe it was just that I'd heard yarns about rustlers cleaning you out one year, and a famine stamping you out the next. Then a plague comes along the third year to kill what you got left. Or, if you have a real good year, everybody else has a good year, too, and the doggone market is flooded. Your price for beef comes down so low that it ain't hardly worth while to make the drive north over the trails to the market!"

Randal Dale listened at first with astonishment, and then with a shake of his head and another smile.

"I understand how it is," says he. "You're one of the very honest people who understand that young men ought not to be given too much encouragement in the beginning. I realize that. I like you all the better for showing me the gloomy side of the picture. But I know that the brighter side is the true side. And now, Mr. Loring, I'll tell you what I wish. I wish that you'd work for me."

Loring looked at him quite a time.

"How long?" said he.

"Oh, forever," says the boy.

"I might work," said Jeems, who had lost all his money at faro the night before, "for sixty a month so long as we get along with one another."

"Sixty?" said Randal Dale. "No, no! I couldn't think of offering the best man in Greensville less than a hundred!"

"Couldn't you?" asked the gunman, thrusting out his long jaw, for he began to suspect that perhaps everything was not as smooth and clear, here, as it appeared on the surface.

"Why, no," said the boy. "You'd be my foreman, of course. And the first thing that I'd ask you to do would be to hire a dozen more men for me!"

"What kind of men?" asked Jeems.

"Your kind of men," said the boy. "That is, if there are any others half as good as you are! Exactly your kind of men, Mr. Loring."

"If I work for you," said Jeems, "leave off the mister, will you? Call me Jeems, and you can use Rancie for your name as easy as anything else. Folks down here, they don't like to get snagged on formal names, not a little bit."

"Don't they?" says the boy. "My real desire is to learn the manners of the country as soon as possible. Of course, you may call me Rancie, Jeems."

Jeems Loring left his employer with a prepayment of a hundred dollars in his trousers pocket, and found Tubby behind the desk.

"Look a-here, Tubby," said he, "this here tree is full of ripe fruit. All that we gotta do is to give it a shake."

"Didn't I tell you? Am I a sucker that can't use my own eyes?" says Tubby.

"You told me, all right. Now, brother, I'm gonna frame this fall guy and frame him good and hard," said Jeems Loring. "But the first thing is for me to hire a dozen more men as good as myself."

He indulged in a vast grin.

"Get 'em," snapped Tubby, with the decision of a practical businessman closing a good deal. "Get 'em as close to yourself as you can, so long as you don't crowd yourself out of first place."

"The kind of a first place that I rate," said Jeems, "it ain't easy to elbow me out of. Who'd you know about town?"

"You know as good as me, except you might not know that Sam Paley and Alabama Joe Hixon are both sleeping upstairs in a back room right now."

"That pair of snakes? Who've they poisoned lately?"

"They ain't been poisoning nobody, and they're looking around for something to get their fangs into."

"I can use 'em both!" said Jeems Loring and hurried off upstairs to see them.

He got them easily for fifty a week. They might have to do a little cattle work, he said, but there would be something more than monthly pay in the job at the finish.

Then he circulated through Greensville and selected ten more of the same type. He was the thirteenth man. When, at the close of the day's work, he thought over the list that was due to report for service the next morning, he assured himself that he had found the twelve toughest men in the toughest town in western America. That is to say, the twelve toughest men in the world.

There was not a one of them that was not a tried-and-proved horseman, a thoroughly stanch warrior with knife and gun or even empty hands.

They were not all of pure American blood. He had an Indian half-breed that should have been living on the Navajo Reservation, except that his criminal record had automatically expelled him from that peace-loving, but stern people.

Loring also had a pair of renegade Mexicans, well-seasoned. They were experienced in all the downs of life, together with a few of the ups that follow successful pieces of knavery on a large scale.

He had a Portuguese wanderer along with an adventurer from France out of a noble family; a French Canadian from the Northern woods, and a Swede with a grin like a hungry cat's.

The rest were Americans, even more unsavory than the foreigners. All were well known to him, either through practical experience or by eloquent reputation. He was satisfied with them, when he thought them over, and carried his report back to his young employer.

Again, he found Randal, henceforth called Rancie through all the West, sitting in his bedroom and working at columns of figures on another large sheet of paper.

"In fifteen years—" began Dale.

"I got a dozen boys that you couldn't match in fifteen years of hunting," said the foreman of the gang. "You oughta see 'em. Not pretty, mind you, but doggone efficient."

"Efficiency!" says the boy. "That's what we want. Really efficient men, able to ride and handle cattle."

"Yeah, or men, even. They could handle men even better than they could handle cattle."

"Could they?" murmured Dale. "That's wonderful! And now we must buy the cattle, you know."

"What kind of cows d'you want?" asked Loring.

"I want your advice," said Rancie Dale. "But I heard somebody speaking today about very cheap cattle to be had from Mexico, cattle that can be driven north over the Chisholm Trail and fattened on the way. Wouldn't that be a good idea?"

"Greaser beef," said Jeems, "ain't any cheaper than gringo beef, unless it's wet."

"Wet?" said Rancie, with a deprecatory smile and a spreading gesture of his hands. "I'm afraid that I don't follow that. Wet beef?"

"Yeah, wet beef," said Jeems.

He pointed through the window toward the darkening face of the Rio Grande.

"South of the river," he said, "you can pick up beef for a quarter of the price of the north shore stuff. If you know how to go about it, and if you can pay cash."

"Why, I can pay cash, all right," said the boy. "D'you know how to go about getting the beef?"

"I'll start tomorrow," said Jeems.

# · 3 ·

JEEMS DEPARTED THE NEXT MORNING, SOMETHING BEFORE
the sun was up, and made a fifty-mile circuit before he returned. He not only rode, but he stopped here and there and
talked. The people with whom he talked were in little Mexican fondas, or in outlying shacks among the hills, or tucked
away in the densely populated small towns. Each man was a
picture worth looking at. They might not have possessed the
reputations that distinguished the twelve worthies he had
picked up the day before, but in appearance they were far
more formidable.

They were the dealers in "wet" cattle. They stole here and
there, and they always had a few head or a few thousand head
tucked away somewhere, ready for the rush through the Rio
Grande. On emerging from its waters, they were bought head
by head for what appeared only a song to a Yankee, but what
seemed to be solid sunshine to a Mexican cattle thief.

The orders of Jeems had been very lax. Exact numbers
were not estimated by his employers. It was simply a "lot"
of cows that he was told to arrange for, and this he inter-
preted liberally. He engaged for seven thousand; he would
not be offended if there were a few thousand more.

After all, he wanted to deploy all the money that he had seen locked up in the hotel safe, and about the disposition of which Tubby had been so foolishly recalcitrant.

He saw Tubby when he returned, late in the evening.

"I got it fixed," said he, "and if we can get the fool to unlimber all his coin and take it down to the bank of the Rio Grande, north shore, I'll arrange to have him relieved of it painlessly before morning. Going to be ready for the play in twenty-four hours, Tubby. And I'm glad that I got that gang together. This kid, he's just been doing my thinkin' for me."

It was, in fact, entirely clear that they would need to have plenty of men if they were to handle the Mexicans who were to bring their cattle to the river and make them swim across.

It seemed to Jeems, whose love of great exploits sometimes almost swept him off his feet, that this was a deal out of which he might make a handsome fortune.

He considered it at length. Once the Mexicans ran the cattle across the river, he would wait until the majority had got over. Then he would start the great herd north and, when the Mexicans demanded payment, he would give it to them in the only form he thought that they either deserved or appreciated; that is to say, he would pay them in lead, in wholesale quantities. He was so pleased by this idea that he felt a song rising in his heart at the idea.

As for the cash in the safe of his friend, Tubby, that money he would secure with as little personal violence as possible. He did not dislike young Rancie Dale. He had, in fact, a kindly feeling for him, as much as he was capable of feeling toward any human being. For out of the fool head of Rancie had arisen this magnificent scheme into the mind of Mr. Loring.

How much there might be, all told, in the safe of Tubby, in that single heavy stack of greenbacks, he could not guess. But Tubby, as we have seen, with great patience, had flicked over the corners of the greenbacks and had made a fair estimate.

Between a hundred and seventy and a hundred and eighty thousand dollars, honest Tubby estimated, was in that pile!

Jeems Loring, when he thought of this, did not regard himself as a criminal.

For there is a point at which murder, for instance, ceases to be murder and becomes glorious war; and there is a point at which common stealing ceases to be theft and becomes statesmanship, let us say.

He felt that work on such a scale as this could not be called crime. He wanted to lift his chin, and he did lift it; he wanted to look the world proudly in the eye, and he did!

He could see that there were difficult points to be considered. As for Rancie, he hardly mattered at all or, for that matter, any action that he might take. What was important, however, was the handling of the Mexicans.

They were almost certain to come in great numbers, and no matter what the story books may say, Jeems Loring knew that a Mexican with a grievance can fight like a wild cat, and no mistake.

He depended upon the hand-picked quality of his dozen rogues, all of whom could fight, all of whom loved battle. In the fracas, blood would be shed, but what of that?

The more Mexicans killed, the simpler the future. The more of his own men dropped, the fewer would remain to share in the split.

It was only too bad that he had had to get this priceless tip from Tubby. Tubby would have to have a good rake-off. Yet the fat man was almost worth his price, considering the fact that he had named the great Jeems Loring as the best man in Greensville!

On the whole, it appeared to Jeems Loring as a satisfactory world but, when the morning came, he received a shock, indeed, a distinct shock.

When he laid the full story of his day's work before the boy, as full a story as his employer's ears could endure, young Rancie Dale declared that he must ride south of the river to see the gathering of the cattle.

Wait on the north bank while they were brought into a great dusty focus in the late evening, and then poured through the funnel of clever riders toward the river? No, no! That would never do for Mr. Rancie Dale. He had to go where he could see the animals in their native habitat, as it were.

He was strangely stubborn. He smiled, as usual, and made his deprecatory gestures with both hands, as though sorry for an attitude in such marked contrast to the usual pleasing ways of Rancie Dale, but, however that might be, he was immovably fixed in his determination to cross the river and mingle with the native Mexicans.

Jeems Loring had lived long enough in this world to know when he was dealing with a man who could not be argued from his point. The whole scheme that Jeems had formed might be bungled by this headstrong decision of his employer, but he saw that it would be a very delicate matter to win him away from his idea. So Jeems accepted it, feeling that his wits were equal to this new necessity.

So he sent out word to his host; he appointed the proper hour, and in the fire of the middle day, that cavalcade of fourteen rode through the muddy waters of the Rio Grande, unobserved, and headed south.

Mr. Dale wondered why they did not take the bridge; and he wondered aloud, so that Jeems was forced to explain to him that they never bothered about the bridge, when the water was as low as this.

Dale accepted the argument, it appeared, until one of the men, the Frenchman, laughed loudly.

"Why did that man laugh?" asked Dale.

Said Jeems loudly: "He laughed partly because he's a laughing jackass, and partly because he ain't got any sense. For another thing, there's a Mexican on the other side of that bridge looking for his scalp, and I hope he gets it."

It will be seen that Jeems Loring could, on occasion, be very severe.

The Frenchman made a motion toward his gun, but thought better of it and shrugged his shoulders.

After all, in certain ways it will be remembered that Jeems Loring was the best man in Greensville!

So they went on through the blinding heat and the stifling alkali dust that burns the lining of the nose, and parches and cracks open the lips. They went on steadily, with little conversation, pulling the silken folds of their bandannas over nose and mouth, and breathing through these.

Rancie Dale did not seem to be much troubled either by the heat of the sun or the steady racking of the horse beneath him. If this was a surprise to the great Jeems Loring, it was nothing compared with the real bewilderment felt by him and the rest of his chosen cutthroats when they witnessed the smooth ease with which Rancie Dale backed his horse.

Alabama Joe Hixon explained to his riding companions: "You take a whole lot of these here tenderfeet, and you'll find out that they've been stuck on the back of a hoss every day since they was six years old, and what they sit on is just a piece of leather that ain't got anything to stick to. They're what you call an English saddle, and an English saddle ain't a saddle at all. It's just a shiny piece of leather, polished up so's the hoss can shed you all the easier. Off an English saddle, a gent rolls easier than a drop of water off a duck's back.

"And that's likely what the kid learned to do his riding on. No wonder that he can sit in one of these here Mexican saddles like he was in a chair, though, if the mustang begins to act up, you'd see Rancie starting right up for the sky. He looks like a regular hoss wrangler, just now, but let the pony give him some fireworks, and he'll come all apart!"

The opinion of Alabama Joe was accepted, but still there was a touch of respect in all their faces as the men looked at the straight back and the easy carriage of the boy.

"If he's half the gent that he looks in the saddle," said one of the riders, "it's a doggone shame to roll him like old man Jeems is sure to do!"

"Anybody that's a real man can take care of himself," declared Sam Paley.

They had reached this easy compromise with conscience when, out of the southern horizon, they saw a dim mist that heightened into a wall, tall and white, and through the lower rollings of this approaching fog, they were presently able to make out dim forms moving.

"There's some of the Rancie cows!" said someone. "The party is gonna begin."

# · 4 ·

THE "PARTY" BEGAN VERY SIMPLY AND EASILY TO THE EYES of the punchers and rascals gathered behind Jeems Loring. To young Rancie Dale, however, it must have appeared more than strange to see the wild men who brought up the herds all through that day. Sometimes there were not more than a hundred cows in a bunch; but in one bunch nearly three thousand came in. Everywhere around the southern horizon, the columns of white smoke arose and stood trembling in the upper sky, melting and then growing closer and closer, higher and higher until, at the base of the moving columns, the dark forms of the cattle began to soak through into the straining vision of the watchers.

They were a wild lot, those cattle. Most of them had come far and had been driven mercilessly all the way but, though they were red-eyed with anger and with thirst, they were not spent. They had plenty of passion in them, plenty of vigor. And their sharp horns were always threatening to this side and that.

They were much smaller, on the whole, than the cattle handled on the ranches north of the Rio Grande. They were smaller, much leaner, and likely to be a little rough-backed and very ewe-necked.

117

Their fleetness of foot amazed young Dale. When a patch of them broke out of the edge of one of the large herds, the cowpunchers had to sprint their horses at full speed in order to overtake the fugitives and work them back into the crowd.

"Are they dangerous?" asked young Rancie Dale.

"Dangerous?" said Alabama Joe. "Why, if you was to hook a pair of horns onto the head of a grizzly bear, it wouldn't make him less dangerous, would it? And them things can do anything that a grizzly can do. They got as much strength in their paws, and, if they miss you with a swipe with a front hoof, they try a sideswipe with a back foot, hard enough to stave a hole through an iron barrel. If they miss with all four feet, they'll bite a hole in you with their teeth. When their feet and their teeth go back on 'em, they got the horns throwed in, all extra. I dunno where you was raised, son, but around the parts that I know best, a longhorned lump of a Mexican steer is called mighty dangerous, I can tell you!"

Young Rancie Dale heard and, as he listened, he opened his eyes until they were as wide and as innocent as the eyes of a child.

The men were growing familiar with this look, however, and they were able to control their mirth somewhat. They simply smiled askance at one another.

They had many other occasions for smiling before that day ended, and seven thousand cattle, more or less, were gathered milling and bawling and screaming like wild cats and buffalo combined.

For Rancie Dale rode everywhere, admiring everything with the same bright and open eye. He said that it was a wonderful sight; but that he did not understand why all the poets in the world did not come to admire this glorious spectacle and write down in words its terror of thundering, clashing hoofs, the white rolling of the dust storm, the flashing of the horns through the mist, those polished horns, beautifully curved like an antique bow!

Rancie Dale expressed himself in words very similar to these, and Jeems Loring and his twelve poisonous companions listened, looked darkly on one another and endured.

Even though they all expected to make a tidy little fortune

out of the spoiling of this tenderfoot, yet it was hard for them to endure until the ending of the day and the final gathering of the herd for the drive across the river.

There was still a batch of three hundred cows, more or less, outlying, when the sun began to redden and puff out his cheeks in the west. And now the rosy gold of the sun's light stained the dust clouds above the milling thousands of cattle, and above the heads of the Mexican riders who circled the edges of the wild horde, shouting, singing, laughing, whooping, sometimes rushing to a distance to head off and turn back the outbreak of a band.

Not until then did the chief cattle thief, the great José Oñate, appear upon the scene.

He was a man of mark. He could not have walked upon the stage of this world unnoticed even as a slave. In a far land, his conversation would have changed the minds of cannibals. His wisdom always would have unlocked the heart of the sternest tyrant, and his hands, a little later, would surely have opened the seven sealed doors of his treasure chambers.

Women could not resist his wiles. Men could not resist his weapons.

If he were a robber, it was plain, not that he loved money unlawfully gained, but money gained by dangerous methods. Nothing in this world had spice for him if it were unseasoned by danger. He had dipped his young hands, already, in a hundred fortunes and, when they were his, he had cast aside the spoils readily. He gave to his companions, to his friends, to his acquaintances, to the beggars beside the road. When the hands of all these were filled, he then gave to his enemies, it was said!

The appearance of this man was such that, at a glance, all eyes instantly understood the metal of which he was made; that is to say, he had the look of steel that will cut steel. In addition, upon the face of him, he was vain, cheerful, inconstant, and as keen as a hungry hawk on the wing.

José Oñate appeared upon a coal-black charger which wore on its haunch a brand that was never printed by a Mexican branding iron. He wore upon his shoulders a little Mexican jacket, brightened by great quantities of gold and silver lace. About his narrow hips flowed a sash which had cost two generations of patient labor, and once had adorned the altar of a church. Silver trimmings gleamed down the seams of his trousers; and at his flaring stirrups there were golden bells, bells of real gold, too! Finally, to finish off his costume, a splendid cloak blew back behind him or drooped over the arching tail of his horse.

He came attended by four men, like a chief who cannot ride abroad unattended. And what a retinue it was! Each of the four looked worthy to be a chief, ruling over a fierce tribe of fighting men!

Each of the four was worth naming. Beginning with the least, they were, first, Pedro Iribas, in whose blood was a plentiful admixture of Apache days, inherited from those days when the terrible Indians used to ride south following the Mexican Moon and whitening their trail, north and south of the Rio Grande, with the bones of dead cattle and dead men.

Pedro Iribas was gaunt and somewhat bent in the shoulders. Hair had never grown on his face, which was covered with small punctures, as though the hair had been plucked forth by the roots. His nose was small; his forehead was broad; his eyes were overshadowed by deep brows; and upon his great mouth there was a continual smile which might have been caused by weariness, or pain, or ferocity, or perhaps a mixture of all three.

He was the oldest of the four, a man of great cunning, capable of leading others in battle, as he had repeatedly done; capable of long retreats and brilliant attacks; capable, also, of all the thousand devices with which the red men of the old days conquered their opponents on the prairies or in the mountains.

At his side appeared Ricardo Girones, a man without color in hair or skin; his eyes, alone, had a dull gray color or, rather, a hint of color, but eyebrows, hair and skin itself were simply dust. He was an albino. He possessed a sort of horrible beauty, with a feminine smile and a rather feminine manner, but no observer was surprised to learn of his bloodthirsty cruelty.

Antonio Cuyas looked like any other peon, with a round face and a brown skin. When one came closer, one saw that his eyes were red and yellow about the pupils, as though they had been inflamed by constantly facing a strong wind. Antonio Cuyas had been longer with the great Oñate than any other of his followers. Treacherous in his dealings with other men, Antonio Cuyas feared his master more, even, than he loved his own well-being.

Finally, fourth and greatest of the lot, there was Arturo Llano, known throughout the length and breadth of Mexico.

It was strange to think of such a man being a follower. All sorts of infamous achievements had been laid at his door; and yet he actually surpassed rumor; he was one of those few men who had performed more than was credited to them.

He was a big man, with a pair of well-squared shoulders, such as one often sees in a military man. And a soldier he had been, to be sure, until the murder of his officer set him adrift. Ever since, he had remained a fighting man and, whether it were battle arranged on a large scale or simply a quiet little knife fight in a dark room, he was sure to be equally zealous, equally at home. The scars he had received were on his body as well as his face, but the face itself had been bullet-furrowed or knife-slashed no less than six times.

Hence, it followed that though he had been a handsome, smooth-shaven fellow in his youth, his face was now covered with mustaches, beard, and side whiskers, a thick growth, but neatly trimmed.

He was the right hand of José Oñate. All four were a part and parcel of him. It was said that he possessed all of their peculiar virtues and all of their peculiar vices. They were himself divided into four separate parts. Yet, it was said, if all the four united against him, there were in Oñate more ferocity, more strength of mind and body than in the precious quartet.

Even Jeems Loring quailed a little as he saw the five coming.

"Jumping Caesar!" said the great Jeems. "It's the old boy himself and his four house pets! There's trouble in the wind!"

## · 5 ·

THERE WAS TROUBLE AHEAD, INDEED! FOR THE FIRST THING
that Don José suggested, after a most cordial greeting to all
of the gringos, was that since the seven thousand head of
cattle had been collected, it was time for some hard cash to
be paid down on them—not the whole amount of their agreed
value, but fifty per cent of the total sum. He said this not to
the purchaser, Randal Dale, but to that other and more famous man, Jeems Loring.

Loring answered: "You see how it is, José. These are wild
cows, and who's gonna tell which way they're likely to run?
After half the coin was paid down on 'em, they might turn
around and run straight for the hills!"

Don José smiled gently on the gringo.

He said, in quite good English, with only an occasional
wrong construction and only a slight lisp in some of the con-
sonants: "There are all your good men and all of my good
men, ready to hold the cows together."

"Yeah," responded Jeems Loring, "but take it this way.
Some of your boys don't speak English, and some of my boys
don't speak no Spanish. Suppose they got all confused and

122

started drivin' the cattle different ways. Look what a mess that would be!''

Don José smiled again, deliberately, and looked Jeems Loring up and down. They had known one another, or about one another, for years. Each was a certain dubious kind of hero. Each knew the exploits which made the other famous. Perhaps no two men in the world more thoroughly yearned to gain further fame and reputation, each by putting the other down. But they avoided giving offense. Ordinary battles they would accept with delight, but for one another, they preferred courtesy until, in the course of time, a pinch should come that would force matters to a conclusion. Not until that moment would the battle come.

So José Oñate, watched and listened to by his four main adherents, merely said: ''That might start a stampede, it is true. Still, I have a great many hungry men and some of them want their pay and wish to get back into the hills. They want their price for their cattle. That is all. Then they will go. Not all their money, but a part of it. You know, señor, that they are men of hard work. They cannot throw time away. They must return quickly to their duties.''

Jeems Loring grinned, but not widely. He knew what sort of ''work'' the rascals employed by the great Oñate were usually engaged in. They wanted to return hastily to the mountains, no doubt, because down here in the lowlands they were likely to be too nakedly in the eye of the law. Mexican law was inclined to be a hit-or-miss affair, in those days, but, when it hit, it landed hard. Half a dozen grim-faced, gaudily uniformed rurales, expert with horse and gun, were liable to turn up at inconvenient moments and explode the penalties of the law like poison gas.

Loring slowly shook his head. ''Friendship is friendship, José,'' said he, ''and I'd like to please you by makin' a part payment now. But business is business, too, and you know that we bargained for payment when the cows climbed the north bank of the river.''

Don José did not frown. He merely steadied his glance upon the American. And his four followers, of one accord, each picked a man and in like manner-steadied glances upon their possible foes. It was a cold, still moment. Jeems Loring did not lose countenance, but there was a icy tingle up his spine.

Then he said: "When it comes down to a pinch, José—"

He did not finish that sentence, and perhaps it was a lucky thing that he did not. At any rate, the tenderfoot, young Rancie Dale, broke in: "And why not pay what they want, Loring? I have the money with me in cash."

Fire shot from the eyes of José Oñate, as from the eyes of a hunting cat.

"Good!" said he.

Jeems Loring turned a look of disgust on his employer.

"That's all right," said he. "That's quite all right. You got the money, brother, and nobody doubts it, but there ain't any use making your greenbacks into a flag and wavin' 'em around in the open air. I tell you what: this here Mexican sun is so strong that it's got a lot of fading power."

The innuendo was not any too subtle, but it did not reach the bland understanding of the boy.

He said: "Is that so, Loring? But still I'm not waving the money about, you know. I have it safely inside my coat pocket."

Jeems Loring snarled with disgust, and shrugged his shoulders.

"You go and do your business in your own way, then," he said. "I've had my say. Now you play your own hand, brother."

Don José was the very essence of courtesy, as he bowed to Rancie Dale and said: "There is the old hacienda where Señor Flandes now keeps a fonda. You can see the sun blink on the windows, yonder, beyond the dust."

"Yeah," said Loring. "It's blinking on those windows as red as blood."

There was a meaning in his voice, but again the meaning missed the cheerful mind of Rancie Dale.

And now Don José put in with: "Four of us, then, should be enough. We can settle everything. I and Arturo Llano, you, Señor Dale, and my old friend Jeems."

He drawled out the last word in a strange voice, and Jeems

Loring pinched his eye narrowly and peered, or strove to peer, into the interesting mind of the Mexican.

Perhaps he would have refused, but now the boy was saying: "Why not here, Don José? I have the money with me. I can count it out to you. It's ten dollars a head, isn't it? Wonderfully cheap, I'd say, and I have a lot more money than that with me!"

A sort of stifled groan that sounded like despair came from the lips of Jeems Loring.

Then the groan was cut off, midway, as he glanced at the handsome face of José Oñate and saw the man wink broadly, slowly, significantly.

A new thought flashed across the active mind of Loring. And he winked back.

"You know, Señor Dale," said the Mexican bandit, "that in my country we mix friendship with business. We put the two together, because we find it very unpleasant when we have to count pesos to no accompaniment but their own clinking. Now, in that fonda, there is some good red Mexican wine, and brandy, too, if you will have it, and excellent cigars and cigarettes. And it seems to me, señor, that I can breathe the scent of roasted kid as it turns on the spit in the kitchen of that fonda. Shall we not go there to finish our little business?"

"Why, of course," said Rancie Dale cheerfully. "Of course, we'll go there!"

He laughed in happy, cheerful anticipation. A moment later, a Colt revolver shone in his hand and he began firing. His target was a lank desert rabbit which had cuddled down in a bunch of grass all this while and suddenly, like his foolish kind, unable to endure the presence of the danger, had bolted out into the open.

Once, twice and again, Rancie Dale fired, his face set, a frown of determination upon his brow, but the bullets struck widely about the little swerving streak of fur and speed that was bolting away toward the horizon. The others smiled grimly upon one another. Then, that conquistador, Arturo Llano, drew a gun, with casual grace, and fired once. The jack rabbit flung up high into the air, fell to the ground, and was still.

The joy and admiration of the boy knew no bounds. He smote Arturo Llano on the shoulder, thereby forever wounding the dignity of that gentleman, and exclaimed: "Why that's simply magnificent! And at such a distance! What chance would even half a dozen men have if they tried to ride you down, Señor Llano? Tell me that. What chance would they have?"

Señor Llano looked him straight in the eye, twirled one end of a pointed pair of mustaches, and finally forced from his throat a faint murmur that might have been taken for pleasure or for nothing at all except disgust with this boyish fool of a gringo who did not know the proper manners which should go with men of the frontier.

"They wouldn't have much chance," said Jeems Loring. "Not if they shot a gun the way you do, Dale. Ever practiced with it?"

"Practiced?" said Rancie Dale, his good humor not in the least troubled by the last sarcasm. "Oh, yes, I've practiced with a revolver a great deal. For hours and hours, in fact!"

He laughed a little. "But rabbits are hard to hit," said he.

"So are men," snapped the disgusted Jeems Loring. "Don't forget that, son. A Mexican is the hardest thing in the world to plaster with lead. They can make themselves smaller than a knife edge, and they can come at you dodging faster than a snipe that's flying down wind, and don't you forget it."

"A very strange thing!" said Rancie Dale, opening his large blue eyes. "Of course, I won't forget it."

Loring was already at the side of Don José.

He said quietly: "You see how it is. There's two of us, and there's two of you. But the fool of a kid don't count. He's nothing. It's me against you and Arturo, and that's too much, if a pinch came. You know what I mean!"

Don José nodded. He was grave and he straightened himself a little in the saddle as he answered: "Between you and me, Don Jeems, there does not have to be lying, eh? If you come over to the fonda with us, we work together—you and

I and my friend Arturo. Look, my friend, there is enough fruit hanging on that tree to fill all our pockets. And it hangs very low. Even a child could pick it!''

Sudden, smooth joy slid over the face of Jeems.

"Yeah," said he, "a kid could pick it off the highest branch. No half-wit, like him, deserves to carry that much freight around with him. José, I'm gonna trust you and make a try at it."

# · 6 ·

TELL ME, SINCE TIME BEGAN, WHAT CROWD OF MORE PER-
fect ruffians ever gathered together to prey upon one poor,
wretched boy. Any one of the three appeared in himself ten
times more than sufficient to overcome any resistance that the
tenderfoot could offer. But there they were, banded together,
the great Arturo Llano, Jeems Loring, famed through many
a land and, last and most deadly of all, that man-queller, José
Oñate! All of these banded together for the plundering of one
boy!

They distributed the task of holding and watching the herd
through the night to the overseership of Paley and Alabama
Joe, and to the attention of Cuyas, Girones, and Pedro Iribas.
Then the four cantered away at the rocking gait of a Western
horse, reaching the fonda at dusk.

It was not an attractive place from the outside and, the
nearer one came, the less attractive it appeared. It stood naked to the bitter heat of the summer, without the suggestion
of a tree about it. There was not even a hill for it to stand
upon to take any chance breezes that might wander by. There
was only a little swale of sand about it, making the place
appear a little higher than it was, in fact. It was simply a

blunt, square, whitewashed lump of a building dumped down upon the desert. There were two stories. That was all, unless one chose to give consideration, also, to the tangle of fencing at one side of the house and a few sheds that were falling to pieces. These were signs that at one time considerable bodies of cattle must have been handled from the ranch house. There was no verdure, no reaching skeleton of a windmill, yet it was certain that there must be a good well, at least, about the place.

The house was old, indeed, built with very massive walls; for it is not easy to raise dobe walls to the height of two tall stories, unless the sun-dried bricks are heaped up like a great mound, rather than a mere wall. Into these walls were sunk a few casements, a very few, and these so small and deep that they looked rather like lookouts of a fort than windows of a house. For the heat of the sun would be besieging this place through nine long months of the year.

Time was telling on the old place; the thick shell of whitewash which had accumulated on it in a thousand paintings had crumbled away near the ground; for five or six feet above the base, the walls were eaten slightly away from the outside, and were the color of plain mud. Winter rains would account for that.

Altogether, young Randal Dale never had come near a place that raised fewer expectations in him than did this lonely outpost, but when they drew up in the very front of it, at the shout of Don José, a battered old door that filled in an archway in the middle of the wall opened its two groaning panels, and the men rode into a large inclosed court.

It was a naked place, as naked as the outside of the building, but the effect was quite different, for around it ran a clumsy dobe arcade, and above the arcade appeared larger windows, set in the deep casements. It looked to young Rancie Dale like a cross between a modern barn and an ancient castle. A sense of time and of romantic adventure breathed through the place.

A peon, barelegged, was leaning against one panel of the gate, slowly walking it shut behind them. Looking out through that diminishing exit, Dale saw the fog of dust rising above the milling cattle and turning dull crimson against the rim of the sky. He made out the dreamlike dimness of the moving cattle, the riders circling on the verge of the great herd, and now, as the second panel of the gate shut out that picture, he heard the lowing of the thousands boom across the air, while the ground seemed to tremble beneath his feet as he dismounted.

In the meantime, the host himself had appeared in the court and was bowing and waving to them with affability, but with a good deal of dignity as well. Servants appeared, active, ragged house mozos, who took the horses by the bridles and held the stirrups as the guests dismounted.

Rancie Dale understood Spanish very well indeed; he understood, also, a good deal of the Mexican dialect, but for a time he found it hard to follow the chatter of greetings and orders, as Don José made himself at home and ordered an excellent dinner, with the best red wine that the inn had to offer. The host, immediately after, was considered important enough to be introduced by name, and it appeared that he was Bartolomé Flandes. He shook the hand of Dale and assured him that the house was at his disposal, at the disposal, in fact, of all of the good friends of José Oñate.

He, Flandes, would now busy himself in the arrangements for their dinner; and his daughter would take them into the garden. They could walk there or they could sit and drink an appetizer in the garden, if they chose.

They would walk, said Don José. Llano, twisting at a mustache, exclaimed: "Señor Flandes, what man in the world is such a fool that he would rather sit and drink than stand up and walk with the Señorita Maruja?"

That was well enough. One expected that a fellow like Don José or fire-eating Arturo Llano would be extravagant in speaking of almost any woman. But Randal Dale pricked up his ears when he heard Jeems Loring mutter: "I seen her once, four-five years back. She was only a spindling brat about fifteen, then; but doggone if she didn't stop a man like a bullet between the eyes!"

At this, in an arch of the arcade that surrounded the patio, a small door opened, and there Dale had a glimpse of the garden beyond, green and glistening faintly in the evening light. In the doorway itself stood Maruja Flandes.

She startled him as though a light had been flashed into his eyes.

Why had not the others prepared him for this unexpected beauty, not black and olive-brown, but golden and blue and tan that was richer than bronze?

He looked at her, smiling, and suddenly his heart laughed in him joyously.

She took the hands of the others; she welcomed them in a quiet, gentle voice, and then Randal Dale stood before her and received a second shock.

He had conceived of her, through the mist of the evening light, as a slender, childlike, winsome creature, and he was wrong. He had thought of her as something that will fit easily into the heart of any manly man. But now he saw that she was quite a different affair.

True, the hair was golden, if it were not too red to be called by that name! And the eyes were blue, but she was no clinging vine. A hundred and forty or forty-five pounds of sun-dried muscle cannot be made into a clinging vine. And that was what she was. No matter how comely, here was one likely to challenge any man in the riding of a horse or the climbing of a mountain. Her handgrasp was firm, with the strength of the muscles behind it. Her very eye was not that of a woman, either overconfident or overshy, but a level, steady glance that went against his face like the scrutiny of any man—not an altogether too friendly man, at that!

It took his breath away. "Confounded masculine creature!" he murmured to himself, and stepped into the garden with the others.

The beauty of the garden itself disarmed him almost at once. It was built against the back of the house and surrounded by a tall wall of dobe bricks. The top of that wall had broken down with the process of time and looked like the ruin of old battlements. Even the garden itself appeared old and battered; while at the farther end of it, only half screened behind a badly worn hedge, he could make out the power beam and the white circle of dust in which the power mule walked in lifting up water from the well.

That was the water, no doubt, that had made this once a good site for a ranch house. That was the water that made the pool in the center of the garden, with its flat, green floats of leaves and the water lilies crimson and yellow and white, giving off a sweet odor. That was the water, too, that had newly drenched all of the garden ground, so newly that one could still, with an attentive ear, hear the sound of the soil, which was yet thirstily drinking, deep and deeper, down to the smallest roots of the bushes and the vines.

It was indeed a battered garden, but this was the best moment to see it, when the dusk covered the bruises of time and allowed one to enjoy the fragrance of the flowers and their dull sheen. There were monstrous blossoms here that Randal Dale could not identify; there were blooms that looked like full moons, shining through clouds, and others that burned through the dimness like flames.

Dale came out of a trance, to hear the brisk, rather hard voice of Arturo Llano talking with the girl.

The other men had fallen back a little, giving Llano precedence in walking down the garden paths with the girl.

Dale heard Jeems Loring saying: "Well, José, it looks as though your sidekicker, yonder, wanted to settle down and start a home, eh?"

As he said this, he laughed a little. "Why do you laugh, Don Jeems?" asked the Mexican. "My friend Arturo would be a good husband to her. He is not one of those who can love more than one woman in his lifetime!"

"They'd have a kind of a peaceful life, wouldn't they?" suggested Jeems Loring. "What I mean is, with the rurales knocking on the front door every Monday and on the back door every Tuesday. Yeah, they'd have a peaceful life."

He laughed again.

"You know, amigo, that happiness is something to be plucked here and there," said Don José. "If it withers in your hand after a few moments, why, let it wither! Everything dies before very long, including ourselves!"

"Well, that's an answer," said Loring. "That's a kind of an answer, anyway. But you know what I smell in the air?"

"Tell me," said Don José.

"Trouble," said Jeems Loring. "I can smell it on the wind, as sure as ever a fox smells wolf and starts home with his brush down."

There might have been more talk. But now a mozo came scurrying and stood panting before them, to announce that dinner was ready.

## · 7 ·

It was a strange dinner. Señor Bartolomé Flandes sat at the table with them, sipping red wine from a massive old goblet, but tasting no meat. His daughter moved here and there, into the kitchen and out again, overseeing the service.

There was that same roast kid, concerning which José Oñate had prophesied. In addition to that, there was a stacking of tortillas and red-hot beans, prepared as only the artists of Mexico knew how to cook that fiery sauce with peppers, green and red. There was plenty of wine to wash down this meal; and there was little talk while the food was being absorbed. There was only a very occasional sharp glance of curiosity directed toward young Randal Dale as he consumed one helping of the beans and then passed his plate for another; and, while he ate a portion that would have wrung tears of pleasure and pain from the eyes of even the hardiest Mexican, it was noted by all that there was not so much as moisture about the eyes of Rancie Dale.

He declared that he never had eaten the dish before, but to his thinking it was the best he had ever tasted.

"You know, Señor Dale," said Flandes, the host, "although you say that you have never been in Mexico before, yet you are able to speak Spanish and Mexican also! How does that happen?''

"When I was a youngster on my father's place in Virginia," said the boy, "a man came and asked for work. He was different from anyone we had seen before. He spoke a rather bad English, but we couldn't tell his nationality, and he wouldn't talk about it. But he got work, quickly enough, because he turned out to be a fellow who could stick on the back of the worst horses on the place. There was only one trouble about him. The horses which he could ride were hardly any easier for others after he got out of the saddle. He had an art of his own in sticking on the back of anything that wore horsehide, and he didn't care at all what sort of a saddle was up. A mere blanket was equally good for him, it seemed. I've seen him stick on a bare back when any of the other boys would have been thrown from a good saddle.

"Well, after a time, a police officer showed up and began to ask questions about this new man of ours, whom we used to call Dick. The policeman was asking for a certain Ricardo who was a Mexican and wanted for killing three men!''

"Aha!" said Landes, Llano, and José Oñate all in a breath. Jeems Loring grinned broadly.

"Did you get him?" asked Landes.

"You see," said Rancie, "I guessed at once whom they wanted, and so I slipped away, got to the stable and warned Dick. I called him by his Mexican name, and I thought for an instant that he would put a knife in me, but then he seemed to realize that I was a friend, and I told him where to hide out on the bank of the creek, in an old cave where we youngsters used to play pirate, you see.''

"Señor, I see that you are a man to have for a friend," said Flandes. Dale, with a smile, waved the compliment aside.

"For three or four weeks, the police were hanging around, searching," he went on, "and I had to slip out from the house with food and bring it to my friend Ricardo. He lived close in the cave, and lived pretty well, too, and I think that those days were about the happiest in my life, because he used to talk to me by the hour about Mexico and his old life.

**135**

I used to get out of bed at night and go out to him, and he'd sit in a sputter of lantern light and tell me stories that raised the hair on my head.

"He had done a good many things that were outside the law, you see. He was an expert robber, and he loved a revolver almost as much as he loved a knife. He used to show me how he handled a gun; and sometimes we walked out into the hills, and he would give me exhibitions of shooting. He was wonderful with a revolver. He was an expert, as you people all seem to be."

He looked about the table and flattered them with an all-inclusive smile. "But with a knife," said the boy, "he was a great artist."

"Ah?" said Flandes. "What could he do?"

"Well, I used to throw up apples, and he got every apple while it was sailing through the air. He used to hold the knife in the flat of his hand and stare at the target, and then there would be a sudden flash, and a line of light would leap from his hand straight into the target, whatever it was! They were small knives, with weighted handles. Have you ever seen such things?"

Flandes looked at Don José, and José at Llano, and all the three of them smiled with understanding. It was plain that they had seen exactly similar things, and understood all about them.

"What became of your friend Ricardo? Did he have a last name?" asked Flandes.

"Oh, yes. His last name was Briguez."

"Hah? Ricardo Brigues?" cried out Don José.

"That was the name he told me," said the boy.

"A short man, with a scar slanting up over one eye and disappearing into his hair?" continued Don José.

"Yes. Did you know him?"

"Yes, I knew him," said José Oñate. "I knew him very well, too."

He broke off speaking and looked rather gloomily straight before him.

"I knew of Briguez, also," said Flandes, with equal soberness of tone. "And he got away from Virginia and the police?"

"A friend of my father ran freighters to Central America," said Rancie. "I knew him, and I took a chance and opened up with the whole story. He was interested. So we smuggled Ricardo down to the docks and shipped him away. That's the last that I ever heard of him."

"The last?" said Flandes, frowning.

"Yes. I never knew what became of him."

"That's not like Briguez," broke in Llano. "He never forgets a kindness done to him. Never!"

"You know him? He is still alive?" asked young Randal Dale.

"I know him. A good many other people know him. He has changed his name a few times, but he is still Ricardo!" said Llano. "If I ever meet him again—"

He stopped. His face was fierce.

"He may have written back to me," said Rancie Dale, "and the letter may have gone astray. I don't know about that. But now, Don José, can't we talk business and get things finished up?"

The meal was ended. They had only the red wine before them, and fruit.

"As good a time now as ever," said the Mexican. "You could make the half payment; that is, five dollars for each head, and there are about seven thousand. Have you as much as thirty-five thousand dollars with you, amigo?"

He spoke softly, but his eyes burned so that he hastily glanced down to the table.

"Thirty-five thousand?" said the boy. "Yes, I have that much and a great deal more. I don't see why I shouldn't pay you the entire amount at once."

He took a wallet from his coat pocket, and out of the wallet he took the same thick stack of greenbacks which Loring had seen at the hotel in Greensville.

There fell a pause. All eyes considered that thick heap, so closely compressed, like the pages of a book.

The girl, Maruja, coming out through the kitchen door, glided on noiseless feet into the dull outer circle of the lamplight and stared down at the treasure, also. Slowly, she began to nod, unseen by any.

"That is a great deal of money," said Don José. "Yes, you could pay for all the cattle now. Why not?"

"Yes. Why not?" asked the boy, very cheerfully.

"I'll tell you why not!" said a voice, so harsh and strained that every one started, because it was not recognized as coming from any of that company. But it was Jeems Loring. "Here's the reason. I made a bargain. Did I make the bargain for you, Dale?" he asked.

"Why, yes," said Rancie Dale, turning with innocent surprise and interest to his employee.

"And the bargain was payment when the cows were drove up the north bank of the Rio Grande, safe and sound. It ain't in the bargain to make even a half payment this far south of the river. But let that go. You can make the half payment all right. But not a penny more. It ain't business. That's what it ain't!"

"And why not?" asked Don José, in the softest of soft voices.

"I guess you know why it ain't business," said Jeems tartly. "If the police or the border guard or a patch of Texas Rangers or the rurales got wind of this and started to—"

"Why," exclaimed Rancie Dale, "and what has this deal to do with the police, if you please? What is there about it that would interest them?"

"Look here!" broke out Jeems Loring. "D'you think that you can buy cows for ten dollars a scalp when the regular price is—"

The hand of Don José, unseen beneath the table, laid upon the arm of the speaker a grip of iron. Jeems Loring was silent.

"Ten dollars," said Dale, "seems to me wonderfully cheap, of course. Is there anything wrong with the cattle, Loring?"

Loring, breathing hard, bent his head and looked fixedly down at the table.

Then he said slowly: "No, there ain't anything wrong with the cattle. You seen 'em. They got plenty of life to 'em."

"Then I don't understand why the police—" began the boy.

"No, you're new to the country and you're green to the country," said the other. "I guess you wouldn't understand. It's only the way that we've got of doing business down here. What I said for the bargain is what I'd stick to. There ain't any two ways about it."

Dale rose with a laugh.

"You argue with my friend," he said to the three Mexicans. "I'm no businessman. I'll walk out in the garden, because I can see a moon beyond that window. Let me know when you've come to an agreement, and tell me what I'm to do!"

## ·8·

HE HAD NO SOONER LEFT THE ROOM FOR THE GARDEN THAN
the host, Flandes, stood up. He was a fine figure of a man
with this peculiar feature—his hair and eyes were distinctly
black, but his eyebrows were distinctly reddish in hue and,
since he was not very closely shaved, the skin of his face was
slightly tinged with red.

"My friends," he said, "it appears that there is business
between you concerning Señor Dale. I hope that he will not
be injured in whatever you may decide."

Then he left the room. It was an odd speech, the sort that
one would never expect from a hotelkeeper, even though the
host were a gentleman born, as was Señor Flandes. When he
had departed, the three rogues who remained looked grimly
at one another.

"He thinks that we're gonna frame this kid," said Jeems
Loring, at last, thrusting out his long lower jaw.

"And that," said Don José pleasantly, "is just what we
are going to do."

He turned to his henchman, the famous Llano.

"How much money was in that sheaf?" he asked.

"Of course, that depends," said Llano. "If there's nothing

less than a hundred-dollar bill in the stack, then there's, why, there may be a hundred and twenty or thirty thousand dollars in that pile.''

He said this impressively, but his chief looked grimly at him and answered: "I saw a thousand, three up from the bottom of the stack. There are a few thousand-dollar bills in that stack, I take it!''

He looked across at Jeems.

"What do you think, Jeems?" he asked.

Jeems Loring was still hesitating. At last he spoke his mind frankly: "It's this way. I got this bird framed. I got him planted, and he's all mine. Then I lead him up and give you a chance to knife him. Why should I do that? Look a-here, José. You're gonna clean up big on your slice out of the cattle deal. You got those cows at not more'n five dollars apiece. You'll sell 'em for ten. That fool of a brat, he don't realize that they're stolen goods. He wants to make his clean-up honest. Why ain't you contented with your cut on the cows?''

Don José leaned his chin upon his left hand and he smiled, deliberately and slowly, into the eyes of Loring.

Then he said: "Jeems, dear friend!''

Jeems Loring stirred a little in his chair. "Don't be a pig, José,'' he suggested.

"Jeems, dear friend,'' repeated Don José. And still he smiled. Jeems Loring grew flushed with passion.

"I frame the whole thing and I work it up,'' said he, "and then you want to knife in like you had joined from the first and helped make the plant. You wouldn't even know how much coin there was in the deal, if the kid hadn't been such a fool as to flash his roll. I never seen such a fool in my life!'' he ended viciously.

"Ah, my dear Jeems, a kind Fate that watches over good thieves,'' said Don José, "only sends to the world once in a long time a great deal of easy money in one loose pocket. Señor Dale is such a gift from heaven to us. Do you think that Providence intends that all of this loot should pass into one pair of hands? Do you really think that you are the only one who should be allowed to dip into the pot?''

Loring answered him savagely: "Whacha mean by that? I

141

got a gang of thugs that'll drain me dry before I'm through with 'em. I got a dozen of the hardest fighting boys north of the river, and you know it. They'll want money and they'll want big money.''

''For two or three days' work, they will not want more than two or three thousand apiece,'' said Don José. ''I also have used some of those very same men, my friend. I know their prices. They are too innocent to think of the sums of money that can be made from simple people like Señor Dale!''

Jeems Loring gritted his teeth. Then, suddenly, he threw up his hands. ''It ain't my fault,'' he complained. ''I was gonna make the play close to my chest. I wasn't gonna make any fool moves. You never would've known that you was next to a gold mine, but that ratheaded brat, he had to flash his whole roll—his whole roll.'' He ended with a groan.

''He should not be burdened,'' said Don José.

''We will help him to do without the money,'' said Llano, nodding his head.

Jeems Loring sat forward, rested his elbows on the table and nodded his head in turn.

''After the beans are spilled, there ain't any use crying,'' he said. ''You know the low-down. And now I'll play with you. We split it all around. I'll need twenty thousand to square my gang, maybe. Count that out, and then we'll cut the rest in three lumps.''

Don José allowed his gentle smile once more to play over his lips.

''I also have retainers,'' said he.

Loring cursed violently, but softly, so that there was a hissing between his teeth.

He answered finally, choking on the words.

''This is a plain holdup, but you have me cornered. I might've known that I'd be cornered when I come to this joint. We'll cut the whole lump in three chunks, then, you robbers!''

''Very hard words, very hard words,'' said Don José and he laughed, looking at Llano.

The latter merely grinned and his grin was exceedingly brief.

"Now, then," said Jeems Loring, "since we've got the case all framed up, what's the best idea?"

"Send out word to run the cattle toward the river. It's late enough now," said Don José.

"All right. That's going to get the rest of the boys off my hands."

"True," said Don José, pinching his lips hard on the words. "They'll be gone north. After the money is split, if you ride south, you might never meet any of them, and you might never have to pay out hard cash to any of them."

He looked hard and straight at Jeems Loring, but the latter did not notice. He began to nod over his own thoughts. "Yeah, better march 'em on toward the north," said he.

Loring went to the door and called to Flandes to send a messenger to the head cowmen controlling the herd, with orders to start them north at once toward the river.

"Is the river clear?" asked Llano, as the other turned and came back.

"I don't know, and I don't give a doggone," said Jeems Loring. "It ain't the cows that I'm interested in. It was simply in getting that fool of a tenderfoot handy on the spot, with all of his hard cash in his pockets. He was telling me that there's a fortune in cattle. Sure there is, if they're worked the way that the three of us are gonna work 'em."

He settled down in his chair, poured out a glass of the thick red wine, then changed his mind and pushed the glass away.

"I gotta have a clear head," he murmured.

"How do we begin?" asked Llano. "Do we simply use a knife or a gun, and then cover up the body?"

"Not here!" said Don José hastily.

"Great heavens, no," said Llano, jumping up in reaction against his own suggestion. "I had forgotten Maruja. She would not like such a thing."

"Wouldn't she?" said Jeems. "She'd like any man that had a third of that money in his pocket, though."

"Suppose," said Don José, "that she may be out in the

garden now, persuading young Señor Dale that the best plan for him is to ride quickly away and forget all about a herd of seven thousand cows!''

"Would she do that?" asked Jeems Loring.

"She would do anything," said Don José calmly. "She is not fond of thieves.''

"She don't know what we're up to," said Loring. "She couldn't know!''

"She has an instinct that warns her of danger when it is still far away," said the great Don José. "I understand her, a very little.''

"She's a straight girl, is she?" asked Loring, interested. "Look here, brother, she's too pretty to be straight, and this far south!''

Don José rested his glance upon Loring meditatively. Llano, when he understood the implied insult, rose savagely to his feet, but with the mere motion of his hand, Don José forced the other to sit down again.

"Do you know what you are saying, Jeems?" he asked.

"Me?" said Loring. "Oh, I see what you mean. No, I ain't reflecting on Mexican girls, José. No, women ain't anything to me. I'm too old for 'em. And they're too young for me. Too young altogether!''

"So!" said Llano, relaxing suddenly in his chair.

"Yeah, and exactly so!" said Loring, scowling at the mustached Mexican.

"Quietly, quietly, my friend. There is only one thing to do," said Don José, "and that is to extract as painlessly as possible from young Señor Dale, that very young gentleman, the money which is now in his pocket.''

"Aw, all right," said Jeems Loring. "I dunno that I care much what happens, so long as we get our mitts on the coin.''

"It shall be done," said Don José.

"You bet it'll be done!" said Loring.

"And why not the butt end of a gun?" asked Llano, thrusting out his chin in such a way that his beard bristled and thrust forward.

"Hush!" said his chief, raising a slender hand, an expression of pain on his face. "Maruja would never forgive us, and her forgiveness means a great deal to you, my friend!"

Llano settled back from his eagerness and squared his shoulders against the back of his chair.

"Cards, then!" he said.

"Exactly," agreed Don José, "and you could win the longest feathers out of the wings of the Angel Gabriel at poker or dice. You are the man!"

## ·9·

In the meantime, young Rancie Dale was strolling through the garden in the moonlight, and he had not gone far before Maruja Flandes came out to him, bringing hot coffee in her hand. He looked at her with admiration that chiefly dwelt on her long, free, easily swinging step, the straight carriage of her shoulders and the way her head was placed upon them, lending dignity to her whole figure.

She told him that he had forgotten the coffee, and dinner was not dinner without it. It was her father's chiefest secret. He made it so well that she, Maruja, had often advised him to go to the City of Mexico and there open a coffee shop. They would do very well at it, to be sure.

Rancie Dale took the coffee cup, and the girl waited for him to finish sipping it so that she could take it back.

He was glad to hold her there in this way, it seemed, with the mist of moonshine about her, making a close, intimate halo in the red-gold of her hair. It was odd to see her by such a light, she was such a vigorous, noonday personality and figure.

"Would you like that better—to be in Mexico City?" he asked.

"In Mexico City?" she repeated, rather vaguely.

"Yes, you'd like that better," said he, venturing to put in the answer as well as the question. "I can imagine that things are pretty dull out here in the desert. In a big town, you could have a good deal more fun."

"Could I?" she answered. "I could settle down as a shop-keeper's wife. What fun would that be?"

"But think of the parties and all the young people?"

"Making a lot of noise is not my idea of a party," she answered. "I've been in Mexico City; I'd rather go into a tomb."

"Really!" he exclaimed in cheerful surprise.

"Yes, I'd a thousand times rather live out here."

"I'll try to believe that," said Rancie Dale. "Will you tell me what happens out here in the fonda?"

"I could tell you for hours and hours," she replied. "I don't sit at home like a silly baby. I ride and shoot and rope almost as well as a man. So I do what the young men do. I go hunting. I can work as an extra hand at a round-up, if there's need of me. I've—I've bulldogged a yearling!"

She brought this out as an exclamation that seemed as much of defiance and shame as of triumph.

"Bulldogged a yearling!" exclaimed he. "Why, I don't think that I could do that!"

"It's a knack," she said. "I wouldn't want to try it again, I don't think. But I stuck at the game long enough to learn how to do it."

She began to laugh.

"You've had your fun like a boy," suggested he.

"Well, more or less," she agreed.

"You could ride, or shoot, or run, or climb like a man?" he asked.

"No, not just the same. I'm pretty good with a rifle; I'm nothing with a revolver," she admitted. "I can hit something only once in a while, I mean. I can run. I can climb pretty well, but a woman hasn't the same driving muscles and sinews that a man has. I can swim, though, better than most men; I can ride as well as a lot of 'em, too."

She added up these accomplishments gravely, without

boasting, and went on: "You see, I can do enough to enjoy the country. Father and I have our good times in the mountains back there. It's a fifty-mile ride to get into 'em, into the good hunting districts. Sometimes we ride there one night, hunt two days, and ride back at night again. When you say 'Mexico City' to me, I wonder what I would do there but wear a mantilla and sit still and talk small talk. I'd rather," she ended, with some emotion, "I'd rather live out here in the desert with no more than a single hawk in the sky than be back there in the big city with half a million people around!"

He still lingered over the coffee, so that he could watch her more closely.

"I can understand what you mean in part," said he. "For the same reasons, I should like to live somewhere in the West—in my own country, of course."

She nodded, but she said: "You have to learn how to live out here, you know. It isn't what it seems at the first glance. Before you can get along very well, you have to be toughened. D'you think that you're tanned enough to stand Western life?"

"Tanned?" said he. "Do you mean colored by the sun?"

"Yes," she said, "prepared for hard use, like leather."

"I think that I could be hardened," said he. "I have the size, to begin with."

There was a stone bench at the edge of the pool of water lilies. She sat down on it and pointed to a place beside her.

"I want to talk to you," said she.

He obediently took the place, turning toward her, holding the coffee cup rather high, perhaps to keep her from seeing that there was hardly a drop of the black liquid left.

"Do you know those three men in the house?" she asked.

"Loring and Don José and Llano?" he asked.

"Yes."

"Why, I have know Loring pretty well for several days. He was pointed out to me as one of the best men in the country."

"Best with a gun," she answered.

"How?"

148

"Best with a gun. A good many dead ghosts know how good he is with a gun."

"He's a fighting man, is he?" said the boy. "I guessed that much. There's a careless way about him that brave men have, as I've noticed before."

"He's killed a dozen men, at least," said she.

She waited, sitting a little straighter. "As many as that?" exclaimed the boy, with enthusiasm. "What a man! All of them fighting people, of course?"

"Oh, they were fighting people, of course," said she. "Couple of sheriffs in the list, I think."

"Really?" said he.

Then he laughed a little.

"He's one of the Robin Hoods, is he?" suggested Rancie Dale. "I could almost have guessed that."

"Robin Hood?" she asked. "Well, other people call him by different names. The other two, Don José and Llano, they're the same kind."

"Of Robin Hoods?"

"At least, they're not working men," said she, and again she waited, as if to let him take the hint that lay behind her words. He merely shrugged his shoulders.

"Some people are drudges," said he. "And some are fighting men who don't like work. They use their brains and their hands in different ways. Some of the most glorious people in the world are of that sort. I've met a few of 'em, here and there."

She paused again and, putting her chin on one strong fist, she stared at the silver glimmer of the moon spread over the face of the water and the big lily pads. On one of those pads a frog appeared and began to croak with a dull, booming note.

"How old are you, Señor Dale?" she asked.

"Twenty-four," said he.

"As much as that?"

"Yes. Why?"

"But you haven't lived your twenty-four years out here, have you?"

"No, of course not."

"Well," said she, "all I can say is that if I were you, I'd spend a few more years in the land before I made up my mind about the characters of the men who are in it."

"And what do you mean by that?" he queried.

"I can't say much more. You ought to be able to guess something from what I've said already."

"Guess?" said he. "Guess at what, if you please?"

She stood up suddenly, held out her hand, and he meekly surrendered the coffee cup. He stood in turn, a big, stalwart form before her.

"I've said more than I should have," she answered. "I only hope one thing."

"And what is that?"

"That you come to no great harm."

"Harm?" he echoed. Then he added: "I understand. You think that I don't know enough to get along in the cattle business. Of course not, but you see that I'm taking in the best sort of experienced men to teach me what to do. There's my friend Jeems Loring, for instance. He seems to know all about cattle. And I'll always have men like him around me."

"Will you?" said the girl more or less dryly.

"Certainly," said he. "When you think of it, it's a grand world where a man can find so much honesty and truth, kindness, and willingness to help others."

A faint murmur parted her lips. That was all. "Even if the cattle business turns out a failure," said he, with his usual optimistic cheerfulness, "there is always the lesson learned, which is something gained!"

He lifted his head as he said this and smiled down at her with such tremendous faith in existence, as it seemed, that she actually moved a short step back from him.

Then, suddenly, she came straight up to him and said, looking up into his face: "Do you know something? I half believe that you don't mean a word you're saying, and that you see through this situation and all of these people as clear as daylight!"

"See through them? See through them?" he repeated. "Why, I see them as they are, of course—free-swinging, honest, open-hearted, genuine Westerners, the sort of men I want to know, the sort of men I want for friends. That's how I see them, and how else could I see them?''

Slowly, she said: ''You great foolish baby!''

Then she turned and went swiftly toward the house. At that instant the door opened upon the garden and the voice of Llano called: ''Señor Dale, will you come in?''

# · 10 ·

Maruja went back into the house, dropped the coffee cup on a table, regardless of whether or not it shattered, and asked a startled mozo where she could find her father.

He was in his own room, so she went straight up to him and found him lying on a couch that was covered with a pair of great sheepskins, reading by lamplight out of a book with a time-yellowed paper cover.

Maruja sat in the casement with the moonlight streaming over her shoulders.

"Father," said she, "what is going to happen?"

"To the gringo?" he asked.

"Whatever he is," said the girl, "he has sat at your table and eaten your food."

"Food that is bought is not food that is given," said Flandes, with a slight shrug of his shoulders.

"You sat at the table with him," she insisted. "Was that right?"

"I sat where I had to sit," he answered. "You saw who was there, giving me orders?"

"I saw three murderers," said she.

He raised a quick hand to stop her.

"That is a very loud word in a very small house," said he.

"Murderers," she repeated. "You know that they're nothing else! Nothing but murderers."

"Nonsense!" said he. "Whatever they are, you know my rule. Through no fault of mine or my father, or his father before him, we have been stripped of everything until we have only this house left. We have done what we could, honestly. We have only the house left. Now, whatever happens, so long as I have no hand in any rascality, I close my eyes."

"That is a weak religion," said she.

"It is not a religion, but a necessity," he answered. "I've argued it out with you before."

"Nothing must happen to this gringo," said she.

"Do you like his blue eyes so much, Maruja?" asked the innkeeper, looking calmly at her.

"I like him well enough," said she. "He is big, and I like bigness. He is handsome, and I like that, too. Besides, there is something else about him."

"His foolishness?" he suggested.

"He may be a fool. I really don't know."

"Think of an idiot willing to trust to José and Llano and Jeems Loring, that cunning fox!" he said, laughing a little.

"I don't want to talk as though I could read minds," said she.

"Go ahead," he suggested.

"But," she continued, "while I was talking to him, a moment ago, suddenly it seemed to me that there was something behind his smile and behind his eyes, as though he were seeing through the whole situation and understanding it perfectly."

The man sat suddenly upright.

"What nonsense is this, Maruja?" he asked.

"It may be nonsense," said she. "But all at once I was afraid of him. I'm not afraid usually, you know that."

"Well, I understand now. It's sentimentality," said he. "He's turned your head. A woman is always a little afraid of a man who's turning her head!"

He waited for a denial, but, instead, she answered: "Perhaps that's it. I don't know, but I don't think so. I've had my head turned before, but it wasn't like this."

"Who turned your head before?" he demanded, sitting straighter than ever.

"Arturo Llano," said she.

"He? A cutthroat! What was there about him that turned your head, if you please?"

"Several things. His scars," she answered. "His fame, his dead men and the fact that he really seems to love me."

"Seems?" cried the father, leaping to his feet. "What do you mean?"

"He wants to marry me."

"I'll strike him dead," began the innkeeper, and then he checked himself.

"You'd strike him dead before you'd let me marry him?" asked the girl curiously. "No, you wouldn't quite do that. Besides, he may still be seriously interested, but I'm not."

"Who else turned your head?" snapped Flandes.

"Don José, of course."

The innkeeper smiled.

"Ah, Don José, of course!" said he.

Maruja leaned her head a little to one side and studied her father, and all men in him.

"That would be different?" she asked.

"Why, Don José—of course, Don José would be different."

"The law will get him before it gets Llano," said she.

Her father waved this suggestion aside.

"Don José is a prince among men," he declared.

"Among mankillers and thieves," corrected the girl.

"My dear Maruja," said the innkeeper, "there is a sense of proportion in all things. Don José is known through the entire country. He is a prince of his kind!"

"Well," said Maruja, "he turned my head for a while, but not for a great time. And I tell you that what I felt about Llano and about Don José was very different from what I felt about Señor Dale."

"Every woman," said her father, "has something in her

that makes her pity a fool and makes her wish to mother him and shield him from the world.''

"It may be that," answered the girl, with her usual frankness. "But a woman is not afraid of a fool."

"Are you really afraid of this gringo?" asked her father.

"In a way, yes."

"Stuff!" said Flandes.

He walked up to her and laid a hand on her shoulder.

"Tell me the truth," said he.

"I always tell you the whole truth," she answered. "This big man, with his foolish, frank way, I'm not so sure that he is so entirely open and frank. That's all!"

"What could be behind it? He's in the lions' den. Do you think that he put himself in with the lions on purpose?"

She lifted a forefinger.

"That," she said, "is exactly what I have been thinking! Only an idea, just a dark shadow of an idea. If he came here on purpose, knowing all of the danger, then he is such a man as I have never even dreamed of. Not even a José Oñate would dare to do such a thing!"

She stood up from the casement, her face alight.

"On purpose?" exclaimed Flandes. "Came here on purpose, knowing what Jeems Loring and José Oñate and Arturo Llano really are? No man would dare do such a thing! You are a foolish girl, Maruja! Go to bed and get these silly thoughts out of your head."

She kissed him goodnight and left the room without another word, but she did not go to bed.

Instead, she went to that upper room to which Don José and Jeems Loring had retired to drink more red wine and tell tales, each man out of his crowded past.

When she tapped at the door, Oñate opened it to her and would have bowed her in, but she remained in the dusky gloom of the hall, hardly touched by the lamplight from the room.

"José," said she, "you are going to take the money from the gringo, is that not true?"

"Of course, it is true, Maruja," said he instantly. "It is a dangerous thing to allow such a man to wander about through the world carrying such a burden. He might fall into rough hands, and then what would happen to him?''

''Very well. I understand,'' said she. ''I don't care about the money. But his life, José?''

''Do you care about his life?'' said José.

''He is such a great young fool!'' said the girl.

José leaned in the doorway, laughing. The metal braid on his jacket gleamed and trembled.

''He is a fool,'' said he.

''And now about his life?''

''Why,'' said José, ''the money will be taken away from him so painlessly that he will hardly know how it left him.''

''Will you pick his pocket?'' she asked.

''No, not even that. Llano is even now taking the green-backs by means of stacked cards or loaded dice, or both. I can't tell which. However, you can be sure that young Señor Dale is rapidly approaching poverty at this very moment. And in the morning, his heart may be rather heavy, but he will be reproaching his bad luck, and not his bad enemies!''

He laughed again. And the girl laughed a little, too.

''It would be strange if Llano failed,'' said she, and turned away.

In the meantime, in the lower room where Arturo Llano and young Dale were together, at this very moment Llano was shaking a box of dice. There was a faint smile under his beard, and there was a flash in his eye as he rattled the dice. He had before him a great stack of bills; and before Dale, at the opposite side of the table, there was a similar heap.

To make up the sum of the last bet, it appeared that Don Arturo had not possessed quite enough hard cash, and now he had laid upon the greenbacks no less than four rings, set with four great jewels. His golden spurs were there, also, together with a number of other trinkets, which Dale had admitted as wagers at two or three times their real value.

''Now!'' cried Arturo, with a ringing voice, and rolled the dice out on the table.

An exclamation of dismay burst from his lips. He had expected, he had really known that three sixes would lie there, looking up at him from their black eyes. Instead, he saw a five, a trey, and an ace.

"Bad luck," said Dale, raking in the money carelessly. "Perhaps your friends will give you another gambling stake, Llano. Or, if you wish, we'll play now for your horse and saddle."

## · 11 ·

Arturo did not answer at once. He stared at the spot which his pile of money had occupied, and then he looked gloomily toward the pile which the boy was arranging.

"We could make the bets smaller, if you wish," said young Rancie Dale. "I'm sorry that you've had the bad luck."

"Luck?" said the gambler. "Luck?"

He made a gesture.

"I have no more money. Perhaps I can get some, though. Will you wait here?"

"Certainly," said Randal Dale. "Take all the time you wish."

He settled down into a chair by the window and seemed to lose himself at once in the contemplation of the moonlight that drifted over the garden wall, beyond, and spilled in silver across the garden itself. Far away in the center of the plot, the face of the water-lily lake glistened like polished silver with the dark design of the pads stretched across it.

Arturo Llano retreated hastily from the room, still dazed by what had happened, and it showed in his face when he reached that upper room where Don José and Jeems Loring were sitting.

On the way, Arturo passed the girl, coming down, and she said to him: "How was the game, Arturo?"

No other woman in the world could have won a single syllable from him, at that moment, but to Maruja, he turned grimly and said: "I have lost three thousand dollars in American money, my rings, my spurs and a few other things. The Evil One was against me."

"You lost!" she exclaimed. "But you never lose, Arturo, except when you're playing against old friends. Is there a demon in this gringo?"

"Demon?" repeated the Mexican. "No, no! It was only chance, and because my fingers suddenly became foolish. That's all. Simply because my fingers grew clumsy and began to stumble. I played like an old fool!"

He gritted his teeth.

"Dice, too," said he. "As though I could fail to throw correctly with loaded dice, Maruja!"

"Loaded dice, and yet you lost?" said she.

"Not one six in three loaded dice!" he complained and hurried on up the stairs, saying over his shoulder: "But I'll get more money and go back and win every penny in that wallet of his, or else my name is not my own!"

He hurried on, and the girl, looking after him, murmured: "If you get more money, you'll have simply more to lose. I was right! I was right! There is something to this Randal Dale. There is more in him than the eye sees in one quick glance. Oh, Jeems and Arturo and Don José, is something going to happen to all three of you?"

She began to laugh, in an odd way, as she went back downstairs. As she stepped into the garden, she saw the head and shoulders of Randal Dale silhouetted against the window. Softly, softer than a cloud shadow stealing over a meadow, as silently as this, she drifted near and nearer, until she was very close. Stepping on a low mound, she was enabled to look in and down toward Randal Dale.

He was looking away from her, into the garden, and his face was blankly and innocently contented in its expression.

There was no triumph in his look, such as a youngster might betray after putting several thousand dollars into his pockets in cash and fine jewels. There was only the calm and gentle absorption of one dreaming over the poetic beauty of the night.

The girl, seeing this, staring hard at him, finally shook her head in surrender. Then she stepped back from the mound. There was a thick bush behind her, making a background against which she must have been totally, or almost totally, invisible. Yet, although in her backward step she made no sound whatever, the man in the window leaped suddenly to his feet and whirled about. A Colt revolver was in his hand, leveled at her down so straight a line that she could have sworn that she was seen. She almost cried out in alarm, then she saw the figure in the window shrug his shoulders, and the revolver disappeared, with one deft movement, inside his coat.

Randal Dale, leaning against the window, stared toward her for a moment, and then turned about and resumed his chair, but only after he had dragged it out of sight within the room.

She, in the meantime, had seen quite enough.

The first gesture announces the celebrated actor; the first note tells the audience the capacities of the great singer; the first blow struck is the sign and index of the fighter. And now the catlike speed with which big young Randal Dale had moved, the deftness with which the gun had been conjured into view and made to vanish again, told the girl all that she wanted to know.

Besides, she was no mean judge of such things. She had seen experts working many a time before this, but never had she seen a speed and a surety of gesture to compare with this tigerish silhouette at the window.

She had dropped to her knees when he first stirred. She remained there for a moment, getting her breath back, covering her eyes, while her brain whirled.

The helpless tenderfoot whom the others were planning to rob was very patently a consummately clever rascal who knew all about how to take care of himself. He was playing a part, the role of an innocent, and before he finished acting, who else would be left on the stage?

What ought she to do—hurry to her father and tell him what she had discovered, or go directly to Don José and the others and let them know?

Something in her revolted against this. She had no love for the Americanos. On the other hand, the thought of warning three celebrated fighters that another man was also a warrior seemed suddenly too absurd, too grotesquely unfair. Besides, they were acting the parts of spiders, and they were enticing the stranger into their trap. Well, let all the ropes and the beams of that trap be strong as steel and cunningly devised, or else the intended victim would escape!

So she did nothing at all, except to remain there on her knees for a moment, turning the whole matter about in her mind, such excitement rising in her breast, it became almost impossible to breathe!

What was to happen? The consummate gambler, the great Llano, was already turned back; but he remained a fighting unit! The other two, would they guess that Llano had been defeated by something more than luck and the vagaries of loaded dice?

That same Arturo Llano now stood before Don José and Jeems Loring, saying to them: "I've heard of luck before, but never of luck that will beat loaded dice. Now, mind you, he did not know enough to roll the dice, at first, without spinning one of them off the table; or else he piled them out in a stack, one on top of the other. But, in spite of having to learn how even to throw the dice, he beat me and my loaded set!"

He threw up both his hands. "Think of it, friends!"

"Yeah, I'm thinkin' of it," said Jeems Loring, "and it's doggone funny. I've seen you make water come out of wallets that wouldn't bleed two dollars a year. I've seen you bring out the hard cash in a flood. But you couldn't tap that tenderfoot?"

"Suppose," suggested Don José, "that he's no tenderfoot at all? What about that?"

"Yes, what about that?" said Llano, grasping at the idea.

"But no, he could not have manipulated the dice box. I was watching him every moment! Every single moment!"

"That's all right," said Jeems Loring. "Don't you gents get excited. I've seen a lot more of the kid than you have, and there's nothing to get startled about. There ain't any real trouble in him, mind you. Not one bit!"

"Is he really a tenderfoot, as he seems?" queried Don José, frowning a little.

"Why, he's so green that a forest fire wouldn't even singe his top branches," said Jeems Loring, confidently. "Only, it's kind of funny that loaded dice should go wrong in a throw."

"They're loaded to go right," said Don José. "What about it, Arturo?"

"They will go wrong, one of them once in three or four times. Two of them once in a hundred times. Three of them once in a million times, maybe. *Hai!* That I should have lost when I already had two or three thousand of his money; then to raise the stakes, as if to favor him in winning back, and then to have him win! Think of it, amigos!"

"Beginners always have luck," said Jeems Loring. "But this streak of luck ain't going to last."

"It won't last," agreed Llano. "Give a thousand or two, and I'll go back and win every penny that he has, because now he is excited, and he says that dice is an amusing game. Hah!" He snorted.

"Yeah. I'll stake you," said Jeems Loring, reaching for his wallet.

Don José held up his hand.

"That won't do," he said. "Never put your money twice on the same horse, unless it wins the first race. You can't make a horse run faster by betting higher on him. No, no, Arturo, your hand is out tonight. Let's try another way with our friend, Señor Randal Dale."

"All right," said Jeems Loring. "I don't mind taking him over and opening him up."

"How?" asked Don José.

"With a gun."

"That is a cruel and blunt way of action, amigo Jeems," said Don José.

"Aw," said Jeems Loring, "I just change into other clothes, speak a Mexican lingo, and change my voice like nobody would know me, with a black hood over my head. Then I step through the door and take the coin away from him. It's simple, it's quick, and it gets the cash!"

## · 12 ·

EVERY GOOD PLAN IS SIMPLE. THAT IS AN OLD TRUTH. AND now it was not difficult for Jeems Loring to gain the approval of the others for his plan.

The clothes were readily got from the innkeeper; and a few moments later, Loring, equipped with fresh trousers and shirt and a black sack to cover his head, with eyeholes cut in it, went down to the room where young Rancie Dale was still waiting for the expected return of his late friend, Arturo Llano.

The door was cast open, and Jeems entered with a gun held before him, a little more than hip-high, and these words growling from his throat in a deepened, husky voice: "Get up your hands, brother, and get 'em up quick, will you?"

Randal Dale hoisted his hands above his head instantly. He rose from his chair at the same time and seemed to be stretching up to the utmost of his power in order, perhaps, to touch the beamed ceiling of the room.

Behind his shadowy mask, Jeems Loring grinned.

It was, after all, even simpler than he had expected to find it. He looked at the strained face and strained eyes of the boy and felt a touch of compassion for him.

"Turn around!" he commanded, not with words, but with a swinging gesture of his left hand.

Terror seemed to have laid hold of the boy, for he wheeled at once and presented his back to the intruder.

At the same time, he said: "I don't know who you are, but I warn you, if you take a penny from me, you're going to curse the day that you were born. I have friends in this place."

"What friends 'ave you got?" demanded the other.

"Arturo Llano and José Oñate. More than that, one of the best men in Texas is my partner. If you rob me, Jeems Loring will never rest till he's run you down!"

At this, laughter well-nigh throttled Jeems Loring. Yet, he was touched with pity, also. Trust always moves us, even in our worst moments. Still, what tenderfoot has a right to so much money as this lad was carrying with him into no man's land?

He laid the muzzle of his revolver against the small of the boy's back: "Don't shoot!" cried Randal Dale.

"Budge a muscle, and I'll shoot!" said Loring.

Reaching around the body of Dale, he dipped a hand into the inside coat pocket and brought it forth again carrying that same sleek, heavy, thickly wadded wallet.

A little sigh came from the lips of Loring, as he grasped that wallet. It meant the consummation of all that he desired. A brighter and a better life he saw extending before him. To be sure, he had just finished agreeing with José and Llano that he would split the profits with them, but why should he be bound by that obligation when, just outside the window, lay the wide security of the night and so many fast horses fit to carry him into it?

"Now, stand fast," he said, "and don't you stir an inch or—"

He began to back away, as he said this, and he naturally tilted up the muzzle of the heavy revolver a little as he moved away, bringing it into firing position.

As he finished saying: "Keep your face shut and your feet still and maybe no harm'll come to you," just, in fact, as he uttered the last of these words, the body of tall young Randal

Dale twitched slightly around, his head jerked about so that he could look over his shoulder, and the long right arm that had been straining so high into the air dropped like a bar of lead.

The balled fist struck across the right forearm of Loring, and the gun exploded and fell to the floor.

Jeems Loring cursed. But he was not a fellow to venture to close quarters armed with a single gun. Neither did a disabled right hand make him helpless. Beautiful and smooth and swift was the grace with which he slipped out the revolver with his left hand, ready for a shot that would smash its way straight through the foolish heart of Randal Dale, but, before his forefinger curled affectionately around the trigger, a great misfortune happened to the expert Jeems Loring.

It took the form of a large, bony fist, which, as Randal Dale kept on turning round, moved in what is known as a left hook, up, across, and then sharply down, with a whiplash jerk at the end, when the big knuckles of the fist found a lodging place on the rim of Mr. Loring's jaw, just beside the point.

He fell neither forward nor backward. He simply collapsed in a heap. When he got the red flame and whirling darkness out of his eyes, he saw Randal Dale seated on the edge of a table holding in his hands both of his guns.

The sight helped to clear the staggered brain of Jeems Loring at once. He was quite capable of hearing the words that ordered him to rise, and rise he did and stood with empty hands before the boy.

"Take off that mask," said Dale.

Jeems Loring plucked it off and, as his bare face appeared before Randal Dale, a random sense of shame came to him, something that he had not felt for many years and made his skin flame hot. But he was amazed to hear no reproofs, no outburst of honest indignation whatever.

"Why," cried Randal Dale, amidst choking laughter, "it's my old friend Loring! It's Jeems Loring! Man, man, it's a good joke! If I'd guessed that you were only playing me a practical joke, I never would have hit you! I'm sorry. I'm mighty sorry. There's a big red lump rising all along your jaw now. I'm terribly sorry, Loring. Forgive me.''

It was difficult, even for the swift brain of Jeems Loring, to understand which way the cat had jumped. At last, he made it out. According to the idiotic understanding of this lad, there had not been any real attack at all. There had simply been a practical joke that had hung fire a little!

Loring cleared his voice, and said grumblingly: ''You might have known me by my voice, Rancie. No need to break a man's jaw for a little joke between friends!''

''I know it,'' complained Dale. ''I'm terribly sorry. It was the thought of losing all of that coin, d'you see? It was that that put me off balance. I saw black—I was so excited, partner!''

''You saw a way home to my jaw,'' said Jeems Loring. ''You could see that far, clear enough. What you wearing on the back of your hand, a horseshoe or brass knuckles, Rancie?''

''Here?'' asked Dale. ''Why, nothing, of course. What do you mean?''

''Never mind,'' said Jeems, caressing his face tenderly, ''but I'm gonna have a lopsided jaw the rest of my life, I reckon. I thought the old gray mule had off and kicked me again, is what I thought!''

''Here are your guns,'' suggested the boy. ''I'm sorry. Just saying it, doesn't tell you how sorry I am!''

He handed back the guns, then, turning and stooping, his face quite away from Loring, he picked up the fallen wallet from the floor.

Why did not Loring cover him again, at that moment, and take the wallet?

It was something which he himself never would be able to explain, in after times. But there was a rediscovered sense of shame, perhaps, controlling him. The thing which he had failed to do, when he was wearing a mask, he could hardly attempt now that his face was bare.

Perhaps, too, the ringing of a bell in his brain had a little to do with the matter. It was still as if a bullet had passed

167

through the base of his skull. What a punch that boy, Rancie Dale, carried up his sleeve!

So, perfectly still, he watched Dale pocket the desired wallet, so sleek, so thick, so filled with fortune!

Then he said: "I'm gonna go and douse my head in cold water. I'm still seeing stars, Dale."

Dale accompanied him to the door of the room, a hand half affectionate and half apologetic resting on his shoulder.

"You're not going to hold it against me, partner, are you?" asked the boy. "You realize that it was just an accident, don't you?"

"Accident?" repeated Loring, raising a hand to his aching jaw, and passing the same hand back across the base of his skull. "Yeah, you can call it an accident. But I'd call it a left hook."

"I suppose that's what is was," said the boy. "You see, Briguez was a great boxer, too, and he used to teach me a good deal about using my fists. A left hook was his favorite punch, and he taught me and taught me until I knew it by heart. I must have used it on you, without thinking."

"Yeah, you know it by heart," said Loring. "What a sock!"

He turned toward the door again.

"No hard feelings, Jeems?" pleaded Rancie Dale.

"Aw, now. No hard feelings," said Loring. "Only, when a joke gets turned around, it ain't so funny, either! I was just gonna raise a laugh, and instead of that I got a bump raised along the side of my jaw. That ain't so funny, either!"

He opened the door. "Wait till I get my head soused," said he, "and then I'll be coming back. So long for a minute, partner, and I'll be right back. We gotta get the business polished off, don't we?"

"Of course," said the boy.

"And we'll get it polished pretty pronto," said Jeems Loring, in a mutter, as he passed through the door and shut it behind him.

Then, in the darkness of the hall, his hand still upon the knob of the door, he paused for a moment, conjuring up a more complete darkness by shutting his eyes, so that his thinking might be the clearer.

Could it be, or were his eyes playing a trick upon him, that at the last moment there was a slight twinkling in the eyes of young Randal Dale?

He opened his eyes again with the question still unanswered. Then he began to climb the stairs slowly, fumbling with his hand for the balustrade, and with his feet for the steps. His mind was still half at sea from the effects of the strong punch.

# · 13 ·

When the great Jeems Loring was halfway up the stairs, he encountered Maruja, again coming down them.

"Are you ill, amigo?" she asked.

"I'm dizzy, Maruja," he told her. Putting a hand on her shoulder, he let her assist him up the rest of the way.

"What's happened?" she asked.

He heard a gasp and a flurry of excitement in her voice, but he could not place the source of it. As a matter of fact, his wits were not operating to the full of their capacity.

So, when they came up to the room where Don José and Arturo Llano were continuing their consultations, she opened the door before them and literally handed him into the chamber.

Arturo Llano stood up and raised a lamp; it was only that he wished to look more closely into the face of his companion.

"So!" he said. "What witch told me that Jeems Loring would come back to us like this?"

He lowered the lamp again. Loring was standing beside a chair, and the girl remained near him, as one anxious to do whatever she could to be of help.

Don José had not risen.

He merely said: "What's happened, Don Jeems?"

"Bad luck, that's all," said Jeems Loring.

He lowered himself into his chair.

"Hello!" said Maruja gently. "Was it bad luck that gave you the swollen jaw, Jeems Loring?"

He looked up at her—and sighed.

"Are you laughin' at me, Maruja?" he asked.

"Laughing?" she said. "Laughing, Jeems?"

He wagged his head from side to side.

"I got him cold," he said to the men. "I stuck him up and had him flat-footed. I could've salted him away. I had him right under my gun, and his hands stickin' up into the air over his head. That was the way of it."

"Great heavens," said Maruja, "and still he was able to do this to you?"

She pointed toward the swollen jaw as she spoke.

"Maruja," said Don José, "you'd better go and leave us alone here!"

"Certainly," said she.

He followed her suddenly to the door, with his wonderfully swift and silent cat's step.

There he held her for a moment with his eye, while she turned about and faced him, her glance upon the floor.

"Look up at me, Maruja!" said he.

She looked up.

"You are laughing," said he.

"Never!" said she.

"Maruja," said he, "I see the laughter in your eyes!"

"Don José," said she, "you are looking too closely."

He laughed softly.

"I never guessed that there was so much deviltry in you," said José Oñate, much pleased. "Will you answer me one thing?"

"Perhaps," said she.

"This fellow, this American, what do you think of him?"

She merely laughed.

"I thought that you might be a little too interested in him," said Don José.

"But why should I be interested?" she asked.

"Because he's alone here, surrounded by danger, with the odds against him; because, I don't know exactly how, he's managed to slip through the fingers of Loring and even Llano!''

She laughed again, outright but softly, at this.

"Let me tell you the truth!" said she.

"Of course. That's what I want to hear."

"Well, then, I was never interested in more than one American, more than one gringo, in my entire life."

"Is that true?"

"Yes."

"Who was that lucky fellow?"

"Ah, Don José, you've had the truth, but now you want names."

He nodded.

"Well, Maruja," said he, "tell me one thing more, and this won't be prying. Tell me if you think that this gringo may be more than he seems on the surface?"

"I couldn't guess what he is," said she, choosing her words with the utmost care. "He seemed to me, when he came in, the simplest fellow in the world."

"When he came in?" pressed Don José. "And what has he managed to seem since then?"

"You know," said she, in answer, "that I've hardly seen him at all since he came in."

Don José grunted.

Then he said: "You know, Maruja, you've grown up so much that I no longer know what's going on in your mind."

"Nonsense, José," said she. "A great man like you, of course, you see through everything!"

He grinned at her, not a smile, but a twisting grin.

"Later on, Maruja," he told her. "Later on, I'll have to try to know you better."

She, with a shrug of the shoulders, turned away, and then looked back smiling, over her shoulder, before she left the room.

Don José rested his hand on the knob of the door, very much as though he were minded to pursue her. But he seemed to think better of this, and presently turned slowly back toward the others in the room.

"What's wrong with Maruja?" asked Jeems Loring.

"Do you think that there's something wrong with her?" asked Don José.

"No. Only she's a little different. What deviltry's got into her tonight?" asked Loring.

"I don't know. I was trying to find out from her, and I failed," answered Oñate. "Go on and try to tell me what was in your mind. How is she different?"

"How's a man different," asked Loring, "after he's fallen into a million?"

"So! So!" muttered Oñate. "I thought the same thing. As though suddenly she had become rich and cared for nothing that she had cared for before!"

"Exactly," said Loring. "But let her go. What's to be done with that fool of a Randal Dale and his money?"

"The last I heard," said Don José, "you had him under the muzzle of your gun and his hands were in the air. Now it seems that all you've brought away is a swollen jaw and no money!"

Loring nodded, with the air of a man who has been too much tried to care about appearances or what others think of him.

He simply said: "I had him covered, and turned around with his back to me. I reached about and got the wallet out of his coat. He was shaking, he was so scared, the poor tenderfoot. He was begging me not to shoot, as I backed away, and then suddenly he turned and slammed me. You know how it is, you get a rat cornered and it'll fight when you don't expect it. He's big and he's fast. He turned around and slammed me. It wasn't no baby trick, either. He knows how to use his hands, I'm telling you."

He caressed his jaw as he said this. Tenderly he touched and stroked it. An absent light was in his eye.

"I went down in a heap," he said, "and when I got up, he was sitting on the edge of a table, swinging one foot, and he had in his hands my two guns. I tell you, he slammed me for fair, and he used only a left hook. He used a hook that that skunk of a Briguez had taught him."

"Briguez?" exclaimed Don José.

"Yeah, Briguez. What of it?"

"Briguez!" exclaimed Don José again.

"What's the use of sayin' that name over and over again?" asked Jeems Loring. "I never liked it much!"

Don José broke out: "Do you hear, Llano?"

"I hear the name of Briguez. What of that?" asked Llano.

"But Briguez was a man who could teach anyone to use his hands like a prize fighter! Briguez!"

Suddenly, Oñate laughed.

"You laugh, do you?" said Jeems Loring, snarling and sitting up straight.

"I laugh," said Oñate, suiting the action to the word, "because I knew Briguez well enough to say that he was lost and helpless unless he had some weapon in those terrible hands of his. Briguez? Why, that murderer could carve out a heart at twenty yards with a knife. But he couldn't use his bare hands to hurt a baby that was put into them. Briguez taught this gringo to fight? The gringo lies, and if he tells one lie like that, he is all a lie! All a lie, do you hear!"

He struck his hands together in excitement.

"Whacha mean, all a lie?" asked Jeems Loring.

"I mean that, and only that!" cried Don José.

Still he laughed. He seemed to be rejoiced by his discovery. Then he said: "All a lie, from top to bottom. He is no tenderfoot. He is one of us! He is one of us! I thought that he sat his saddle like a man who had been there before! Tenderfoot? Hah-hah-hah!"

He fairly roared at this point.

"You mean—" began Jeems Loring, and then paused, while a very ugly look spread over his face.

"I mean that," said Don José. "And for such a man, why, amigos, there is only one thing that I can do for him."

"And what's that?" asked Llano.

At one stroke, all of the laughter, all of the good humor departed from the face of the Mexican.

He said grimly: "You'll see, or at least you'll hear, what I do to him. Come down behind me and guard the door of the room. I'm going in to talk to him! Do you realize that by this time the first cattle of the drive are sniffing at the waters of the Rio Grande, and we, my friends, have not had one single dollar in pay?"

# · 14 ·

Now, when Maruja had at last gone down the stairs, stopping to laugh to herself now and then on the way, she paused and tapped at the door of the room where the inn's American guest was staying.

He called out, and she entered. There was still laughter in her eyes, but her face was grave enough.

So were the words which she spoke, saying: "Señor, you have done very bravely and well. But now it is time for you to go."

"Time for me to go?" said Rancie Dale. "But why should it be time for me to go, señorita, when I have not yet completed the business of the sale, and when—"

Cheerfully, she smiled on him.

"I understand," said she. "I think that I understand a great deal more than you suppose."

"Such as what?" said he.

"That you never intend to pay one penny for the cattle!"

"I?" cried he, touching a forefinger against his breast.

"No," she answered, "not even a penny!"

"Ah, Maruja!" he said reproachfully.

"I think," she went on, "that is the truth. You don't intend to pay one penny for them. Will you confess that, Señor Dale?"

"A terrible thing, Maruja, if you are calling me a thief!"

In fact, he looked as though his large blue eyes would start out of his head in sheer horror.

"You have told them only one true thing!" she declared.

"Only one?"

"Yes, only one."

"What is that?"

"That Briguez is your friend."

"Ah, Maruja, only lies—all the rest that I have said!"

"Well, there are lies and lies," said the girl. She leaned back against the door and regarded him with obvious approval in her eyes.

"You reckless scamp of a man!" said she.

"Reckless? Scamp?" said young Randal Dale. "Maruja, what are you saying to me? Who has been talking about me to you? Because that would anger me!"

"My own wits have been talking to myself," said she. "That is all. No one else guesses, I hope, though they may soon. You've made complete fools of two of them; they may have begun to guess by this time. Only, I hope not! But I, Don Rancie, was outside the window, a little while ago, when you heard a whisper in the dark."

She paused. Randal Dale, in a single instant, lost the look of innocence and made a long, feline stride toward her, his head drooping a little forward, his shoulders sloping also. He checked himself at once and straightened again.

His right hand made a gesture toward the bosom of his coat. "You were out there, when I made a fool of myself? You saw?" he asked her.

"I saw," she said. "I saw it all! I have watched the best of them handle their guns, but no one more skillfully than you, Don Rancie!"

Suddenly, he shrugged his shoulders.

"Why should not one friend know another?" he asked her.

She waited, making no answer to this, but with her eyes fixed very straight upon him.

"It was the sound in the dark, or almost something less

than a sound,'' he explained. ''It startled me. I turned around, hardly knowing what I was doing!''

''As if you were out on the hills,'' she suggested, ''with many men hunting you, and suddenly a sound outside the rim of the light of your camp fire—''

''Many men hunting me?'' he quoted, with a frown.

''Why should not one friend know another?'' she demanded quickly.

He smiled at her.

''You are a bright girl, a good girl, Maruja,'' said he. ''But it is foolish to talk of some things, is it not?''

She made a small gesture.

''As you please,'' said she, her face growing colder.

At that, he went up to her and took both of her hands in a sweeping gesture into one of his.

''Suppose that it is true, then,'' he said. ''Suppose that I, also, am a man that the law wants. What would you think, Maruja?''

''I would think,'' said she, ''that partly for your own sake, and partly for the sake of Briguez, you have attempted a terrible thing for any one man to do!''

''Coming here?'' he questioned.

''Yes, coming here. Partly because you wanted to make some money; partly because you wanted to harm these people for the sake of Briguez.''

''Briguez?''

''Yes. You are the sort of a man who would never stop trying to avenge a friend.''

She, watching him very closely, saw his nostrils quiver, and there was a faint gleam of perspiration across his forehead.

He merely said: ''You have good eyes and a mighty clever mind, Maruja.''

''That is all I have,'' she answered.

She felt a pressure that prevented her from withdrawing her hands.

''Am I to take you into my whole confidence?'' he asked.

''I haven't requested that,'' said she.

''You wish it, though.''

''Yes,'' said she. ''I wish it. Is that beast, that Briguez, really a friend to you?''

"Yes, really a friend," said he.

She sighed. Her eyes, this time, opened, and she stared at him.

"Briguez!" she murmured.

"They cheated and robbed him when he was helpless," said the tall American. "They betrayed him, and the government caught him. There is only one way that I know of to get him out of danger."

"Money?"

"Yes," said he.

"But your pocket is filled with money!" said she.

"One or two bills on top are honest, and three or four on the bottom," said he.

"Ah, ah, ah! Wicked fellow!" said she.

In spite of her words, she laughed and clapped her hands together.

She was fairly dancing, her body as well as her eyes, as she looked up to him.

"Señor Dale!" she said. "You have come here with counterfeit money, and you are making thieves try to murder you for the sake of it! Why?"

"Because," said he, "there has to be time for the cattle to be driven through the river. Once they are on the north bank, I may manage to handle them!"

"And the men who are still with them?" she asked.

He made a quick gesture with his hand which was free.

"There must be a chance taken," he answered.

"So you have put yourself into the trap, and you are the bait?" she suggested. "You are the bait that they can worry, while the cattle are driven north of the river into your country? Ah, señor! That is a terrible madness. Because you have dealt with the other two, but you have not dealt with that Don José!"

"No, he's left for the last," replied Dale. "I know that. And it's the way I would have it. What does poor Briguez care about the other pair? Why, nothing at all. It's only because of Don José that he's eating his heart out—that beautiful lying man. Tell me, Maruja, how it comes about that you are able to resist such a face and such a pair of eyes, and such great fame!"

She shook her head.

**178**

"I have been waiting," she said, and she looked into the eyes of the American in such a way that he started a little.

Then he bowed over her hands and kissed them.

"Maruja," he said, with his eyes fixed low on her hands, still, "I'm a worthless thief of a man, a gambler, and all the rest. And I'm not worthy of a glance from you, really. But tonight—"

He paused. And she answered: "But tonight you could use my help. Is that not true?"

"That's true."

"For instance," said she, "if I were to get together the best horses in the stable, and saddle a pair of them—"

He pressed her hands again.

"Would you really do that, Maruja?"

"See if I read your mind correctly."

"Very well, then, but I think that I hear someone coming down the stairs."

"That will be Don José. Señor Dale—"

"Yes, Maruja."

She went rapidly toward the window, and he followed her, as though compelled by her strength. She was whispering: "If I saddle the gray horse and the black horse, then take two more of the best on the lead, turn loose the rest from the barn the instant that I hear—a noise from the house?"

She gasped.

"Then, Maruja, you and I will ride around the world and laugh at other people, laugh at 'em, d'you hear?"

She closed her eyes. The color flooded up into her face.

"But you, señor, you have faced enough danger for one night. If you go now, there will be time to fly away from them. I'll show you."

The steps on the stairs came nearer, and now, in answer, Randal Dale lifted a finger toward her.

Maruja understood. There was nothing that she could do or say, at this last moment, sufficient to convince or to persuade him.

With a sigh that was half a moan, she slipped suddenly through the window and was gone silently into the moonlit gloom of the garden.

## · 15 ·

When Don José rapped against the door, young Randal Dale called out at once in answer, and Oñate entered to find the gringo seated by the table, near the lamp, reading a time-yellowed newspaper printed in Spanish.

José, entering, closed the door softly behind him. When he saw that intent figure, he was on the verge of snatching a revolver on the spot, but something restrained him.

He said: "You have found a long bit of news, amigo?"

"News," said the other, "that you wouldn't believe, except that one sees it in print and on paper. And print doesn't lie very often, I suppose, Don José?"

"Not lie?" said the other, smiling. "Oh, well, that may be so, also. I have found lies enough in newspapers."

"But such a thing as this, and about you, Don José!"

"Hah? About me?"

"Yes."

"What is it?"

"Slander, I say."

"Slander, eh?" said José.

And he brushed his knuckles across his chin and smiled a little grimly. He knew that newspaper. He had read it two weeks before, thoroughly, down to the advertisements, as a bored man will do. There was in it not a single word about José Oñate!

"Yes, horrible slander," said the boy, putting down the newspaper and looking up with a sigh and a shake of his head toward the Mexican. 'I never read such a thing."

"And what is it about, Don Randal?" asked the robber.

"Why, about you, and about Briguez. It connects you with poor Briguez in a terrible way."

"In what way?" asked Don José sternly.

Dale made a sign for silence and stole to the door. He slid the bolt of it home, still with his fingers to his lips.

José, in the meantime, watched like a cat, and once, twice, his right hand flickered down toward a revolver, and each time came away.

He seemed to be thinking to the bottom of this situation, and finding a great deal in it that was worth pondering.

Now Randal Dale stood again beside the table; then he sat down upon it, swinging one leg and shaking his head as he looked at Don José.

"Of course, there's nothing in it," he said.

"I hope not," said Don José.

He added: "Then, what's the story?"

"Why, the story's a thing to burn up the heart of any man," said Randal Dale. "You see, it says that at one time you were the friend of my old friend, Briguez!"

"If the newspaper says so, the newspaper must be right," said Don José dryly.

"And then it says," continued Dale, "that you were with him for a long time, that you learned a great deal from that old master of knives and guns."

"A master of fists, too, eh?" asked Oñate.

For a moment the glance of Randal Dale steadied upon him, but he returned no direct answer to the last remark. He simply went on: "The account says that after you had learned all you wanted to get from Briguez, you found yourself short of money, and it was then that you remembered, very strangely, that there was a price of twenty thousand pesos upon the head of poor Briguez, dead or alive. Is it true?"

"There was that price on his head. Go on," murmured the Mexican.

"Therefore," said Dale, "you sent advices to the rurales. And they came in the night. They came while you were supposed to be on guard, watching the camp. They surprised Briguez, and captured him before his eyes were open. It was not until their hands were on him, that you opened fire and shot your bullets into the air! You ran, and they pretended to chase you, but in due time, at the appointed place, you got your reward, half the blood money that was on the head of Briguez!"

He paused. All the sham was abandoned now. His blue eyes flared with wild fire, as they stared at the outlaw. Yet Don José endured that glance steadfastly.

"That stuff," he said, "is fit to be written in a newspaper. But it is not fit to be repeated by a man who is about to die, Señor Dale!"

"Am I about to die?" asked Randal Dale, smiling coldly.

"You are about to die," said José Oñate.

"I am glad to know it. It gives me time to say a few quiet prayers for the repose of my soul," said Dale.

"You sneer, señor," replied Oñate. "However, I'll tell you one other thing. Briguez was once my friend; it is true that he is my friend no longer; but it is false that I betrayed him. Not one penny of blood money has ever come into my hand. I, José Oñate, tell you this thing!"

"You, José Oñate," said Dale, "are a bloodsucker, a sneak, and a killer. I, Randal Dale, tell you so. Now fill your hand, you rat! You handsome-faced rat, you!"

He said it through his teeth, but the other merely smiled.

"When the time comes, I shall kill you, señor," said Oñate. "Be sure of that. I am not a Llano or a Loring."

"And I shall work on you with something other than loaded dice, or my fist," said the boy.

"How did you manage Llano?" asked José.

"It was simple enough to palm his dice and put in my own. My own were honest. That was the difference."

"Ah, then you were taking chances."

"I believe in chance-taking, señor," said Dale.

"You are the more fool," replied Oñate. "You were taking

chances today, also, when you tried to play with the three of us, like three mice in the paws of a cat. Now I am to show you how great a fool you were.''

"I wait for you, Oñate," said Dale. "Afterward, I'll have the pleasure of meeting your two friends. They shoot straight, I understand.''

"They shoot straight," agreed Oñate, "but not as I shoot.''

"My own bullet is for your head, Oñate," said the boy. "Briguez, he'll die happy if he knows that you've gone before him!''

"If he needs that to make him happy, then he'll die miserably. Tell me, how does it happen that they keep him alive, so long?''

"Oh, a little matter of torture, amigo," said Dale, his voice careless, but his eyes filled with fury. "Of course, you didn't dream of that. You thought they would order out the firing squad for him at once. It would cut you to the bone to know that they preferred to torment him, first, in the hope of extracting useful information from him. That would be a cruel thing for you to learn, Don José, eh?''

His teeth snapped upon the last word.

"I learn it now, and it is wine to me," said Oñate. "Is that all that you have to say?''

"I'm finished.''

"I've finished, also," said the Mexican. "Only I cannot help reminding you what a fool you were to bring a fortune in hard cash south of the river and into my hands. It was kind of you, but a little foolish, señor.''

"Fortune?" said the American, smiling. "You don't understand, poor Oñate, that it is all counterfeit? Fifty cents' worth of counterfeit. Hardly that, hardly worthy of being called more than stage money!''

Strangely enough, the insults that had preceded had not moved Oñate, but the sting of this remark caused the blood to rush to his face and turn purple in his cheeks.

"You lie!" said he.

"In the meantime," said Dale, "the cattle belonging to the poor, foolish tenderfoot have crossed the river, and are running north, where I shall pick them up. They are all running safely north of the river.''

He laughed.

"You will never reach them," said the Mexican.

"As soon as you are dead, I ride."

He held up his hand.

"Listen," he said. "The horses are being turned out of the stable, now."

In fact, they could hear through the open window the snorting of horses, then the rattling of hoofs, speeding away toward the horizon.

"By heaven!" murmured Oñate. "You have brought up helpers, eh? You are not the hero I thought, after all."

"I brought no helpers, but I found one here!" said the boy. "The lady you were raising under your own eye, the loveliest girl south of the Rio Grande, or north of it, for that matter! She has turned the horses loose, and she is saddling, now, the best of them all for herself and me!"

"You lie! You lie!" screamed Oñate, and he leaped at Dale, tearing out a gun as he sprang.

It was a stupid move. If he had not been bedeviled almost to the point of madness, he would never have dreamed of springing in like a blind bull at his enemy instead of standing firm and making the draw.

Swift was that gun flash, nevertheless, but Don José saw before him, forever imprinted on his very soul, the calm smile of the other and the glint of the jumping revolver that sprang into his hand. He saw that, but, even as he thumbed the hammer of his own gun, he heard a thundering report in his very face and was knocked flat backward into darkness.

Instant pandemonium broke out in the hall beyond the door.

"José! José!" shouted his two friends.

Regardless of the hands that beat on the door, Randal Dale stooped over the fallen man and regarded a long, ragged wound that ran down one side of Oñate's skull.

He shook his head as he straightened again.

"A miss, only a graze!" said Randal Dale. "Who will believe it, at such a distance? Will poor Briguez believe it? Will he ever forgive me for it? Damn my luck; I can't shoot a helpless man!"

# · 16 ·

When Llano and Jeems Loring broke down the door and rushed in, they found their friend lying with eyes wide, but with the faculty of sight only gradually returning to them.

"Maruja!" said the wounded man. "The black demon has stolen Maruja from us. Get horses, ride, ride with wings, tear the souls out of the mustangs, but get Maruja back from him!"

Llano howled like a wild beast when he heard these tidings and fairly flung himself out of the house and toward the stable, but when he came to it there was only one horse to be seen, and that was a lame old gray mare, hobbling about near the front door of the barn.

On her bare back, Llano flung himself and fastened his spurs in her flanks, but only at a hobbling lope could she go over the plain, and it was only the frantic yelling of the rider that overtook that thievish master of men and women, Randal Dale, as he galloped smoothly along on the tall black stallion which the girl had saddled for him.

He looked back over his shoulder, murmuring: "They have started, Maruja, but you see they're already falling back."

"José!" she cried. "Did you kill him? Is he dead, Randal?"

"José? No, there's only a glancing surface wound down one side of his head."

"Oh, I'm glad of that," cried Maruja.

"Glad that rascal is alive?"

"If he were dead, there would be blood on my hands!" said she. "And he was always kind to me. How did you manage to do it? How did you overcome him? And not one scratch on you, not one!"

"It was a matter of talking, Maruja," said he. "Talking will bring guns out of the holster before their time, and talking will dim the eyes, and make them see more red than light. He came at me with the best intention in the world of killing me. He came in, running so fast I almost missed the easiest shot that I've ever tried in my life—like a snipe flying against the wind, and I barely grazed him. Maruja, if only I had Briguez out of prison, I would make him start at the beginning and teach me all over again how to shoot!"

"Was it true that he taught you?" asked the girl.

"Every word or almost every word. I left out that when he went to Mexico on the boat, I went along with him."

"With Briguez!"

"Yes, with Briguez. And I wish I had remained with him. There would have been no dog of a José Oñate to betray him, then!"

"Oñate betrayed him?" cried the girl. "Oñate hated him, but he was so far from betraying him that—why, Randal, he killed that traitor with his own hands, when the dog came sneaking, to hunt for a reward!"

"*Hai!*" cried the boy. "Is Oñate such a man?"

"He's a hero!" said Maruja. "There is nothing mean and small about him. Oh, I know him like a book!"

"A little too well, Maruja, to make me entirely happy."

They rode on, stirrup to stirrup, over the undulation of the desert, and now there was a sting of alkali dust in their nostrils, a sudden, far-off promise of coolness in the air, and they knew that they were drawing near to the river valley.

Through the night and into the first gray of the morning,

which turned the moon into little more than a luminous wisp of cloud, they still rode on and found, at last, the widely trampled bank of the river where the great herd had gone down, and the beaten, broad way on the farther side where it had climbed onto the territory of the United States.

They were quickly over the ford and straight on into the rose of the morning before they found the cattle. They had traveled all through the night as fast as wild horses would travel, not at all as heavy-sided cattle might be expected to amble along. Now, in the morning, while a few riders on the points kept the herd spreading peacefully over a wide, grassy hollow, the rest were gathered about a small camp fire to boil coffee and drink it down, scalding hot.

Toward them galloped a single rider. Maruja kept far in the rear, and Randal Dale, as he galloped, was shouting: "Help! Help! Saddle and ride! Don José, Jeems Loring, Llano!"

A dozen guns were out, covering him, when he came up. But they recognized no real danger from a single horseman on a foaming horse.

From them all, he picked out the lean, ashen face of the albino, Ricardo Girones, and flung down at his feet a revolver.

"It is from Don José!" shouted Dale, waving his arms frantically. "He sent me off when the danger came. He gave me this gun to hand to you, as proof I was from him. Danger at the inn. At the fonda of Bartolomé Flandes! They—"

The lean hands of Girones fastened in the throat of Dale.

"Fool!" he shouted. "Tell us the truth, did Flandes betray them and did—"

"No, no, but the rurales have come. They have beseiged the place. A dozen rurales, I think. They are shooting and it is terrible. They are shooting with rifles. They are shooting to kill. And Loring and Llano are in there with Flandes to keep them off—I don't know how long they can manage it. Go, go! Ride in the name of Don José. He's already wounded. I saw his blood. Look! This is his blood drying on my hand!"

He held out his hand, and the flickering light of the fire showed the stain clearly enough.

It is said that there is always a certain honor among thieves. At least it is true of Western thieves, be they Mexican or American. There was one general shout of rage; one general imprecation against the rurales of all times; one vow to wipe this band from the face of the earth, and then the brave riders who followed Don José and the men of Jeems Loring—that handpicked twelve!—mounted their horses, and rode, whooping like Indians, across the plain, back to that land of sunshine and knives.

Randal Dale waited for Maruja to ride up. Together they sat down to a pot of hot coffee, and sipped it at their ease.